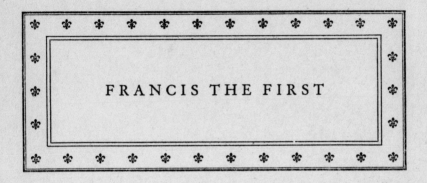

FRANCIS THE FIRST

FRANCIS I
From the Painting by Titian in the Louvre
(*Braun Photograph*)

FRANCIS THE FIRST

By Francis Hackett

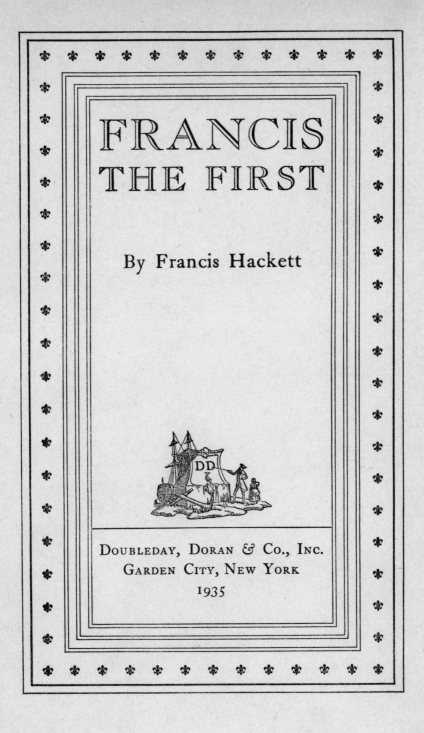

DOUBLEDAY, DORAN & CO., INC.
GARDEN CITY, NEW YORK
1935

PRINTED AT THE *Country Life Press*, GARDEN CITY, N. Y., U. S. A.

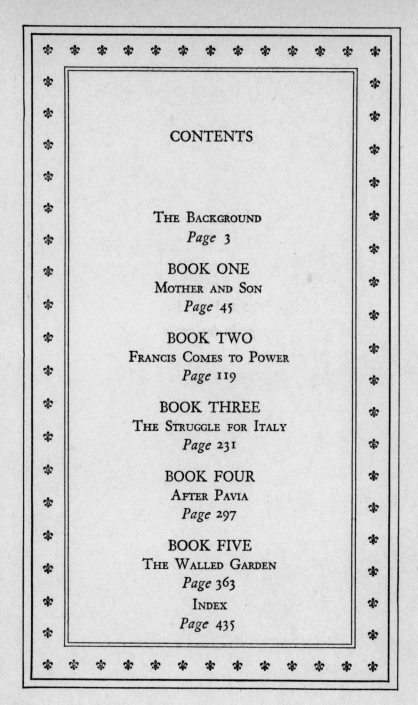

CONTENTS

THE BACKGROUND
Page 3

BOOK ONE
MOTHER AND SON
Page 45

BOOK TWO
FRANCIS COMES TO POWER
Page 119

BOOK THREE
THE STRUGGLE FOR ITALY
Page 231

BOOK FOUR
AFTER PAVIA
Page 297

BOOK FIVE
THE WALLED GARDEN
Page 363

INDEX
Page 435

To
S. F. H.
perle des perles

ILLUSTRATIONS

Francis I   *Frontispiece*

Louise of Savoy   *Facing page* 144

Francis I   *Facing page* 176

The Château de Chambord   *Facing page* 180

Françoise de Foix, Dame de Châteaubriant
Facing page 184

Guillaume Gouffier, Seigneur de Bonnivet
Facing page 192

Queen Claude, about 1520   *Facing page* 216

Charles de Bourbon, Constable of France
Facing page 268

Marguerite d'Angoulême, Queen of Navarre,
about 1525   *Facing page* 320

Francis, the King's Eldest Son, Who Died
in 1536   *Facing page* 324

Henri d'Albret, King of Navarre, and
Husband of Marguerite d'Angoulême
Facing page 332

Francis I   Facing page 376

The Emperor Charles V   Facing page 404

*Francis I on Horseback, about 1540
Facing page* 408

*Anne de Heïly de Pisseleu, Duchesse
d'Étampes   Facing page* 416

Francis I, about 1544   Facing page 424

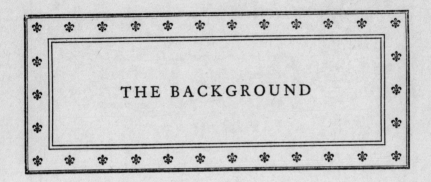

THE BACKGROUND

THE BACKGROUND

Stand on the boulevards to-day and you may see a Francis go by. He may be travelling fast, himself at the wheel with a blonde girl by his side. He is the athletic type, the lithe attractive male, broad-shouldered and thin-legged, with his hat raked at the jaunty angle of a military cap. His life, the joy of life, glints as he flashes past, maybe on his way to Mont-Oriol. He is a type of Frenchman not yet extinct nor likely to be extinct for centuries.

Those who wish the ampoule to be opened and a gallant like this to be anointed once more at Reims, with the oil that the dove brought from heaven, do not choose to see him as a human being so much as a King, a mysterious throb in a force that streams from the Eternal. They think it vulgar to see the blonde at his side: history should be blonde-proof. History may select the facts, but they must be worthy of History, must be dignified.

Yet observe this long-nosed personage with night-life in his narrowed eyes, eyes that have wept for the broken Virgin, eyes that have faced battle, caressed and lusted, heavy with cupidity, glazed with surfeit, once expectant as the sky in May. The curve of this personage has its own peculiar grace. But when you take him as the head of a European state, with millions in his power, his intrinsic character is too important in its tiniest detail to be veiled

3

in obedience to power-historians who rule out the human being.

The craft of ruling certainly glints in those incredible eyes. If he were just a Big Boy, a Big Bad Wolf on the boulevards, his character would be of human interest, in its own way. Make him King and it is of poignant social interest. Set him on the throne of the most powerful single nation in Europe. Endow him as a multi-millionaire. Give him a strong army. Ask him to guide the nation with a handful of councillors, no representative assembly, no potent public opinion. Then require him to deal with the great surges of human vitality which make themselves felt both in religion and in the plain struggle for existence. What he is, what he inherits, how he feels both as man and King, become then of supreme significance for the Europe he has to mould during the full third of a century that he reigns.

Francis was the absolute monarch with whom John Calvin collided. He was Rabelais' patron. Erasmus and Machiavelli disputed him. His sister at once befriended Calvin and wrote the Heptameron, standing in the dizzying cross-lights of Renaissance and Reformation. It is not enough to see him as a monster, simply because he was a sensual male. Our judgment of him must take in an immense variety of Europe, action whirling into counter-action and the chaff almost smothering us as we try to sift the wheat of reality. But that reality cannot be taken as merely political: the basic stuff is human.

How delightful it would be if Francis were a more dominating figure. To arrest historic attention—that is, to become world-famous —one must make a block reputation: be a conqueror like Cæsar, a vamp like Cleopatra, a greatheart like Abraham Lincoln, a virgin Queen like Elizabeth, a non-Virgin Queen like Catherine the Great, a steam-roller like Napoleon . . . Francis I did not, in this manner, stamp himself on his epoch. He was not man enough to do it. But if he were not a superman, he should not lightly be made the puppet of high moralists, the Bad Wolf execrated by Bishop Stubbs or vilified by Victor Hugo. Those great condemnations of the nineteenth century were not history so much as pamphleteering. Francis was no monster, any more than his contemporary Henry VIII.

He had, curiously enough, much the same personal problems as his rival Henry VIII, but he went about them like a Frenchman.

Had he married his mistresses, as Henry did, and then cut off a head or two, he would have added several interesting women to the historical waxworks and himself into the bargain. But though born within three years of Henry and dying within three months of him (Francis 1494–1547, Henry 1491–1547) he did not push coincidence as far as he might, and he was not forced to, since he was a Frenchman.

His two most eminent mistresses were just as fitted to be queened as Anne Boleyn and Kathryn Howard, but Francis lived under another star. His art of marriage, his art of politics, his art of life, were different. Consider the obstinacy that brought Henry VIII into collision with the Vatican over the question of divorce. French politics inside the Papacy had already arrived at the stage where no such collision was necessary: Louis XII divorced his wife quite simply. French "mistresses," on the other hand, had romantic sanction from the days of the troubadours. Jane Shore, dishonoured in England, had her counterpart in Agnes Sorel, to whom Francis later wrote a poem. This royal suppleness could elevate a King's mistress without mortally depressing his wife. As for Henry's use of the axe in dealing with his nobles or his ministers, Francis did not risk it except with his treasurers. He had to preserve a delicate balance with his nobles. He had to find clever ways of managing them, as well as his Church and his parlement. His political state was exposed more dangerously than England's was. Its connections were intricate and its methods had to be nice. You observe French solicitude for its own well-being driving it against the pressure of its neighbours and stirring its neighbours' neighbours to hostility. The political stress and strain created a system correspondingly pliable and recondite. Since the circumstances were so different, it is unwary to judge the Frenchman's conduct as if he had been circumstanced like an Englishman.

2

One may best identify Francis by glancing at his family tree in its barest outline. We go back to Charles V, his immediate royal ancestor.

In this family tree there is the usual lamentable paucity of

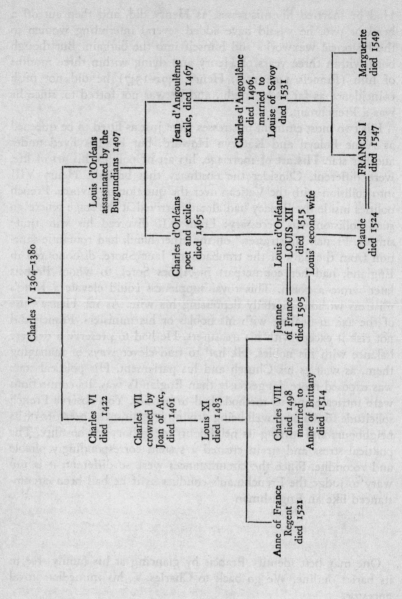

Charles V 1364–1380

Charles VI
died 1422

Charles VII
crowned by
Joan of Arc,
died 1461

Louis d'Orléans
assassinated by the
Burgundians 1407

Louis XI
died 1483

Charles d'Orléans
poet and exile
died 1465

Jean d'Angoulême
exile, died 1467

Jeanne
of France
died 1505

Louis d'Orléans
LOUIS XII
died 1515
Louis' second wife

Charles d'Angoulême
died 1496,
married to
Louise of Savoy
died 1531

Claude
died 1524

Marguerite
died 1549

FRANCIS I
died 1547

Charles VIII
died 1498
married to
Anne of Brittany
died 1514

Anne of France
Regent
died 1521

Christian names. We have six men called Charles and three called Louis. In addition there is one Louise. Few things make French history so confusing as these loyal echoings, but we may now bow three of the family off the scene, Charles V, Charles VI and Charles VII. This narrows us down to the generations immediately preceding Francis. He was of the younger branch, so we may turn to the Orléans. In his Orléans origin we find the clue to the æsthetic man in Francis, prince of the Renaissance, patron of art, builder of castles. Francis was not on the main line: his was a quite minor branch of that elegant family. He was born in shadow, the son of a mere princeling.

3

Deep in the heart of France was the home of his father, Charles d'Angoulême. His favourite castle was seated in the small town of Cognac, on the amiable Charente. This was a castle in the true feudal sense, dominating the feudal town. Its twin stone towers, its moat, the drawbridge with the heavy gate that rumbled and quivered down, spoke of private war and direct dominion. It was from here that Charles d'Angoulême would actually bear arms against the crown, and it was not half a century since the English had held Bordeaux. Yet inside the courtyard the fortress was already breaking into the smile of the Renaissance, venturing into open windows, outside staircases and balconies that accepted the world. It was a castle like all castles, a stubborn statement of power, but from inside, changing from isolation to social grace, it would give its glimpse of another nature, of trees and the river, and of flowers.

This household of Francis's father had its history. For over a hundred years the county was something more than a district in the wine region dotted with provincial hamlets and feudal domains. It had become an apanage of the crown. By the privilege of maintaining younger royalty it took on the proud feeling of importance that goes with money-spending castles and the divinity of kings.

Francis's grandfather, Jean d'Angoulême, held the apanage. But it had been sadly wasted by war. Azincourt was accountable for it. At that remote battle (1415) the armoured nobility of France had stood engulfed in mud and English arrows had mown them down. At one moment, when treachery was suspected at a distance, a prompt massacre of the noble French prisoners had been ordered. The Duke of Orléans had a close shave. Eventually he was dragged out from under heaps of dead, the most valuable of the spoils of Azincourt. Jean d'Angoulême was his young brother. He escaped the massacre by already being a hostage of war.

These two brothers were held in England against ruinous ransoms that could not be sweated from their estates, Charles for a quarter of a century, Jean for over thirty years.

The pall of war debt still trailed over the life of the Angoulêmes fully seventy years later. But for France, and for Francis I, there would be deep significance in the spiritual qualities that long exile developed in the two Orléans, voicing itself especially in the poems of the elder brother.

Another voice, a young vibrating voice, would be heard in the same period—at home in France. Sometimes in the country one wakes suddenly in the middle of the night to hear the cry of a bird. It gives a queer poignant cry straight from the heart, harshly real, infinitely lonely. And as one listens it recedes, carried across the swamps and over the woods, still urgent, still plaintive. There is something like that in the voice of François Villon. He wrote of the snows of yesteryear. One can see him by a bridge, the flakes drowning in the black river as that miserable scallywag with pinched face and purpled hands waits exiled from the fireside, while across the river Notre Dame uplifts its blunted arms. Out of the blood of Villon, blood with a cruel drop in it, came a native cry steeped in real and independent and outcast feeling, the cry of a midnight bird.

The poet in Charles d'Orléans, who would later welcome Villon to his court and speed him from it, had another accent, that of urbanity. Villon was dispossessed. He could not have thriven outside Paris, and in Paris he could only be free in a floating population, that of outcasts and criminals. There he could give himself to his own singularly vivid appreciation of everything that happened to him. His taut, alert nerves communicated with a brain that was freehold, not one cell mortgaged to the group, and all of it alive. But his experience of other people dominated this plastic nature, and his response was shaped by a passionate recognition of the beauty of his direct and unreserved adventure. He was Prometheus who had defied the gods, and his liver was eternally devoured by experience. So must poetry be lived, except by those who know that the attenuation of experience has its own slender adventure, just as putty-coloured pottery has its own charm, and pewter its lustre.

Charles d'Orléans had a song to sing precisely because he refined away from harsh experience.

Actually Charles's life had been a terrible adventure. His father had been murdered by the Burgundians, 1407, and he was left to avenge the murder. He had been married to a queen while yet a boy. He fought, was wounded, made prisoner of war, separated from his adored mistress, exiled in the bloom of youth and then by mean compromise restored to his Touraine. Yet here was a man whose tragic emotions could not be liberated in poetry. What he had actually suffered, seen, endured, was more catastrophic than anything that had befallen Villon. But Charles d'Orléans was a poet whose social mien was fixed. He achieved his life through an apparatus that included a duchy. He gave free play to his ingenious intelligence, but not to his temperament in collision with life. He was incased in his code. He was not on speaking terms with his naked soul. The outcome in poetry has none of Villon's emancipation. It has only the clear docility of order, the exquisite resignation of taste. But if power makes for prudence, and prudence for platitude, there is another beauty in subdued emotional life. Some nations, Japan and Greece and France, have within themselves this curious fineness which turns the folk clay into porcelain. The senses have become attentive and critical. There is a light in jewels which is like the crystallization of the light in wine—that pellucid quiver on which the eye muses as fragrance spreads itself and as liquor warms the palate and the heart. And as the jewel is a captured delight, a fine sensation crystallized, so a subtle poem may become the capture of a harmony which, until the poet made a jewel of it, was a fugitive in human experience.

The poet within Charles d'Orléans was thus attenuated and delicate. In this life he knew the garden he had lived in, from which he was exiled, to which he returned; he flew in hovering caprice among flowers in kind weather, touching death and love with the same lightness, grace in his very elusiveness, beauty in his wings. The gentleness is not of the heart. It is a gentleness of the nerves. He drew it from luminous Touraine and his own delicate attentiveness to perception.

He obeyed the first of aristocratic necessities, a denial of the romantic heart. When he was poor, poverty was his panache. He did not rage or rebel against the hard fortune of war. Ingloriously restored to the rich court of Orléans where he builds a wing, he takes life on its shrewd hereditary terms. He merely admits, with the least tremor of his voice, that he shivers in winter, that spring captivates him, that his heart opens to pretty women.

His brother, Jean d'Angoulême, came back, not to Blois but to Angoulême. He was longer in exile, and returned a depressed, reflective man. To marry a Rohan, on account of Brittany, was as natural a duty for him as for Charles to marry a Cleves on account of Burgundy. But it was no road to a brilliant career. His penury and his politics cut him off from court. He settled down into his county as a domestic bird into its coop. He governed faithfully. He copied and annotated religious and philosophical manuscripts, giving himself to the inner adventure, a man of gravity and probity. Religion for him was perhaps as formal an exercise as poetry for his brother Charles. His library did contain Chaucer and Boccaccio. But his intimate friend was Boëtius. With Gerson and d'Ailly, Anselm and Augustine, he enlightened himself about the conciliar movement. He pondered his theology, his whole life passing on the sunless slope that ran on from the Hundred Years' War.

4

The poet Charles d'Orléans had no heir when he returned from exile. Near the end of his life a child was born of his union with his bride from Cleves. Was it his own child, or the offspring of his steward Rabodange? No one could say. But this single boy, Louis d'Orléans, would live to be Louis XII. Like Charles d'Angoulême, the son of Jean d'Angoulême, he would be ranged with the opposition so long as Louis XI was on foot.

One may imagine him in the year that Francis was born as a rather genial young dissident who would never write a poem in his life. "He has a small head with not much room for brains in it," said an observant Florentine. All the room in it, at any rate, was taken up by Milan. A rather skinny youth, with a small face, a prominent Adam's apple, blond and blue-eyed, Louis d'Orléans regarded himself not only as heir to France but as heir to Lombardy, through his maternal grandmother, the alluring red-haired lady who had been married to the poet's father. This latent claim had never stirred the poet, but it would dominate his son's soldierly life. And Louis XI viewed with acid disfavour this self-assertion of the Orléans.

5

With hardly more favour did Louis XI view the other young Orléans, Charles d'Angoulême, who was early left to tutors when Jean d'Angoulême died. Charles d'Angoulême quitted Cognac for the royal court as soon as he could bear arms.

At that unprincely Court he was a true sprig of the Orléans, in dire contrast to the workmanlike King. From life the Orléans family sought a multiplication of intimate experiences, and the command of the means to procure them. The dark side of their method was the appalling selfishness with which they purloined or debased public resources for private ends. But if by public standards the Orléans family was wasteful, it had at least the virtue of pursuing its own delectation. Good beds, after all, are a social achievement. To advance from leather sheets to bed linen is a step upward. A château, in its own limping way, is a social experiment if it develops the vegetable garden and improves the stallion. To say it is light and trivial, superficial and airy, is not altogether to condemn it: a good omelette is light and airy, and yet a monument of civilization. The amenities of life are not so impressive as the acquisition of territory, but territory in the end must house amenities or seem a waste. The Orléans, epicurean by nature, had in them something of their Milanese ancestress. They were at once softer and finer than Louis XI. In a sense they had arrived, they were achieved; he was a pioneer. And the best pioneers are not epicurean.

6

Louis XI's Court was definitely a political workshop. What he was making of France, against the medieval grain, was an implement of European power. God, art, woman, war, gold—nothing could distract him from his purpose of moulding his dynasty. It was a master passion, and he brought to it a master hand—the grasp of his opponent's goal, quickness in tactics, economy of resources, and merciless absorption. Sometimes his nerve broke and he misbehaved, but his mind had a cruelly gay lucidity. He drove himself. He drove France. He overrode habit, disregarded honour, so that he might complete his design for France within the scheme of Europe, and this not with the valorous insanity of the Burgundian Charles the Bold, but with a steadfast obedience to his own political engineering.

His policy had two aspects. He wanted to centralize and consolidate France as a unit, seeking to base his dynasty on a productive people and a subject nobility; and he aimed to surround this secure centre with diplomatic bastions.

His mind was hag-ridden by the disunity of France. He knew, from the inside and by his own act, the disruptive forces with which a royal master has to contend. He had himself behaved with fierce animal jealousy of his own slow-going father. But during the twenty years he reigned he showed himself extraordinarily alert, restlessly resourceful, in the promotion of that power for which his nation was ripening. Time was hugely important. The European nation that first bore princely harness could gain an advantage not only by outdistancing its rivals but actually, for the time being, by blocking and even crippling them. This hope nerved Louis to intensify his nationalism. He was first in the modern field. He led the procession that Maximilian and Ferdinand were to follow. By a natural development from the Hundred Years' War, with the aureole of Joan of Arc still circling the head of France, this impulse to unify itself was throbbing in the nation and this was seized on by the tough, ductile Louis XI.

Inside France his methods were single-minded. He outwitted his feudal lords. Outside he showed the deep peasant acumen of the French people. He looked on his neighbours with one idea in his head, their power to do him evil. This belief in their power and their intention to do him evil was the mainspring of his craftiness. He did not rely on war. He relied on money. He bribed right and left. He refreshed his allies in Catalonia. His members of the Eng-

lish royal council he paid for and took their receipts in writing. He
had his secret agents in Burgundy. He had his well-oiled party in
Liége. He had his hirelings in Ghent. He corrupted Breton noblemen. He debauched Savoy. It was an underhand, vigilant policy:
but Louis XI had a plan.

His first political object was to wedge a French Savoy between
Burgundy and Milan. This would block the Germanic Empire; this
gave the Swiss importance to him: and this would overshadow
Lombardy.

Savoy held the key to Geneva, Burgundy and Lombardy. Turin
was one of its chief towns, but it ran up as far as Bresse and its
windows opened on the Saône as well as on the Po. Louis concentrated on it. England and Spain and Italy he watched out of the
corners of his slithering eye. He wanted to brace himself against
the Pyrenees, and even in Catalonia. And he was aware of Brittany
because his back was exposed to the Duke of Brittany. But his incessant and tireless preoccupation was with the East. He was governor-
general of Dauphiny in his formative years, and he had asked
nobody's permission to marry the personage whom his policies
marked as of supreme importance. Charlotte of Savoy was never a
woman to him. She was a hostage. Her brother Philip of Bresse
was his agent. And Louise of Savoy, the infant daughter of this
agent, was a little nobody to be used for a marriage. In consigning
Charles d'Angoulême to Louise of Savoy, Francis's parents, he
would fence a frontier. He would have scorned to think of them as
human beings.

Louis XI's great moment arrived, of course, when Burgundy
overreached itself under Charles the Bold. This was just as young
Angoulême came to Court. Charles the Bold was a soldier with a
very combustible imagination. Burgundy was a long wedge between
France and the Empire, a buffer state, but he saw himself an Emperor, conqueror from Antwerp to Milan. Yet when he bit on the
gritty Swiss, when those wild, poverty-stricken, pocketed mountaineers turned into a cohesive and ferocious army neither Charles
the Bold nor his nobility was able to withstand them. They captured his treasure at Granson. They took his silver to be pewter, it
was in such plenty, and sold his dishes for a penny apiece. A priest
bought his greatest diamond for three francs, the diamond of the

Great Mogul, and it had its own adventure from the time it was picked in the mud, changing hands in the early nineteenth century for over £20,000. Gold coins were poured from the Burgundy coffers into the hats of common soldiers. The Swiss were drunk on the fat juice trodden out in the Netherlands, by the commerce and industry that this medieval prince could tap. His defeat by the lowly Swiss goaded him to fury. He who had breakfasted on linden tea and conserve of roses, Commines tells us with awe, changed to the fiercest wines. His unmeasured policy united the Duke of Lorraine and the Swiss against him. He retreated along his corridor. They followed him to Nancy. There, in white anger, with a handful of an army, Charles the Bold flung himself into battle (1477). He was left a naked corpse on the frozen field.

Louis XI praised his God. Burgundy was at his feet. He saw Dijon revert to France, for lack of male succession.

7

It was precisely at this point, with Burgundy destroyed, that modern France and modern Germany may be said to have come into existence. Louis XI's aim to aggrandize himself brought him into collision with another power, the Habsburg, that aimed at a similar aggrandizement, each basing his policy on his neighbour's infinite capacity for evil.

The Téméraire, as the French called him, had left an only child, a daughter. Mary of Burgundy was a princess out of a fairy tale. "She is small," Maximilian would say, "much smaller than Rosine, white as snow, hair black, a tiny nose, a small head, a delicious face in spite of eyes a little tired and a mouth too big."

Louis XI had only one son, his little gnome Charles, who would later be Charles VIII. Louis wished to pin the great heiress to this unshapely boy aged seven. But Mary of Burgundy had a will of her own. She had chosen the Habsburg. He would be famous as Maximilian I. He was a tall, romantic prince of sanguine spirit and charming airs. He would always be poor. He was now too poor to come to his bride-to-be. But she hastily sent him money for linen and fine apparel. And so, equipped by his bride, he rode to his wedding.

Chivalrous though high-handed, gallant though miserably poor, Maximilian became lyric about Mary. "If we only had peace," he moaned, "we would be in a garden of roses." But he would never have peace till he joined Mary in his mausoleum.

Two children would be born of this union, Philip the Handsome and Margaret of Austria. Mary was to give birth to a third child, when, thrown from a spirited nag, she died at twenty-five. This was in the year 1482—the year before Louis himself died, 1483.

8

The one French prince who was really eligible for Mary of Burgundy was not the unfortunate heir to the throne but Charles d'Angoulême, freshly arrived at Court. Louis XI could have forced Charles's suit on the forlorn princess, and it was just the sort of stately marriage to which the youth aspired. It would have restored the fortunes that Azincourt had sapped. It would have revived the younger Orléans. But a cool schemer like Louis XI desired no such resurrection. He was building up France for his own family. He wished to diminish the Orléans. He took young Angoulême by the ear and led him to his future bride, Louise of Savoy. She was an infant, two years old, and she would inherit scarcely a penny.

Young Charles d'Angoulême could not resist Louis XI. He feared the King who barely tolerated him. He feared the agents that Louis XI had around him, the dungeons he had in his castles, the cages in his dungeons. Louis XI had grimly nerved himself to certain savage executions, actually decapitating Arras as if it had but a single neck. His fangs could set in a horrible yellow grimace, and no man living terrified his nobles more than he. But it suited his humour to incarcerate the young Angoulême in an impoverishing marriage, rather than in a cell at Loches or Bourges.

It was exactly the decade in which babies were murdered in the Tower. Louis XI inclined to less self-damning methods. He had brains with which to outwit his dynastic rivals while avoiding the wet footprints of melodrama. To tie up young Angoulême in a penniless marriage was an effective way of blocking the Orléans, while he had sterilized the older branch by forcing the poet's son to marry his crippled daughter Jeanne.

"Holy Mother of God," exclaimed the little duke's mother, "must my boy have this cripple for a wife?"

Louis XI sniffed with amusement. "It will not cost these two a great deal," he said to a crony, "to rear the children of their union."

Such was the Great Man in action. Had he possessed a male heir on whom he could have solidly relied, it is unlikely that he would have been at such pains to frustrate the younger branches of the royal line. But he was in a cruel predicament. Of his three children two were crippled. Charles VIII, who succeeded him at the age of fourteen, was perhaps not technically an idiot but to be three-quarter witted is scarcely enough. Jeanne, now Duchess of Orléans, was a pathetic hunchback with the lovelorn eyes of a spaniel. Only one child was strong and straight, like himself. Anne of France, who became Regent in 1483, would brace her little brother against the storms of the minority, since both Louis d'Orléans and Charles d'Angoulême would have asked nothing better than to snap off this dynasty at the root, and themselves take possession of the crown.

Like many another warm-blooded human being in his class, therefore, Francis I was destined to be born of a cold-blooded marriage. Neither his father nor his mother would desire this marriage. But what was soft human desire to the witty, crafty Louis XI? Some forty years later Machiavelli would distil his handbook for princes. Louis XI needed no handbook. He took as his own the task of unifying France, and to lace up France with a string of enforced marriages cost him no sentimental anguish, nor did his cunning mind dwell on the human consequences. He occupied himself with his supreme object. He was willing to break eggs to make an omelette, to break heads to make an agreement, to break hearts to make a marriage.

9

Before one condemns Louis XI, however, one must consider the Europe in which he found himself and the forces with which it seethed. One must glance, first of all, at the breakdown of the Church, which was heading for the Reformation. One must see that France would have to withstand the great powers that formed on either side of it: the Empire under Maximilian, the Spain of

Ferdinand the Catholic. And one must further take into account the Italy on which France, Spain and the Empire were destined to converge.

In so far as Louis XI provoked war by his malignant selfishness, he may have been held to have handicapped Francis I. But the Europe into which he was born was undergoing rapid transition, and in periods of rapid transition it is the audacious men who affirm themselves, the lawless and ambitious men who surge into leadership, impious and ruthless save in those days of happy accident when a magnanimous man arises, to steer by the stars.

Europe was still under the tutelage of the Catholic Church when Louis XI was born, but throughout the fifteenth century, especially in the Germany-Italy of the Holy Roman Empire, there ran tremors of enormous dissatisfaction, an anti-pope appearing, then three Popes all at once, mounting into the great attempt of the Councils to control the Pope, and then subsiding reluctantly with guttural foreboding.

These moods, or rather storms, of dissatisfaction, springing largely from the betrayal of the poor people by the wealth-fattened clergy, rose into popular expression. Strange and powerful beings who faced the moral adventure of life—Joan of Arc the nationalist, the nationalist John Huss—sought to lift the people above the confusion and misery of the times. Joan of Arc and John Huss caught the people's imagination, and of their nationalism came a temporary liberation. But revolt is death in life to the ordinary man. Savonarola would soon emerge in Florence to renew the agitation, but his disciples would be called "snivellers," and his ashes would go sifting down the Arno.

In this period of poignant contradiction between the Church as a theory and the Church as a going concern, what was the main fact in politics? Throughout the fifteenth century there could only be one answer. The Grand Turk fought the Christians, as he fought Persia and Egypt. Spain fought the Moors. Austria fought Hungary. Hungary fought Bohemia. Burgundy fought the Swiss. The Swiss fought Austria. England fought France. France fought Brittany. France fought Guelderland. Florence fought Pisa. . . . The list could follow the Spaniards to America or the Portuguese to India, an endless list in red.

So far the futility of Christianity. What Europe had accepted, and what had been sanctioned for it by its thinking from Plato to Aquinas, was this incorrigible institution of war. Far more powerful than any other tendency in Europe, stronger than diet, cortès, estate-general or parliament, stronger than piety or humane impulse, stronger than anything except wet winters and empty coffers, this feral institution towered over the Church, gripped the state, bled the universities, monopolized the nobility, whetted the bankers and enslaved the people. Wars on principle, wars without principle, defensive, offensive; history became the story of wars brooded and matured, declining and putrefying. There were intervals for rest, fallow years or fallow months. There was no relinquishment. It was just as much a matter of course as flood and the plague. It was accepted like the pains of childbirth. It was advocated as a law of nature: Mars and Jehovah rubbing noses across the boundary. The pattern of war was ingrained in the very brain of Europe. The Church, conflicting with the Emperor, had frankly abandoned the ethics of Christ in the crusades, and it used every lethal weapon against the Emperor. The nobility of Europe, illiterate, athletic and ferocious, was only too glad to block the path down which came the dreary saints and sages. They had with them millions of years of prehistory, the natural craving for power, the love of hot sensation and God knows what endocrine secretions. War was invincibly established as a European method, while at the same time the expansion of trade and the invention of the credit system were to supply grand motives and new means for pursuing it, at the moment that the Church was to fling away its moral authority and itself join the rude scramble for power.

The key that would open the gate of medievalism was golden. Men staggered out of a fixed class system, out of immobilized hierarchies, into a wholly novel autonomy, credit autonomy. This unexpected escape from the heavy trammels of orthodox society was a blinding intoxication. Both Pope and prince were to become drunk with it before the reign of Francis I. The ruling class succumbed to its new opportunities for spending energy and releasing desire. The pious might dwell on Vincent Ferrer preaching six-hour sermons but, while the simple Bretons listened to Saint Vincent, the rest of the world would dwell avidly on Alexander VI.

In such a world, where goodwill lost the one method it might use, the civil state based itself on force and took war as the prime condition of its freedom.

The French state, in particular, embraced war. From Louis XI onward, the French state was a hard fact, one that Calvin himself could not bend nor twist. Within the system, the native could frolic at will. He could create works of art, he could pursue unruly and extravagant pleasures, he could exercise his mind, he could be as severe or as gay as he chose. But this activity was just as much plunged in state-necessity as a fish is in water. In other countries, still amphibian, there could be fantastic variations. In France the man who disputed power with the state was tragic because fore-doomed. And he was fore-doomed because he lived in a political society definitely based on securing power by arms. At the heart of France stood the noble as soldier. He alone held France into place and against his implicit dominance every counter-aspiration, re-ligious or social, artistic or amatory, broke into a shower of spray. To see France as other than military would be to blink its supreme characteristic. It was not scientifically martial. It had no thorough recruiting. Yet its ruling class were conscripts of a state of mind, and their women the conscripts of conscripts. Escape from this servitude was impossible.

The beauty of France, both in climate and in physical endow-ment, enormously increases the verve with which Frenchmen are French. Human beings love the accustomed. The Arab is no more passionately attached to the desert than the Icelander to his night-capped island. But France is so situated that bare existence can be secured without rigid discipline or asceticism. The vine is an excess of fortune, the laughter of nature, and France has this merriment in abundance. The land itself has for ever invited the people to enjoy life, to improve the soil, to live in the open, to profit by a kind and fertile climate, with the uniformity of a temperate sun and the multiplicity of a continent. From the olive to the elm, from the fig to the apple, from the panniered mule to the cow of Nor-mandy, France ranges across the seasons and beyond the limits of a type, equipped for every experiment.

But this vast experiment, granted the rich varied country and the dangers from outside, directly induced French statecraft to unify.

Local intimacy could not be disputed, and every district was deeply rooted in provincial differences. But the unit would not grow out of federating these differences. It had to subordinate them. Because of its vitality from seething Marseille and throbbing Lyon to endlessly active Paris, it had to be an arbitrary simplicity. It called not for goodwill so much as for a white intellect. And when the consommé was made, when experience was sieved, the result would be an absolutism. The French people themselves might have enthusiasm, but the châteaux were fixed points in every community, obdurate first claims, and out of them, on the sure footing of prose, ran Roman roads of the will, hard and durable, paved for military communication. The aristocracy devoted itself to war, but it brought brains under its service, and neither the universities nor the professions nor the great traders nor the artists could keep from being pinned down by the châteaux which, subordinate to the King, would soon confederate with the abbeys and the cathedrals. This did not contradict the variety of France but subdued it to military intelligence.

In the days that preceded artillery the whole people were as capable as any other of exaltation witnessed by sainthood and religious art. But the trade of war became a class trade. The monarchy became above all a military institution. Hence the singular formality of aristocratic culture, in which refinement was a means of exclusiveness which in turn was a manifestation of power. The French were too intelligent not to turn to Italy to acquire and adapt the arts, but they would long refuse sympathy to even the greatest genius who was outside their aristocratic idiom. This narrowness was part of military defence. The intellect became foremost because, with finely organized natures, to feel is to be vulnerable. The dominant class, the class that gave the nation its stamp, submitted its lyricism, its mysticism, its luxuriant emotions, to the test of survival by war.

And this military "necessity" would also decide its use of parliament. The Tudor parliament, after all, had a certain free and popular aspect. It was an institution by which local communities could feed public discussion to its members, and those members, untrained in the law but responsive to class interests, stolidly deaf and solidly dumb when need be, took the materials that suited

their book and made law out of it. This law the same ruling class
had a chance to administer as magistrates, passing the bigger in-
fractions to policy-makers called judges. And the Tudor King, who
had kept his parliament fully aware of his preferences, managed to
wag his judges by the ear. In this circular process, making law and
making criminals, the Henrys were able to favour certain social
tendencies and to hamper others. But precisely because the strong
groups in every community had an actual means of applying pressure, a punitive instrument in their hands, their emotions and
their judgment could be made known, and the English parliament
could be made to feel the impact of popular opinion.

The French parlement was a very different institution. Louis XII
would not disguise his paternal superintendence of it. He might
have gout, he might be bed-ridden, but he would ride in on a plank
and plant his bed in the very centre of parlement. Its members were
not elected. He appointed them, out of a close corporation. They
were a corps of lawyers, not a corps of representatives. They had
no direct link with local communities. Their business was to frame
laws as well as to dispense justice, manipulating the needs of the
nation and the demands of the monarchy. When it came to the
point, parlement had a certain integrity of its own. It was too
human not to develop a spirit of workmanship. Hence France
obtained laws that were accepted throughout the land, laws tending
to become calculable, the first need of a community. The visage of
the law-makers that the public beheld tended to be severe and even
repellent. Yet behind the scenes the King, who made the makers,
could put final pressure on them. The very shin-grinders and nail-
rippers and thumb-screw and bone-wrenchers that they would use
for "justice" could be turned against themselves. In this struggle
between parlement trying to run straight and the King managing
to flex it the people were held outside. The King had his place, the
law and the Church, the nobles and even the merchants. But public
opinion, the vertical art of discussion which cuts through every
class and is one of the ultimate satisfactions of a free parliamentary
system, a relief for feeling if nothing else, could not be enjoyed in
France except in rare Estates-general. Perhaps this led to its amazing activity in mere speculative conversation.

Everyone can see that superb means for self-satisfaction exist in France. It was made to be pleasant to live in, and its beauty became the refrain of every visitor in the sixteenth century, even the grudging Venetians. The "admirable industry" of Paris was praised from the first, just as much as the laughter, the gaiety, the zest of the South. So, together with the mortal insecurity of the nation, and the incessant remorseless reminder of war, there went this natural expansiveness and liberation. But it was not liberation and expansiveness through the state as much as under the state. The religious epoch was over: the political epoch had arrived.

The cathedrals remained as popular monuments, a florescence of energy and a picture of the group-mind. With the progress of the new century the cathedral became obsolete; the idea of propitiating the deity gave way to the idea of propitiating the monarchy. The biologic realism of the French continued to be based on a neighbourhood to death, but the outlook on life became more aggressive, the thrust more pointed. Self-protection can be solved as the oyster solves it, doing its best to look and act like a stone. But when homo sapiens is far removed from the oyster, as the Frenchman is, when he has ardour in him, he must be very nimble and clear-minded to protect the beauty and the sensitiveness that he has developed. When all the popular energy that had gone into the cathedrals could no longer flow into them, it had to go elsewhere. Aristocratic France, capturing the state, asked France to have the vivacity to defend it. The people said "carpe diem," or, turning to theology, sought innovation. But there they met the elder statesmen, hostile to every experiment that could impair the national egoism. The outcome, in Francis's time, would be the marriage of war with nationalism, which breeds absolutism.

10

The more France became its triumphant self, as Louis XI proposed, the sharper became its intimidation to other dynasties. Louis XI did not himself wage great war, but by his merciless affirmation of self-interest he generated future wars and made them unavoidable. Those wars, or most of them, would bear on the empire, that is to say the Habsburgs, whom Louis outraged.

A ridge runs through French history between yesterday and to-day. On the far side the Norman Kings, the Hundred Years' War, and Joan of Arc. On the near side is the national military state. It was Louis XI who made the watershed.

The national state, what Machiavelli was to call the Principality, the thing formed by a prince, was destined to come into existence everywhere. Once a keen observer saw the first ridge formed by Louis XI he might have foreseen Maximilian and Ferdinand. The core in each case was a dynast, stimulating war and promoting martial efficiency. But where France would become as true a national state as Spain or England, sprouting its national literature, growing its national army, and in a sense budding a national Church, the condition east of the Rhine was so complicated by the Holy Roman Empire that the Habsburgs opposed to France not a true national state, but a congeries of alliances. One glance at the Habsburg family tree shows the nature of the difficulties that would surround Francis I.

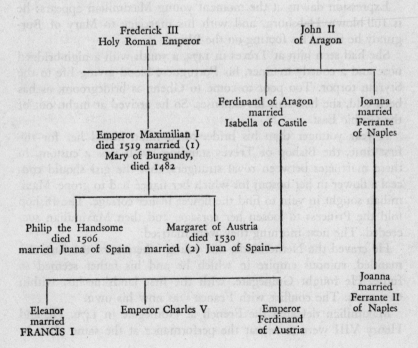

The clue to this family tree is Maximilian. Maximilian's father, the Emperor Frederick III, certainly had no means by which he could have deadlocked with France. Frederick, who ruled from 1440 to 1493, was neither by nature nor by equipment an aggressive man. He had come from Styria into power, precisely because Germany wanted a weak Emperor. He had small means. With Hungary, Poland and Bohemia to create problems for him, with Germany intractable, Austria disputed and the Turk an unceasing menace, it was hardly surprising that he crawled through his career like a river with no fall of water, sluggish, opaque, meandering, utterly inglorious as an Emperor, but, with passing years, more significant as a Habsburg and destined to bequeath his AEIOU to an energetic son. His futility is a delusion. An entr'acte is not a breakdown, it is a white space between one positive fact and another, and the blank expression on Frederick III witnesses the end of the Holy Roman Empire and the beginning of the Habsburg dynasty.

Expression dawns at the moment young Maximilian appears: he is full-blown Habsburg, and with his marriage to Mary of Burgundy he found his footing on the Rhine.

She had seen him at Trèves in 1473, a youth with a high-bridged nose and a courtly manner, his Portuguese blood giving life to the Styrian torpor. Too poor to come to Ghent as bridegroom, as has been told, she had sent his expenses. So he arrived at night, out of the Gothic East.

A year younger than his bride, Maximilian kissed her for the first time, the Bishop of Trèves standing by. It was a custom, in these marriages between royal strangers, that the girl should conceal a flower in her bosom for which her fiancé had to grope. Maximilian sought in vain to find the flower in her corsage. The Bishop told the Princess to loosen her corsage, and then Maximilian succeeded. The next morning they were married.

He craved the Netherlands, this young inheritor of the vast, dismantled, ruinous empire in which he and his father seemed so futile. He fought Guinegate, with the first landsknechts, within two years. The conflict with France was now his own.

Maximilian defeated the French at Guinegate in 1479. He and Henry VIII were to repeat the performance at the same place in

1514. During the long years between these two unimportant battles, Maximilian would conduct an incredible number of similarly futile operations—nearly all of them, so it seemed, ambitiously conceived, badly organized, absurdly conducted and ridiculous in conclusion. As a general he was master of fiasco. He failed almost unfailingly. And yet this Emperor who could not even defeat Venice was the one man to consolidate the Habsburgs in Austria, to see them joined in Spain, and so to weave a network around Francis I.

It is true that the Netherlands rejected him. They wanted peace with France. They resisted Habsburg influence both in the town and in the castle. The burghers objected for reasons of municipal privilege and the nobles for reasons of state. Maximilian found himself the prisoner of the good citizens of Bruges, an Emperor's son locked up in a grocery. And Ghent, which dominated Bruges, played into Louis XI's hands by despatching his little daughter Margaret of Austria to the puny French dauphin. Maximilian, in a word, was cut off from power by the willingness of the burghers to sacrifice him to peace with France. And France did not rest with dominating Ghent. By working with all its allies, the la Marcks of Sedan, Bourbon at Liége, Cleves and Guelderland, it soon dug its frontier down the familiar line through Bethune and Arras and Cambrai, from St. Omer to le Cateau. This line would be vigorously contested by Maximilian. And when Louis XI died, the next offensive by Maximilian was to become engaged to Anne of Brittany. This was in 1488, carrying the contest to the Loire.

Here Maximilian ran into Louis XI's true heir, Anne of France. The late King had acridly honoured his daughter by terming her "the least foolish woman in France." She was Regent for the most foolish man in France, Charles VIII. But the clear-minded girl had sense enough for two. Where her father had used all his cunning to do away with Burgundy as a danger, she now took it on herself to deal with Brittany. It obliged her to meet every opposition brewed by the policy of Louis XI—not only Maximilian, the affronted enemy without, but Louis d'Orléans and Charles d'Angoulême, the affronted enemies within. For nearly a decade following on Louis XI's death a tremendous struggle was thus waged to confirm the French unit. It owed its vigorous prosecution to Louis's daughter.

The struggle with Brittany was obviously of the first importance. For every nascent national state, there lurked this question of the weaker neighbour. England had its Scotland, Spain its Portugal, Denmark its Sweden. To absorb the weaker neighbour called for a degree of internal unity hard to achieve in the fifteenth century, and even harder to moralize, in a period of perpetual belligerence.

So long as Burgundy and Brittany could make common cause Louis XI had to temporize. By a caprice of fate, however, each of these dynasties came to hang on the life of a single girl heiress. To cut the thread in Burgundy had failed on account of Maximilian. Would the same man, now a widower, be able to secure the heiress of Brittany? This was the conflict pressed on young, hard Anne of France.

To go forward to meet an awkward situation takes a resolute character: this she possessed. She had no fear of the Duke of Brittany. Not strong himself in mind or body, he had a strong minister. The daughter of Louis XI decided on action, and on warlike action. A good French general was vitally needed. After trial and error, he appeared in the person of la Trémoïlle. For the rest, a knock-out blow would tell the story.

There was of course the underlying population. But this population, anchored to its humble life, was like rooted seaweed swayed back and forth in the dynastic tides. Its power was social but not political. It could, almost, be ignored.

The Bretons were a nationality without being a nation. The passion of nationality was just as inherent in them as in the Bohemians or in the Irish. The Breton peasants were inured to a Celtic way of living, farming the land and farming the sea. A Celtic language held them apart in their peninsula, with a climate clinging like a wet net, and a history whose mesh was woven by Druid hands. To assault this virile people, to disturb the languid tenacity of pious custom, to arouse the sense of difference and alarm primitive instinct, to stir even the turgid provincialism of the remoter aristocracy—this might involve deeper struggles, longer accountings, than Anne of France had bargained for. A prudent young woman, she had the astuteness to search out and bear down on the point that, in the case of the Netherlands, had been bungled by Louis XI, namely: the weak link in the dynastic chain, the girl heiress herself.

The strong minister was got rid of—killed. The decisive battle was fought in 1488. The feeble duke died. Everything now depended on whether Anne of France could rescue the girl duchess from Maximilian.

Maximilian was immensely handicapped. Held back in Flanders by the agility and resolution of the French, he was forced in turn to repel Matthias Corvinus in Austria. He could not come in person to Anne of Brittany. They could only be married by proxy. The young Breton duchess, passionately aware that her fate was staked on this union, went through the ceremony on December 6th, 1490. She was then fourteen years old, with a lively dynastic sense and a pointed will of her own.

The next year saw the struggle decided. The Bretonne's subjects were in the field, rallying round their Duchess, and she herself was something of a fighter. It was clearly impolitic to conquer Brittany by force of arms. If it could not be absorbed dynastically, there must be conflict with peasant customs, seizures of property, quarrels with the Pope, alienation of the pro-French barons and the pro-French priests, floods of French administrators, provosts, truculent magistrates, military police. In a word "occupation" of Brittany. It could not be undertaken. Brittany could not be conquered: it must be seduced.

Hungary called Maximilian away in 1491, and the French army was powerful enough to encircle Anne of Brittany. Then began diplomacy.

The Bretonne's dream of an independent nation was still bitterly tenacious. She held to it as a peasant to his acre of sod, as a peasant Celt to her virginity. It was her life and her honour. But the Regent prepared a way out: she would make Anne of Brittany the Queen of France.

The bridegroom would be Charles VIII, now twenty-one years old. He was not a handsome bridegroom—his eyes on stalks, his head a lump, his ear disfigured. Anne of Brittany resisted. If her face always kept a look of strain—a big bomb of a forehead, a sharp nose and a pinched mouth—part of this strain came with her defeat at Rennes. There are events in life that make a human being their convict, that burn red-hot into memory. Her enforced marriage was of this searing character. She held off the French through the loyalty of her Bretons and the skill of her councillors. Her own courage was unshaken. But with gradual and implacable movement the more powerful monarchy narrowed the circle round the young girl until, cut off by the tide, she stood without escape. To engulf her in France, to swallow her into a greater order not hostile but hugely indifferent, became the drama of those three days at Rennes. They terminated the history of Breton self-direction. But the quelling of Anne of Brittany, a little woman of obdurate pride, was not without spiritual cost to the conqueror.

II

The first cost was the ugly breach of faith with Margaret of Austria. This blithe child, with gossamer hair and the bluest of eyes, had been joyously betrothed to Charles VIII when she was three, and she had been reared at Ambroise as "Queen of France." Louis d'Orléans had made much of her. She was an early love of his. "Do you remember," he asked her years after, in diplomatic cajolery, "when I used to smack your behind?" More vivid certainly was the realization that France had done the same thing and not in tenderness. It had been cruelly necessary, in order to link Brittany with the crown, to repudiate her marriage to Charles VIII.

Anne of France could scarcely help herself. It was Louis XI who had recklessly poisoned relations between France and Maximilian when, at the end of his reign, he had cynically annexed little Margaret of Austria. Her eventual repudiation inflicted a personal insult on the Habsburgs. It was one of those dynastic grievances that always become septic since the damage to human dignity is ineradicable. Such were the imponderable deficiencies of Louis XI's nimble statesmanship, to be paid for when Margaret's nephew became Emperor Charles V, and when Francis I was to find himself his prisoner.

The enmity of the Habsburgs fed on this insult, and when France marched on Naples in the August of 1494, the duel of Habsburg and Valois was decided.

This duel would affect everything in French life, from the accent of its poetry to the curve of its architecture, from the cut of its clothes to its worship of God. And the person whose influence would count for most in bringing about this duel would be the man whose eccentricity, whose unreliability, whose poverty and whose fantasy made him over and over again the laughing-stock of Europe. Maximilian, the weakest monarch of them all, did more to manœuvre France into a difficult position than any other king in Europe. It was his animosity which brought into the balance the new Spain that Ferdinand and Columbus had created, with the abnormal aggrandizement of Castile.

There are some fine edifices in this world which are expressive in front but blank in the rear. One of them was French policy in the East. Anne of France preferred peace with Brittany to Margaret of Austria as queen. On the Brittany front this was admirable, but the side turned to the Empire was a blind surface, no light in it, bald and provisional.

The actual deportation of little Margaret of Austria, to make way for Anne of Brittany, was entrusted, among others, to Francis's future father.

In the distance could be heard the growlings and rumblings east of the Rhine.

"Rather would we depart from this world in peace and blessedness," Maximilian's father declaimed, "than suffer so unchristian-like and foul a deed to remain unpunished and the Holy Empire and the German people to put up with this scandalous and irreparable injury under our rule."

These hot words marked definite enmity. As for Margaret of Austria herself, she said little, as she rode with her gracious escort to the border.

Her personal attendants wept to part from her, and one of them did her best to console the princess.

"Madame," she bent to her, "you ought not to be put out. You are the daughter of a great King, and the sister of a great prince. You cannot fail to be a great princess, and if you have missed our King you will have another. There are lots of other Kings!"

Margaret was not consoled. "This has come upon me," the child had told the weeping Charles VIII, "through no fault of my own."

She met her fate with pride, but not till life had given her many a hard lesson did she forget being rejected as "Queen of France."

12

The seduction of Brittany was humanly outrageous, but it was practical politics. The last to deny it would have been Ferdinand the Catholic who had just spent ten years in the conquest of Granada. He was rounding out Spain, and he comprehended that Anne of France should round out France. He did his best to hamper her, but it was not whole-hearted. But since France, at the same time, had given the Habsburgs a grievance, it was most important that it should not give them an ally. Yet the moment the Regent retired to her own great domains, to allow Charles VIII to rule, the fatal step was taken.

The little King, Charles VIII, had a wholly united Kingdom. He thereupon launched forth on an enterprise that, whether it succeeded or failed, was bound to enrage Ferdinand. This could only result in drawing Ferdinand and Maximilian together. And in the pincers between Ferdinand and Maximilian France would be unmercifully squeezed.

There is something a little mad, or at any rate quite out of fashion, about this French invasion of Italy. The claim to Naples, like the claim to Milan, was simply dynastic, and these claims do not cohere with the sensible acts of self-assertion nearer home, which all went to round out the national state. To the bourgeois mind, with its definite picture of France-in-Europe, these dynastic impulses seem almost grotesquely primitive.

Yet this invasion, which took the French so far from home, costing them so much effort and involving so much vital conflict, was fantastic only in the shape it happened to take. The impulse behind it was very little different, so far as Europe was concerned, to the impulse behind the national state. On the face of it, this invasion was set in motion by the urgent desires of a few avid men, but it really sprang out of a complex of forces, generated in Spain and Germany and Italy. It was in fact the great opening gesture of the one mature national state in Europe. To launch Charles into Italy, just as to launch Francis into the world, needed the development of a long train of circumstances, under the management of Providence but clearly having a bit of assistance from the devil. And while Charles rode forth with a scroll of dynastic parchment in his hand, and the banner of a crusade held before him, the thing that drove him forth was definitely modern. His invasion of Italy was the opening chord of that terrific warlike national symphony that Europe has been playing ever since.

In 1492 Ferdinand of Spain was exhausted. The conquest of Granada had taxed him. But it was not conceivable that he could allow France to annex Naples. His sister had been married to King Ferrante. His bond with the so-called Aragonese dynasty was of the closest. If anyone was to take Naples, it was himself. This was elementary. In every negotiation with France this was the underlying motive. Once Charles VIII revealed his desire to conquer Naples Ferdinand set in counter-motion. A minor move was the pledging of Catherine of Aragon to England. One of the most important would be his proposal to Maximilian that both Maximilian's children, Philip and Margaret, should marry into the house of Spain. This would be a direct outcome of the invasion of Naples. Its consequences would be dire. And there was one other element destined to accumulate huge importance as the years rolled on. That was the activity of Christopher Columbus.

In fourteen hundred and ninety-two, so says the little ditty, Columbus sailed the ocean blue. And he sailed it, like many a man before and after him, because he had an idea in his head. He was born within a year of Leonardo da Vinci. A weaver by trade and pronged forward by poverty, he had the energy to sustain a grand conviction outside himself that bore on the science of life. He was, in a word, one of those Renaissance Italians in whom there burned a beautiful and passionate certitude about the immediate world, a belief that what he imagined he could prove real. The globe was round. The Western ocean had cast up strange timbers and the bodies of strange human beings. As he followed the sea, from Iceland to Africa, the Genoese reasoned that if others had crossed the ocean, so could he, and if he sailed long enough west he must come east again.

On this he was prepared to stake his life, but no one was prepared to stake his money. There was plenty of money for silk, for pyxes and chasubles, for dowry and for artillery. But Columbus could not tap anyone, not even in marine Portugal. The King of Portugal was unconvinced. Henry VII was too prudent. Anne of France was sceptical. The hard-headed Spaniards found nothing to countenance it either in Saint Thomas or in Saint Augustine.

Columbus must have expostulated without mercy to Geraldini, another Italian at the court of Spain (later Catherine of Aragon's confessor). Geraldini had the courage to discredit the great saints as great geographers. The Spanish wavered, pondered, and eventually agreed. Columbus was given his ships. He went into the known seas, then into the unknown, bearing with him words of greeting to the Grand Khan.

He sailed through despair. After five weeks on the waters he came to land in the night. It should have been a glowing Asiatic city, lifted in splendour, with bells ringing to welcome him, the soft voice of an old civilization to greet him and palaces to visit. Instead he was to grope in the primitive, with savages who feared him, tangled in the roots of life. This rude, fertile land lay across his way to Cipangu but it gave him trophies to carry back to Ferdinand and Isabella, wonders to excite the grudging mind.

That mind hardened as time went on. Kneeling bareheaded at the feet of Kings, Columbus had begun by promising miracles, as only imaginative men can promise miracles. What he had really discovered was an acorn, and the oak could not grow in a decade. He completed four rounds of voyage in this decade, groping in the unknown, trial and error. He strewed Spanish names on the map, Hispaniola (Haiti), Juana (Cuba), named for the Infante, Dominica after Sunday, Venezuela after Venice. Then, wearied and overwhelmed by circumstance, he was discarded—and died fulfilled. He had provided for his son Diego, he had found reality for what he had imagined, he had broken through the chains of the world.

Pope Alexander VI drew a line down the new hemisphere, half for Spain, half for Portugal. Not many years later, the sceptic Frenchman emerged in regard to this division when Francis I said he should like to see the paragraph about it in Adam's will.

It was to concern Francis, because the consequences to Europe were immeasurable. By linking two groups that had not touched each other since the floors of the earth subsided, Columbus gave

Europe a new neighbour and new offspring. The results were more than to upset the currency, to divert shipping, send syphilis to Naples, though even these things would not be indifferent to Francis. The signal political result would be the marriage of America to Castile. America, the greatest heiress the European family had ever seen, would come to benefit the Spanish crown. Into the system of dynastic marriages that regulated the politics of Europe entered a new bride, deaf and dumb, a metal bride whose fortune grew out of a crown monopoly. By thus reinforcing Castile, not all at once, but year by year, the military balance of Europe was to be transformed, the political balance to be given a new axis. And with this change for Spain there would be a complete upheaval in the history of France.

13

Nothing was more remote from Charles VIII than these vast repercussions. He was a little dynast from top to toe, and he proceeded on the simplest dynastic lines. Naples was his legal heritage!

With Brittany no longer the focal point of international dispute Big Head saw other worlds to conquer. For personal reasons Venice and Milan and the Pope had been urging him to invade that distant kingdom. He believed that by making concessions to his rivals he could buy off their enmity. He employed 1492 in cooking up peace treaties. By the end of it he had placated Henry VII (promises of cash). He had restored to Maximilian the Hainault and Artois that were Margaret of Austria's dowry. As a last resort he had given back to Ferdinand the two morsels of Spain (Rousillon and Cerdagne) that Louis XI had pulled away from it. Then he sallied forth, to make history.

But in the year 1492 there were more important events than Charles VIII's distribution of consolation prizes. By January Ferdinand had completed the conquest of Granada. In April Lorenzo de' Medici had died. In August a new Pope, Alexander VI, was elected. Each of these unconnected events bore on Charles's invasion. The death of a unifying Italian, the accession of a Spanish Pope, and the freeing of Spain to look across the Mediterranean, combined to magnify the dangers to a French invader.

Lorenzo de' Medici was extremely important as an Italian, precisely because he was a banker and negotiator. He was not a prince; Florence was a city state and could not give him the army that would have made him a prince. His career, in any event, turned on the fact that he lent money to princes at fifteen or twenty per cent. But he had two healthy organizations that decided his importance; his political grip at home and his correspondents abroad. By a facility of nature and a versatility of gifts, he manipulated the city government, the guilds, the clergy and the men of letters. He was a true Florentine leader, shrewd and easy and subtle, with a very high order of personal charm. In a city that was ripe in every faculty, he understood the creative mind. It was not in his character to dominate the Italian situation. He was a banker, and insinuation was his art. He went to the greatest lengths to ally himself with the Papacy by marriage and to have his Giovanni (who would be Leo X) made a cardinal. But he comprehended the dangers to Italy of the enmity between Naples and Milan. He took his life in his hands when he went to see King Ferrante at Naples. Without being a great Italian, he was a good Italian, and his early death (he was forty-four) removed an international intelligence.

Savonarola saw him on his death-bed, but Savonarola was proposing to an epicurean the stations of the Cross. What Lorenzo had favoured in Florence was that richness of strength and sensitiveness which Pagan Europe has always desired, that state of well-bred anarchy which makes life a joyous and dangerous adventure to its ruling class. Savonarola was a medieval saint. He was an agitator, harsh-voiced, steeped in the Bible, the centre of throngs of workers whose white glance flashed in their dark faces, pouring out their response to a clarion of the Lord, the voice of denunciation and prophecy. This, in its essence, was the old cry for theocratic government. Few bankers heed the cry, and there was little for a Borgian Papacy to do but kill Savonarola.

In April, then, Lorenzo died at his lovely villa outside Florence, to be wept over by lenient churchmen and by his Platonic Academy.

The election of Roderigo Borgia as Pope Alexander VI came in August. Alexander purchased the office of Pope, giving his heaviest bribe to the Milanese Ascanio Sforza. He was a man of great ability. A Spaniard, born in Spain, deriving huge revenues from

Spanish bishoprics that never caught sight of him, and managing, when his uncle became Pope Calixtus III, to rise in importance, he soon proved himself one of the ablest though greediest of papal chancellors. Borgia was a buoyant, coarse, vigorous man, with a power of work in him, a will in magnificent order, a keen sense of the way of the world, Spanish frugality at the table and the extraordinary sexual gusto that, in certain hearty men, is equally Spanish. He possessed, almost to an inordinate degree, the paternal instinct. It was perhaps one of the reasons he was thought to be a Jew. Though Pope, he loved and bred a big family, and he used all the power that came to him as Pope to thrust his family ahead. Borgia did not begin his career as a criminal. But he was one of those urgently active men who are tempted, by very reason of their wile and prudence, to play a dangerous game and to get into corners from which the only exit is culpable. To put it in a word, he was a prince in Pope's clothing.

With the accession of Alexander VI, the Papacy itself was in the balance. Not so long before Pius II had stood on an eminence, gazing out to sea at Ancona before he launched the Crusade against the Turks. He was near enough to have given a firm fatherly rebuke to Borgia for the looseness of his morals; and yet he was already a million miles removed. The Papacy was passing into the hands of a new series of Popes whose methods would vary—one a criminal, another a soldier, a third a diplomatist—but all, whether criminal or violent or suave, bent on worldly power. For half a century the saints would be out of work. Savonarola's heroic efforts to teach as the Bible taught, in a world where "the power of princes is nowadays so greatly increased by artillery," could only invite his destruction. Italy was entering on a new path and the Popes with it.

The list of Popes for a hundred years traces the rising curve of princeliness, to end with Paul III and the Council of Trent.

1455 Calixtus III (Alfonso Borja)
1458 Pius II (Æneas Sylvius, Piccolomini)
1464 Paul II (Piero Balbo)
1471 Sixtus IV (Francesco della Rovere)
1484 Innocent VIII (Giovanni Cibo)
1492 Alexander VI (Roderigo Borgia)
1503 Pius III (Francesco Piccolomini)

1503 Julius II (Giuliano della Rovere)
1513 Leo X (Giovanni de' Medici)
1521 Adrian VI (Adrian Dedel)
1523 Clement VII (Giulio de' Medici)
1534 Paul III (Alessandro Farnese, died 1549)

It is a period of spiritual eclipse, in spite of its grandeur in art, and even in the art of the greatest of Italians one may read the decline of Christian ideals. What moved the tragic geniuses like Michael Angelo, brought up under the Catholic dispensation, was a passionate sense of the clash and groan of warring worlds. He painted ceilings, one might almost say, because he dared not look down. His heart was twisted by the squalor of princes and the ingratitude of peoples, by the seductive beauty of the universe and its constant betrayal down below. He had within him the chalice of the artist which is filled both with delight and agony. As a venerable man he broke with life. He laid down his mallet and took death's cold hand.

14

But Charles VIII's Great Enterprise was exuberant, not tragic. If France waited until Spain girt its loins, Naples never could be captured, and the apron of Lombardy never could be French. So the expedition was decided on—speed, dash, victory, with a compact army of 40,000.

Francis I was born at Cognac, on September 12th, 1494. And on that same day it was swelteringly hot at Asti. The greatest confusion reigned in the town, especially in the mansion where little Charles VIII had been installed. Passing in and out, through doors that were never closed, there streamed war-lords, members of the council, nobles, princes, pages, couriers, priests and pen-men. It was the royal muster of France. Most of them had found lodging nearby but the army had to be accommodated all through the neighbour-hood—an army including Gascons and Bretons, Germans and Spanish, Swiss, Normans, Italians, men from Lorraine, from Liége, from Picardy. Some were gunners and pioneers, well trained to artillery. Others were thieves and murderers, scallywags from every corner of France. Mingled with them were the camp-followers and the prostitutes, kept in order by provosts who dealt savagely with disorder, hanging as many as twenty soldiers a day. But there was nothing sombre about the expedition that had crossed the Alps for the invasion of Italy. It had guns the like of which had never been seen before. It crackled with excitement, with audacity, with gaiety. It was coming to conquer and, to the infinite amusement of this French army, the Italians stood petrified, filled with consternation.

The company that thronged about the little King gleamed with colour and distinction. One could pick out a dozen men already notable and a score whose careers were now beginning—the modest and spirited la Trémoïlle, fresh from his brilliant exploit in Brittany; Gié, a prudent Breton who had early sided with France, a solid councillor with a dogged acquisitive nature; Gilbert de Montpensier, a heavy-headed person, father of the future Constable; Giuliano della Rovere, the leonine cardinal who had been urging this invasion with mighty vehemence, and who would be Pope Julius II; Philip de Bresse, Louise of Savoy's father who had joined at Turin; the boyish Chevalier Bayard; those and innumerable others, a whole flood of them, and, floating on this sparkling and agitated tide, the little cork whose name was Charles VIII.

Nature had played a trick. Charles was the precise opposite of his calculating lion-tamer of a father. The lions now roared around Charles VIII and he stood trusting and optimistic. Their muzzles brushed against him and he petted them. He was off to conquer Naples and recapture the Holy Sepulchre. He had dreams. He heard his Voices. And around him crushed interpreters of these voices, a few of them definitely alarmed for France, some of them pitying him a little, some of them mirthful, all of them vibrant with personal gain that must flow from this daring expedition.

In the midst of them, fixedly smiling, stood Ludovico Sforza, il Moro, gold and olive in complexion, with a glittering black eye and a flesh that had the texture of marzipan. He had come by himself to this intolerably hot hotel. But it was not the heat that made Ludovico Sforza wrinkle his nose with the utmost displeasure at the scene before him. He had arrived to discuss matters of extreme importance with the King of France, and Charles VIII had made no effort for him. Charles expected him to stay on hand in this noise and dirt and confusion.

Ludovico Sforza, a portly gentleman, who for years had made people address him from behind a barrier while he stood so far away they had to shout to him, was now jostled in a crowded room where Charles VIII, who in his beauty-loving eyes was a person of peculiar ugliness, began dictating, first at one man's suggestion, then at another's, then at the suggestions of both together, his advisers getting excited, contradicting, shouting. Not only did they interrupt their half-illiterate King without ceremony but they brushed up to him from tables where some were eating and others playing cards. In the midst of this oppressive clamour Ludovico champed in irritation. He watched Charles out of his black eyes, saying to himself as he said to the Venetians later, "The Most Christian King! Young and foolish, with little presence and less mental power."

Charles VIII collected his manners and led his guest out of the room where everyone was talking and eating and spitting. But even this he mismanaged. "More than once," complained Ludovico, "more than once he left me alone in the room like a beast, to go and dine with his friends."

What made it hard for the ruler of Milan was in part his sense of dignity. He had come from Milan with Beatrice d'Este, his young wife, who was quivering with interest in the French. At a castle nearby, Ludovico's headquarters, Leonardo da Vinci was planning an entertainment for the next day, but the French, to whom Ludovico il Moro was lending 200,000 ducats, were vague with him, in spite of his collusion, and uncertain when they would go forward toward Naples.

But Ludovico had greater reason to be uneasy. He was, to the eye, a stately figure—richly clad, his long hair well combed, his hands heavily jewelled. He had surrounded himself with loveliness at Milan. He had built with lavish zeal. He had employed Bramante. Leonardo he understood and had rewarded with a lordly stipend. He had created a great farm, with as many as eighteen thousand cows, and administered it with science. Yet his duchy, one of the richest in Europe, had the anatomy of a pancake. It was exposed on every side. It forced its ruler into every form of cajolery. He had, besides, the inevitable uneasiness of an intriguer. He had planned the downfall of Naples, but his own affairs resembled Leonardo's equestrian statue of his father—a huge clay model, still under the master's hand, not yet cast in bronze. It would never be cast, Michael Angelo said bitterly, it was a failure. Ludovico's dukedom was also in the foundry. He was planning to dispossess the hereditary duke. Could the metal be molten and poured into his mould?

What concerned him most deeply was the arrival of Louis d'Orléans. Louis d'Orléans had inherited Asti from his Italian grandmother, Valentina Visconti. Visconti, in the middle ages, spelled Milan. No one could have any illusions in France about the family tree of the superb Ludovico. His dynasty was two generations old. His father had been a plain fighting man, a magnificent condottiere, who carved his fame with his sword and grafted his stock on an illegitimate Visconti. Louis d'Orléans, on the other hand, felt himself to be a dynast in every bone of his body. For all his campaigner's heartiness, he was born elect. Asti was his territory, inherited from his illustrious grandmother. Milan, in his opinion, was also his territory. He had come to Italy with his royal cousin, but he was going no farther than Lombardy.

And around these French invaders with their royal claims and their superior air surged an army of forty thousand, backed by the best artillery in the world.

Charles rose with cheerfulness to the enterprise before him. Like a distracted child in fairyland, he really wanted to see everything of the treasures in dazzling Italy. He had just come through Turin where the zanies had been sent out to greet him, and where the Duchess of Savoy had lent him her jewels. Italy enthralled him. He had just been met by eighty ladies at the castle outside Asti and had stood on his toes to kiss every one of them. This was an occasion that the Italian princesses had awaited with a thrill, since it was a strange French custom. Meanwhile, deep in his indolent body, Ludovico Sforza quivered at the turn his diplomacy had taken. Venice was stirring unhappily. Florence was ready to prostrate itself. The Pope, Alexander VI, nervously packed and unpacked his policy from hour to hour.

While these events were preparing, Beatrice d'Este, in a captivating new red hat, was waiting to receive Charles. Beatrice was a fearless, spirited, buoyant young woman, anxious to play her part in European politics. But Charles could not come. He fell ill. In a month, however, he was on his way to Naples, "to the sound of violins, marching on branches and on flowers." So the little King rode down a prostrate Italy, his charger as glorious as his costume, his gay plumes nodding.

At Florence, where Savonarola welcomed him, the Medici fled. Here Charles and his advisers made open declaration of his great reason for proceeding to Naples. He wished to conquer the Turk. It was a Holy Enterprise. God was his Witness that he sought to spread the glory and the benefits of the Christian religion.

Charles wanted particularly to enlist the Sultan's brother Djem, now a prisoner at the Vatican. With Djem by his side he would attack the Sultan Bajazet in Greece, rallying Djem's partisans.

But the Pope, Alexander VI, had not been reckoned with. As early as July, Alexander had himself enlisted Bajazet against the French. The Holy Father secretly begged the unspeakable and perfidious Turk to strike at France through Venice: he did not want France in Naples (where one of his sons was now allied by marriage) and he secretly sought the Turk's confederacy against the new Crusader.

The Turk responded gratefully to the Holy Father, proposing however that the simplest method would be to have Djem murdered, for which he was willing to pay the Pope three hundred thousand ducats.

Meanwhile the Pope received Charles VIII paternally, lifting him from his knees, embracing him, making Briçonnet cardinal, naming Charles Eldest Son of the Church.

The French nobles swarmed over the Vatican. Their disorder, their "mocking and satiric gaiety," their insolence, deeply troubled the wardens of propriety. The Pope stumbling through an unfamiliar special mass, giving Communion to the wrong people, appearing in a white biretta—everything upset the custodians of tradition. And as for little Charles, the master of ceremonies wrung his hands.

Djem, the melancholy Turk, was taken from Rome to accompany Charles to Naples. In a few days he mysteriously sickened and died. Cesare Borgia, the Pope's son, who was also accompanying Charles, sneaked home, disguised as a groom. "Those underhand curs," Charles exclaimed, "and the Pope the very first of them."

15

Such was the temper of that strange, that reckless, act of aggression that was to bring France into Italy. It was a maggot, no doubt, in the brain of the French King, but the French King was simply a bit of agar in which political microbes could multiply, a child credulous enough for empire or pious enough for crusade. Plato speaks of those "fierce and crafty natures" who surround a feeble ruler. They fostered the capture of Naples. An army of forty thousand is not set on foot by a youth who has been reading fairy tales. It was a great composite enterprise. Innumerable practical men pulled the wires.

And from this act, throughout Francis's adolescence, would roll up storm after storm, the weather of his young life. But just because Charles VIII and Louis XII had ploughed in Italy, Francis I would reap in it. It would make a soldier of him, battling on the plains of Lombardy, but no less would it mould him as a Renaissance prince. Just as Charles V would be steeped in Spain, so he would be saturated in Italy. His horizon was widened by the wars.

Yet, under his feet was the national state that Louis XI had ordained. It began with the elimination of Burgundy and the absorption of Brittany, the abandonment of Christian leadership by the warring Popes and the brutal unsocial code of absolutism.

What no man could have foreseen, unless he had drilling gaze of Machiavelli, was the danger that would come from disregarding Ferdinand. It would turn out incalculable and appalling, once Spain and the empire united under Charles V, to veneer Italy with the Habsburgs for hundreds of years. In those terms the struggle for Italy would have to be waged by Francis. And this struggle was initiated on the day he was born.

But he is not yet born, the long-nosed prince. We may now leave the vast complications of European history to glance at his future mother. She is Louise of Savoy, and she is at Amboise, under the chilly hand of the Regent, Anne of France.

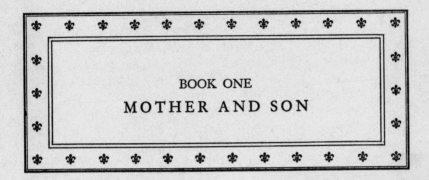

BOOK ONE

MOTHER AND SON

❖ ❖ ❖ ❖ ❖ ❖ ❖ ❖ ❖ ❖ ❖ ❖ ❖

MOTHER AND SON

Down the corridors of Amboise, in the year 1487, a subdued little person went to mass every morning. The fingers of light that barred her path, and that ran across her as she proceeded, lifted at times to the face of a child, round and immature. But this was not the open face of childhood; already she knew the world and was as much oppressed by it as her small body was hampered by custom. She moved in long skirts, a miniature woman, wearing the full habit that is still perpetuated by nuns.

In 1487 the castle at Amboise was still medieval. Like its solid compères nearby, at Loches, Langeais, Chinon, it was a castle intended for war, with heavy masonry built for a siege and windows tight with suspicion. It was, of course, still the good old times, the age of Christian faith and Gothic cathedrals, but this child was no less sombre because the age was Christian.

On one single fact depended her whole life: she was a ward of the Regent. In a strict court where a great and devout lady presided she was a little nobody. She was in the shadow of a protectress, sheltered by her, and cut off from the light.

The great lady, Anne of France, was the daughter and true heir of Louis XI, and no one could have better looked the part. She stood straight as a lance. Her brown eyes were direct in their gaze, clear and prominent. They flinched from no problem of state. One could not say that the Regent was beautiful, with her thin lips, her thin hands, her haughty nose, her prudent chin. But even at her present age, twenty-seven, she was already a noble priestess of power. She had that beauty of precision that is seen in a shapely blade, and this blade had been shaped by Louis XI. But when the crooked father has a straight disciple in his favourite daughter the lesson is only too well applied. Anne of France translated her father's realism into an aristocratic code, which she herself was soon to write down. It would quote Socrates and St. Paul. It would set forth St. Thomas and St. Bernard, St. Ambrose, St. Augustine. Vanities, delights and wild pleasures would be gravely rebuked. Blandishments and signs of love would be disowned. Confidences would be distrusted and jests frowned upon. No man would be allowed to press a maiden's hand or touch her foot. The woman of forty would be denied cosmetic. What would be permitted, besides three Our Fathers and three Hail Marys every morning and evening, would be the humility of the Christian, the mild manner of the honourable dame, the cold assurance, the affability, the good repute. Anne of France would counsel a serene control of eye and tongue, a sense of rank, a pure discipline of the heart, in the interest of a dominance which aimed as much to lessen friction as to direct the state. Shrewd, self-sacrificing, foresighted and formidable, the Regent ruled Amboise for her little brother Charles VIII with a dignity that was royal to its core.

Her ward, Louise of Savoy, was kept in place. She had the robes that the Regent thought fitting for her condition. She had her modest corner in the tapestried chamber, hearing tapestried stories, embroidering, learning the lute. No glamour invested the child. Her destiny was to marry an impoverished count and to become Countess of Angoulême. For three years her prospective husband had been a rebel. She hardly knew him, and he took not the slightest interest in her. This made her even more negligible in the eyes of the Regent. She was a minor figure whom Anne of France surveyed, and in this school of power, so well housed at Amboise, the girl was learning her lesson. This was her true education, more than her Latin, more than Italian, more than her needlework or her prayers.

She perfectly consumed the lesson as she learned it. On her young face, to judge by her early portraits, she had something of that institutional look which is best observed on the faces of found-lings and orphans in large and comfortless orphan asylums. It is a face filmed with caution. A look of wary obedience is on top, and just underneath the nip of intelligence, calculating the hazards of disobedience.

Yet below the institutional surface resided a richly emotional Louise. She had a full imagination, crude, hungry, in love with marvels and prodigies, tenacious and superstitious. Beneath the imagination, or running through it, there was actual desire, ardent and positive, the whole nature founding itself on a rock of will. So, at any rate, might be guessed by anyone who took an interest in the youngster, but of this complete personality only the least tip jutted above the planing surface of Amboise. The exposed character was well guarded, and the eyes obediently round.

The thing that kept the girl most subjected was her Savoy family. Her aunt had of course been married to Louis XI, but Queen Charlotte had been afraid of her shadow, chivvied by Louis with his teasing malignity, bullied almost into imbecility. Louise could not escape the atmosphere in which a dismal family fortune envelops a child. But she did not bow to the suggestion of failure. There was something strong in her fibre that resisted it, a kind of obstinacy and patience. Perhaps she had a saving memory, a far hill with a touch of sun on it, which would be the place she was born in, the castle of Pont d'Ain in Bresse.

The drama of her life, at any rate, was now cast in France. It was not in the wide nation, the richest and strongest single unit of Europe, but inside the castle, inside the caste, inside the family, with formal religion to accompany it, and sinewy human motives to guide it. And so one imagines her going and coming, a veiled, enigmatic child, in this company of the royal wards at Amboise.

2

Charles d'Angoulême was betrothed to Louise. It had helped to make him a rebel. But as a rebel he lacked three useful things—

an army, the resources that feed an army, and the programme that rallies it. So he rather invited defeat.

Anne of France herself rode out of Amboise in the summer of 1487, taking the malformed little King with her, as a chancellor might take his seal of office. Her first task was to mop up Charles d'Angoulême. He nimbly retreated before her. She advanced. She nearly swept him into the Gironde. Managing to evade her, he slipped away to a neighbouring château. But it was hopeless for so feeble a rebel to continue his Mad War. The feudal game was finished. One of his satellites brought in his submission, and this was what the politic Regent wanted. To divide Charles d'Angoulême from his naughty cousin Orléans would enable the Regent to turn all her attention to Brittany. She made it easy for Charles. She offered him the governorship of Guyenne. Then, having padded the blow, she stunned him with the demand that he fulfil her father's plan by marrying Louise, aged eleven.

It was a shock. When Charles took to the martial life in 1485 he had cheerfully put Louise out of his mind. Not only had he a child by his mistress Jeanne de Polignac, but to this little brood he had incontinently added two other children by two other women. These, with Orléans insouciance, he had brought under Jeanne de Polignac's wing. To include a wife, aged eleven, was complicating. But the Regent was obdurate. So again Charles submitted.

Such was the courtship that preceded the marriage of Francis's father and mother. No one knows how the approaching wedding was announced to the child. No one knows her emotions, whether panic or dismay or relief, resignation or curiosity. But so began her career as a woman, giving her a home in the Angoumois.

3

Louise began actually to live with Charles as his wife between fourteen and fifteen. At no time did he disguise his existing establishment. Jeanne de Polignac lived with him at Angoulême. So did Jeanne, their little girl. Souveraine and Madeleine, mothers unknown, could not be hidden away in a cupboard. They were indeed bastards, as was René of Savoy, Louise's own brother, but though chastity did not seem to be violently characteristic of court circles, the extraordinary thing about the Angoumois establishment was the cheerful dominance of Jeanne de Polignac.

She was, in every real sense, the châtelaine; and when the young wife arrived at Cognac, she was embraced by this presence, which must have been disarming. Instead of a battle between wife and mistress, with traditional dignity and animosity, there was, instantly or very soon, a durable attachment between the elder woman of inferior rank and the friendless girl from princely Savoy. Jeanne de Polignac flowed round monogamy with a serene disregard, becoming the permanent ally of Louise and the faithful guardian of Louise's children.

Beneath this generous ease there was, of course, a worldly and immoral practicality. Nothing like it would be counselled by Anne of France in her spotless Instructions to her Daughter. And yet it was this correct Anne of France who had encased her ward Louise in the loose household at Angoulême.

Louise's early life at Cognac has to be inferred from a few bare facts. Her ex-rebel of a husband, governor of Guyenne as well as Count of Angoulême, had no more than 10,000 francs in revenue plus her own 3,000. How he could ever have raised 40,000 francs to lend to his cousin Orléans when the latter was besieged in Novara is hard to understand. His household, no matter how much Guyenne added to the original income, was by all accounts never an affluent one. It could not afford the hunts and banquets and tournaments which made the Loire a centre of royal festivity and could so easily ruin an exuberant noble. Cognac was constricted. It was on a small scale. Its falcons, its horses and its hounds were, beyond doubt, as good as rank demanded, but there must have been a constant struggle to keep up appearances.

The hero of this struggle could hardly have been Charles d'Angoulême. He was evidently an easy-going man. Whether in the early thirties he was already fattish and grey, with a longish nose, is only a guess. His portrait has not been indisputably identified. Though he went on frequent long journeys and took part, because of his rank, in all high ceremonial events and reunions, he never really broke through the merciless snobbishness of historic inattention.

At Cognac, however, goodwill clearly kept the establishment going. Jeanne de Polignac was not misplaced. She was not Louise's rival, since she was not of a rank to marry an Angoulême. A Polignac would marry a Larochefoucauld, and the Larochefoucauld château would be of a soaring elegance, but Charles d'Angoulême had been prohibited from marrying Jeanne, daughter of a Chabot, by the clutch of his ancestral ghosts. He existed to uphold a tradition, and his obedience to that tradition glorified him at the expense of subjecting him. Charles d'Angoulême enjoyed loyalty because his father Jean d'Angoulême had had it and his grandfather Louis d'Orléans had had it and his great-grandfather Charles V had had it, roi de France. It warmed the heart of servitors and archers and grooms and valets and their round-bosomed wives and their round-thighed daughters and their round-eyed infants to look up at the Great Lord as he strolled around the kennels.

In such a society, so sincerely aristocratic, Jeanne de Polignac submitted to the Angoulême tradition, and her alliance with it was completely flexible. We soon find that it engaged more than the handsome Jeanne herself. We find her brother Jean as maître d'hôtel, and her brother Elie will be Francis's chamberlain. Also, under her wing, were warmly and firmly sheltered the Count's two other children, and the amusing fact is that, for all the irregularity of origin, a certain humane unity was successfully fostered under the tenacious management of Jeanne. A Russian novelist could not resist the full realities of such a household, but we only see it through the greying distance, far away, with little knowledge of the natures, lacquered by politeness, with which Louise of Savoy came to deal. Yet how well the lacquer will make them wear! In spite of every prejudice and every disadvantage, Jeanne de Polignac will act as mother not only to her own Jeanne and to Souveraine and to Madeleine, but will go on with Louise into the upbringing of Marguerite and Francis. It is in her room and under her care that Francis will spend his first seven years. The triumph of this relationship is a triumph of compromise, of clear perception, of a convinced exclusion of the ideal. Louise of Savoy and Jeanne de Polignac make friends against obstacles that no romantic attitude could have surmounted. Aristocracy required it.

Charles had indeed tried to escape his handicapped marriage. But

to be an aristocrat implied some marriage of convenience. A freak-
ish person might marry for love. Or a proposed marriage might
be too grotesque. Anne of Brittany, for instance, had just put down
her girlish foot when she was offered an impossible widower, the
florid, stunted, grunting, hobbling Alain d'Albret. But when one's
livelihood rested solely on inheritance, and when inheritances could
solely be acquired by marriage, marriage had naturally to ignore
"nature" and to obey calm intelligence.

This put a strain on the time-honoured sacrament. But French
nobility had to survive, and they had to marry on the basis of
power, which would be the right combination of property and class.
They did not start with love, which might be illusory. An heiress
might have a squint or a sharp tongue, but there is another beauty
in châteaux, acreage, market towns, toll gates, bridges, fishing rights
and the salt monopoly. Out of these established goods came social
amenity. Conflicts sprang out of unneighbourly disagreements
which could reasonably be solved by marriage. Deficiencies in plate
(wars have to be paid for) could be remedied by the dot. Noblemen have to live at court. There would be no chance for them to
repair their fortunes except by combining with the fortunate. And
if this applied to the lesser aristocracy, it was the supreme rule for
royalty. The whole of dynastic Europe was committed, and had
been committed for hundreds of years, to the notion of reasonable
marriage, duty marriage, power marriage, marriage on the lines of
policy and politics, marriage for revenue.

It was in this state of affairs that Jeanne de Polignac presided.

If marriage based on reason could, with Anne of France, rise
to an exquisite circumspection, it is idle to suppose that it was
usually circumspect. The Heptameron, written by Francis's sister,
would be evidence on the other side. Outwardly there would be
decorum. Not only would strawberries and apples play their part
in the garden, and violets and carnations in the flower-beds; not
only would the shrubs behave in the park, with deer and boar and
snipe and carp fitting into the cast, but so would guests and hosts
have the same elaborate alphabet of decorum. Yet the whole formal
performance would have its compensatory protest. The humour
of the cuckold, the ribaldry of the lascivious wife, would in their
rough way declare allegiance to an instinct that refuses to fit into

a system. The château could not respect free personality, yet it bore within itself a quaint duplicity, its vitality overflowing, its superb manner concealing the burble and gurgle of an instinct. From master and mistress, down to the matted scullion, there would be a constant comedy of spontaneous human feeling; the unconquerable desire of each individual to bring life into conformity with his own self-esteem, his own sensibility, his heart. Here the duke and the chimney-sweep would be at one: each thrusting against the walls that corseted him. And sometimes, when the allée was black under the moon, and the river swum silver below the silent terrace, there would be hardly one human being in this whole contraption of prestige who was not either richly indecorous behind the arras or else bitterly or nobly tormented by contradiction.

But Jeanne de Polignac lifted contradiction into the light. She made easy the noviceship of Louise of Savoy.

4

Louise herself had been to a good school. She took her new bearings carefully, and on her own side she deliberately allowed Jeanne de Polignac to slide into the position of her friend. The trump-card, after all, was hers, and she was shrewd enough to know it. She was going to have a child. Where Jeanne's child and the other children could only be advanced by favour, hers would have status. That gave the fifteen-year-old girl her vital advantage. She needed only one thing to have supremacy even with her husband. She needed an heir.

The change from the subdued orphan into the confident little châtelaine was not long in shaping itself. Louise divided her heart from her head without agony. What most occupied her was for her ardent prayers to be answered, and a male heir to arrive.

She believed she was to come to her full reward in 1492. Everything depended, however, on the help of providence. A disappointment befell her. At Angoulême in April she gave birth to a mere girl. This unimportant daughter was Marguerite, who was named after the doddering grandmother. Louise still needed a male child to fortify her within the tradition.

5

Charles VIII was now married to Anne of Brittany.

It was this new Queen who absorbed Louise. Anne of Brittany might have a limp, just as Jeanne de France had a limp and Alain d'Albret had a limp, and little Suzanne de Bourbon. As the only good doctors, so far, seemed to be the Italians and the Jews, the limping procession would go on and on, with enormous faith in relics and no faith in science. But even if the little King Charles VIII had a grotesque physique, even if young Anne was a skimpy creature, everything would depend on her power to increase and multiply. Louise of Savoy, now sixteen, knew that between her own official husband and the throne of France there still stood no one but Louis d'Orléans, married to a cripple, and little Charles VIII, himself deformed. Behind her inferior status and her prudent manner there pushed this vigorous consciousness of a dramatic possibility. Her husband might easily, easily become King!

The birth of Marguerite did not reinforce her. But at sixteen she could look forward to a male heir. Only, what would happen with the new queen at Amboise?

The new queen promptly answered Louise by giving birth to a sound and substantial boy.

This gave the throne a dauphin. The child was christened Charles-Orland. Charles VIII had refuted dismal croaking. Anne of Brittany flounced her Breton cloak over duchy and kingdom.

Louise was young but stirring with positive force. Had her nature been a tenth as gentle as that of the baby she was putting out to nurse, perhaps she could have controlled her tension. But she was not gentle by nature. She was hot, narrow, confined. She had vitality. The thought that fortune had given a male heir to her rival, shutting her out from glories and splendours, whipped up depths in that darkness where her imagination and her desires fermented. Louise was very young. Life still shook out fresh green leaves around her, and she could no more keep from aspiring than a lark from soaring. She suffered, so far, only the fresh premonitions of her ambition. But already her heart shrank at the mere name of Anne of Brittany. She felt toward that newcomer an inexplicable, an ineradicable, hostility.

One of the aids that Anne of Brittany had sought for procuring a male heir was the prayerful intercession of the Good Man, Francis de Paule (Paola), who was to become godfather to the dauphin. Francis de Paule was pushing on towards his hundredth year. He had been brought from Calabria by Louis XI in those last terrible months when every royal nerve cried out against the King's going to his accounting. The saint had soothed Louis, sitting on a mat apart from the agonized King. He was simple and detached, deep in prayer. He wore almost nothing. He pushed aside the gold bowl and ate out of his wooden one. He wanted nothing more luxurious than fruit—and not as much as the vegetarian Emperor Frederick, Maximilian's father, who had just died from eating eight entire melons. Francis de Paule could not avoid a great reputation as a saintly man. He had inhabited a cave in Calabria and nothing was easier than to find a cave for him on the chalky banks of the Loire. To him there went in pilgrimage all the women of the royal family. The expectant mothers begged for male children. And Louise, visiting Amboise, besought Francis de Paule and left him, with holy candles.

But the midwife had no chance to light a candle for her. She was at Cognac in the September of 1494. Her husband had just come from Lyon. It was the twelfth of the month. Toward the close of the day her pains began as she was out of doors. She was hurried to a quiet corner, under a tree, according to tradition. There, in the open air, she gave birth to a well-formed son and heir. Francis would be his name. The young mother gloried in him.

6

The birth of Francis, on September 12, 1494, was an event of great importance at Cognac and Angoulême. It was fêted, at the moment, in the generous liquors of the country. It was celebrated at the christening. The châteaux talked of it. The country people discussed it in warm detail. But outside Angoumois it was of less startling interest. The Italian war completely overshadowed it. On the very day that Francis was born, Charles VIII was at Asti, meeting Ludovico Sforza. He had departed from Lyon with an army of 40,000 for the conquest of Naples. Francis's father had said good-

bye to him at Lyon, returning to look after Guyenne. The Angoulême family were out of it, even in wartime.

7

All during that summer of 1495, there was unusual activity at
Amboise. The castle was rebuilding. The work had been sent forward by candle-light through the winter, against the King's coming home, and it did not slacken as summer followed spring on
the Loire.

Everywhere, in the grounds, up the ramps, by the windows,
could be seen the quick figures of directed workmen. Crouching
artisans laid parquet floors. Thick walls were pierced for light with
crowbar and sledge. Joiners framed the open spaces that would
look out on new gardens. Neapolitan stonemasons brought into
relief the gracile foliage and the joyous arabesques that spoke for
them of Naples, their brown hands working deftly the creamy
stone. For them it was an art as well as a craft, and they strutted
about the castle, being Neapolitans. Some of their kind would soon
cross the Channel to Westminster, where the insular craftsmen
would grumble against the foreigners. The French craftsmen did
not love them, but the French were nimble-minded, and when the
booty that had escaped the battle of Fornovo arrived with the dust
of Italy still on it—tapestries, marble, porphyry and manuscripts
and paintings—they unpacked these treasures with their brains in
their finger-tips, instantly detecting the new spirit—the vibration of
Greece, the something of the flesh that is imperishable, the beauty
from the other side of Galilee. The Italians had opened both arms
to embrace the antique; France on the Loire was now embracing
Italy.

This work at Amboise was a passionate response to profane in-
fluences, a direct outcome of the great French attempt to dominate
the Mediterranean. It was a change in idiom, as when crusaders
had brought back the Byzantine for the glory of Chartres. But it
was more than that; it was a change of ideal. Sedate France, confirmed in medieval stone, was yielding to a new delight. The king
had begun to decorate his own house rather than the house of
God. The cathedral was ceding to the château.

This change that began with Amboise found its natural home on the Loire. Though the rose, seen in Persia by a wondering voyager, was destined to be brought north to the edge of ice, it is not everyone who can foster roses. The luxurious Renaissance would flow from Italy into every land in Europe, but it could only thrive where wealth and peace could nourish it. Hence in France, which is the crossroads of the world, tense to preserve itself and yet alert to change, there were resistances in some communities while in others there was prompt and suave adaptation. Paris was not the first to offer itself. Paris was still a municipal porcupine. The princely Renaissance sought a home more pliant to its will, and found it in this valley of the Loire.

A copious river gives a living character to the land through which it broadens down. The Loire valley of itself would be charming, if one could imagine it without the river, on account of its openness, fringed by long woods and melting into easy hills. But the river makes it resplendent. Bosomed with debris torn from the upper reaches, the valley still presents the very picture of equable and beneficent fertility when the summer sun gleams on vine and cornfield, bathing its dikes, its yellow sands, its tufted islands, the forests blue-green in the swimming distance and beyond everything the spreading waters that move onward with a slumbering grace. The light sparkles in summer. The heat is strong but caressing, with a whiff of the ocean in it. Nature hides its effort; it says little of grey days and lashing rain and grey green waters: this river which has taken its rise at a point further south than Milan seems to change its course by intention, to gather a whole territory within the generous crook of its elbow, to turn it toward the south and the sun.

Nature has favoured the Loire, bringing the spaces about it into kind harmony with its own movement and expanse. But not nature alone has ordered Touraine. Such a river in Canada or deep Africa would have the same happy proportion: what would be missing would be the mind. The Loire has served its apprenticeship to a developing nature. Mile by mile, the river enrolls the adventure that has no other name but French.

This adventure was already a prolonged one. The Celtic tribes had once gazed across these waters or had burned human victims in its groves. Rome had challenged the Celts on these river-banks, and in its shallow pools Celtic blood had mingled with that of Cæsar's legionaries. At Orléans the merchants of the Empire had been massacred. At Orléans the swarms of Attila were later held in check, while in the years that followed blunt Saxons had anchored at the mouth, and Vikings behind striped sails had sailed up and sailed away. Through these disputed centuries the valley was moulded by a distinctive desire, an individual discovery, a creation that is France. In the very year that raiders had stood on the prow with bare steel, the cross was raised on a high spire, and pillared temples had gone over to the god of Martin. Slow vessels had lumbered along, heavy with stone and iron, deep with corn and round with wine. These were the materials of a new delight in living. The tributary rivers brought down rich earth and towns lifted their walls above the river. Lean river-men cried hoarse cries as they steered in shifting channels, or they lingered for weeks by the waterside when the capricious river was parched. The waters in full flood were tamed under graceful stone and wooden bridges. As the dangers of invasion subsided, the handsome cities multiplied. High escarpments began to blossom in a new architecture. And soon, like a peal of bells, from one white terrace to another, Italianate castles would ring the change from feudalism to the Renaissance. A predatory class would adopt new ways of mastery, deferring pride, ambition, energy, to the beauty of their visible existence and to the dominance of an absolute King.

The news of these changes reached Louise of Savoy and Charles d'Angoulême in their province, and they observed the changes when they came to the Loire. They were, in their way, like children outside the festive window.

8

In the late autumn the workmen went silent at Amboise: the little dauphin was mortally sick. Charles VIII was still at Lyon while his wife, Anne of Brittany, was with the Regent at Moulins. The King's arrival at Lyon was the last stage before the reunion of the royal family, but the news from Amboise was always reassuring. Charles-Orland had been left in the best of hands. He was a robust and self-reliant child, quaintly forward for his age. He had excellent physicians. His godfather alone, the holy Francis de Paule, was enough to ward off every misfortune. No one was disquieted.

But as the days went on the emaciated godfather could only bow his head. The child lay feverish in his deep cradle, with concerned faces peering down at him.

The Bourdichon portrait that the fond father carried away with him to Italy showed what Charles-Orland was like. He seems almost the universal child, the little nose, the chubby face, the small plump hands. He is not squared to the artist, he stands askew, he clasps his beads with the unevenness and unsteadiness of a serious two-year-old. His bonnet might be a peasant bonnet. His bib is the bib of a promenading, plopping, grubbing infant, whose eyes look out with a guarded wonder while his mouth is open between living breaths. This is not the combed and perfumed darling who is to appear in the next generation, the beads banished and a coquettish spaniel in courtly hands. In the next generation the bonnet will become a plumed hat, the bib will be a rich velvet surcoat with finely pleated shirt and cuffs edged and frilled. Charles-Orland is still near the nursery. His hair is not neat. He is not a symbol of princely affluence; he is a child, connected with the plaintive and submissive simplicities of human nature.

One of these simplicities is to die. To the alarm and horror of the physicians the little dauphin was to lose his fight. He was three years old, and it was to their dead child that Charles VIII and Anne came home.

It was not Charles VIII who was grief-stricken. The death of the dauphin scarcely rippled his nerves. With Anne it was very different. Anne was a serious human being. She was now eighteen. The loss of her boy, coming on the heels of foolish reassuring letters from the physicians, shocked her in her soul. Was she to blame? Was this a punishment because she had broken her betrothal to Maximilian? She cried bitter tears, beside herself with grief and anger.

The royal physicians rattled their brains to find some distraction for her. It was December, the month of Noel. They were at their wits' end. They urged the royal household to think up something new—games, mummeries, masquerades. They invited in particular the King's royal cousin, Louis d'Orléans.

9

Louis d'Orléans came at once from Blois to take his part in distracting Charles and Anne. After his imprisonment at Bourges, he had sworn amity on the True Cross both with Charles and the Regent. He was reckoned a friend, and he had bound the King to himself by the hard campaign in Italy. There was every reason he should fall in with the suggestion of the Court physicians.

But these physicians did not count on one fact, that the death of the little dauphin made Louis heir apparent to the throne.

It was only too human that Louis should palpitate at having come nearer to the throne. Already the throne soared in the landscape just as a solitary peak rears itself, even in a hilly country, to catch the eye at every angle, to hold itself austere in its isolation, mysterious in its simplicity, bold and dominant and inescapable, already deified because standing above everything. The wonder was that an eager man who had watched Richard III could sheath his violent desire.

He came to Amboise. What to Anne and Charles VIII was a painful effort was a festival to Louis d'Orléans. Never since the royal marriage had he forgotten that the one obstacle between himself and the glistening throne was this royal baby. Louis was by no means a brutal man. But he had himself been deprived of heirs through the malevolence of Charles's father; it was too much that he should be expected to feel benevolent when Charles VIII was deprived of heirs. He came to Amboise in mimic grief.

And, when he had drunk his full in the warmed hall where the music was playing and the dance was spinning, his hilarity got beyond his control. He mocked, danced, laughed, pantomimed outrageously. His immoderate gaiety, to Anne's shocked nerves, became exultation at the death of her child. The fury that she had felt with the physicians turned on Louis d'Orléans. He was ordered from Amboise.

10

No delicacy had kept Louis from betraying that he was madly excited. The same avidity gripped the quiescent family at Cognac. They were further off than Louis. He was in the parterre on the Loire: they were in the poor back seats in Angoumois. But they alone had a male heir. Louise of Savoy was as sturdy as any country girl from Bresse. Twice already she had defeated the obstetricians: she was the mother of two beautifully healthy children, and her own slim person, with straight back and quick head, gave her the prospect of a flourishing family. The Angoulême prospects gleamed once again, with the dauphin gone.

It was cold at Cognac in December, but the news was too stirring to be contained alone. With secret thoughts bubbling underneath, they prepared their funeral clothes and funeral faces. The whole family would reunite at Amboise around the little coffin.

Out of the castle at Cognac started the count and Louise, following the rough road under bare boughs through inclement December.

They had hardly reached Châteauneuf on this pious journey, toward evening, before Charles d'Angoulême was suddenly bent double with pain. Carried from his saddle, put instantly to bed, he was seen to be in a high fever, whether it was from pleurisy or pneumonia. Messengers were sent back to Cognac for a physician, then to Angoulême, and then to Poitiers. The emergency changed Louise of Savoy into a nurse. Directing everyone about her, taking immediate and complete charge, she never spared herself for a moment. He could not be moved. The doctors came, one colliding with the other. Louise had no romantic reason to devote herself to her husband; but as he lay in bed, stertorous, grisly, grim with fever, she applied herself with all the forces of her nature to an arduous and desperate task. For two weeks she stood by him, through a Christmas ironically forlorn, never undressing or going from his side. By this time she had made hospital around her invalid. Physicians, counsellors, priests were with her. They compelled her to lie down. But her husband grew no better. Would he die? He believed it. He made his will in her favour. He found bare vitality to indicate the many small bequests he had in mind. By the morning of New Year's Day, 1496, the experienced observers shook their heads. Francis's father was sinking. The parchment was put under his hand. He made his great effort: he signed his will. Then he died.

II

Louise returned to her children at Cognac. To have lost her husband, who was only thirty-six, could be taken as a personal sorrow, and some of her servitors were tearful and sad, but the loss of Charles d'Angoulême, stripped of all gesture, was enough to weigh on the young widow. She was not yet twenty. His death was shockingly sudden. It cut off a fruitful marriage, narrowed her hopes to a single son, and left her alone to guard the flame. At Cognac she could count on warm partisans, and did count on them, but at court she had no powerful friends. Her wealth was limited. Her husband's will did not entrust Francis to her. She was not in a strong position to direct their fortunes.

If she was apprehensive, she had good reason for it. Louis d'Orléans had an ally who urged him to insist on the full control of Louise's household. It was a quiet move in legal order, adroit and foresighted. The boy might one day be King. To mould him from the beginning could be a source of inexhaustible power for the man, or men, who could do it. Louis XI could have done it; Louis d'Orléans and his adviser, the Marshal de Gié, imagined themselves as masters of that same political wile. Gié had been a page to Louis XI. He was a Breton, stubborn and positive, but his mind and his hand were heavy. He loved the game of power, but greedily, not subtly. In the long contest that he now opened with Louise of Savoy he gave no great promise of outplaying his opponent.

Louise had gone to a school of power. She was a woman, but neither timid nor yielding, far from expecting indulgence or goodwill. And now she had something passionate to live for, with ageless instinct in her bones. Outwardly, she was a demure countess in mourning, but actually she stood over her young like a healthy animal, alert, dangerous, with a magnificent gift for preserving what was hers. She was not merely a primitive mother protecting her young, she was the proprietor of a male child in whose destiny she stubbornly, even frantically, believed. Had not the Good Man, Francis de Paule, told her that her son would one day be King? She had that mystic "apprehension of truths beyond the understanding" which can never be argued or even denied.

She demanded the payment of her dot. That was a practical retort to Louis d'Orléans which he did not care to counter, so she remained the actual guardian of her boy.

To marry her off would get her out of the way. But the young widow had her own ideas on this score. Marriage for her had been penal. She had served her term. Now she had something to which she could give herself without fear and without scruple. To have loved her husband would have been worse than tragic, it would have been ridiculous. But her son was born within the citadel of the ego. He was her own.

No one could call this young mother commonplace. She was one of those whose light never lances out of the personal, but within the limits of her spirited nature and her clear interests she lived with an intensity that no one near her could neglect. She was a tough cortex around the life of her son. Louise was the mother, not of her two children, but of her male child, the heir. Marguerite she treated with the calm proprietorship which mothers have for good children whom they take for granted. Francis she never took for granted. She fluttered, twittered, ululated over the cradle of her darling. She did not live in him because she loved him. She loved him because she lived in him. He was more to her than a person who held her by charm. Alluring he had already become for the tender little Marguerite, who personally loved him. For the mother he was the air she breathed. She could not detach herself from the career that he was to lead, the triumph he was to win. His career would be her own, his triumph hers. She possessed all to herself the key to the greatest monarchy on earth. The very uncertainty of the inheritance aroused in her all the protective impulses, even the animosity and suspicion, of which an energetic nature is capable. Big stakes call out fangs and claws. Louise was well equipped to take care of herself and to protect her conqueror.

And she had a loyal personal entourage to count on. She and

her satellites, the Saint-Gelais and the Polignacs, would hold their
ground against every interference.

12

At first the widow's life narrowed down to the necessities of her
small court. Her husband, insignificant as he seemed, had really
been master. Now she had to adminster Cognac and Angoulême,
Romorantin and Melle.

Louise was pretty as a young widow. Her eyes were of that
slatey blue which have gravity behind their inquiry, but she had
the light auburn hair and the fair skin which go so well with
mourning. An earnest young widow with an inviting mouth, small,
blonde, well-formed, she was emerging from the dense shadow of
her childhood as a not insignificant person.

But her first years of widowhood were absorbed in her family.
Charles VIII's council decided that Louis d'Orléans should be
merely a sort of supervising guardian, countersigning her expenses
and kept aware of the changes in her household. She retained Jean
de Saint-Gelais as her chamberlain, and the Polignacs were not
disturbed. Her life was therefore staidly preoccupied with her
establishment, her widowhood dashed with noble resignation.

Those who spied on her soon began to speculate on her chamberlain, Jean de Saint-Gelais. He was much too sprightly, too gallant
and insinuating and facile, not to be regarded inevitably as dangerous. A young and smouldering widow, an experienced and adapt-
able chamberlain of forty who was in and out as he wished, what
could keep them from fidelity to nature, or the "filthy and
abominable wickedness of the heart"? It was already clear to the
burly Gié that the chamberlain meant too much to Louise of
Savoy. He would have banished him.

The widow's court at Cognac developed as a miniature of royal
existence on the Loire, and no one could have said that the new
Amboise was a model of propriety. Charles VIII was surrounded
by spirited young soldiers of the gayest type. The adventure of
Clara Gonzaga, recounted in the Heptameron, could outdo anything that Louise ever imagined. All one could say of Cognac was
that it carried on the light Orléans tradition. Her artists were not

great. Her bishop Saint-Gelais voluptuously translated Ovid. Her illuminators melted clean Flemish clarity into a sort of Boccaccian missal. Her circle softened the austerity of young widowhood, with Anne of Brittany disapproving, and Anne of France disdainful. But, as its actual term wore on, it became evident that if Louise of Savoy was anybody's mistress she was also her own mistress. Her mother-in-law's death in 1497, her father's death at Moulins soon after, gave life even more completely into her hands. With Francis's destiny those hands were devotedly occupied.

Yet, if the temper of her establishment was young, she was in her own way a great lady, and by nature and training she insisted on form. Her model was essentially Florentine. The very words that Lorenzo il Magnifico had used at Florence—*libri et liberi,* my books and my brood—were adopted by Louise. But her resources were provincial. We do not see a Michael Angelo at her table. She is not a connoisseur, educated by contact with genius, receiving with loving hands the bust of Plato, the bust of Hadrian, cameos, lustre ware, Greek vases, jewels, treasures from Arabia. Few men equalled the eager receptivity of Lorenzo in his rôle of magnifico. His farms, his herds, his pheasants, his racing stud, his gardens— these went with his shrewd ubiquity as a politician, his frank patronage and exploitation of the Church, his familiarity with philosophers and poets, his understanding of ostentation, his personal frugality. Though a commoner, whose vulgar origins would be reproached to his family for generations, the quality of his spirit was really magnificent: he had created a pattern of a culture that only kings could afford to follow. Louise could not rise to this creativeness of Florence, but her spirit was alive to it and Cognac coquetted with the arts.

Her coquetry, however, was never at the expense of her mission. When it came to Francis, she was the wary, quick protectress who underneath is the maternal wolf.

13

Perhaps by reason of her bereavement Louise remained outside the court. Anne of Brittany was deep in maternity, during these years with Charles VIII, and Charles VIII was deep in beautifying

Amboise. The Neapolitan campaign had turned out to be a miserable fiasco, yet one effect of it was that Spain took steps to meet French rivalry. Ferdinand arranged the double marriage with Austria. Margaret of Austria was to have the Infante, Juana was to have Philip the Handsome. While this political structure was being designed by a man as wily as Louis XI himself, the young French King and Queen were glorying over the exquisite chapel of Saint Blaise.

The little King was sad over Naples but elated over his Neapolitan gardeners. His oranges flourished. His peach tree bore fruit. His Italian craftsmen fashioned feather, concocted perfumes, carved alabaster. These diversions occupied him while Anne did her best to give him an heir—another boy, again christened Charles, who died in less than a month, and two others unnamed. The little King busied himself with jousts and tourneys, embellished his possessions, saw ambassadors and heard grievances, while the idea of Naples kept flitting like a swallow through the open belfry of his brain. But as the two parties in the council came to grips to gain control of him, an accident changed the reign to an interlude.

In the spring of 1498, Charles was escorting his wife to see a game of tennis that was to be played in the grassy foss, and on taking her by a low door into a sort of barn that had a gallery upstairs in view of the game, he struck his head against the lintel. He still took her up the ladder and sat chatting, when suddenly he went into a fit. An old mattress was dragged out. They laid him on it. Every one came as he pleased, to gape at him. There he was from two in the afternoon, life flickering once or twice, until he expired at eleven at night. It was a humble death that filled even the most veteran courtiers with awe. Louis d'Orléans broke into tears when they brought him the news at Blois.

14

Louise was with her children at Cognac when this sudden death occurred. Immediately her heart uplifted. Four sons had been born to her rival, Anne of Brittany, and all of them had died. This was the end of Louis XI's dynasty. The crown now passed to the genial Duke of Orléans, her husband's fellow-rebel, who would become

Louis XII. His fruitless marriage to the crippled Jeanne left the way
clear for her own Francis. Such a stroke of fortune, when widowhood had left her so defenceless, gave meaning to a life that had
no other outlet for feeling or self-respect. Francis was now dauphin,
and Louise could thank God that he was still in her hands.

She lost no time scanning the prospect. She aspired at once to
the vacant dukedom of Orléans for him. Energetic and aggressive,
but still demure in manner, she promptly arranged her affairs and
got ready for a journey to Paris to congratulate Louis XII. Her
chamberlain, Jean de Saint-Gelais, would accompany her, while
Jeanne de Polignac would stay behind to look after the children.

Strong heads buzzed with strange rumours. The crown had indeed passed to Louis d'Orléans, but he was outside the dominant
party in the council, he had been a rebel and a traitor; could he be
opposed? There was a throbbing pause for calculation. Had the
Bourbons been ready to seize power, had Francis been more than
four years old, the intriguers would have jumped at the chance to
dispute the crown with Louis. But Anne of France came forward
from Moulins and made the decisive gesture: her husband waited
on the new King. France drew a full breath and acquiesced in
Louis XII.

15

It was evident to Francis's mother that Louis was no longer a
robust man. Only thirty-six years old, disease had worn him. He
had suffered great hardships at Novara, had been in prison, had
gone the pace in every sport: his body, though wiry from hard
exercise, was already scorched and seared. His eyes were too bright
and prominent, his lips too thick and dry, his neck too goitrously
swollen. He quite possibly had Graves's disease. He ate frugally,
mainly boiled meat, and he kept regular hours, but it struck every
one who observed him that he was undermined. When he was
worried he became testy and explosive; generally, however, he
stayed on even keel; and, when his health permitted, he was
friendly, easy-spoken, open.

The advent of this new King, so far as the outer world was concerned, would immediately express itself in appropriate pageant.
His predecessor would have a costly public funeral, to revive the

feelings of his reign, and then there would come the new King's consecration and coronation, with banquets and a state entry into Paris, new initials on the hangings, new colours on the grooms. The old personnel would go. The new could clamber into the light, move gaily in freshly decorated chambers under brightened chandeliers. Ambassadors would sort out their tears and smiles, condoling one day, congratulating the next, and under these honourable appearances making notes and taking stock. To the old hands it would be a routine, sympathetic or the reverse, but following an established rhythm, stage-managed and obedient to precedent. But the young observers would re-create it in their own fresh eyes. They would feel its significance instead of its banality. They would lend to it their own adventure and their innocence. And to the King to whom it was happening it would also have the adventure and the innocence of a unique event. It would lose its trite, stage-worn, hollow character, with hirelings and mummers crowding the assembly. It would become real. God would lean from Heaven to bless it. The nation, overflowing with magnanimity, would lift up its heart and every one of the weary symbols would lose their apathy to arise in touching witness to a hope. No King could see his predecessor interred and find himself blessed and crowned without the capsule of custom breaking in his heart and all the old sweetness of his imagination flooding his veins. Even a cannibal, the King of the Cannibal Islands, could not be inaugurated without borrowing the flags of sunrise. And when it came to a monarch in this civilised nation, he had complex emotions drawn from a thousand associations, each of them as faded, perhaps, as an old battle flag, hanging dusty in the palace, yet suddenly seized by the reverent memory of his race, and trooped and paraded through his soul. This strange creature, man, who has invented a soul, has also invented Kings to incarnate a facet of it. Louis XII, permeated by the usages in which he had been bred, could not at times help— not lending himself, but giving himself to the complicated fiction, and so converting his fiction into the only certainty we have, the certainty of its acceptance. It is the triumph of imagination over habit, the leap in the dark which, when a monkey took it, made a man of him.

Louis d'Orléans had been a rebel and a scallywag, but the rôle of kingship steadied him. It was, however, one of cold adjustment and hard choices, and soon the sunrise mood was passing. The outer world that had revelled in the pageant could hardly tell what drab daylight must reveal.

16

Louise of Savoy went to Paris demanding the dukedom of Orléans for her son. She did not quite understand that Louis XII was already plunged in the first unromantic task of any ruler, trying to keep the claimants in line. Anne of France, Anne of Brittany, Louise herself, were pressing on him their flat expectancies. So do the colours of sunrise go morose.

Anne of France not only came down on the crown for a dot that had once been allotted to her because of a marriage that had never taken place, but she also put forward her vital demand that her title to the Bourbonnais should be cleared. That was her price for patriotism. Anne of Brittany, swathed in mourning, the complete Celtic widow, asked only to go home to her still independent duchy, carting away everything she could legally lay hands on. After this, Louise was almost modest merely to ask for the House of Orléans.

Louis XII was good-natured but frugal. He at once went into council with his two best advisers, Georges d'Amboise and Marshal de Gié. These two men, one a priest and the other a soldier, had no doubt about the course to advise. To name Francis as duc d'Orléans would be the least of the King's troubles, if he intended to remain within his childless marriage. But how about Brittany? Anne of Brittany, that upright, serious young widow, whom he had once courted, was on her way to her independent duchy. This must be stopped, and it could only be stopped by Louis marrying her himself. He was already married!

Every Frenchman who came into Anne's dampening presence from the tingling vivacity of France felt her oppressive particularism. But Brittany? Brittany must be absorbed. The French policy was not to administer Brittany; it was to wed the Bretonne.

Anne of Brittany instinctively resented a crude move from Charles VIII to Louis XII. It was indecent. But Louis already had a motto: "Let Georges do it." Georges d'Amboise was his partisan.

He had endured prison for Louis d'Orléans. He was a churchman, and only a churchman could compose the right febrifuge for Anne of Brittany.

Louis XII's own attitude was gentle, mournful, humane. France needed an heir. Without it, "it would come to quarrelling and finally to ruin." Louis sighed heavily, "in great pain and perplexity." He hated to hurt his crippled wife, Jeanne de France. "I'd rather die childless than displease you," he gallantly told his spouse. At the same time he privately swore to marry Anne within a year or give up the four fortresses that France held in Brittany. And at the same time again, still sighing in heavy pain and perplexity, he secretly ordered his captains to hold these Breton fortresses at all costs. Louis was in travail: he must leave it to Georges. Georges turned to the Pope, and luck presented him with the right Holy Father.

Alexander VI was the pontiff with whom Georges d'Amboise had to deal. And this, as Louise of Savoy ruefully discovered, made all the difference.

17

What Louise suddenly beheld, even with her boy Francis as sole heir to the throne, was the quick development of a grandiose policy that reduced her to utter insignificance.

The new King had two motives that Louise was quite powerless to affect. One was his need for a divorce. The other was his claim on Milan. As duc d'Orléans his claim to the fat duchy of Milan had been the luxurious day-dream of his family. His grandfather had not only received Asti and half a million crowns when he married Valentina Visconti. He had also inherited a clear title to the duchy of Milan. The war-lord Francesco Sforza had disputed this title, having married a bastard Visconti himself, and Louis XI, not possessing the claim, had ostentatiously made friends with the war-lord. But now that an Orléans had become King of France, the claim to Milan became a national obligation.

It became a royal claim all the more readily because Italy was weak. The Italy that Louis XII was planning to invade he had surveyed in the year that Francis was born, and it was made to be exploited from outside. A small stellar system violently busy within itself, it was hopelessly uncorrelated with the greater systems around it. There it was, at the end of the fifteenth and the turn of the sixteenth century, dangerously unstable and uneasily self-contained, its development carried to high pitch where prodigies of art were possible, and yet these very prodigies of art seeming actually to deny obedience to a durable political order and a common end.

The Italians lived beautifully. They brought everything, even religion, even the pursuit of wisdom, even warfare, into harmony within each principality that could be an economic unit. But these units of harmony, reeling round in their dizzy and eccentric orbits, were inevitably swinging within the pull of greater power. The Medici lent money to France and inevitably Florence was drawn into the French system. The duchy of Milan pulled against the kingdom of Naples, so that Naples was driven into the orbit of Spain. Venice, bland as its lagoons, held itself detached, but its land buttresses encroached on Milan, and once the oriental trade began to be diverted by Portugal to Antwerp, Antwerp was ready to work against Venice through Maximilian.

The proximate enemy of a free Italy was modern artillery. Walled towns were the municipal equivalent of armoured knights: and where walled towns could withstand the old catapults with the same calm superiority as that with which the knight could withstand a mace, it was a far different story when guns came into action that could shoot iron balls and wallop lumps of granite, hundred after hundred, into the stomach of a squatting city.

The Italian municipalities had given their vitality to something beside ballistics. They had built their duomo and their city hall. They had painted frescoes in their cloisters. They had wooed statues from the brown forms of lads diving gaily in the Arno. They had sung at sunset in a pang of reunion with their God. They had imagined flights of angels, or springtime in flowing garments, or a cornice that was a ledge on which the blue heavens could lean. Life in Italy might have lost the simple chastity which, like a candid robe falling from throat to bare ankle, gave its unequivocal beauty to an earlier art; but the blossom that now unfolded was radiant and glorious. The arts awoke to their full powers in unison. Unfortunately, they were joyous behind ramparts that were not built to stand off gunshot, and it is the peculiarity of all life that it aims to flourish at the expense of every well-nourished and badly protected organism that walks the earth. Had the Italians been living in mud-huts, wearing little didoes, they would have been in no great danger. But they were worth despoiling; hence, in a Europe military at heart, certain to be despoiled.

It was not, however, as loot that Louis and his advisers conceived Italy. They were political-minded. They definitely saw Italy as something which, if they did not assert themselves, must fall to the lot of Spain. Ferdinand had had his eye on Naples before Charles VIII had put his hand on it. Ludovico Sforza at Milan had imagined he could use Charles VIII to crush Naples, and then could use Maximilian to oust Charles VIII. A fat dowry, dug out of the black earth of Lombardy, had induced Maximilian to marry Bianca Sforza. But the sleek Italian had thus invoked tremendous rival forces, forces charged by the fiercest of ambitions and the most ruthless of impulses. Louis XII was now responding to them, and Ludovico was to go diving down, a bit of driftwood in a vortex, the victim of swirling principalities.

The claim on Milan was, in reality, a mere acid that France contributed to the fate of Italy. There was an alkali at Rome, the caustic Cesare Borgia. And by pouring Borgia's unlimited ambition into Louis XII's family claim, Georges d'Amboise would unexpectedly make an astounding effervescence. It was Louis's need for a divorce that started it, but the Borgias traded on this need to use the French in Italy. And so, to unburden himself of Louis XI's daughter, and to acquire Milan, Louis XII went deep into business with the Borgias.

18

Cesare Borgia was the Pope's eldest son. He had been popped into the cardinal's college at an early age, before the family had waked up to its political future. Cesare watched his insupportable younger brother go cavorting as a duke while he himself was tonsured and skirted. Then, on a dark night, the Duke of Gandia was stabbed to death, and his body flung into the Tiber. The Pope was at first stunned by the murder of his favourite son but soon, with that extraordinary verve of his, between laughter and tears, he was exulting in Cesare. He could not resist anything that exulted a Borgia. He was extremely reluctant to follow Cesare's reasoning that it was France which could help the Borgias in Italy: but the death of Charles VIII brought Pope Alexander around and a bargain was struck with Georges d'Amboise in the summer of 1498.

Cesare was to be released from holy orders first of all. Twin affidavits had originally been prepared by the Pope concerning his son's birth. The first proved that he was born in wedlock, to enable him to become a cardinal. The second proved that he was the Pope's bastard, to disqualify him as a cardinal. Cesare now produced the second affidavit and resigned as a cardinal. The sacred college eventually left it to the Holy Father, who released him from his vows. Everything was perfectly in order. So Cesare departed for the court of France, armed with a dispensation for Louis's new marriage, equipped with a cardinal's hat for Georges d'Amboise, ready to receive a dukedom from France and a bride suitable to his rank and fortune. Then would come a military agreement with Louis XII and the invasion of Italy.

The divorce suit was painful. Jeanne de France was a tragic human being whose flame burned in a twisted vessel. She was weak. She was born with her limp, one shoulder higher than the other, her legs and arms attenuated, her head set awry and her lips thick and unsightly. Very early her father Louis XI had thrust her out of sight and mind.

The divorce trial had as its judges Georges d'Amboise's brother and another bishop equally indebted to the new King. Troops of aristocratic witnesses were ready to back up Louis's contention that physically the marriage could not be consummated. Rabodange, Louis's reputed father, came forward. The earliest anecdotes were recalled. "Ho, Master Salmon," Jeanne had bemoaned to her doctor, "I have not the person for such a prince."

Jeanne's own testimony was that of a wife who believes herself in the right, but knows she is to be disowned. She refused to be examined by physicians. She left it to Louis to state on oath what the facts of their married life had been. The genial Louis, to her extreme astonishment, affirmed that she was not made for married life. His story prevailed. It had to prevail. His plans for marrying

Anne of Brittany had already been mature for months, just as the Papal dispensation had been in Cesare Borgia's pouches since his departure from Rome. Jeanne received the news with floods of tears. A Catherine of Aragon would have had the stubbornness to contest the papal decree. But Jeanne de France was a French-woman. She had not the rude intransigence of a Spaniard. She was caught in a finer, subtler system. She broke her lute, the one joy in her forlorn life. She retired to Bourges, where popular sympathy followed her, and sought the solace of founding an order of nuns.

19

Until this divorce was decreed Louise of Savoy might go on hoping that her son would be Duke of Orléans. Louis XII was cordial. While the divorce suit was pending he came to the great castle at Chinon, and there Louise was installed with her children. The new King sat in their chambers, chatting with Louise and playing with her children. He liked Marguerite and the personable boy. Francis was four. He had a dog! Marguerite was six, a great reader. Louise, in the bloom of health, could not fail to be at home with so affable a man as Louis. But his mind was really absorbed by one sole purpose. He wanted to have a stable, well-ordered country behind him to enable him to pursue his heritage in Italy. He was a self-willed soldier and Milan was his policy. He intended to have Milan. This was no airy project with prodigal expense and headlong haste to mark it. The new King, clad in plain black velvet, went to Louis XI for his model of efficiency. With a strong hand on the treasury and close confidence in Georges d'Amboise and Gié, he gave up frivolity and put first things first.

This could not hurt Louise, who saw eye to eye with him on French expansion, both in Naples and Milan. As for the intrigues with Rome, Louise was not like Anne of Brittany. She had no illusions about the Church militant. The Borgias were already notorious for their excessive greed, helping themselves with both hands. Louise saw with revolted indignation the contrast between a Borgia and her own Francis de Paule. But where they did not see eye to eye was in relation to her boy, who was now technically dauphin. Louise submitted painfully to the King's project for his own remarriage.

She had to be content with the dukedom of Valois for Francis. Anne of Brittany would not allow Orléans to go to him. But Louise's revenues were increased, her prestige magnified, her household set on a grander footing.

Louis's bishops gave him his divorce, through the shameless agreement with the Pope. The King could now found a family. He, too, appealed to the saintly old man from Calabria, and presented him with a mule. The saint retorted by giving him twelve holy candles (for the midwife) and a hair shirt for himself. Louis passed on the hair shirt.

And no sooner was the divorce decreed than Cesare Borgia's grand entry to the French Court, with papal hat and papal bulls, was announced to be at hand.

20

The entry into Chinon was no mere courtly pantomime. Cesare Borgia is one of those hard points on which history pivots. His was the arrival, with sounding silver bugle, of the change in French destiny. So far Charles VIII's foray had not precipitated upon France the impact of the empire or the weight of Spain. It had been a simple and exterior adventure. But the arrival of Cesare Borgia brought Italy to the Loire. It was, for Francis, a flourish of trumpets to open his personal history, and he might have heard in it strange minor accents, the plangence of rebecks and the sombre omen of the drums.

At Chinon, on the day of Cesare's entry, two children of the same age of four were presumably watching the pageant with sparkling eyes. One was Louise's Francis, the other Francis Rabelais. The two of them, each in his way, sprang from this genial region. In the doctor's intellect that Rabelais would mature there would be a buoyant, emancipated nature, one of the boldest that France would ever nurse. In the prince there would surge the same true capacity for enjoyment, the gift of vitality and an accessible heart. Yet a political alliance was now being hatched in the cynicism that passes for statesmanship, and from it would spring disaster and degradation. An adventure was opening that would beckon Francis for ever. Its harbinger was this young Italian who now entered Chinon.

Cesare Borgia was bitterly intelligent. He knew exceedingly well that his evil reputation had run before him into France, flashing its sinister light into every face that regarded him. He came advised. He had deliberately loitered at Avignon and Lyon. He had hung himself on the neck of Giuliano della Rovere who hated the Borgias. Disdain was a long French suit but he had played an ace against it, refusing to touch the Order of St. Michael from any hand except the King's. He was wantonly rude to minor courtiers, and he met pin pricks with a glance like steel. He knew exactly the hierarchical world he was living in.

The mere fact that he was the Pope's son, and admitted to be the son of the Holy Father, was enough to stir attention in an orthodox world. But his paternity was not the only thing about him. He had been a cardinal. He was whispered to have loved his sister. He was a Lucifer, baleful and fascinating, and the most startling thing about him was his age. He was not yet three and twenty, and already he set himself in political perspective like an arc de triomphe.

His entry into Chinon was correspondingly planned for effect. He knew that King Louis would be watching him from a high window. He knew that great captains and gallant ladies would be there to view him and comment on him. He could not come as a soldier, brandishing arms. He must come as a courtier. What he aimed at was an effect universally and eternally besought by every great showman who understands the theatre. In Siam he would have spoken in elephants. In Mexico he would have spoken in painted bodies. Rome had staged innumerable triumphs, proud white figures golden in sunlight, legions ripe as cornfields, and their captives drooping in chains. But here the young visitor could only flaunt an inordinate wealth. He sought the effect of transcendent luxury, of overwhelming expense, an ecstasy of colour, a cascade of jewels, music that makes the heart jump and the blood beat in unison. This showmanship demanded that the climax of pride and ostentation must be himself, beyond good and evil.

Georges d'Amboise, well-fed and impassive, crossed the bridge to greet Cesare and ride back with him. Before them, along the bridge, went pattering the first visitors from Italy, four detachments of shapely mules that had been shipped to Marseille. The first two dozen, with emblazoned red cloths, were joggling sacks and boxes. The next three batches had arrogantly bizarre trappings, in red and yellow, in striped yellow satin, in cloth of gold barred and smooth. These gaudy mules preceded war-horses glinting with gold, pages on fine coursers, six crimsoned lackeys leading caparisoned mules, and after them two nobler mules, on whose backs were the splendid coffers that contained mysterious valuables, whether papal bulls or clean laundry, Cesare's breakfast mug or his silver chamber-pot, or the cardinal's hat.

Then rode thirty noblemen, in cloth of estate, with minstrels, brave clarions, another batch of lackeys, and at last the two principal personages, Georges d'Amboise and Cesare himself.

The churchman, portly and thin-lipped, rode low on his mule, watching his familiar world with smooth ecclesiastical face, a vigorous yet unpenetrating strategist, still elastically young. The Italian, straight-backed and lithe, bestrode a charger whose red satin overall was bordered with pearls and stones more or less precious, while he himself rode stiff with jewels, his flat bonnet picked out in a constellation of huge rubies, red as the eyes of war.

The French watched intently. They knew it was Cesare's' visiting card, ostentatious beyond all proportion, deliberately florid, deliberately insolent. Thirty noblemen, when the trappings called for at least a hundred and twenty! Mules in cloth of gold! Eighteen pages for a dukedom such as Valence! The French sniffed. And Chinon, a drop on the end of its nose on this wet December day, glued its eyes on the Pope's offspring.

Louis XII had been informed that the young man had not been complaisant. But Louis, fresh from Reims and the chrism of Clovis, beamed on him and embraced him.

What Louis really embraced was the Italian adventure that Cesare had come to arrange for, which gave Georges d'Amboise his whiff of the papacy, and sealed the doom of Milan.

The French Court, Gothic in spite of itself, stiffened against this alien Borgia. But while he came hot into a cool mild atmosphere, his white face, with the scorched eyes of a man eaten by disease, was still beautiful in its stony contempt. Behind his effrontery there was a brain, and in his glance a capacity for sharp decision. Cesare had made up his mind to a drastic programme in which he needed the French. He wanted the Romagna. He wanted to marry into Naples. Once dominant in the Romagna and Naples, the subjugation of Florence was foreshadowed. He could count on France to deal with Milan, Genoa, Venice. By a series of operations, each of which led to the other over an abyss of improbability, he could thus become master of Italy by stealth and speed. It pointed to a man with nerves like steel springs and a heart of ice. Cesare was the man. He was an untamed animal, capable of unlimited ferocity but seldom striking until his victim was disarmed. Among criminals, the Cesare type detaches his heart from his will. Here was the predatory male, restless, suspicious, dangerous and solitary.

His arrival at the French Court, his blatant display of wealth, was calculated to upset the nerves of everyone but pawnbrokers. He wore his bank account on his neck, on his arms, in his ears, in his beret, on his fingers. He represented tangible assets from the top of his head to his horse's golden hoofs. And before breakfast everyone knew that he had come provided with a brocaded nightstool. The French, accustomed to decorate royalty in this fashion, were silently revolted by the profane use of a precious metal. Dry officials and sensitive matrons smiled sparingly at the parvenu. Cesare Borgia did not flinch at this wintry reception. He was not courting the French. They were courting him.

For his bride Cesare nominated Carlotta of Aragon. She was living at this court. The Neapolitan princess was in love with a Breton. She declined the honour: she said she did not care to be known as "Mrs. Cardinal." Cesare scowled, whereupon King Louis produced another worthy lady. She came out of the Landes, the daughter of Alain d'Albret. A larger dot was promised. (The facility with which unreasonably large sums were readily promised was one of the foibles of the French.) And Cesare promptly married her. It was not unlike him to provide for her, to get her with child, to leave her in France when he set out on his great adventure, and never to see her again. He was not bourgeois.

This great deal with Cesare Borgia turned Louis XII to Italy. His first campaign, that of 1499, captured Milan. His next captured Naples. His hands were full with the affairs of war.

This would have left Louise of Savoy in a pleasant position, with increased wealth and increased prestige, had the Marshal de Gié not existed. But he did exist, and from the first returned to his early contention: he kept urging that Francis be leashed.

Now that Louis was King, Gié ruthlessly suggested that Louise be placed under surveillance at Blois. This he broached to Georges d'Amboise, to the cardinal's brother, to another friend who had served under Louis XI. They united in pressing the King to survey Francis's mother. Louis assented. One of Gié's most trusted handymen was immediately attached to her household. From Chinon to Blois, very reluctantly indeed, the guardian-mother moved with her family. Blois, however, was actual incarceration, with its throngs of plumed archers and its Scottish guards. She detested it and made no secret of her dissatisfaction. And in 1499 the family, still including Jean de Saint-Gelais and Jeanne de Polignac, was allowed to settle at Amboise.

The King's marriage to Anne of Brittany had meanwhile been consummated, and it was going to be a success. The Queen was honest by nature, though straitlaced and a bit of a shrew, and something benign, something indulgent, permeated the King's relation with her. He knew how rare a virtuous wife was at court; he valued Anne precisely because she was virtuous, and he did not combat her fidelity to Brittany any more than her fidelity to himself. Her patriotism was in dire conflict with his own. As Duchess of Brittany she behaved just as though her actions did not involve France. There must have been times when, in secret talk with the cardinal, Louis's profanity reached considerable lengths. He was a very dirty-spoken, hearty man, when talking in his cups. But he and the cardinal knew that the only way to get round the Queen would be to wear her down. They were prepared to be kind as well as patient.

So, in the beginning, was Louise of Savoy. When the King went off to Italy, Anne of Brittany was expecting her first child of the new series. Plague was raging at Blois, the smells of the tanneries afflicted her, she wanted human refuge and she turned to her antagonist. Louise was in the cool woods at Romorantin. She gladly welcomed the Queen, and there Claude of France was born, the girl who was destined to marry Francis.

If anything could have cemented goodwill between the two women it would have been this human bond. But pride, which demands misunderstanding, was nourished in each of them by hopes that were irreconcilable. Anne of Brittany yearned to found a royal family, and so did Louise. To the narrow mind of the Queen, Louise's desire was profane. The air was ribald with ambition, fortune was blowing bubbles and the world dancing for them. The old discipline, on which the Queen prided herself, had long fallen like a grey robe from the bare young shoulders of her rival. Anne did not quarrel with her, but no human tie could bind these invincible rivals.

The Bretonne, moreover, had never resigned herself to being merged with France. She was a Celt, with a true Celt's hidden tenacity of personal purpose. The birth of Claude, a rather sickly infant, inflamed in her the separatism that her forced marriages so far had thwarted. Claude would be Duchess of Brittany, and the proper husband for her would not be a Frenchman, but an independent prince. So the Queen grimly decided. And for the next seven years a tense drama of the palace would grow out of Anne of Brittany's dynastic rigor, with strange consequences for Louise of Savoy.

Louise had to assert herself as her son's protectress. It was the most important crisis of her whole life. She knew that Gié had a soldier's prejudice against a woman's household, not lessened by the new successes in Italy, and she knew that a woman like herself was not supposed to mould the dauphin's childhood. But the mother was more aware than ever that if she were set aside when he was six years old she could have no intimate rôle in his subsequent career. Her experience had already taught her how insignificant a wife and mother could be. Her aunt Charlotte and her aunt Bona were very clear in her memory. Hence the encroachments of Gié, tacitly supported by Louis XII, ran into a steep resistance. She knew that this was an implacable combat. The firmness with which she undertook it showed how masterful she might become.

Francis was thus the centre of a wearing intrigue. It was one of those long, unsparing, stealthy dramas in which a softly moulded young face becomes tense to the bone. If anger flashed, it had to be flanked into a smile. If a move had to be made, it must be a lightning dash from correctness to stolidity. Fortune and reputation were involved, but the principals in the drama could never afford to drop the mask until that fateful moment when every hand is bared.

Marguerite and Francis would sit gravely at the chess-table, moving their little chessmen, while the great game was going on over their heads. Marguerite would play dolls with a little girl from the town, Françoise by name, while Gié would try to baby the young prince. Marguerite, swinging her legs, her chin cupped in her hand, would sit for hours in the library, living the bright days of chivalry, while her mother would listen with pricked ears for the arrival of a marshal of France. Louise might go away in 1501 to attend Margaret of Austria's wedding in Bresse. But she was seldom absent, knowing she was encircled by animosity. She practised vigilance.

This animosity, at its height while Gié was in favour, owed not a little to the real character of Louis XII. Louis had an easy smile, a genial surface. He had the good sense not to bleed his people or to trifle with Brittany. He liked a broad story, was a stout sportsman, a soldier who had stood the worst and a master who could demand extreme cruelty in warfare to gain the day. But this spare, ungainly person with prominent eyes and fever-bitten look was quite incapable of the comfortable magnanimity of his legend. "Make up to him," Jeanne his wife had been urged, and she answered, "I wouldn't dare to. He has no use for me." He could not be counted on for bonhomie. If he could leave difficulties to his advisers, so much the better. He could thus keep his genial surface and preserve appearances.

Gié and Georges d'Amboise, working through this slippery master, shared in directing the nation. Each of them had a host of relations to provide for. Each of them was intent on manipulating Louis. But while Georges d'Amboise worked for the most part abroad, Gié stayed at home. He did not seek a way of guiding

Francis with Louise's consent. He believed he could bully Louise. And the King, evasive master of a vigorous steward, delegated ugly duty to a man who was building his fortune.

The marshal's château at Verger, like the Cardinal's at Gaillon, testified to healthy acquisitive instinct. These men served France, and they collected millions for doing it. It was a process with which the frugal Louis could not quarrel. They were voracious but indispensable.

22

One tempting matrimonial proposal after another was brought to Louise. She could have had an Italian spouse, Alfonso d'Este, whom she relinquished to Lucrezia Borgia. She could have Henry VII. But she was not susceptible. She sat in her window, plying her needles, her mind as busy as her hands. There was something in that concentrated gaze, that firm mouth, that clean chin, which did not spell Christian resignation. She saw through Gié's pressure with an unsparing clarity. He dined in all friendliness with herself and the children. People even smiled and said that Gié would marry her. Louise looked at him with that steady comprehensiveness which streams from an unshakable woman. Her heart had received a terrible shock early in 1501. She was watching Francis astride a pony, given to him by the marshal, in a field at Amboise. The pony bolted. For a few moments the mother was certain that the child was to be killed. In that instant, as the pony flew across the ground, the mother saw the end of everything—her boy's life, her own hopes, her love. Could God be so cruel? Could He abandon the widow and her orphans? God relented, and Louise's heart beat again. But she knew that her life was bound up in Francis and she would leave him for no kingdom on earth.

When, some time after, Jean de Saint-Gelais sidled in with the news that Anne of Brittany had had a son, born dead, Louise did not think of God abandoning Anne of Brittany. She thought triumphantly of God as her own protector.

But Gié was increasingly exasperated by her stubborn will. He resorted to pin-pricks. He kept insisting that Francis sleep in a room with one of his sons. Louise refused. She wanted to have her

children safely with her and to rise in the morning without ceremony. Gié then ordained that an officer should call every morning,
knock on the door and conduct Francis to Mass. This arrangement
worked well until, in the absence of the regular officer, a good
fellow was posted at the door who did not understand the art
of pin-pricks. He knocked. He was told that the young duke was
not going out. But he had instructions to escort the duke. So he
raised his voice and reiterated his summons. Getting no answer, he
stood back, took a mighty breath, lowered his shoulder, and burst
open the door.

A guardian angel was waiting for him. Louise had a tongue. She
gave him the benefit of it, she pursued him to Gié, then to the
King. Her fury was unanswerable. The zealous gentleman was
disavowed and recalled.

It would have gone hard with Louise had Gié stood well with
Anne of Brittany. But fate had juxtaposed this ex-Breton to the
most unyielding of his countrywomen, and between them there
was an impassable gulf. He looked on the Bretonne as a fanatic.
He could not conceive that anyone could desire anything but the
unity of France. She looked on him as a traitor; she could not see
how any Breton could work against the sole princess of his house.
Gié shrugged his heavy shoulders. But if anything ever happened
to the King, he was resolved not to let the grass grow under his
feet before he seized Anne of Brittany. He was ready to pounce
on her, and to take Francis under his wing.

23

Francis was thus growing up, in these formative years, partly
under his mother's wing at Amboise, and partly under the direction of Gié. The men of the tribe did not propose to leave the boy
to women. How are Kings made? "The father answered that they
were such as had more valour than any other in the world."
Francis was perhaps not to be the Parfit Knight of the Grail who
"hath a head of gold, the look of a lion, the navel of a virgin maid,
a heart of steel, the body of an elephant, and without wickedness,"
but he was to be a Man. And it was for this, as well as for surveillance, that Gié was made captain of Amboise.

The campaign went from Milan to the great Neapolitan campaign and already the boy's imagination was caught. There was something about French valour in the earlier years in Naples which made the heart thrill with its vainglory and its hardihood. The immortal Bayard had emerged. The Combat of the Eleven, the Combat of the Thirteen, Bayard's duel with Sotomayor—these episodes had pride in them, the pride of gentlemen. They must have made Marguerite's eyes fuse into generous fire, and they must have stamped on Francis's heart that faith which he wanted to live by—not the Christian faith which was a matter of course but his keen private faith, "foi de gentilhomme."

The courtly system takes the young tree and makes it an espalier. With Francis, who could not be deprived of the ardent solicitude of his mother, there was active comradeship at Amboise with chosen companions from the best houses of France. It was, in its way, the equivalent of a school, and it made intimates for life of the youngsters who played together. Among these Francis stood on his own feet. His mother indulged him, but he was not indulged by his companions.

Robert de la Marck was from the Ardennes. He arrived at Blois, aged ten, to offer his sword to the King for the wars in Italy. Louis laughed, "it's a little soon," and sent the "young adventurer" to Francis at Amboise. They were almost of an age. For all their courtly upbringing, they struggled together with the equality of cubs. Two days after he reached Amboise, leaving his inn, the Sainte Barbe, to live at the castle, young Fleurange wished to show Francis that he was just as good as he was, and fought to be first out of the litter. He was a sinewy, deft, indefatigable boy. His mind was absorbed in Italy and the fine things that his heroes were doing there. He soon knew the army from top to bottom, with everyone's rank, everyone's equipment, everyone's duties, everyone's perquisites, everyone's pay. The "young adventurer" was brave as a lion, literal as an almanac, dull as mud. But he took games seriously and he worshipped the greatest game of all. Anne de Montmorency (pronounced Annay) was with him. He came from Anet. He had as much stamina as Fleurange, an upright boy with a steady gaze, a tight mouth and a general air of strong determination. With them were Chabot and Montchenu, a spirited company of the best bred, liveliest, most emulative of a noble tradition.

There is a virginal freshness, a rare and exciting quality, about this upbringing. Young cocks always fight and these were too French for anything but equality in their ardour. What the boys learned was knighthood, formal combat, personal prowess, bodies beautiful and finely trained. The minds played on every point of the game and every detail of war and tournament. To win—that was the intoxicating dream of the very hardest of these young chevaliers who, by the time they were thirteen or fourteen (1506—7), spurred their steeds and poised their swords. They flung themselves into a career which asked of them to defy the instinct it exalted. Out of this dual rhythm they grew in pride. No man is as quick as the soldier to study the weak point in his comrade, yet these quick appraisals, which breed the sportsman, remain on the schoolboy level. Francis and his comrades were confirming themselves from day to day in that iron infantility which is the supreme characteristic of the military mind. To clothe this infantility in patriotism, or in the proud dynasty which goes by the name of patriotism, and to serve this infantility by every art and craft known to experts in games of skill—it could hardly have been called maturity, but it was the degree of it to which this little group was attaining. With it went the charm, the verve, the buoyancy of France, a radiance that came into their whole aspect when they addressed themselves to their comrade Marguerite, and that created, if only for the moment, a certainty that nothing was more a pass-key to honour than their "foi de gentilhomme." Francis had this true faith. Honour and glory were his dreams.

Their games pointed straight to real war. The boys had armour before they were full grown. They shot with bow and arrow at ten. The war was blown to them on the wind from Italy. La Palice was wounded before "Venouse," and they heard of the bit of bone, four inches broad, taken out of his head. The Spaniards "treated prisoners badly." The boys discussed Cesare Borgia. He was a wicked man, men said, but in war he was "a good comrade and a brave man." The prowess of the French had been proved on countless fields, and each youth dreamed of the day when he would

mount his charger, caracole before the ladies, and ride away. To be
soldiers, to win victories, to command great companies, to have
ensigns and trumpeters, to be gallantly caparisoned and grandly
plumed, to have a little horse as wonderful as Savoy that saved
Charles VIII at Fornovo, to see those brown Italian towns, to lead
French artillery across the Alps and manage the culverins—these
were the passionate imaginings of young Fleurange, of young
Montmorency, of young Brion, of Francis. Their brown eyes
sparkled at the sight of veterans. How often had armies sprung
from French soil like great chestnut trees in plume, to flaunt their
bold branches in summer, to be whirled bare in autumn, and in
winter swept down in sodden rags. The French had strewn their
bones from Apulia to Asti, on those very plains where, a season
before, their pikes had danced. But it was not the outpouring life,
the hardship, the squalor, the profanation of human spirit, that
came into the minds of Francis and his good companions. It was
valour they dreamed of. They wanted to taste adventure, and to
ride on flowers. No dream of conquest could be too naïve to engage
them.

In the mild twilights on the Loire, the wine of Chinon warming
her blood, Louise could see troops of elephants kneeling to her
Alexander, and camels obsequious, and circling slaves resplendent.
The gleam of a limitless empire swam before her dilated vision,
and in these resilient hours even the youngsters were drunk with
chimera.

24

The real war in Italy, meanwhile, went on parallel to this
passionate adolescence. And rather different was the real war.
Sandro Botticelli wrote its epitaph on his picture of the Nativity
now in London, painted in 1500 "amid the confusions of Italy at
the time prophesied in the Second Woe of the Apocalypse, when
Satan shall be loosed upon the earth." By this Satanic enterprise
Milan was settled. Milan was occupied.

King Louis and King Ferdinand did business together. They
agreed to partition Naples. But by the middle of 1503 Louis had

awakened to the fact that he must come to grips with his partner. Part of his Milanese conquest, Bellinzona and the territory about it, had been torn from him by the ravenous Swiss, and he was forced to cede it permanently. This concession meant that he was bracing himself for hostilities elsewhere. He went again to Milan, shared his days and nights with his friend Cesare Borgia, treating him like a brother. An immense effort to smite Ferdinand all along the line was ready for the summer when in August, 1503, out of the sultry air of the Campagna, death struck down Cesare's father, Alexander VI. This was a grand political crisis. Georges d'Amboise, confident of Cesare Borgia's help, drew away part of the French army to hover near Rome. He failed to become Pope. King Louis was furious when the news came to him. Even in the presence of Anne of Brittany he exploded against his pal Cesare Borgia. "That son of a whore," he said in pure moral indignation, "has prevented Rouen from becoming Pope."

Every offensive against Ferdinand went wrong. By the end of the year Naples was untenable. Georges d'Amboise saw Pope Pius III die within a few weeks, and Giuliano della Rovere, the Terrible, opened his resounding career as Pope Julius II. Then arrived the French capitulation of Gaeta. And Cesare Borgia was despatched a prisoner, to go to obscure death in Spain.

Louis, already sick in body, shut himself into his room at Blois, to give up his soul to the gall and misery of defeat. He had immeasurable contempt for his captains. He would not lift his finger for his beaten army. The remnants that fled from Naples came up the coast to Rome, black stumps of military companies, hordes in the tatters of discipline, straggling units without a stitch on their backs, bare-footed, empty-handed, thin, diseased, desperate, the last months in the swamps having eaten away their quality as men. They found themselves naked in mid-winter on the outskirts of Rome, with no place to sleep and not a rag to cover them. And these wretches who had gone so soon from fame to infamy, could only dig themselves into the warm dungheap to keep heat in their bodies, already company for worms, while hundreds of them, no longer able to crawl, were strewn in naked death, grinning at the sky above them, far from the France that had sent them out a proud army. Louis from his sick-bed sent hard orders to punish his dishonest paymasters and to cool his defeated captains in Milan.

25

Gié profited by the disasters abroad. Following the death of the gallant Duke of Nemours in Naples, he had married the duke's pale sister, the great Armagnac heiress. He was now named the Duke of Nemours. (His son, to make everything solid, married her sister, thus becoming his father's brother-in-law.) And when the King fell seriously ill, at the beginning of 1504, the new duke rose to the occasion.

He had parked artillery at Amboise. He had his sons dotted as captains in the vital fortresses along the avenue of the Loire. He had sworn the archers, in the little chapel at Amboise, to give him blind obedience. At the word of Louis's death, he cut off Anne's road to Brittany and gave orders to seize Louise and Francis.

The alarm was false. Louis was not dead, only comatose. Very soon he opened an eye, and then it was too late for Gié. He had fatally exposed his hand.

Louise and Anne were not natural allies, but they had equally fretted under the blunt domination of this ducal policeman. Now, with his schemes betrayed, they let loose their anger. Louis XII had to go on living with his wife. He left the marshal between the crossfire of the two little women whom he had scorned and despised. They fell on him, and it was the end of him.

There was no melodrama. An admirable judiciary cooled off hot passions in the long slow coils of the law. But Gié was finished at Blois. He was heavily fined, and banished to Verger. And Georges d'Amboise blandly concurred.

Paris turned it into a farce, making an "âne" give a "maréchal" a kick that landed him in a "verger." No sense of historical dignity!

This college-boy farce, and the story of a pet monkey that leaped on Gié's shoulder, in the middle of a tense interview with Alain d'Albret, and plucked at his beard, deprived his fate of tragic atmosphere. He was a defeated bully. Anne of Brittany grimly

announced that she preferred to have him disgraced rather than
executed. It would, the Christian lady said, prolong his suffering.

26

Gié had been crude, and he was laughed out of court, but this
did not mean that Louise had been sanctified. If an heir appeared,
her boy would cease to be dauphin, and everyone knew the political
evils that might spring out of this disappointment. The young
Louis XI had tried to disrupt France. So had the young Louis XII.
It was the natural outcome of dynastic frustration, and one glance
at Louise of Savoy showed that she was capable of it. The suave
Georges d'Amboise, who now took up the governorship of Francis,
was perfectly aware of this ugly contingency, and he proposed to
match his brains, both against Louise and against Anne of Brittany,
to clamp Francis into a marriage with Claude, the King's daughter.

Louise did not want it. Not only would it exclude her from
authority over Francis, but it would subordinate him to an inferior
marriage should a male heir be born. Moreover, she saw Claude
as a fat, torpid, deformed child with a limp, almost another Jeanne.
She emphatically did not want it.

Neither did Anne of Brittany. Her one hope for Brittany was
to see Claude married to an independent prince. She had selected
the Archduke Charles (the future Charles V), and this had been
arranged long before.

As a boy of seven Francis had stood at the King's right hand,
while Louise of Savoy and Anne of France and Cesare Borgia's
wife, escorted by six pages with green candles, offered sweetmeats
in gold compotiers to Juana. She was Mad Juana, the mother of
Charles, on her way to Spain, and this act of deference followed
the betrothal. The betrothal still persisted, but King Louis's shaken
health made it positively dangerous, and the cardinal meant to
break it.

27

The King was much too afraid of his wife to present her with
anything except a coup de théâtre. He had been sly enough, when
Claude was bestowed on Charles, to prepare a secret document pro-

testing that his consent was not in earnest. This was the usual
politician's device of an-oath-that-is-not-an-oath, a bit of pious
chicanery. A more delicate comedy had now to be enacted. Georges
d'Amboise had the formula: the irresistible Will of the People. The
King summoned the Notables to Tours.

Louis's desperate illness paved the way. His second collapse in
1505, coming so soon after the first, stirred the whole of France by
its seriousness. News was gravely awaited. Public prayers were
offered up. Public men went on pilgrimages. The Queen set out
for Brittany, to visit the holy places. Louis was delirious, asking for
a sword in his delirium. The elder statesmen crowded to him, in
the hush of anxiety and apprehension. And when, out of the sick
room, came a word of hope, it was accompanied by the solemn
pledge that Claude, the King's only child, must at once be married
to Francis, heir to the throne.

Anne obstinately sought to prolong her absence in Brittany. It
was in vain. The marriage was decided on.

Louis emerged from his illness emaciated and touchingly feeble.
A great orator from Paris came to him in state, as he sat limp
amid princes and councillors. The orator intoned his praises, calling
him Father of the People. His humble subjects begged him to give
his daughter to Francis. The King's eyes filled with tears. The
humble petition would be entertained. In five days the Estates
assembled again to learn that Louis had acceded. The official orator
again rose to the occasion, expressing exalted joy. Two days later,
Francis and Claude, escorted by their mothers, were joined in marriage by Georges d'Amboise.

Francis was twelve and Claude seven. Anne of Brittany was
glum, and in private Louis had the audacity to chaff her clumsily
about the stag at last deposing the aggressive hind and deciding
himself to wear the antlers.

This marriage of Claude and Francis was not easy to explain east
of the Rhine. Maximilian had been espoused to Anne of Brittany.
His daughter had been espoused to Charles VIII. His grandson had
been espoused to Claude. The French had violated all three pacts.
When the news of this last piece of legerdemain reached Maximilian his fury was unbounded. And Margaret of Austria, his
widowed daughter, had her own thoughts about the French.

28

But the Ship of State has gay passengers as well as careworn crew. Marguerite and Francis were at last at home on it, and while it carried them to Blois, for Francis's betrothal, their own lives had a motion all its own, like free will inside determinism. And this movement, in Marguerite's case, was already touchingly feminine.

Georges d'Amboise had been too busy to keep Francis as his ward. He had passed him to Artus Gouffier, lord of Boisy. Gouffier was a superb gentleman, of charm and mature ability, a Gascon in a great chivalric tradition. Louise probably had a voice in choosing him. He had a young brother Bonnivet. And Francis's marriage brought Bonnivet to court, as well as everyone else, since it was one of the most sumptuous of princely celebrations.

Bonnivet was a Gascon who had his career to make, fearless, lively, well-built, dashing. One may imagine him swaggering at Blois in the insolent charm of a young soldier, his head full of projects and his eye ravaging the scene. One of the first persons on whom it alighted was Marguerite, the sister of the boy bridegroom, now a slender and aerial girl of fourteen.

Though he was himself neither of a rank nor of an intimacy to make advances to the maiden, Bonnivet found her so intensely to his liking that he could not take his eyes off her. Through his brother he could meet her, but when at last he did meet her, for all his glib Gasconade, he could not muster a word. Marguerite was too young, floating too lightly in the ether of this princely gathering, to note her admirer's tenseness. She smiled on him, as she smiled on the world.

The girl of whom Marguerite made a most intimate companion was a small heiress little older than herself and not famous for her looks. Knowing her closeness to the Angoulêmes, Bonnivet made up his mind to court her. In this he soon succeeded. His proposal of marriage was accepted, and with perfect shy deference he made so winning an impression on the innocent Marguerite that very soon she confided to him her own most precious secret: she was in love, not with the dull young Duke of Alençon, whom her mother was choosing for her, but with the one really romantic young chevalier who had come to court from the south, Louis's nephew Gaston de Foix.

Bonnivet thereupon decided to make as much of Gaston de Foix as possible. He and Gaston de Foix and every other young courtier at Blois lived under the glamour of approaching war. The young Charles de Bourbon, who had ousted Alençon as the candidate for Suzanne de Bourbon, was another superb figure at Francis's betrothal. All of them swirled and bowed and pranced and preened, in the glory of youth and arms. And when Bonnivet was off to Italy, following his marriage, he had pledged Marguerite to let him have news of her through his bride, her own lady in waiting.

This was the gallant idiom of the life now opening both to Marguerite and Francis.

29

The other idiom was that of the soldier. Francis, at twelve, ached to join the campaign of 1507, that was taking a brilliant army to Genoa. Genoa had "revolted," and Louis was bringing it to submission. It was part of the glowing conquest of Lombardy.

Only a year before the greatest of Genoese, Christopher Columbus, had died in Spain. He had just taken his little part in welcoming Philip and Juana. Genoa knew nothing of its great citizen except down on the water front, under the gossiping arcades, where the oily sea rolled dingy fruit and straw against the wharves, and the air licked up the smell of onions, and old seafaring men wrinkled their eyes. But Genoa knew that Philip the Handsome was dead. It knew that Louis was about to confer at Savona with Ferdinand of Aragon. Once Genoa gave in to the French King, Georges d'Amboise arranged the adroit, the fatal, interview.

In a great window looking out on the sea, while Louis chatted with his niece, who was married to Ferdinand, the real business was worked out by the sleek cardinal and the astute founder of the Spanish Empire, sitting close together in another window. Each of them agreed to regard Italy as theirs to dispose of. Ferdinand had Naples. Louis had Milan. Now who was to have Venice? To carve up Venice was the subject of this particular Peace Conference.

So France committed itself to further wars in Italy. And so did it take a new partner, Ferdinand.

"He fooled me twice," Louis would later protest.

"He lies, the drunkard!" Ferdinand retorted, "I fooled him ten times."

30

Louise at home in France had her own views of Georges d'Amboise's policy. She never approved of it, but she had no voice in public affairs. And even the one private affair that gave her such bitter satisfaction, that Anne of Brittany could not have a son to survive, now forced her to separate from her own son, the acknowledged dauphin. It was firmly ruled that he was too old to remain with his mother. He must come to Court.

Louise hated it. It had just been proposed once more that either she or Marguerite marry the decrepit Henry VII. A diseased old gentleman! Marguerite in particular did not hide her feelings.

"England is a far and strange country," she said gravely, "and its king is somewhat elderly for a bridegroom. If, perchance, my brother were to become King, I might then find a young, rich and high-born husband without going over the sea to look for him." Was she thinking of Gaston de Foix? Her thoughts, at any rate, revealed a candid heart. She could not be forced to go away. But it was high time for Francis to leave his mother.

In August, as the mother long remembered, the formal separation was made. She swept past her daughter to cling to the boy who was departing—the warm southern mother clinging to her son.

Louise was now a vigorous mature woman of thirty-two. Her solid carriage and her well-cut chin augured ill for anyone who opposed her. She had the positive, self-confident, energetic character, the vital force, of the true southern matron, bold in judgment, brisk in argument, prompt in action. How like her it would be to look at the folio of the Round Table, on its stand at Blois, and to turn to the valet: "That young people should waste their time reading such idiocy!" As against this decisive woman who took him as hero as well as son, Francis was amiable and pliant. His own tongue was quick, his glance lively, his nose amusingly long, but the Orléans quality in him made him less direct than the Savoyard. She did not intend, however, to domineer. She was sure of him. Another southern mother would, indeed, keep her Valois so long that he would remain a spoiled child for ever, in frills and ear-rings, not quite sure of his sex, a perpetual darling. Louise was too sensible for that, and Francis too much a male. But parting came hard. When he left, the little matron walked through their familiar rooms at Amboise saying, "All alone! All alone!"

She had only fifty or sixty persons under her thumb, and was not twenty-five miles from Court. But the childhood was actually over, the nest empty.

Francis, however, carried with him the anchor of his childhood. He was, above everything, the son of his mother. She had made herself central for him, and this dominant little woman could not let go. She had set him on the slope that caught her own bathing sunlight and drew him down from the inimical winds. The personnel around him had been directed by her. The gay dialect of her court, that curious special language of a household, was naturally lisped by Francis after her fashion, in droll contrast to the stiff idiom of Anne of Brittany and of Claude. Louise's primacy in his moral system, her power to stamp with approval or disapproval the acts no one could combat within her dominion, made him very much her child, incapable of transferring that unspoken allegiance on which, with a fierce instinct, her own purposes were built. Her husband was gone. She, the Latin mother, was the one disinterestedness he knew. And this circumscribed him.

Francis was French in giving to his mother a peculiar respect that he could never give in the amatory realm. There he would remain self-centred while with Louise he knew disinterestedness, taking his tone from her, too gay, too lively, not to be sceptic about anything she disdained. He might oscillate between his own romantic chivalry and this scepticism, but his escape would be into frivolity, into light inconsistence, and, when he was avid and experienced, into the pursuit of sensation. It would not be an easy thing for him to give any other woman a true allegiance. He was kind. Cruelty was naturally abhorrent to him. But his romance was his mother, and it would be view-halloo with other women.

He would be keen in this gallant pursuit. He said "yes" to life. He shot outward, made for action. He would have the quality that most arouses interest in women—the quality of being madly interested in them. He was already, even as an untouched boy, one of those youngsters who ripple attention as they go by. The offence that unbounded vitality gives to polite taste would certainly be offered by Francis: his buoyancy would seem conceit, his gaiety animal spirits, his zest would seem vulgarity. It was noted of him by the attentive within a few years that he was becoming rather coarse-looking. But what Marguerite loved in him at first and always would love was his boyish responsiveness, his delight in the gift of life. For herself she was born saying yes-and-no. He could forget himself.

Sensuousness was the simple lyric rule of the new generation. The commandments raised barriers that were leaped by high spirits. The drama of life might be handicapped by Anne of Brittany's precisions, but there were a number of extremely urgent males in Francis's company. There was the example of Bonnivet, who attracted Francis. There was Gaston de Foix, white swan on a dark pool, a natural prince. These were the generation just ahead, but soon no frolic could dismay either Montchenu or Chabot de Brion, Francis's intimates; and Anne de Montmorency and Fleurange, soberly devoted to Francis and the main chance, were at any rate destined to action. In this swift life warm glances rained on attractive youth. The young were sure of themselves, confident of good fortune, at once greedy and aspiring, purely devoted, hotly passionate. And the Court was the centre of this allurement.

Francis, a boy of fourteen, joined the court at Chinon. He had hardly arrived there before he and his young lords went on a joyous romp to Fontevrault, where the King's sister was abbess. In the garden he was clouted on the forehead with a stone. This was the sort of news that the loving mother really apprehended. And on the heels of it came news of Anne of Brittany. The wooden bridge at Montsoreau had collapsed under her litter. Such an accident, happening to a woman with child, could decide the succession. It was in the midst of this sort of drama that Louise nervously existed. What was inside Francis's head was not so much to the point, but to have it banged by a stone was catastrophic. She knew

these things were written in the stars, she believed frantically in
lucky stars. But which they were she was not sure, nor what could
be the good Lord's intentions.

31

Away from his loving mother Francis surprisingly throve. It
was enlivening, in every sense, to be at court. Very different from
the little hothouse in which he was reared, it was amusing, less
restricted, less subtle. Anne of Brittany had been forced into marriage before her senses were ripe, and she seemed to rebel against
sensuousness her whole life through. Her poets—for she favoured
the scribes—sat bolt upright in the pew. She liked them there, as she
liked her Bretons on the perch facing her window. Pedantic,
censorious, rigid, she was safe from the leniencies of the Renaissance but she lacked its flexibility and gave no play to temperament. As queen she was immensely serious. Her dames and maids
of honour she supervised severely. She prohibited a marriage for
love with a hardness that revolted Marguerite. Louise's children
viewed her ironically.

Had Francis been King Louis's son, his initiation into affairs of
state would have been allowed; as it was, he was treated like a
schoolboy.

Margaret of Austria was this year beginning to govern the
Netherlands, her eye constantly on her nephew Charles. This
solemn boy, born in Ghent, reared at Malines, would be elbowed
by burghers from the start. Antwerp swelled with commerce. Industry was dinned into his ears by the hammers of carpenters, of
hoopers, of shipwrights, of coppersmiths. The sun of the Low
Countries took a serious view of production, expected workmen to
burrow and barter under sombre skies. But on the Loire there was
another life—hunting, feasting, war and women. The sun issued
invitations that Francis would be the first to accept. He stood on
the brink of the Renaissance, eager and sensuous, yearning to be
old enough for war. And Marguerite, his loyal sister, stood smiling
by him.

The King loved hunting, so that Francis, who fretted to be a
man, had his chance to join in the sport of kings. There was noth-

ing particularly French about this ardour. All over Asia and Europe
the map was dotted with forests consecrated to wild beasts. Everywhere princes and dukes and counts pursued horned and antlered
creatures, and everywhere the walls of palaces sprouted with the
dry bones of once magnificent animals. Russia, Hungary, Persia,
Arabia, Denmark, America, China—it was world-wide, the mark
of a caste. A prince, surrounded by pikesmen, armed with sword
and dagger, or equipped with bow and arrow, sought as a matter
of course the poignant thrill of hunting. Maximilian adored to
hunt the chamois; one sees him like a figure in a tapestry, the
chamois leaping, Maximilian leaping after. Ferdinand lived and
died a hunter. His son-in-law Henry VIII was already hunting
assiduously in 1509. The fat Leo X would soon trot out to hunt,
dressed in green leather, with a feathered hat. Hawks, falcons, grey-
hounds, wolfhounds, Neapolitan horses, Spanish horses, Irish
horses, Arabian horses—the princely class worked inside these
themes of excellence as a poet works inside a sonnet or a composer
inside a sonata. To adapt a means to an end—preferably a beautiful means to a useless end—gave the lords of the earth some of
that ultimate satisfaction which abides in being a lord. In this, as in
so many respects, the princely life of the sixteenth century has its
counterparts in India of to-day—the same wealth, the same ostentation, the same formal religion, the same cruelty, the same beauty,
the same lascivious extravagance. Sport an end in itself, and sex a
pastime. . . . One can see the young Francis as a budding Maha-
rajah, happening to be a Catholic.

But the essence of good sport is prowess in danger, and this is
the school in which King Louis trained him. Louis prepared for
the next year's campaign by leading the hunt from Blois, and
Francis, already a good horseman, was allowed to follow him.

Those days in the forest, plunging through the underbrush, racing under the trees, down steep inclines, up the banks of ravines,
with the tang in the air, the heart galloping, the tongue dry—those
days, so full of glorious effort, so rich in amour-propre, so eloquent
in opinion—Francis adored them. "No matter how old and ill I
may be," he would come to say, "I will have myself carried to the
hunt. And when I die, I shall want to go there in my coffin!"

His book education tried to edge in, between such excitements.

The abbé who was told to equip him did not propose to arouse his young intellect, he proposed to furnish it; and the harness did not come out of French life or in the French language, it came, heavy and solid, from the antique grammarians, from the mummified Greeks and petrified Romans. Francis's mind was not encouraged to discover itself, or to relate itself to its experience. It would have to survive dead formula. As it was his intellect pushed up between the slabs of his education, like bright glass between implanted stones. To estimate what was done for the European mind by Rabelais and Erasmus, Rabelais in insurrection and Erasmus in independence, it is only necessary to see them in their early monkish years, still tied in the stall. Francis had Budé to countenance his own attempt to enter into humanism. But his most sincere use of Budé was to employ him on an embassy and to have him translate The Art of Hunting. He had been too well discouraged at the start, too closely companioned by illiterates like Anne de Montmorency, ever wholly to overcome this sterile system, though he mastered Italian and proved to have a prodigious memory for every sort of fact. Marguerite had intellect—she could penetrate the abstract rules. Francis had facility. He could join in any conversation on any topic, especially on the days he was not hunting.

32

One day in church he found himself looking at a girl whom he had not noticed before. She was a hazel brunette, small, refined. Yet she was not a lady of the court. He went back to Marguerite full of this girl whom he had seen in chapel and whose glance had caught his. Who was she?

It suddenly came to them. She used to come and play dolls with Marguerite herself. She was Françoise! Marguerite listened delightedly. Their own butler was married to Françoise's sister, and Françoise had come to live in a house on the square in Blois. She was just sixteen, a year older than Francis. Marguerite instantly decided she must be asked to court to the great feasts and assemblies. She had the air of a charming little princess.

She had, as it happens, all the qualities a boy demands. He had actually known her, in the warm diffuseness of infancy. And yet she was coming new into his vision, a discovery of his own. That he could forget her made him remember her all the more: she touched the tenderness of the nursery. And a creature who had belonged to this earlier sensuousness, coming back subtly strange, awakened in Francis's fresh veins a delicious excitement.

Just because she was from the town, just because she was plebeian, she had what his timidity demanded. Being Orléans, soft metal, Francis was easily lapped round his mother's authority. But he was urgent and his sister would not have it in her heart to suppress it. John Calvin—Jean Cauvin—was at that moment being born in Picardy, in 1509. But the attempt to keep the male chaste was no serious preoccupation at the court. Francis's loyalty to his mother was too assured to condemn him to chastity.

Françoise, shy and admiring, saw her effect on him. When she changed her place in church, the long-nosed young prince would shift his seat and turn on her his eyes. This fluttered her heart with misgiving and delight. She knew he was "doux." But she could not see herself acquired and then given up. Her own place in the court was abundantly clear: she was a "worm of the earth." Francis, whose face had still the roundness of boyhood, was on fire with her; but, a true bourgeoise, with her own house and her own land, she did not succumb to the glamour of the court. On her squat domestic altar there burned the little lamp of pride. To give herself to him would be to lose herself; Françoise read the young prince with direct French eyes.

The duel could not go on in chapel. Françoise went to mass elsewhere in Blois. Her disappearance troubled and incited the boy. Through the butler he discovered where she lived. He was not free to find her. His mother had come to the court and he was afraid of her sharp supervision. But he thought of a plan that would actually bring him into the girl's bedroom. He took his big horse into town and, in the square on which she lived, went through his most dashing paces. Then he managed, in front of her house, to fall off, into a puddle. His attendants saw him caked with mud. He limped and groaned. To carry him into Françoise's house, and upstairs to bed, was instantly manœuvred, while a messenger was sent for a fresh costume.

When he was brought upstairs, Françoise, who must have been

watching his performance, hid herself in a remote room. He asked
for her; her half-sister and the butler hunted her out: she had to
come. She stood alone with him, pale and trembling. He, lying in
bed, took her cold hand.

"Why do you fly from me? Why do you torture me, Françoise?
I am not wicked. I won't devour you. Why won't you let me see
you?"

His hand pleaded but the girl held back. Everyone had seen him
come into the house and would never believe that she had not
given herself to him. She was quivering.

"No, Monseigneur, no. What you want cannot be. I am a nobody
beside you, but I would rather die than give in."

He despaired. She could not like him!

God knows she liked him. "I am not so stupid, so blind, as not
to see how handsome, how lovely, God made you, and the woman
you love will be the happiest in the world. But . . ."

He waited.

"It would be madness for anyone of my kind to think of you.
Yes, you could amuse yourself telling all about your little conquest
to your mistress, but in your own house I learned what love is,
where my father and mother served you. If you want women for
pastime, there are plenty of them far prettier than I in the town,
who would not make you plead so hard. It is not lack of love that
makes me hide from you. I love you better than my life, but I do
not not want this to be on your conscience or my own."

Francis kept pleading. They knocked on the door to say his
fresh clothes had come. He made them wait. He urged, prayed,
argued. At last, for fear of his mother, he had to make haste to
return for supper. Françoise, her heart torn, stood firm against his
pleading.

His gentleman of the bedchamber he took into his secret. The
older man understood these things. He could settle it. Money!
Question d'argent! But Francis's treasurer was his mother, and he
could hardly ask her for money without hearing "what for?" He
must find it by other means. By hook or crook he scraped together
five hundred crowns. His courtier took it to Françoise, with his
lord's compliments. She laughed at him. He lost his temper. She
laughed at him again. He returned to Francis, furious with the

girl, saying it was an insult to him, she must be broken. But Francis, on account of his mother, did not dare do anything violent.

To catch her by a trick he asked his butler to decoy her to his vineyard, and there he would join them, in their little house. The butler was willing. But here again the boy had to get round his mother. She happened to want his help, and Marguerite's help, for a room she was decorating. All the time that Françoise was being delayed in the little house in the forest, Francis was having the extreme pleasure of dancing attendance on his mother. By the time he was released and leapt on his mule to ride to the forest, the girl had discovered the trick and returned home, resolved to leave Blois altogether.

Meeting her in church, where she could not escape, Francis managed to draw her aside and to heap her with reproaches. She stood firm. Then he saw his defeat. He gave in; he would pester her no more. And, when the time came for her to make a match, which she deferred until he would sanction it, he had perfectly forgiven her. He always looked out for her and her fortunes.

33

This first affair had his sister's warm indulgence. It sprang in part from her own yearnings. Her hero Gaston de Foix was much in her heart, and Bonnivet was very much in her mind. He was remaining in Milan with the cardinal's nephew Chaumont, and constant letters from his wife brought girlish messages from Marguerite herself.

In spite of Marguerite's charm, Bonnivet was far too gallant to waste his golden opportunities in Milan. His love adventures in exile were peculiarly vigorous and resourceful. He was afraid of nothing, and he let nothing stand in his way. A woman to him, whether wife or maid or widow, was something to be captured by his expert address as a soldier. He believed in possession as nine points in the amatory law, and the game was conducted with a great flourish of gallantry. Once secured, his loves lasted no longer than "the flowers of the field." But he did not forego the greater conquest on which he had set his heart, the sister of the heir to the throne, soon to be wife of Alençon.

He returned to France very little between 1506 and 1512. But on his first return he took particular pains to pay court to Louise of Savoy. The Gouffier family stood high with her. She had the same delight in him that had Francis, and he was "trusted like an angel or a holy man." His feeling for Marguerite was hard to conceal. "The flame that was in his heart rose so high that he could not hinder the colour rising in his cheeks or conceal the flashing of his eyes." Too wary to approach her directly, he found his way to pledge himself to her platonically, but with such passion that this time he aroused a definite feeling in the girl herself. She gaily seconded his affair with a maid of honour but it went so well that she was jealous.

"In serving your pleasure," she said sharply, "you preserve my honour!" But he was called away before he could make any further advance.

Her own marriage to Alençon would probably not have taken place if Georges d'Amboise had not found other designs for Gaston de Foix. But Gaston's natural alliance would be with Spain, since his sister had married Ferdinand and since his claim to Navarre made a further Spanish connection imperative. Marguerite resigned herself to Alençon: his lawsuits with the royal family could only be wiped out by a royal marriage. "God be praised," she said of herself, "but she would rather have received death." She tried to carry off her wedding at the end of 1509 without betraying her feelings, yet "so strongly did she constrain herself that the tears driven inwardly into her heart caused such a flow of blood from the nose that her life was in jeopardy."

Her first years of marriage were "living a life scarce better than death." But when Gaston de Foix was killed at Ravenna three years later her idyll was extinguished and "from this time she resolved to keep God always before her eyes."

Bonnivet's return to France, however, opened a new chapter for Marguerite. He came so suddenly, late at night, to see her mother, that Marguerite flung her arms about him. This embrace had in it her passionate regret for Gaston de Foix, yet it almost admitted her desperate readiness to receive Bonnivet as a "true and perfect lover." But just as he prepared to receive his conquest, with his devoted wife in attendance on Marguerite, the news came that he must go to the King. He collapsed. "His brain well nigh fell into distemperature." Urged by Alençon himself to comfort the invalid, Marguerite went to him alone. "'As far as honour allowed she would give him her love." The Gascon, feigning collapse, "let himself fall into her arms." She held him up. "The medicine she gave to cure his sickness did but increase it." He managed to lie upon her and "fell to seeking for that which the honour of the ladies forbids." Marguerite cried for help. Bonnivet's brother came and was sent for restoratives. While he was gone the indignant lover, forgetting platonism, burst out, "Now that you are married and your honour in safe keeping, what wrong is this I do you in asking what is my own?"

Marguerite was torn between her own desire for this passionate devil and "my honour and my conscience." His assault on her ("love is the most unbearable of all the passions") shook her to the core, but she saw him as the conqueror of women and she fought against her own conquest. Yet when she had repulsed him, while the night went on, "she did naught else but weep."

His next return meant that he would face her in pure anger for her "nice points of conscience." He would try to rape her. "Though you were but bones," he would cry with flaming face, "I would hold them close to me."

But Marguerite was escaping from the first of her "prisons." Her passion for Bonnivet, or her lust for him as she plainly termed it, made her ready to defend herself against her own blood. Had he found his way to her tenderness it might have been very different. The wistful Montaigne would have been a more dangerous man than this Gascon who breathed flame and pawed the ground. Yet the soldier did stir Marguerite to the marrow. She was his partisan against the fine ladies he seduced in Milan. She would not hear a word against his charm, his flowing discourse, his fire, his bravery.

Louise of Savoy, the crafty and experienced matron, did not oppose Bonnivet's suit for a moment. Why should she? In the Gascon she may well have seen a man who could give her daughter what Alençon had failed to give her—the heir to a duchy of supreme importance. What could indelicacy, infidelity, matter in comparison with this intrinsic service? Louise embraced Bonnivet as a son. And when Marguerite cried out for her mother, in the throes of another assault that was too earnest, Louise hardly thanked her. She could not refuse to hear her, but she was content with explanations as flimsy as Marguerite's costume.

34

While Italy was making soldiers of Francis's comrades he was a "fine young gentleman" at home. Anne de Montmorency had left at seventeen, light of heart and of purse, to learn hard lessons in danger, rough living and fatigue. Fleurange would soon earn nearly fifty wounds in one engagement, to be picked up by his own father and brought back for dead. Gaston de Foix would go down in glory, the meteor of these campaigns. But no matter how Francis chafed, he was the Second Person and his place was in France.

Big-bodied, agile, with the most agreeable voice in the world, Francis naturally did not lack distractions. He and Marguerite and their mother constituted a trinity. Marguerite was his best ally. She was part of his natural environment, his "mignonne." Of course he loved her. He not only loved her, he credited her to himself. And this she accepted with the easy indulgence of a radiant girl who has the power and the need to love. To her he was a law unto himself. And so he was for his mother. But his mother observed her boy rather with the eye of a trainer. The big event in 1511 was Francis's fever. The poor boy had a tertiary fever on June 22. By July 15 he was almost well at Valence. And now, in 1512, the poor boy was ill again. This, however, could not deprive him of the great chance that had at last been offered to him, to go to the front. He told his mother about his "mal" on his way to Guyenne. Henry VIII's troops had landed at San Sebastian or thereabouts and Francis was to command the army that would secure Navarre.

The army was a big one, passed in review by him in October. But the campaign was a fizzle. A tardy advance by La Palice ended in the frustrated siege of Pampeluna. The advance had given Francis his first sight of another country and opened his eyes to warfare, but of all the soldiers he served with—Lautrec, Longueville, La Palice, Bourbon—it was only Bourbon who had the intensity and the exactitude that war required. Lautrec's sister, a strong brunette with vivid eyes, made more impression on Francis than anything else. He found her opulence alluring.

The little kingdom astride the Pyrenees, Navarre, was now cut in two, and France had to make secret terms with Ferdinand. Meanwhile, not yet knowing his father-in-law, Henry VIII had decided to invade France in the north, helped by the practised old Maximilian. Maximilian had fences to mend on the Flanders border, and Henry came, fiery to do it for him.

This was the second campaign in which King Louis was willing to engage his heir. He commanded Francis expressly to do nothing except on the advice of his seasoned captains. This Francis undertook. And if the loss of Thérouanne and Tournai was inglorious, and the flight at Guinegate disgraceful, Francis was little more than a spectator, with Louis a wreck carried on a litter, divided in misery between the demoralization of his armies and the gout in his limbs. He was on the point, in fact, of taking all as lost and flying to Brittany.

35

It had been no part of Louis's plan to make Francis a famous captain. The young man certainly did not burst on the world as a military genius, and even as against Henry VIII, brightly busy at Tournai in 1513, Francis was not in the picture. But as the armies disbanded and as Francis went home, he was no longer the mere amorous boy who had left his mother in 1512. He had been away from court, actually soldiering, and he had been fast ripening into manhood. Not being wealthy, he was not yet resplendent. But inside his status as dauphin, where he still was on trial, he had acquired favourites, he had sparkled. And even in statecraft he was feeling his boyish way. Two of Louis's ablest councillors, Duprat and Robertet, were constantly in touch with him. Louise had made a close ally of Duprat. Robertet, who had been steadily undulating forward, courted the dauphin obediently and was going with him to Cognac for New Year's. Louise and

Marguerite would be there; so would Alençon who had fallen off a horse and broken his arm.

The buoyancy that sustained the youth had long since deserted the ageing king. Louis XII was sick in mind and body. His enemy Pope Julius had died in the beginning of the year, having long defied his doctors. But this welcome death and the election of a Medici, Leo X, could not change the defeat at Novara and the loss of Milan. Dijon was saved from the Swiss only by making a perjurer of honorable la Trémoïlle. The war against Henry VIII had been dismal and half-hearted. Navarre was gone. And the unpopularity of the reign was now surging from below. France was politically isolated. The people were depleted and discouraged. Louis's officials were grinding them, and the strong feelings that had been stirred by the war against the Pope were blending into a deeper national resentment against the King himself. It was a morose man, surcharged with debt and gout, who rejoined his wife at Blois, bringing troubles to a market already glutted.

Anne of Brittany herself was far from well. She was not happy about Louis's wars. She was urgent for reconciliation, bent on using every means to win the new Pope. She was certain that the Emperor could be alienated from England, and she sent for Fleurange to take messages into Germany. But in the middle of these pressing anxieties a terrible attack of gallstones assailed Anne of Brittany. For five days she was in agony and then, on January 9, 1514, she closed her eyes for ever.

Anne was not old. She would have been thirty-eight a fortnight later. But ever since 1511, when she had lost a male baby, her health had been shattered. Though she had stood her ground, always the Breton princess, sharp, unyielding, dictatorial, it was impossible for her to survive. Her Brittany was as fixed an aspiration as Louis's Milan, something instinctive in both of them pushing them to these goals, but the dream that had been first embodied in her betrothal to Maximilian and that she had renewed in pledging Claude to Maximilian's grandson had been nullified by the policy of France. She was a defeated woman and her baulked ideal had turned her to recrimination. Her intransigence had made her fling the mantle of her pure faith around Brittany,

equally convinced of the injustice of fate and the justice of Providence. She "mortally hated" Louise of Savoy. She would not tolerate
the marriage of Francis to Claude. That young man, with his
gleaming eye and his naughty smile, seemed to her a wolf about
to ravish her lamb. Had she known more precisely what the
future was to bring she could only have been more forlorn. Not
only would Francis marry Claude within four months but her
sorrowing widower would be remarried within nine months, and
her little Renée, now three, would at last wed the son of Lucrezia
Borgia and end by being a Calvinist. These were the blows that an
inflexibly righteous woman was spared: it was hard enough to go
out in lamentable pain, the cope she was making for His Holiness
Leo X remaining unfinished.

Louis had known his Anne for a quarter of a century. He cried
over her like a child as she lay in her coffin with her face uncovered, its expression calm and young. "Go make the vault big
enough for us two," he said brokenly. "Before the year is out I
shall be with her, to keep her company."

36

At Cognac there were no tears. On one day the news was galloped from Blois, and Louise and her family were overjoyed. Their
road was cleared. From the time that Anne of Brittany had
married Charles VIII, Louise had lived in tension. She had
watched the death of Charles-Orland, the death of her husband,
the death of Charles VIII, the birth of Claude, the birth of a male
heir, the pledging of Claude to a Habsburg. Five children in all
had been born by the second marriage, four by the first, and each
of them had harassed Louise like an injury. They had forced her
to encase herself in hardness, but with Anne's death the shell broke
and Cognac burst into joyousness. It was not enough for them to
share the great news with the Chabots at Jarnac, Francis walking
lovingly by his mother's litter all the way. Louise had literally to
celebrate. She gave him a pompous entry into Cognac when he
returned within the week, the crude triumph of the living widow
over the dead queen. Then with their masks adjusted the family
arrived at Blois to mourn.

37

The long procession that left Blois for Paris was a singular testimony to the enhancing of the Angoulêmes. Francis and his mother and his sister walked after the hearse through all the towns and villages, trailing black weeping trains from their shoulders; and through the wintry countryside they followed the body on their house-led mules. This was the second act of the forty-day ceremonial that would take the queen to her rest at Saint-Denis.

Another of the emerging relations was stern Anne of France. At this ebb tide all the family was restored to view. Anne of France, her head a little bent forward, stood there with Suzanne, her lame daughter, and Charles de Bourbon, her son-in-law, the apple of her eye. Bourbon, a black, smouldering young man, had already made his mark as a soldier. The most powerful feudal noble in France, he appeared over against Francis as a formidable personage, and once the widower dried his tears at Vincennes, Anne of France sank her grave voice to discuss with Louis the ominous cloud of Angoulême. The queen's death made Francis's union with Claude inevitable. But there were other possibilities, and every head was filled with them. Louise was too combative to leave the field to Anne of France. To conciliate Leo X was a policy on which everyone agreed. His envoy was coming to France; and the marriage of Louise's sister to the Pope's brother Giuliano would be the first of the fateful marriages with the Medici. But there was another marital alliance possible, that of King Louis himself. Under the dead herb this little shoot was pushing.

Francis, in the midst of these schemes, blew a grand fanfare of youth. All the economies of Anne of Brittany had been for Claude's benefit, which now meant his, so, with a burst of satisfaction, he consulted his desires. Royal by birth but parched by three generations of penury, his narrowed eyes were now drunk with the sight of healing waters. He dived, rioted, scattered in gorgeous abandonment. There are many things that a prince of the blood might crave who had been slimly financed. Francis knew them. With quick hand he signed promises for 10,000 crowns, for 20,000 crowns, for 40,000 crowns, for 80,000 crowns. Diamonds, rubies, pearls, enamels, superb harnesses, heavy golden spurs, costumes that danced with golden spillikins, swords inlaid and ceremonial, bucklers, gold vessels for the table and for the sideboard, the finest of linen, the loveliest of chemises, the most exquisite perfumes— he devised for himself with his blood singing of proud days and nights varied in delight. It was youth crisp and audacious, swaggering and superficial. It had in it the passion of the Renaissance, if not something almost Assyrian, and Francis made no pretence of restraint.

From his invalid's litter, his blood sluggard in old veins, Louis glumly watched this performance. "This big fellow will spoil everything," he muttered. A jealousy of blood that was bounding swiftly, a hatred of hope that betrayed itself indecently, made Louis clamp his weary jaws and tighten his knobby hands.

Soon the bishop of Canossa would come from the Vatican to see Louis, and then would go over to London. The outcome, worked by Leo, by Canossa, by Wolsey, and by Longueville, would be a deft political transfer, the transfer of Mary Tudor from the boyish Charles at Malines to the decrepit King of France. Had it been possible to take away Claude from Francis this might not have happened, but a decade of pledging and planning had made the marriage inescapable, and Louise of Savoy was now heated at postponement.

Francis had not a shred of sentiment about marrying Claude. He saw her as she was, a limping girl with a slight squint in the left eye, white-faced, low-sized and extraordinarily fat. She was fifteen and though a great heiress and duchess of Brittany as uninspiring to Francis as stale bread. He respected her. She was good. She was pious. But she recalled her mother, and, as his friend Fleurange put it, speaking of the mother whom Claude worshipped, "she was ever against Francis's doings and never a day but those two houses were bickering." Francis was too human to forget that disapproval. He would marry Claude, but without ardour, as a step in his career.

The niche that awaited Claude, azure with fleurs-de-lis, would make her queen. She would give Francis children, direct the court, sustain ceremony, entertain Europe, wear a crown. But at this moment, very much alone, her heart was laden with dismay. Marguerite looked on her with instinctive tenderness and perception, but the girl had only her religion to support her in a painful crisis, with her mother dead and her father visibly dying. Behind darkened doors, under a vault as mysterious as the sky, she could bring her sorrow to a silence and raise her spirit to another sorrow, at once sublime and ultimate, the humbling reminder of sacrifice. Acquiescent where her mother would have rebelled, Claude did not dispute with fate. Whether she wore cloth of silver or whether she stood in kirtle and apron, a fat plain little woman with internal complaints, she would be clay in the hands of her husband, but only because, in her own way, she would always be beyond his reach.

Her father prolonged his mourning, even though the wedding approached. "I am going to be married," Francis suddenly announced to Fleurange at Amboise, on May 10. Louise and the bridegroom set out that day to Saint Germain-en-Laye; and there, in the freshness of spring on May 14, Claude and Francis were married in mourning.

The bridegroom next day absented himself from his wife to go on a hunting trip.

It was in this month that Louis XII, on the suggestion of the Pope, began planning his remarriage.

38

The remarriage of Louis XII was a brilliant political move, worthy of the most flexible and resourceful schemers in Europe. So long as he could be held upright in the saddle, he had tribal importance, and to marry him again carried the game forward. He might slump dejected, aching in the sepulchre of his own body, but he could be prodded up to perform, and he could lend himself to the performance. Mary Tudor had been consigned to Flanders. Two years had been lopped off her age to bring her closer to Charles, "Prince of Castile," whom she had been destined to marry in May. But Henry VIII had been deceived by Aragon, and all Mary's fine sheets, all her feather beds, all her cramoisy and arras, all her "perylls" and "braselets of provune gollde," could now be shipped to France. England married to France served notice that Italy was not yet Ferdinand's to dispose of, and Leo X saw in this change a widening of the prospects of the Medici. Himself the unhappy periphery of a gnawing disease, Leo could distract himself in great plans for his family. As for Mary Tudor, she was assured that Louis was dying, and her brother promised her that when Louis was dead she could marry her own fancy. She was easy to control.

For Francis, and for Francis's family, the remarriage was disastrous. Louis in January was extinct. He could only look at Francis with a sigh, his vision leading from his own obsequies at Saint Denis to Francis's anointment at Reims. It was all over. After years of voyage more precarious than Columbus's, Francis had touched shore. But with one foot on the land this new marriage broke the realization and they were all at sea again.

Francis had not been in the least hesitant or tentative about his own policy. His closest associates were Lautrec and Bonnivet, Boisy, Duprat especially. He meant to renew the Italian adventure, resolutely, comprehensively, the word gloire shining for him like the quivering sea-ribbon of the sun. Women were dalliance, delicious and provocative, but his supreme end would come with the assertion of arms. He played with voluptuous pleasure but he was six feet, broad shouldered, powerful, nimble, and the thought of leading his own army, the first army in Europe, was his indisputable end. When it came to war, there was no levity in Francis; or rather it was the great levity that swallowed up all the little levities that amused him. A need for action burned in him, and he had plunged into expenditure with youthful folly, but as he moved about Blois, towering in height over most of his company, he was the young soldier and nothing else. He was scarce-bearded, red and white of skin. His eye was quick. His long nose gave him that quizzical look that made him almost grotesquely human. With his eyebrows quirked upward and the nose shooting downward he was a gay devil gazing benignly at any little morsel of a woman. And now to have life flare up in Louis's old carcase, with a new dynasty possible, was almost too much to bear.

Perhaps because Francis was less alcoholic than Louis had been, or perhaps because the resilient Duprat and the prudent Robertet were near him, he made up his mind to sit out this game with death. His marriage to Claude would be fruitful, he had reason to hope. The outcome of Louis's marriage he could only guess at. But, en principe, Francis had good sense. He could force himself, that is, to give the classic frontage to his behaviour.

39

Yet at twenty, and married, Francis was inflammable. Had his head opened on a hinge, the first thing to pop out would have been a woman. He had discovered in the army the facility with which a handsome lad could be amused. One glance from him was enough to skewer a pretty girl. He was a young faun, his ears picking up that keen vagrant music which is inaudible to the Christian citizen. At twenty exigency usually goes with timidity, but Francis shed timidity, and he was richly equipped to satisfy himself. By the time he was twenty he had reached the foothills of curiosity. Every amatory triumph brought him to a little height from which lovelier hills were visible. He had verve, the lightest step, easy energy. To be captivated by new prospects was as natural for him as to savour wine, or to love a thing of beauty. He was still an amateur. There comes a time when the itch is merely tedious, when a door cannot open or a woman pass without whipping weary nerves. The hardened professional with his flaccid flesh and his pouchy eye slips bit by bit into the darker streets of desire. In Francis the lilt of the blood was spontaneous. He began straightforwardly, as Marguerite sympathetically recorded, and his first affair after his marriage had the same natural eagerness. True, he was married to Claude, but this was scarcely free will. It obliged him to be considerate, "foi de gentilhomme," but unless she had the punitive vigour of her mother it could not hold him.

And Francis, who often had indulgent feelings towards his good little spouse, was not held. At one of those Parisian marriage feasts which the court sometimes honoured, the most attractive figure was the new wife of an advocate, Disomme by name. Disomme was elderly, eminent and fatigued; his wife young, provocative, fresh and dissatisfied. When the roving eye of Francis alighted on Jeanne le Coq, a single instant swam them into audacity, a few words from him and a few ardent responses from her opening a delicious and palpitant intimacy. She was near him in her glance

but far in her station, well outside the inquisitive court, his survey-
ing mother, or inconvenient scandal. To go to her, late at night,
into the warm coverts of the bourgeoisie, excited his acquisitive
heart. Her husband was the sole obstacle, but Francis was already
audacious.

It would not do for him to be waylaid by the marauders who
made Paris dangerous at night. He needed companions to take
him into the quarter but not beyond a given point. The rest was
a question of their returning before daybreak.

Once at the advocate's house it was the husband who greeted
Francis. Sufficiently Gascon to be fluent, the young prince improvised. He explained his unconventional visit. No one had such good
legal judgment or such proven fidelity as Disomme. It was a desire
for the advocate's counsel that had brought him—for that and for
a drink!

The flattered advocate bowed Francis in: he summoned his wife
to serve her prince on her knees. Francis in his lordly way barely
noticed her. When the husband was fetching his best wine she
whispered, "the first door on the right." Francis took his wine, consumed the advice, recommended the good wife to dwell on her
fortune in having so sage a husband, and then insisted on· departing alone as he had come.

The door firmly closed, he slipped into the little room on the
stairs. In that seclusion, with his nerves singing in excitement, he
waited, and then the escaped wife stole in to him.

Their discovery of each other was passionate. But a short-cut
had to be found for their intimacy. Behind the advocate's house
there was a vast monastery. Through these grounds Francis could
pass, if he made it his custom to visit the chapel for prayers. A
solitary figure, cloaked and kneeling, soon became familiar to the
monks who clattered in for matins. He remained with eyes cast
down, absorbed and reverential. The abbot regarded him from a
respectful distance. The nose? Could it be the duke? A lesson to
every one.

Not until the abbot breathed this edifying spectacle to Marguerite,
and not until Marguerite, who knew her brother, looked him
straight in the eye, did he burst into irresistible laughter. The sister
laughed with him. In her there bubbled comprehension of her

gaillard, dry amusement at the monks, cool perception of the matron. Marguerite loved Francis enough to include all of him.

40

In September, Louis had been formally plighted to Mary Tudor. He had held her childish letter in his hot old hands, and now the dauphin had to go north ahead of the King to escort the bride to Abbeville.

Mary Tudor was arriving at Boulogne, under the loose wet loom of autumn cloud which portends grey-yellow seas and a miserable crossing. Her maids of honour and Mother Guildford were with her, her valiant blue-eyed, stiff-lipped knights. She herself was a dewy English rose, scarcely more than a bud but opened in the warmth of her brother's young court. She spoke a quaint halting French in her fluting voice. Her manner could be arch, her gaiety impulsive, and she could dance as prettily as she played the lute. But her mission was not easy. Suffolk, her brother's favourite, had a stubborn magnificence in the tourney that was only surpassed by his overwhelming direct prowess with women, and Mary had succumbed to him. Her heart was no more than a frightened bird in his hand. She meant to make much of the old gentleman she had to marry, but she was a spoiled, passionate child who had left what she loved in England.

As Francis saw her, on her white palfrey, with her crimson hat cocked over her left eye, she seemed a coquette of rare attraction. At first he was ceremonious but hardly had he explained in detail how Louis was to ride out to their casual encounter than she and he were gay together, talking freely and laughing.

Louis had arrayed himself for the occasion to match his Princess's toilette and came jouncing on a lively Spanish steed. There was no nonsense about his greeting. She had graciously removed her hat so all the better he "threw his arms around her neck and kissed her as kindly as if he had been five-and-twenty."

Francis and Claude gave her a ball at Abbeville that evening. She was arch with her "son-in-law," he sparkling. A lady so lovely, all in gold and diamonds, frankly delighted him. As against an advocate's wife in the alcove, Francis found his imagination enlivened by this princess from afar. When at last, after feverish festivities, she came to the altar with her King, "feeble, old and pocky," Francis stood behind her, her heavy crown in his hands, and her tremulous body close to him. He was already amorous of her, with the facility that conceives all women facile.

The eye that Francis bent on Mary Tudor was that of a handsome gallant. The world saw them riding together, on the road to Abbeville, under a broken sky. They would be paired in a number of brocaded processions, which would be faithfully described by the chroniclers and be watched with stinging curiosity by a populace keen for diversion. But Francis took official pageantry as a routine, a duty that he discharged because it fell to his lot as a craftsman. He rode beautifully: and he dressed in costumes that amused him because they were parries and thrusts in emulation, a way of dazzling the world, asserting oneself, a happy art in which one's own body became an adventure in beauty, catching for an instant the flash of crystal waters, the glow of sunshine, the buoyant colours of a young meadow, the pride of a bird of paradise. But this glory of the eye, that aroused the spectator, was only the histrionism of his rank. His enjoyment of it, never ceasing, merged in his enjoyment of its register in the eyes of women. There he really found himself, enhanced and released, as if he had passed into a boundless elasticity. Fully alive to the rôle of France in Europe, quite able enough to outline his own scheme to the Venetian ambassadors who waited on Louis, he was still powerless, and he lived at present not to round out France but to round out Francis. His was the alert and eager spirit of a gay adventurer, quivering with the life inside his head. He was young, blithe, personal, indefinitely expansible. The universe was a mechanism to which he resigned himself with simplicity. He could not run his hand along its little arm.

Louis loved his new doll. He popped his jewels to her one by one, as if they were bon-bons, chuckling and asking kisses for them. Mary played up to him but when she heard that Mother Guildford was to be sent away, leaving her all alone with the French and her old gentleman, she fluttered into panic. But her spouse was firm. A strange woman hovering around his bride, standing in corridors, lurking behind screens, giving little coughs

—never! He might be ageing but he was king in his household and he very plainly and sensibly dismissed her. The person he could not dismiss, however, was his heir. Francis had established himself in Mary's graces. He did everything he could for her. The jousts he was arranging were solely for her eyes and he intended to shine in them. His "mother-in-law" enjoyed him. At the same time her liberty was gone. Francis and Louise of Savoy had quietly placed their own people in close attendance on her, day and night. Every act of her life was spied on.

Taking his friend Fleurange aside with gleaming eyes Francis gripped hold of him. "Adventurer, I'm happier and easier in mind than for the past twenty years! Unless people are lying very hard, I now know that the king and queen cannot possibly have children, which is made for me."

But even with this assured to him by his mother's confidants, Francis could not keep away from Mary Tudor. She enchanted him. His mother watched his infatuation with growing alarm. If he really seduced her, the throne might pass to his own son, and this at a moment when Louis was visibly wilting! The old King's tenacity was feverish. He sat through banquets. He dragged himself to his feet early in the morning, new satins hung on his frame. But the whole world watched him, as they might watch a wretched dog pawing his way against the current. His plight seemed comic. "This hackney that the King of England has sent is jogging him along very pleasantly, whether it is to heaven or to hell."

Suffolk arrived, Mary Tudor's stout friend. And Francis, who took him under his wing, found him lodgings with the le Coqs, his mistress's family. No one could have been warmer to him than Francis. But of course the English had not failed to put Francis in his place when they arrived first of all for the wedding. They kept insisting on addressing him as "the duke," meaning the duke of Brittany. This deposed him as second person in the kingdom to make him Claude's husband. Francis did not let it pass, and when he wrote to Henry VIII immediately after he allowed himself the irony to offer regrets that "the *duke* of Angoulême might not come to your presence, to bear the *aarl* of Angoulême's heart to you." The English went hunting the boar with Francis, and here again they snubbed him. They thought him a braggart. As for jousting, Francis had new armour that he could not even adjust without their advice. Pride with nerves did not find favour with pride that could conquer nerves. Suffolk, a human turret, withstood every shock of Francis's lance, and Francis retired with an injured finger before the end of the tourney. His lavishness, even, made a rather unfavourable impression. And he was unsportsmanlike. He actually introduced an unnamed bully of huge and savage dimensions to dispose of Suffolk. But, as luck would have it, Suffolk knocked him silly. Thus the islanders went home to tell the tale.

The hollow gallantry of Louis's marriage was not long to be sustained. The king desired an heir more than he desired life itself, but unless everyone was in error it could not be managed. Louise of Savoy, almost grey with anxiety, could not remain on the scene. Marguerite had also gone away. Francis stood by, and so did Anne of France, the succession still of consuming interest to her. Louis was bent over and sagging, thin and worn, eroded by the disease that had deranged him since 1500. He left Paris for the country, to try a change of air, but by Christmas he was at the Tournelles, on the broad of his back, barely able to smile at the young wife that diplomacy had sent to him.

He called for Francis, to say he was dying. Francis tried to reassure him, but the old soldier knew it was fraudulent. He made his confession and then grimly gathered into himself the last energy to break with the long habit of life.

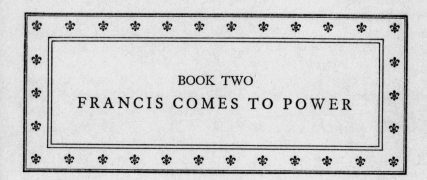

BOOK TWO

FRANCIS COMES TO POWER

FRANCIS COMES TO POWER

FOR A MOMENT the past clung to the future in the hôtel des Tournelles: Louis XII dead, Francis I living. Then the present set them apart and Francis went to the Palais.

It was black when he left the deathbed to begin his new life. The streets were pot-holed and the storm had lashed them into lakes of mud, but instead of the crackling movement of daytime Paris, the swarms of pedestrians in the roadways, the wagons, the litters, the mules, the bells, the cries, there was a laden and suggestive stillness.

Francis's course wound down to the Seine through the twisted streets, and above him the houses lifted in melancholy oblivion. They crowded together, those secretive tenements of Paris, some with timbered fronts lurched forward, some leaning back in dinginess, as if to conceal a destiny limned in grime: silent witnesses, those oblique houses, to the immense and oppressive struggle they had spanned. They were now steeped in midnight. They had cradled the child and bosomed the invalid, held end and beginning, and with each divided effort, each passionate recapitulation, they remained an obdurate monument of perishable man. Even if the thatched houses rose to mansions and the rich and steep-roofed mansions mounted into magnificence, they brooded the same human obliteration. A boss of glass might glow hot from a tavern

window or a candle quiver in a bedroom, yet this mute city, the
greatest, richest, the most populous in Europe, gloomed above
Francis in indifference. Francis was nothing. No one man could
seem to it more than a leaf to the tree, the little flutter of an implacable repetition. And as the houses converged on the bridge, the
city parting for the river, an even deeper indifference swept along
in its current.

But the spleen of Paris, the detachment of the river, could not
touch Francis I. He and his archers made an oval of light, swaying onward in the pool of the dark. Under his long nose the
torches flared, and under his bonnet seethed his young imagination. What was he thinking of? France had just come to him. He
had craved it. It was his. He possessed it, in so far as any man
possesses anything, in the degree to which it would work in him
and use him. But what was in his head, what hummed in his
veins, what was he feeling?

He was nothing, a flicker in the night. And yet he was everything, palpitantly human. Those houses, he could move them. That
row of brothels nudging the church, he would see it borne away.
That tower, he would give it to Cellini. He would open a purse
and a hospital would spring out of it. He would sign an ordinance
and the towered and dungeoned Louvre would disappear. The
river itself, he would give it a harbour, le Havre de Grâce. . . .
But these would be prompted or capricious acts, not the clue to his
nature. The processions to Notre Dame, the funerals, treaties,
banquets, the executions, these would not explain him, or reveal
his inner quality. In Paris, throughout France, in Europe or in
Canada, wherever the waves of his own impulses would surge
from him, waves that insinuate and resist, destroy and remould,
there would he leave the memorial of his existence. Everything
turned on those impulses, on the real inner quality of his being.

France had had a hand in him. Europe had worked on him.
The race, in fact, approved of him. He was one of its masters, a
soldier and a prince. He sat firm in his saddle, having been at it
since he was six, erect, correct, big torso, long legs. He had the
right cut of a French soldier, could wield a heavy lance or a two-
handed sword with a light and nimble wrist, could kill a boar
or fly a hawk, could run and jump and wrestle with any man.

This solid physique, bravely framed, did not limit itself to arms. He could eat and drink like a hunter, a man of warm substance and superb immoderations. With these generous physical traits, funded for life, went his quick but subsiding temper, a confident mood, a need for affection. He was only twenty, still docile to his mother and enthusiastic about the men she sanctioned. That loyalty, indeed, would largely dispense him from using judgment. It would deliver him to Lautrec and Bonnivet. It would be akin to his religion, the religion of tribal conformity, loyal to the legends.

Already he had seen something of the world, scanned history and romance, written bad verses, dabbed at languages, met ambassadors and tried his wits on them, spread out the map of Europe. That was his schooling. And now, the young master, he was moving to the centre of the stage.

It was a proud stage and he rode on to it naturally. Buoyed by the class behind him, he could look back on a tradition that had known no fatal break, and held a place in Europe he could strengthen. Confident, gay, affectionate, he was still everything that the Swiss priest said of the French noble, "orgueilleux et glorieux et triomphant." And this crisp defiance Louise had fostered. He had been shaped in the army and the council, by tutor and governor, but she had had the first hand in him. She had been his nursery and in him had favoured the two supreme tendencies of the nursery: the generous approach, and the desire to seduce the world into indulging him. It was from this immature centre that he would rule France.

So had Louise initiated him into worldly wisdom. All his life he had listened to her, a conspectus of political Europe, and he knew everything that this great lady had drily and sardonically revealed. She was, in effect, his touchstone. Cupboards had been opened to him and old bones rattled. His innocence had been erased and he had blithely adopted a stale, bitter tradition of survival. So far, he was a woman-made man. And with his mother's archaic shrewdness had mingled her perfect indulgence of him, so that he saw no difficulties, no real disadvantages, in getting his own way. This he took to be the way of France. From Louise, and from Marguerite, he had imbibed his self-confidence, inferring a universe to captivate. Just as his body was moulded for sport, so was his mind shaped for agreement, either to be dictated or to be won. They had not frightened him of the world, they had encouraged him. He was stimulated by dealing with human beings. Their expectancies quickened him and their contact vivified him. It gleamed from his eyes and flowed from his hands. But this social skill, this mobility and facility, would convince him that he could win anyone by courting him. He had, in fact, the makings of a politician.

But his politics would go to serve his kingship, and his kingship made him a soldier. The brave man in him, genuine and direct, started from this self-assertion. He proposed to leap over the timid restrictions under which Louis had apparently laboured and this with what he called honour. At the same time, and here was his strength and his weakness, he was beguiled by his rôle as a Renaissance prince.

It was by no means strange that France disappointed Machiavelli. For all its military dash, which attracted him, it was not deeply imbued with his antique Roman faith. What undermined this Roman virtue in the French was just that savour of human enjoyment which makes power a means and not an end. Philosophically the French might despair, actually they relish. With their natural force they could long since have conquered both Naples and Milan. They could have colonized. They could have administered. But clear as their vision might be, and hard their claims, a love of beauty, a love of women, a love of France itself, could lure them from the dire persistency of the Roman. Francis I, soldier as he was by outlook and prejudice, would have a natural sympathy with the arts, a fresh curiosity, an opening mind. He would feel the caresses of the new Spring, the marvellous resuscitations of the individual encouraged by the legends of Greece. A feudal lord within him would grope toward a larger idiom, and Marguerite would be near him, Marguerite whose flame would tremble in the unknown.

But any cut-throat of this midnight Paris, glowering from his lair, would thirst for the rare pleasures of which the passing prince was the mirage: and so would Francis. Out of this crass appetite would flourish his Court and his courtliness. It would leave him shallow and make him positive. He would spend his vitality, and endless vitalities inescapably enslaved to him . . .

He had gazed on his dead predecessor at the Tournelles. Now he turned to the future. Tonight he would sign letters announcing his accession. From thinking of Louis his mind may have veered to Louis's widow. Life opened vistas beyond Jeanne le Coq, and he gazed down them in that extraordinary avidity of the senses that made him at once daring and shrewd and voluptuous. It was this vista that beckoned as he rode across the Seine. Hope exhaled from him like his radiant vapour in the cold. It flung from him like the blobs of light that slewed up and down the walls. And then the palace engulfed him, and the dark houses closed in.

2

Before he had crossed the Seine his courier was ploughing to Romorantin on roads scarred by the winter. Louise, a hundred miles away, was waiting in impatience. Nineteen years ago to the day her husband had died, and during those nineteen years she had endured every vicissitude of the anxious, pining to see her son on the throne. It was now within reach, and she was not yet forty years of age. But Mary Tudor? As her mind hung over the chasms of uncertainty, those abysses that ambition digs in the heart, the courier lashed toward her. He had the big news. He was the chosen one, the elect of the mighty. He covered his hundred miles without mercy for himself or his horses. He knelt to Louise, muddy and exultant. And hardly was he wined and comforted for this commendable effort than the King's mother was herself on the road.

She ached to be by Francis's side. She was brimming with management. She must see Duprat, must hasten the funeral. Her Cæsar must be definite with Flanders. Her Cæsar must eat in solitary state.

Meanwhile the firm hand of custom had guided Mary Tudor, no longer queen, from her palatial Tournelles to the hôtel de Cluny. There, sequestered for six weeks, she would be la reine blanche. It was just long enough to give the last accounting of the biological union she had shared with the old king; any child conceived before that six weeks had elapsed could still legally be ascribed to him. But was she with child? Francis's first concern would be to probe into this danger. Meanwhile the young widow was guarded from temptation.

3

She lay in bed. The daylight was excluded from her room as she enacted la reine blanche, the sorrowing widow of Louis twelfth of the name.

Wolsey had written to .her in the knowledge that her husband was dying. She had read the pompous consolation in ecclesiastical polysyllables, and then the plain warning to let nothing pass her mouth whereby any person in these parts might have her at any advantage.

"And if any motions of marriage or other fortune to be made unto you in no wise give hearing to them."

Re-marriage! Mary Tudor could only grip the coverlet in desperate anxiety at the thought of such pressure. Her one hope, Suffolk, her stalwart compatriot, her sweetheart, would not be in France till the coronation. Meanwhile she was anchored in the Cluny. English monks would break in to warn her that her friends Wolsey and Suffolk were in league with the devil. It was Wolsey and Suffolk who had given Compton his running sore in the leg. Mary had dismissed them, but she was shaken. She was a political puppet. A ruthless practicality had been shown in espionage by day and night. The loss of liberty she felt, the unknown terrors she imagined, rose from time to time into an actual crisis of her nerves, her whole body taut like a vibrating bow that cannot shoot its arrow. Her breath came short and her natural pallor turned to rose. This anguish, this fever, invaded the nerves of her teeth until she was aware of nothing but physical and moral misery, until she broke into tears. Meanwhile she was treated with courtly ceremony.

Francis came to see her. She could quickly reassure him that she was not with child. In this small room, with herself perched in white on the canopied bed, the new King, towering in violet costume, smiled his kindest smile. The Venetian ambassador who had just seen him with his Mephistophelian smile and his long purposeful nose had remarked with a certain awe, "He looks like the devil!" There was, perhaps, just a suspicion of horns budding on his young head as he smiled at the princess. She looked at him, breathing short, blue of eye and rosy of cheek. A tall devil in silk, with long slim calves and long tapering hands, not a very Christian apparition. Such was the make-up. But of course he was a devil of a gentleman.

How did Francis suppose her? She was not a jeune fille. He had kissed her hand and danced with her and held her gaze. She had come from England with a bevy of sophisticated girls, one of whom, Mary Boleyn, would be called a "hackney." Mary Tudor's intimate friend was a French girl, Jane Popincourt, who had been with her for fourteen years. Jane had become Longueville's mistress while he was prisoner in England, and when Louis had heard what she was like he had refused to have her in France, mumbling that "if the King made her to be brent (burned) it should be a good deed." Since Longueville had given his own account of Henry VIII's court to Francis, and since Mary's sister Margaret was a scandal, the mood in which Francis came to her was naughty. If Mary was pretty, with a beseeching manner, virtually defenseless, she could only appeal to her visitor as practising the art of defence. The corresponding art is attack, and this was Francis's.

Had he been coming for himself, he could have wooed. He was tender for a woman. But she was a political personage. She was destined to draw 80,000 francs a year as Louis's widow. If he could win any advantage when so much was at stake, as Wolsey foresaw, he would certainly do it. And he now had his mother to advise him.

So he took her in hand. If she went back to England, he told her, she would be married into Flanders, to young Charles. This made her cry out in naïve horror. Better a convent than that! Francis urged her to let him arrange for her. The Duke of Savoy he named, which would bring herself and her jointure straight into his mother's family. That did not answer. He next tried the Duke of Lorraine. Since Lorraine was the blond giant whom Francis had brought forward to knock Suffolk silly it was not the happiest of proposals. But why would she not remain in France? He would give her the revenues of Blois. Still she did not respond to him. Then, before long, he was confessing that Claude could be rejected, just as Jeanne de France had been rejected, and he leaned over to propose himself.

When Mary reported this to her brother she put it this way: she spoke of "the extreme pain and annoyance I was in by reason of such suit as the French King made unto me not according with mine honour." She spoke of it again as "his malfantasy and suits." And again she feared he would "take courage to renew his suits unto me."

England was vital to this debonair youth, and Mary Tudor enchanting. With his ardent face and pleasant voice, a rare perfume floating from his linen, he could be a princely lover. But Mary was hysterical, Mary had the toothache, and Mary was in love with Suffolk. The more he pressed her, the more he frightened her. At last, her prudence giving way to the alarm that this false courtship was exciting, she had to burst out with her secret, to refuse him on real grounds.

"Sir," she begged him, "I beseech you that you will let me alone and speak no more to me of the matter, and if you will promise me by your faith and truth and as you are a true prince that you will keep it counsel and help me, I will tell you all my whole mind."

She then told him how she stood with Suffolk, how Wolsey knew of it, and how she had written to her brother Henry that, having obeyed him by marrying the old king, "now I trust that you will suffer me to marry as me liketh for to do."

With this confidence poured out to him, the fluid sincerity of Mary's heart, Francis ceased being a prince and became a gentleman.

But Mary Tudor had had a glimpse of a hard audacity. She was "weary and afeard" for Suffolk.

His little treachery to Claude was neither here nor there. He pledged himself to help Mary, but bound her rigorously not to give him away. She promised, not without treachery herself. But by making love to her, by driving through her defences, he secured something to retrieve to his mother, the inside knowledge of Mary's intentions. He had wanted her, palpitating as he gazed on her, with her wisps of blonde hair under her cap. But if he could not win her, he had learned how she stood with Flanders. So much to the good. He could make a farewell as well as any man. And as he rode from the Cluny to the Palais, in the mournful January twilight, he could smile down his nose and plume himself on the audacity that had denuded Mary's heart and given Suffolk, clumsy in this tourney, right into his hands.

4

Francis misunderstood Mary Tudor. She had never encouraged him: if she had been sweet to him, it was because of Suffolk. But Mary was too young to see that Francis had his own great motive. He was plotting for Milan.

To enjoy himself—he could not suppress his instinct for it. He was intoxicated by women. He burned for enjoyment. But in between the innumerable papers to sign, the conferences to hold, the councillors to heed, he was certain of one object that gave meaning to his kingship, and that was the reconquest of Milan. It was elemental. It came straight out of the intentions of his predecessors and straight out of the teachings of his Savoy mother, sharpened by her contempt for the princes who had failed. Milan was as much to him as it had ever been to Louis XII, but he designed to build on the security promised by writing a new treaty with England and by eliminating Mary Tudor.

The moment he was sure of this he did not hesitate to see Charles's envoy. He took a high tone, to show he was no novice in monarchy.

"I shall be a good friend to the Archduke," he said loftily, "because he is my vassal."

He had been his vassal for about forty-eight hours.

The envoy bowed. "Sire," he retorted, "I would have you know, no 'friend' or 'vassal' can do you more harm than he can."

This left Francis unmoved. He had a kingdom behind him, the first in Europe. He believed in it and in himself. And with this power behind him, at the least reminder of rebuff, there came his bugle of insolence.

But this was young insolence. From the moment he got out of bed and looked at the sky to see the weather, an unshaven youth in his nightshirt, he was now surrounded by flattery. The courtiers that flocked into his bedroom, and saw him wash and heard him spit and watched him dress, the men whose fortunes he was making and who were shaping his fortune, knew on which side of the boat to paddle. It was headed south, and England and Flanders must be "practiced." That was a necessity. Henry VIII should naturally be allied to Flanders, the market for his wool, but he could be bound by fresh promises of gold—the payment of French debts that somehow straggled back so far as to include his own father's ransom. Francis inclined to jibe at Henry in private, but he knew his importance, and Mary's importance as a link with England.

And his courtiers, the new men, echoed the tall talk he indulged in. The older men, who had been at Agnadello with Louis, were now standing by their old master. They were seasoned Frenchmen who knew a little about war and Italy, and even about life and love. But their old master was in the coffin, soon to be lapped in lead. They had little to say. They were not in the new circle. They were in mourning.

5

It was on January 2 that the servitors had borne Louis's body downstairs. His physicians had disembowelled it and embalmed it. Then into one stiff claw was put a royal sceptre, into the other a heavy club, while he was laid in a coffin with the meagre face exposed to view. A rich cloth now draped the coffin. In by one door came the stream of faithful subjects, with twelve archers on guard, and out by another door they departed. The monks, paid by the day, kept vigil the round of the clock and high requiem masses were intoned every morning, very piteous for to hear.

Francis could see no point in sustaining this expensive wake for forty days, so on the eleventh day criers were sent through the streets of Paris, twenty-four of them, armed with the arms of France. "Pray God for the soul of the very Christian Father of the People, the magnanimous Louis, to-day to be brought to the great church of Paris. Pray Jesus take his soul!"

From every corner of the city, poor and rich came hurrying to the funeral of a king. Jacobines, Carmelites, Augustines, Bernardines and Maturines and Minors pattered in front of his funeral procession. Through streets hung in black marched the horse, the foot guards, the officers of the law, the criers blowing bugles, the trumpeters trumpeting, the heralds of Brittany and France, the blazoned officers of the city, the city archers and bowmen, the members of the university. The master of the horse came with three riderless chargers, a white cross on black velvet trappers that trailed to the ground. The Swiss guards carried their standard and swords. The archers of the guard were in mourning, carrying their standard. The servants of the palace marched next, the twelve archers who had guarded the body, black staffs in hand, the mayor of the city and the rector of the university; after them the grand master of the horse with the sword of state and five riderless chargers. At last came a chariot drawn by six horses in black velvet, led by pages in black. On this chariot was a great cloth of gold, each corner held by a marshal of France, with twelve gentlemen on each side of the chariot; and under the great cloth of gold lay the coffin, while above it, on a frame, extended a waxen effigy of Louis.

Behind the dead walked four princes of the royal blood; Alençon, Bourbon, Francis de Bourbon and Vendôme; and over these mourners a canopy was perambulated by the officers of the city.

The tail end of the procession, civil and military, followed in equal state from the Tournelles to Notre Dame.

Before the funeral had started, unfortunately, the mayor and the rector fell into a dispute as to the order of precedence. It was sincere and heated. And it could not be adjusted until someone cleverly ran for the lawyers.

At Notre Dame the body was placed in the centre of the cathedral. There, with myriads of candles flinging light into their faces, rows of clergy in white rochets, some saintly, some mundane, some diabolic, pealed out the office for the dead, while behind them the grey pillars lifted themselves sublimely to hold aloft the roof.

The next day, as drizzle threatened, the funeral started in the same order for Saint Denis.

The religious of Saint Denis waited at the outskirts of their town and when the chariot and the chief mourners reached the spot where the lieutenant of the abbot was attending, he raised his voice and asked, "Who is it you are bringing to us?"

"It is the body of Louis, twelfth of the name."

The prior advanced. "Is it the very body, or another?"

"By my faith," answered la Palice, breaking into tears, "it is my master's own body."

The monks surged forward at these words, laying sudden hands on the great cloth of gold. "That belongs to us!" they cried, beginning to drag it from the coffin.

The twelve gentlemen of the household pulled it from them. "We who served the king when he was alive," one of them shouted, "have a right to this." Whereupon a brawl began with high voices.

"We refuse to chant," bellowed a monk, "unless we have the cloth of gold."

Bourbon, knitting his black brows, stepped right into the mob. "What is amiss?"

Explanations poured out to him. It belonged to the monks, the pall did, it had always been the perquisite of the monks. Two old quavering monks, parchments of tradition, were pushed forward. "By our faith," they wagged, "it is ours of right."

"Are there no other elders save these?" Bourbon demanded.

An aged priest spoke up. "I have always understood the pall to appertain to the monks."

Bourbon waited. No one spoke. "No one is bold enough to say them nay. It is their pall by rights. Now let the dead have his rights."

With that Louis XII was remembered and the abbot, sobbing appropriately, began the "Libera me." But by that time the day was falling in and torches had to be lighted. The rain began to come down. With much grinding in the ruts the chariot, drawn by those six horses in black velvet, lurched forward, jammed under the strain and finally stuck in the mud. Something had broken. The gentlemen of the household scurried to find a wheelwright. Old campaigners gave good advice. The carriage was hammered. It was now seven in the evening, the bells tolling and tolling (at the cost of sixty livres) while Louis laboured to come to his tryst with Anne of Brittany.

Great candles were left lighting round the coffin for the night. In the morning was the final service, and then the body was gently lowered into the tomb.

La Palice, a black staff in his hand, raised the cry, "the king is dead!" Throwing his standard into the tomb, the other standards were thrown in with it, and after them, to the same hollow cry, the great banner of France. Then, instantly raising aloft the great banner, la Palice exclaimed "Vive le roi! Vive le roi!" So the heralds of Brittany and of France took up the cry throughout the church. "Vive le roi!" And thereupon the great lords and the princes of the blood turned their backs on the altar and went to dine.

When grace had been pronounced up rose la Palice, who had served Louis so faithfully.

"All the servants of the late king, are they here?"

A chorus of voices shouted yes.

"My lords, here and now I proclaim to ye that the king our master, Louis twelfth of the name, has passed from this sphere to the other. Our master is dead. Our master is no more. And as we no longer have a master, which each and every one of ye is able to see for yourselves, in sign of the truth I break my staff and throw it to the earth."

With this the grand master broke his staff. And as he did this the vast hall of men, great and little alike, with one voice cried a mighty cry, "Long live the king!"

6

After this royal feast at Saint Denis the great lords jogged back to Paris, and thereupon, in the afternoon, came the first big political move of the new reign. Charles de Bourbon appeared at the Palais to take his oath as constable.

The oath itself was tremendous, "jusques à la mort inclusivement," putting all the brakes of religion on the engine of politics. Bourbon stood up solemnly, swore to think solely of the king, his honour and his profit, and the well-being and service of the kingdom. He also swore to bring any "machination ou conspiration" to the royal attention as well as uphold military and civil discipline. With these stiff pledges he became commander-in-chief of France.

The brakes, however, were far less likely to hold him loyal than Francis's entrusting the army to him. Bourbon was of royal blood.

He was much more of a captain than Francis. At nineteen he had fought boldly at Agnadello. He had been heroic at Ravenna. He was the one keen soldier in the Navarre campaign. He was recently assiduous in Burgundy. The whole of the nobility had been watching the new king to see how he would deal with this rather wire-edged, high-strung, black-browed young prince. Bourbon's appointment as commander-in-chief was the answer: it took him into camp. It was Louise's way of counteracting an opposition, bringing Bourbon and Angoulême into equilibrium.

The real personage to be placated was less Bourbon than his mother-in-law, Anne of France.

She was now a matron of advancing years, a figure of great dignity and integrity. She stood sufficiently apart from the throne, sufficiently supreme in their own dominions, to exact a prudent, even a nervous, consideration. And this young man with princely gravity and liquid black eyes, his father sleepy Montpensier, his mother passionate Gonzaga, was the sword of which she was the scabbard.

When Charles de Bourbon fulfilled her wishes by marrying her only daughter, the malformed Suzanne, there were conjoined, with legal sutures, vast territories in the centre of France: duchies of Bourbon, Auvergne and Chatellerault; counties of la Marche, Clermont-en-Auvergne, Forez, Montpensier and Gien; the dauphiny of Auvergne; viscounties of Carlat and of Murat, lordships of Beaujolais, of Combrailles, of Roannais, of Thiers, Bourbon-Lancy, Annonay, Le Roche-en-Renier. This block of France, so solid, so extensive, was no accident of inheritance. Interlocked by subtle toil, it was a masterpiece of acquisition. Wills had flagged and hearts rebelled, but Anne of France had persisted. Hers was not a work of art that carries into assuagement; it was rather an incrustation of the human spirit which, by its deference to the stuff in which it works, gains a power as terrible as the power of the ascetic. Anne of France had remained pre-Renaissance. She lived islanded in her possessions, with her law, her army, her artists, her architects, her gardens and parks and menageries. She was herself not entirely unlike the giraffe she had requested from Lorenzo il Magnifico, a giraffe browsing on the top leaves of the genealogical tree, and, implacably upright, desiring to perpetuate this form of nourishment for her family. The problem was difficult, because at each acquisition in this forest of acquisitions, there had been evasions. Hence to give Bourbon and her daughter a secure holding on this superb domain was her covert preoccupation. So much of France registered in a single name meant a mortgage even on kingship. It was power in perpetuity. The title might be disputed, but Anne of France had devoted to the Bourbonnais that same intensity and lucidity which she had devoted to France as regent; an indomitable woman, and convinced of the wearing quality of a dukedom. Lesser mortals might want the syrup of amusement in life; Anne of France asked to build a great family, based on the pedestal of vast property, and to do this as an architecture aristocratically understood, a monument that had in it something more invincible than mood or time, the cold music of power, the triumph of status.

By making Bourbon constable, by naming him governor of Languedoc, and accepting him as heir to the Bourbonnais, Louise was far from gratifying her personal emotion. She looked with favour on Bourbon as a man, but nothing could wipe out her early subjection under Anne of France's glacial regime. Her method in life, however, was to submit until a balance could be shifted. If Mary Tudor had to be managed, for the sake of Milan, so with Anne of France, and so with young Bourbon. Hence the collaboration at the Palais.

7

But the advancement of Bourbon could be partly squared by another process, and an agreeable one. All his life Francis had suffered from the poverty of the Angoulêmes whose county, abutting on the Bourbonnais, was hardly more than a cottage at the foot of a manorial hill. Now that could be changed. For his grandfather Jean it was too late to do much, except to ask Rome to beatify him, one of the final steps in the celestial peerage. But his mother he could enrich, and his sister, and his sister's husband. And this was the first joy and benefit of being king.

To his mother he gave the duchy of Angoulême, the duchy of Anjou, the counties of Maine and Beaufort, and the barony of

Amboise. Not so bad, for a beginning. To his sister and Alençon he gave with high hand the disputed county of Armagnac. He also gave them the right to name a master in every trade throughout the kingdom. These were his first benevolences, to secure the independent wealth of his family and their heirs for ever.

The next was to entrench his adherents. Marguerite's husband was now Second Person of the kingdom; he was named governor of Normandy. Lautrec was made governor of Guyenne. René of Savoy, his mother's bastard brother, was made governor of Provence. Artus Gouffier, known as Boisy, Guillaume Gouffier, known as Bonnivet, René of Savoy and la Palice were given the right to name certain officers of the law, a profusion of saleable appointments.

To milk a kingdom requires a double art, the art of decreeing and the art of extracting revenue. Happily for Francis, taxation in France did not carry representation with it. The commonweal was in the hands of officials, and if he could manage the officials he had license.

The character of the new regime soon shone out in the building of châteaux. One by one, as candles are lighted on an altar, there began to bloom the exquisite châteaux of Francis's officials. Florimond Robertet had Bury. Antoine Duprat became seigneur of Nantouillet. Bonnivet would have Neuville. The huge château of Artus Gouffier, Oiron, grew out of the funds made available by the gentlemen of the long robe, but they themselves did not fail to follow suit. Berthelot, a president of the treasury, flowered into Azay-le-Rideau, the most charming of domiciles, while a Bohier-Briçonnet marriage gave birth to the proud establishment of Chenonceau. The list would run on, over years, and no one could be blind to its meaning: the class of officials inestimably important to Francis would roll into wealth and assert themselves in the most beautiful of idioms.

The new chancellor was the key man. Antoine Duprat's mother was a Bohier. For some years this plump man had been growing in the confidence of Louise of Savoy, and even while he was president of the parlement of Paris he had taken over Francis's education. Louise's judgment stood her in good stead when she picked this little Auvergnat. He might have been a churchman; he would in fact end as a cardinal. He was a stout, resilient person of energy and keen insight, understanding from the start that Francis's absolutism demanded the firm control of parlement and the strong manipulation of the Vatican. As a by-product of his skill Duprat would become a multi-millionaire, but this because he was a merciless special pleader, with that hard French mind that can triturate diamonds. Louise, by no means as able as himself, could work perfectly with him. When he differed with Poncher, the archbishop of Paris, in the last year of Louis's reign, it was to Cognac he betook himself. There he undoubtedly combined the mother's with the son's education.

Francis's machine of absolutism would require soft metal as well as hard, and in human engineering this is always a problem. Duprat despised gentle Semblançay, Semblançay shrank from Duprat. It was a case of surgeon against physician. Semblançay in his time had served both Louise and Anne of Brittany, and never lost either woman's favour. He understood the art of elongating ends until they meet. As a spendthrift's treasure he had now the most delicate position in France, and Duprat was unjust to his resourcefulness. He was a wizard. And with the easy affection that is bestowed on wizards in the families of the great, Francis called him "father." He meant, Father Christmas. Semblançay was his indulgent Santa Claus.

There was another wizard in this establishment. The "pivot of the court" before Louis died had been Florimond Robertet, a native of Forez, a born secretary of state. He had been with Charles VIII before Francis was born, had carried across to Louis on the bridge of Anne of Brittany, had found favour with George d'Amboise, knew German and Italian and Spanish and English, married a Gaillard who brought him 100,000 livres, saw her brother Michel marry into the Angoulême family (the daughter on the left, Souveraine), was treasurer of Normandy before becoming financial secretary, knew everything, saw everything, foresaw everything, moved like glycerine through the intricacies of the law, and was able, sick and old and half-blind, to slide the springs of diplomacy.

But the machine had wheel within wheel, all interlocking. The Gaillards were cogs of national finance. Another Gaillard was married in Normandy. This Gaillard lady would have a son-in-law

who, first as Marguerite's chancellor in Alençon and later as head
of the Rouen parlement, would prove serviceable. And this family,
too, would have its second close tie with the Angoulêmes. Louise
of Savoy believed in utilizing the by-products; so, when Francis
saw his mistress Jeanne le Coq become a widow, a son of the Gaillard lady in Rouen was happy to come forward and marry her.
Thus, through the Gaillards, Francis's mistress and Francis's half-
sister were intertwined with Marguerite's chancellor and his own
secretary of state, the financiers, the parlement and the treasury.
It made, in its quaint way, a bourgeois dynasty, bound to the king
not only by interest but by personal ties, and able, in the secrecy of
the heart, to feel itself a backstairs royalty. Edward IV let Jane
Shore sink to a wretched old age but Francis let France pay for it
and dared public censure.

He was hardly on the throne when he nominated a place in
parlement to Jeanne le Coq's brother. There was no vacancy among
the lay seats; whereupon he demanded an ecclesiastical seat for
him. This was intolerable. The interlocking families, the Briçonnets,
the Ruzés, the Huraults, the Ponchers, the Beaunes, the Bohiers,
stiffened under this youthful imperative. Every one of them, of
course, knew of Francis's escapade and his liaison. But to give
Nicole le Coq a cleric's seat was too much; they had the courage to
keep him waiting until there was a lay vacancy. It was opposition.
Francis measured it.

All of Paris knew of his adventure with the advocate's wife. It
became the subject of a farce that rocked the Place Maubert with
laughter. The names le Coq and Dix-hommes suggested a sort of
dumb-show in which Francis was symbolized as a salamander.
"Une poulle portoit sur elle une chose qui estoit assez pour faire
mourir dix hommes." The news of this hilarity crossed the river to
the court, and one night a handful of Francis's cavaliers betook
themselves to a tavern near the Place Maubert. They merrily invited the author of the farce to amuse them. He did his best for the
noble gentlemen. Then they set on him with belts and beat him
furiously before putting him in a sack to throw him in the river.
But because he showed his tonsure, or because the patrol arrived, he
escaped with his flogging. Yet Francis had served notice to the
town. He would not stand ribald critics.

8

The restiveness of Paris did not greatly agitate Francis. He had no popular parliament and no direct public opinion. To wage his war he must control the law and control taxation, even if his commoners were to be let build châteaux. He did not intend, like Louis XII, to wheedle France. He was sure enough of it to dominate it. But he held to the organization of privilege.

Just by virtue of ascending the throne he found himself a magnate of the first rank, perhaps the greatest in Europe. Nothing in the nation was too big or too little to escape his sway. No herring could go into Rouen without owing him tribute. No pound of beef could be sold from a butcher's stall without adding to his wealth. The rivers and the forests were in his debt. No one could use a pinch of salt or eat a crumb of bread until he had had his share of it. He controlled the mints. He manipulated the coinage. He decided who would lodge troops and who would hold fairs, who would repair bridges and who would profit from prisons. No counsellor of the parlement, no notary, no master of a craft, could be named without squaring him. The street-singers of Paris, the washer-women in its arcades, the fishermen on the Seine, the barbers, the sign-painters, took their licences from him and paid for it. And with the privileges that looped every town and village, every trade and profession, every natural utility and every product of skill, there went his power to loosen bonds, to give exemptions, to instal favourites, to depress classes, simply by the transfer or extinction of these majestic prerogatives. To dispute the prerogatives was out of question. The Ghetto might declare to the world that the Jews were segregated, but the Jews were only more desperately segregated. France was a vast congeries of Christian ghettos, where ingress and egress cost money, where the citizen stood and delivered. The Church was his only legal rival. The nobles, it is true, by reason of their war services, paid no taxes. But the burden of war fell on the shoulders of the commoner, and the nearer he was to earth the heavier the load, so that the poorest class was flattened like the straw-thatched huts that stabled them.

Every sharp-eyed citizen who wanted to advance himself turned his eye to the King. No matter how small he might be, the citizen's one hope, in a system of privilege, was to win privilege for himself. This applied to abbeys that wished to spare themselves the derangement of feeding an army. It applied to universities that sought revenue, to towns hampered by imposts, to courtiers wanting captaincies, to the exporter asking for the easing of a tariff or the parasite seeking an estate or a borough. Like a water-tower sucking the stream into its arrogant height and shooting it into every outlet with new and powerful pressure, Francis concentrated in his own will the decisive distribution of national revenue. It flowed to him by franchise and privilege: by gift and by exemption it poured from him. Through this means he was empowered, without the check of any representative government, to nail the obedience of his subjects and make them slaves of his will. He was literally master of France. His pen alone could sign the ordinance. He grouped round his absolute power not only the army that upheld it but every class from his peers to his poets. An idyll could be sung of him as the monarch who safeguarded the national well-being, the good shepherd who protected against wolves. But to merit this shepherd, his people had to be sheep—to be pastured, to be sheared. The relation of subject to monarch, of sheep to shepherd, had consequences in every prayer, in every petition, in every lyric of their existence. He would, of course, fight the wars he created. But since war rotted citizenship, homicide ruled the land. The roads were so villainous in winter, the chance of policing so small, that bandits terrorized every traveller who was not ready to fight for his life. The forests harboured predatory man. Every influential noble strung up the culprits who were brought to him as marauders. The penniless soldiers replenished the ranks of either criminals or executioners. And this branch of anarchy, one result of starved citizenship, was paralleled by sheer indifference to municipal routine. The plague, an annual visitant, was merely the public herald of neglect. When he blew his horn, every one fled, king, queen and royal family. Men like Erasmus detested magic, but magic was privilege's romantic sister. To have plodded out cause and effect in any field would have created common sense, and to common sense every absolutism must turn its brocaded behind. Francis, in many ways, was as artless as the islanders who make love as they will and do not relate it to the arrival of babies. He did not enter into explanations. So the new deal would be a patriotic one.

The cold scrutiny of an expert might have found fault with the methods by which he had provided for his mother and his sister, and the light-hearted way in which he ordained the sale of new seats in parlement for 6,000 livres each. But these were preliminaries to his domination of Italy. He brought to this task that had baffled France for a score of years a wholly new confidence and enterprise. But this had to be lubricated. To drop Château-Thierry into the lap of Fleurange was merely typical of the high spirit in which he was encouraging his captains. His hand was on his heart, and even more frequently in his coffers. The army! That was the mainspring. All the jousts and pageants with which his accession was to be celebrated were only the frosting on the cake. The real performance was to be in Italy.

All his nobles were ready for it. His young hopefuls, Montmorency and Fleurange, Brion and Montchenu, were no less ready than Bonnivet and Lautrec. And Lescun, Lautrec's bishop brother, swopped careers. He lost no time giving up his round hat to become a soldier.

It was only the first tattoo of the drums, a gay little patter of sound, a tap-tap-tap in the distance. But it was the real meaning Francis found in kingship. And it was patriotic. Had not France been recently humiliated?

9

But God must be conscripted by good governments. Hardly had the dilution of parlement been arranged for, and the bounties handed around, than the whole world, by horse and mule and litter, streamed off for the consecration at Reims.

The oil had been brought by a dove from heaven on Christmas Day, 496. Perhaps one or two were thinking of a more recent miracle, when a girl from Lorraine had led the King to Reims not a hundred years before. In the same vast cathedral, but now prosperously attended, with the peers revolving in rank, came Francis to touch hands with Clovis, and so with the dove of heaven. Naked

to his loins, very white of skin and black-bristled, this young man
with startling red lips stood up to be dabbed on his forehead and
his broad back, his armpits and his navel. Those who loved him
gazed raptly on the youth. Marguerite, absorbed no less in her
brother than in her Deity, watched with mystical intensity the
consecration of that precious human body. As his silken shirt and
his outer garments were restored to him, a pang was left of frail
mortal flesh. But with incense, with music, with intonation, the
Church now proclaimed its power to set him apart from ordinary
mortal, to link him with divinity, to knit him to purposes as pure
and mystic as its own. And the whole congregation, rather more
than less archaic, felt as if a directing spirit came in unto them.
Many resolved to love chivalrically, and battle nobly, and be for
ever valiant and loyal. They then went to the royal banquet, as
from the funeral, with the appetite that comes from high resolve,
and before evening a great generosity shot them with lascivious-
ness, a glory singing in the blood.

It was in the trail of these hearty celebrations that Suffolk
arrived from England, to interview the King.

Francis had been to Saint Marcoule, which gave him the power
to heal the king's evil, so that he was exalted by old vintages of
the spiritual order, as well as earthy wine. He greeted Suffolk
lovingly and familiarly, having now known him both for himself
and through Mary Tudor.

Suffolk was given public audience in which he conveyed Henry
VIII's formal thanks to Francis "for the singular comfort he had
given the Queen in this her heaviness." The word "singular" was
no doubt due to Wolsey. He had been to her, Henry said, "as a
loving son should be to his mother." Francis responded in the
same humour. He modestly affirmed that he might do no less with
his honour. "And how lovingly I have behaved myself to her," he
said, "I trust that she shall make report herself."

That was witty enough, but when Francis had Suffolk alone in
his bedroom he looked at him down his nose.

"You are come to marry the Queen, your master's sister."

Suffolk floundered. "I trust your grace would not reckon so great
a folly——"

Francis cut into his protestations. "As you will not be plain with me, I shall be plain with you. Have you heard this word before?"

It was a secret word from the love code between Suffolk and Mary Tudor, a little bite of a word, that Mary Tudor had revealed to Francis.

Suffolk blushed crimson. But Francis thrust out a friendly hand. "By the word of a King," he said, having been a King three weeks and four days, "I shall never fail unto you but help this matter betwixt her and you."

Suffolk's relief was instant, yet at once his mind ran to his master. "But I am like to be undone if this matter come to the King my master."

"Let me alone for that," said Francis grandly. "The Queen and I both will write letters to the King your master, in the best manner that can be devised."

Yes, Mary could have her way. After all, Henry had promised it. It would make a fast friend of Suffolk. It would remove her from royal alliances. Should England break with France, the revenues of Saintonge and the rest, Mary's 80,000 francs a year, could be suspended. It was a happy and honourable solution.

Francis thereupon turned his mind to the approaching tourneys, the royal entry into Paris, the marriage of young Diane de Poitiers with Louis de Brézé, and all the other glories and festivities in the middle of which he would be no less "beautiful and triumphant" than he had been at the consecration. But first he had to meet the ambassadors from the Archduke Charles. This would be at Compiègne.

10

Francis had been condescending to young Charles, but there was a reason for that. On New Year's Day, without any warning whatever, Margaret of Austria had been deposed and the fifteen-year-old boy placed at the head of his government. She made dignified protest to her father, but she could thank old Maximilian's wariness, her own flirtation with Suffolk, her anti-Habsburg nobles and the pro-French chancellor Chièvres.

Charles, as yet, was not an imposing figure. A pale, thin, melancholy boy, with his mouth hanging open and his gaze floating vaguely about him, he seemed more like the village idiot than a future emperor. But Chièvres, who was with him night and day, and no less French than ever, was capable of steering both Charles and the council. Maximilian would consent to let things be, for 150,000 florins and an annuity of 50,000 livres. Margaret of Austria could only bide her time while Nassau and his companions went to do fealty for Charles.

Francis, it must be said, did not avoid a somewhat patronizing tone. But a French marriage was agreed on. Charles had already been affianced to Claude and to Mary Tudor. He was now offered Renée, Claude's four-year-old sister, with a big dot and the duchy of Berry. This decided on, soon to be embalmed in oaths, Francis turned to his royal entry.

II

A royal entry was important. It bore a strong likeness to the funeral, but the largo had become allegretto gracioso, and the mood was proud. Here were red silk and scarlet mantles, banners and escutcheons and standards, cloth of gold and scarlet on crimson. Here were heralds with trumpets and ladies smiling from their carriages, ladies on hackneys, princes of the blood. It was the royal ancestor of the circus parade, even to the drums.

And Francis was the centre of it, "wholly accoutred in white and cloth of silver." A canopy was provided for him but his horse would not stay under it. "Ca ha, he bounds from the earth, as if his entrails were hairs." And everyone admired his continual curvetting and prancing. "There were good horses and riders," wrote her envoy Gattinara to Margaret of Austria, "that did marvels to attract the notice of ladies."

Daytime Paris was rich, decorative, Gothic. Its windows were crowded. The tailors had been frantically busy to the last minute, and prices had soared. But it was a sight for every one who had not yet seen the king, and it ended royal mourning. He was applauded. It was a triumph.

There was, indeed, no white elephant, such as had recently been sprinkling holy water in Roman festivals: and in this gay procession, as against the funeral, the religious note was absent. The monks had arrived, all ready to start, but the minute Francis caught sight of them he had given word to detach themselves. So they flipped along side streets while the decorated ways were left to the King and his officers and his men-at-arms.

Mary Tudor's quarantine was over. She and Suffolk were able to watch the entry together. And they did so with a great secret throbbing between them.

The municipality had first place in honouring the King. The provost and the councillors trotted in full feather, the officers of the Châtelet, the men of parlement, the archers, the heads of the guilds and the town guards. However the populace might veer in its fancy, the great city owed the King a magnificent welcome. And, while the entry could hardly rival the funeral, which had cost 31,670 livres with 4,000 to the clergy, it was still one of the pageants that gild the crown.

A great banquet followed. And Mercurio Gattinara was not invited. He was deemed anti-French. It is the people who are snubbed, after all, who ought to be listed.

12

The bills might depress Louise of Savoy, but the court was soon presented by a greater economic problem, and this by Mary Tudor. That fervent young woman made away with a diamond.

She had not restrained herself when Suffolk reached Paris. She flung herself on him. She would have no other husband, and he must marry her within four days. "Sir," Suffolk excused himself to Wolsey, "she said that she had rather be torn in pieces than ever she should come to Flanders; and with that she wept. Sir, I never saw woman so weep." So he had yielded. An unknown priest married them, Lent or no Lent.

To resist a second indecency like her marriage to Louis was apparently Mary's uncontrollable desire. She had been forced into the embraces of a scrofulous old man whom Saint Marcoule had not empowered to heal himself. She had endured it. She had survived it. But she would not repeat it. Something passionate and wilful in her made her put Suffolk before anything else.

This biological excitement about Suffolk would not impress the French. Mary was young and beautiful. She was royal by birth,

doubly royal by marriage, and by the death of her husband provided with a great revenue. Europe was at her feet. Maximilian,
it was reported, sat in a maze before her portrait for half an
hour. Even if she were narrowed to Lorraine or to Savoy, hers
could be royal strategy and ascendancy. The French court would
coolly ask, what was a man of low birth like Suffolk as against
this? Louise of Savoy would not exclude him as a lover, but Mary's
insistence on marrying Suffolk was ignoble, the caprice of a child
badly brought up. When Charles of Austria, promoted by Chièvres,
tore a love letter from the bosom of his sister Eleanor, and berated
her for dalliance with a count, he showed a princely sense. Noblesse
oblige. Mary Tudor was selfishly thinking of herself, not of France,
nor of England.

But Mary Tudor, Queen for three months, had of course thought
of France and England. That is what she had been meditating in
the Cluny. And what happened to princesses who gave up their
own preferences? Mary had not watched Catherine of Aragon for
nothing. Anne of Brittany, Anne de Beaujeu, Jeanne of France,
Claude, what had they had? The snow-cold Diane de Poitiers
might accept an important husband. But Margaret of Austria would
never marry again, to please her father. Why should she, to please
her brother? Even Louise's own daughter Marguerite, bound to
Alençon, had the feverish, strained, nervously sparkling manner of
the intelligent woman exiled from satisfaction. The self-willed Mary
Tudor was contemptible to Louise of Savoy, she had insisted on a
preference. And now she had put her low choice beyond argument.

The diamond was missing, however, and that renewed her importance.

It was an unusual and very costly diamond, with a pendant, given
to Mary Tudor by her fond elderly husband. It was the Mirror of
Naples, one of the superb heirlooms of France. To appease her
brother, Mary pinched this precious thing from her treasure box
and smuggled it post-haste to England. It was a bribe. Unless she
bribed Henry not only with her annuity but with her plate and her
jewels, Wolsey had written, Suffolk's head might pay for it. Mary
knew her brother. She sent it, then clung to Suffolk, waiting for
the worst.

The French do not like pranks with their property. According

LOUISE OF SAVOY

From the Drawing attributed to Clouet in the Uffizi, Florence

to their law, they said, Mary could not have the plate and the
jewels unless she paid her late husband's debts, which would have
taken much plate and many jewels. This was food for discussion.
Meanwhile, could Suffolk arrange with his master for the return of
Tournai? To ask Suffolk for the moon would have been equally
kind. He could not arrange it. Francis thereupon frowned. Louise
looked very solemn. Duprat rolled a wicked eye.

For the next two months Mary and Suffolk were sorry they were
wintering in Paris. God's anointed kept asking for his Mirror of
Naples. They were formally married by the end of March, to be
married for the third time on their return to England. But when
the jewel was admittedly not to be called back from the royal deep,
Francis was furious, and grew curt with Mary. And then, as
Duprat acidly pointed out, there were eighteen pearls, worth at
least 10,000 crowns. They too had found their way across the
Channel. It was "sale," dirty, unspeakable. Francis forgot his bedside manner. Suffolk was tremendously uncomfortable. Mary ached
for home.

At last the masterly hand of Wolsey steered England into a treaty
with France. This ensured Francis for his descent on Italy. Mary
and Suffolk were free to leave their "stinking prison" of Paris.
Their book of words, expressing penitence to Henry and giving
their fortune to him, was forwarded by Wolsey. They learned it by
heart, paid mountains of bills, and rather tremulously set out for
Calais. There Mary Tudor, who had married an upstart instead of
Flanders, had to hide from the mob.

13

Francis was on a hunting expedition in the middle of March, as
the new Venetian ambassadors for France and England drew near
to Paris. By lucky chance the Marshal Trivulzio, on his way to
Lyon, was able to stop long enough for a visit at their hotel.

When this hard-bitten veteran opened his mind about Francis to
the two absorbent Venetians, something very like the truth emerged.

Was he going to descend on Italy? Trivulzio said it only
depended on his first establishing himself in the kingdom. He had
squared himself with England and Flanders. Spain would be more

difficult. The Swiss were on the war-path but he could arrange with Genoa. "I have laboured strenuously at the council," said Trivulzio, "to persuade him to undertake the expedition without delay and his majesty is all for it."

"And what is his majesty like?"

The old veteran's wrinkled eyes screwed up.

"His extreme liberality to every one," he said, curtly, "will drain the very blood from his veins."

"But who controls him?"

"His mother applies all her energy to accumulating money. She lays claim to managing everything, not allowing him to act without her concurrence."

"And who else?"

"Boisy, his former governor, now Grand Master. Francis defers to him greatly. You might say, he is still under the rod!"

"And who else?"

"Next to him is René of Savoy and the Constable and Lautrec. But it is his mother, with Madame de Bourbon, and Boisy, who really manage everything. It is a great pity to see him under petticoat government. But what can you expect, the way he lives. He does not get out of bed till a little before noon. Then, after dressing and hearing mass, he goes straight to dinner. Immediately afterwards he withdraws to his mother. Then, after a short while with the council, he plunges into amusement which goes on incessantly until supper time. It is extremely difficult to find an opportune moment to transact business with him. And there you are!"

With this inkling from the hardy Trivulzio, the Venetians came to audience on March 25 at Paris, where Francis, all in white under a canopy, sumptuosissime, rose to greet and embrace them with every cordiality. After the usual exchange of ceremonial addresses in Latin, Francis took them into a window embrasure. "Very shortly will I come in person with a powerful army into Italy," he declared. He lucidly explained the position of France. Guelders, Liége, Hainault, Lorraine and the Palatine could be counted on to embarrass Maximilian. The King of Spain, "crafty and a vessel of manifold deceit," was not so contained. Francis spoke with realistic contempt of England's impotence, unless Flanders and Scotland joined with it. As for Tournai, "I can have it whenever I choose," he said with a flourish. Once treaties were signed, he added, he could unite his troops.

Louise, "the Most Christian King's most illustrious mother," told the Venetians that Francis would prove "the greatest and most faithful friend" Venice ever had.

"Had the deceased King not failed the Signory," said Louise incisively, "his affair would not have come to so disastrous an end."

Anne of France drily concurred. She dwelt on England's impotence. She even paid a grave and formal tribute to Francis, "young and powerful, much beloved by the entire realm."

Francis frankly admitted, in a long and prudent discourse, that he must prepare. He was serious. Placing his hand on his breast he said, "On the word of a gentleman, a year from this day, or thirteen months at the utmost, the Republic will recover her whole territory. Even at the risk of losing my own crown, I would not abandon her!"

14

Francis's pledges were for effect. When he laid his hand on his heart, looked at the Venetians with his slanting eyes and said, "a year from this day!" he knew the words would be repeated in England. His actual scheme was to reach Milan sooner.

Pope Leo was nervously aware of this, and behind him Cardinal Bibbiena was linking up a Holy League against the Most Christian. "It will be a lesson to him," said the malicious humanist piously, "and will teach him to be moderate in this as in all other matters."

But Francis did not aim to be moderate. With his high colouring, his high cheekbones and narrow eyes, he made a picture of incomparable young insolence. The Pope had invited him to waive his claim on Naples, in the month of March, and Francis had responded in "an abrupt and offensive manner." He had suffered the fatal moderation of Louis XII: he had framed his own programme.

And he was not hiding it. In the bosom of the family he did not spare his departed father-in-law. Sir Robert Wingfield bemoaned him. "He is young, mighty, insatiable," he reported to Henry VIII, "always reading or talking of such enterprises as whet and inflame himself and his hearers." He seemed deplorable to the old school. "He keepeth no silence," noted Wingfield, "for his common saying is to all that he speaketh with, that his trust is that by his valour and industry the things which have been lost, lettyn and spoiled by his ignoble predecessors shall be recovered, and that the monarchy of Christendom shall rest under the banner of France, as it was wont to do."

It was a critic speaking but it told Francis's mind. Henry might go on holding Tournai at present, and Ferdinand could hold Navarre. He was waiting to settle these things when he conquered Lombardy. But his mother already saw him as Emperor. She had sent a messenger to her kinsman the Elector of Bavaria urging Francis as a candidate at the next imperial election.

Louise was aggressive for her son. Less aggressive but even more benign was Marguerite. She was always her brother's partisan. Alençon, her draw in the lottery, was certainly not an exciting person. He was a faint duke. But that gave her more right to be near her brother. She was 23. Her straight look, her direct talk, her straight tall figure, made her "to be loved by men and gods." Any intelligent man who watched her could hardly help being moved to vigorous delight. One ugly fellow, a poet named Marot, would soon say that no one ever, no woman ever, had filled him with such ultimate satisfaction. Before her he was nothing, but "against the superiority of another there is no remedy but love." Alive in her own way to this amiable impression she created, Marguerite had that radiance of the inspirited young, that intrepidity of the sensitive which at once dazzles and enchants the older observer and reminds him that roses dare to bloom again. She was leading the whole court for her brother. Her pious mother-in-law, her fat inarticulate cousin Claude, her positive mother—all of them she charged with her gay generosity. She had not yet had a child, in spite of her wishes, but she was undaunted in endless activities. The incessant royal hunts, the tournaments that delighted Francis, the foreign receptions, had her presence and her lively countenance. She was the first serene creature, the first really affluent one, in a royal society tense with ambition, often insipid out of prudence. She had a heart. In her eyes, her face, her bearing, her words, she had some fund of spirit that those poor beggars around her needed to

share. But her blind devotion to Francis demanded its own ob-
scurantism. He had imbibed her sympathy and fond admiration
since his childhood, took her as a plant takes the air. She was part
of his natural environment, his "mignonne." Of course he loved
her. And if he gave her territory, she endowed him with virtues and
all gentleness.

As spring approached, she and Louise knew that he would no
longer stay in Paris to play the statesman. He needed Touraine. It
was the first of those immense migrations that were to distinguish
Francis's court—the King, the Queen, the ladies, the great officers of
the crown, the archers, the gentlemen, the courtiers, the councillors, the treasurers, the ambassadors, the huntsmen, the dogs, the
horses, the artists, the poets, the upholsterers, the farriers, the prostitutes, the doctors, the priests, the kitchen. And damn the expense.
When the trek was complete, it took three thousand horses.

The outer world saw him go to Blois—by river to Melun, by
land to Gien, and then by royal barge down the Loire, with music.

At Blois he had a vast forest, eleven leagues by four. Here, with
the hunter's delight in expertise, he would chase the stag into the
bay that the archers made with canvases.

This sort of thing would cost 150,000 crowns a year, but it went
with military preoccupations. The two parts of France he had
visited, the north-east, and the south-west, were reservoirs of disbanded soldiers, and Bourbon went north for him while he sent
Pedro Navarro into the Basque country. Meanwhile, toward the
end of June, another military operation was gracefully effected at
Amboise when the Duke of Lorraine married Renée, the Constable's sister.

This wedding called for royal diversion. Francis, to amuse the
ladies, sent his trappers into the forest to catch a boar, "un vert
sanglier de quatre ans." He wanted to take the arena himself, to
slay the pig in the courtyard before every one. Louise, Claude, Marguerite, implored him not to attempt it. He yielded, but he insisted
that dummies should be worked by wires to see how the boar
would attack them, while everyone could hang from windows with
the staircases barricaded. He gave the signal. The boar rushed from
his box, slavering and frantic. He was unused to the court. He
bolted for a staircase, broke through, and ran madly up, stam-

peded into a gallery. The spectators scattered, half a dozen courtiers
stepping in front of Francis. He cried to them to make way, and
went for the boar with his sword. His thrust was true. The boar
quivered, turned downstairs, to fall stone dead in the courtyard.

"I can tell you, ladies," narrated a glowing eye-witness, "that of
all the nerve I ever saw, the good King's was the boldest."

So thought Claude and Marguerite and Louise. They had been
thoroughly frightened. And they knew that the wild boar was a
gentle symbol for other work before him.

At three on the morning of June 29 he stole from his room at
Amboise. He did not want to agitate Claude, who was soon to
have her first baby. His departure was quiet, but his mother he
found ready and waiting for him. In the hush of the morning they
started south, mother and son going side by side as far as Romorantin. She was to be his Regent. He stayed long enough to arrange
every detail. Then he departed for Lyon, and his stout-hearted
mother knew what it was to see her King go to the wars in Italy.

15

Francis entered the city of Lyon triumphantly on the twelfth of
July, 1515. By this time the holy relics at St. Denis had been taken
down and exposed because a King of France had gone to war.

Lyon was a nerve centre. It stood at the meeting of waterways
and at the crossing of highways, drawing merchants and bankers,
attracting craftsmen of many races, with a free grouping of thinkers
and artists and poets. Here Rabelais, at 40 livres a year, would be
physician to a great hospital, a hospital worthy of his scientific soul.
Here Etienne Dolet would bite his thumb at his enemies. A merchant city, it had that touch of the cosmopolitan mind, that flick of
liberal thought and free speech and hospitality, which compensated
for the superb consciousness of a capital. Its women were reputed
beautiful, probably because alert with intelligence. But the arrival
of the army brought home a crisis to Lyon which its Italian bankers
could best measure. Young women might admire the jaunty horsemen, or pout at the impudent archers and gunners. But the special
kind French quality that Erasmus found in his Lyon inn, the clean
sparkle, the honest delicacy, the mother and daughter so vivacious

and comprehending—this was the very quality that the war would tax, more than the wine and the viands. Milan was eventually to engulf 10,000,000 crowns. The bankers were watching at Lyon. The news was soon read on the Thames, on the Tiber, on the Tagus.

But this army that converged on Lyon was obviously redoubtable. Its magnificent artillery had Galliot de Genouillac for master. Pedro Navarro had recruited ten thousand men, Basques and Gascons, on the quiescent borders of Spain. From Guelderland and Sedan poured landsknechts in their madly scolloped hose. The Black Bands, enfants perdus, were heralded, but were still eagerly awaited. There were 3,000 pioneers, equipped to make roads and build trenches. In addition there were 8,000 Bretons and Picards and 2,500 gendarmes. In the train of this lithe host came commissary and camp-followers, vagabonds and filles de joie. It was artillery and lance, arquebus, arrow and pike, tailing off into pantry and circus. The biggest unit would be the 22,000 landsknechts, with Sedan, Guelders, Guise and Lorraine proportionately important.

The French people were not a military people, invading Italy. Their part in the business was to supply taxes for the adventure, which the aristocrats would lead. This war would raise the price of salt, the price of black bread, the price of herring, the price of wine. It would be collected by speculators who farmed the taxes, or by officials who doled out salt. A very humble drama of sweating extra cash out of the peasantry and out of the towns would later be occasioned by this enterprise, to be left to the generals of finance. The actual game of war was carried on by virile poverty-recruits, fanged and whetted like wolf-dogs, and preferably from outlying regions. The nobles directed the show, gleaming in the perfect insolence of vitality, proclaiming valour in their swagger and their clatter, bearing open arms. And Francis had them swirling about him, each of his great nobles having his own company of gendarmes. Fifty or a hundred little squadrons of eight would be reckoned simply as fifty or a hundred gendarmes, and at the head of them these armoured captains of territorial fame. The leading soldiers: Bourbon, rough Lautrec, the Neapolitan Galeazzo San Severino who had served with the Sforza, bluff Humbercourt who always began battle by opening a flap behind, the grizzled soldiers Trivulzio and la Trémoïlle and sage la Palice, the agile Bonnivet,

Lorraine, Guise, Sedan, Fleurange, solid young Montmorency. And on another plane, Bayard from Dauphiny. France to him was a mistress in the medieval sense. A soldier already a legend with friend and foe, he was so ready of wit, so innately clear, so indifferent to money or to privilege, that even his extreme pride of rank and his exclusive sense of honour became metaphysically imposing. Bayard struck through malice with the same sword that cleaved the enemy. To the word gentleman he gave an austere and spiritual meaning. Poor, reasonably chaste, nobly obedient, he took France as his Grail. His type was far more flourishing in Spain, much nearer to its Holy War. In France, since Louis XI, it was already archæological.

There was hardly one important churchman in Francis's entourage. Since Alexander VI, especially since Pope Julius II, the French aristocrats were changing their orientation. Yet all the bold games he had ever played, the chase, the joust, the sham battle, had prepared for this. Pampeluna and Guinegate had been manœuvres, but here, with virgin artillery around him, with thousands of fighters in movement, with hot news arriving of fresh troops on the march, he could feel his crest rising. His blood rippled with war.

His mind seized the main purpose; the encountering of the Swiss. But if negotiation could disarm the Swiss, it must be managed, to leave him free to march on Naples. If not, challenger would meet defender, a clash into which all the resources of the season would be poured—men, money, munitions. France was not the Roman Empire. Only this campaign was in view, one trial of strength, a duel.

The campaign, in truth, was an improvization. By reason of the resources he could skim, owing to the size and riches of France, the young King could naturally aim to break the Swiss, with Venice to support him and with the Pope to bide his lesson. But he was not a truly professional soldier. His army was largely mercenary and alien, hired by the month, and too expensive to keep long under arms. No French army had yet been moulded and hardened into legionaries. This in reality was an extravagant foray, and he was a wasteful young amateur. He would have his panache. His plumes would curl like young ferns. He was extremely concerned about the style and beauty of his armour: San Severino had promised him a German suit with blue-enamelled devices, charmingly designed, and this excited him. It was a glorious prospect—to arrive like gentlemen, to conquer like heroes, to dazzle by nerve, to subdue by fortitude, and then to have the prospect of including Naples. It was more resolute than Charles VIII's expedition twenty years before, but the element of hazard was still extraordinarily high. Louise at home, watching for portents in the heavens, was on the same level as her Cæsar.

But Duprat at Francis's elbow, aided by Robertet and Semblançay, was an abler craftsman than Briçonnet or de Vesc. He was building a powerful tool for his master within the terms prescribed by war. He was welding a system, resourceful manipulator of absolutism.

16

Dauphiny is shaped like a section of orange, the Rhône flowing along its straight side and the crescent wedge rising to a desolate frontier, then descending to the plains of Piedmont.

Up this wedge, grooved by deep rivers, Francis had to push his army: the Constable taking the vanguard, himself the main "battle," and Alençon the rear. On the Italian side the Swiss were ready for him, posted at the mouth of the valley near Susa, down whose narrowness he must descend either from Mont Cenis or Monte Ginevra.

But Trivulzio had gone to Dauphiny in March, precisely to find some way out of this trap, and the keen-eyed old man had been led to a wild, precipitous, impracticable pass, known to the hunters of chamois, which the labours of pioneers might sling into shape for an army. It was a countryman who vouched for it, and the sieur Morette, whom Holbein was later to paint as a bearded diplomat, vouched to Trivulzio for the peasant.

On the way up to this seam through the Alps, often a mere discontinuous ledge hanging on the abyss, there were no centres for provisioning the troops, only a few clustered towns whose inhabitants fled like mountain goats at the approach of an army. Once these lonely habitations were left behind, the army must traverse the echoing mountains, where cascades would undermine the foot-

ing, where tree trunks must bridge ravines, where sudden chasms
would descend, and only desperate effort could plane a passage
broad enough for men to clamber. But this improvised path must
accommodate horses as well as men. And where no human effort
could haul the guns along the ledge, they had to be swung along by
ropes, piece by piece, until safe hands could clutch for them. While
this was going on, the troops had to brace themselves for surprise,
and to work their way, sweating in the keen air, pulling, shoulder-
ing, climbing, stumbling, with no drink save water, and bread and
cheese for diet. At times a rush of sound, a cry, would tally a false
step, horse and man plunging down a chasm.

But this audacity was rewarded. Humbercourt, Bayard, la Palice,
d'Aubigny, pushed on before the others, following Morette, and
found themselves near the headwaters of the Po. Close by, in a
walled town of no importance, was quartered the commander of
the Pope's forces, Prosper Colonna. He had been warned that the
French were coming but he no more expected them, this lazy
August noon, than he expected an avalanche. Just as he was sitting
down to dinner, his doors burst open and in swarmed a hot-faced,
grim troop, by the windows as well, crying, "France, France," and
"rendez-vous!" He reached for his sword.

"My Lord Prosper," said Bayard, "the fortune of war! Lose one
time, win another."

The Roman swallowed hard. "Would to God——" Then he controlled himself. A prisoner to France, and without a blow struck.
He recovered his manners. "It is a country I have always wanted
to visit."

Surrounded by his captains, the general was hustled out. A rapid
pillage secured thousands of ducats. Scarcely had the French got
in the saddle before the Swiss came at a trot, but the booty was
safe, and it was nothing compared to the general. As the French
would learn later, when he had ended his visit to France, he was
the wiliest campaigner in north Italy.

Francis was still waiting at Embrun when the great news crossed
the mountain. He was overjoyed. By this time the Constable was
in motion. The Swiss stood alert with whetted pikes at the outlet
by Susa, but the whole French army took Bourbon's trail, safely

debouching to the west. The exact spot at which Francis crossed seems to have been by the Argentière peak (6,545 feet high). He left the deserted hamlet of St. Paul on August 14. He reached Demonte in Piedmont on August 16. The bleak landscape was new to him. He found it "strange." For two whole days, even more strange, neither he nor his suite had a drop of wine.

The Swiss hurriedly retreated toward Milan, cursing their luck, lugging their heavy guns.

17

Francis had only been leaving Lyon when he was overtaken by an English embassy, with an admonishing message from Henry VIII. This had not glued him in his tracks. But once in the plains of Italy he spared no effort to negotiate himself out of a battle. As the Swiss retreated he advanced. Lagnasco, Scarnafigi, Carmagnola, Turin, Chivasso, was the line of progress. He was angered by the ruthlessness of the retreating army, but his goal was the vital city of Milan, and he was prepared to amend Louis XII's treachery after Dijon, and to promise admirable terms, if the Swiss gave him a free hand in the duchy. With Milan secure, and an army of 40,000 at his disposal, he could conquer Naples. Already the force he had sent to Genoa under Aimar de Prie had linked with his army. To buy off the Swiss was imperative. He could then deal with the Pope and the Spaniards.

The Swiss were tempted. To be given cash in hand, to be honourably released, to have an annuity guaranteed to the Duke of Milan, opened the way to profitable retreat. Some of them were for it. But the majority of them demurred. They had come a long way since Granson. At that time, driven to smite the Duke of Burgundy, they had hardly known their power. They were rough, impoverished mountaineers maddened into defensive warfare. Since then, within forty years, they had become a power in Europe, selling their services to one side or another yet gradually extending their territory, and well aware of the stinging defeat they had inflicted on Louis's army at Novara. Louis had not thought it "honourable" to ratify the agreement by which la Trémoïlle had induced them to quit Dijon two years before. They were still smarting under this deception. Much as they loved their pay, they might gain Milan for themselves, and all the rich crops that their mountains denied them. This was a greater bait than French silver.

For several weeks, in spite of the cost, Francis delayed battle to press his offers on the Swiss. Those from the Low Cantons were disposed to come to terms with him, but the High Cantons, guided by Matthias Schinner, the Cardinal, awaited new contingents, 20,000, and argued loudly against peace. The Duke of Savoy was in touch with both sides. At last the more discreet Swiss gained the upper hand. If Francis paid them before Ferdinand, they would go home. Within ten hours, scouring his camp for coin, and precious vessels, Francis gathered 150,000 crowns. The bullion was sent under arms to Gallerate, where Lautrec and René of Savoy were framing the treaty. On September 8 this was provisionally signed, but required general ratification.

Meanwhile, Francis had never relaxed as a commander. He had great bodies of restive troops to encamp and keep in trim. From time to time they got out of hand, brawling, straggling, looting. At the first sign of outbreak he himself would leap to the saddle. He knew the risks of demoralization. On one occasion, pursuing the culprits, his horse stumbled and he was thrown. A fugitive soldier saw his plight and stopped long enough to help him remount. This delighted Francis, but his rescuer would not come to take a reward. He was only a looter, not a courtier.

September 12 was the King's birthday. He was twenty-one. A big youth with a scanty beard, the Venetians who visited him in camp were struck by his sumptuous attire, by his prompt and easy sentiments, by his circumspect speech, by his affability. He arose from table to greet Alviano, whom he called "Lord Bartholomew," and his manner was caressing. He warmly appreciated the rapid advance that had brought his ally's Venetian army to Lodi.

Francis was circumspect because uncertain. The Swiss to the number of 40,000 were now swarming in Milan, but their decision was still in the air. They had little to hope either from Lorenzo de' Medici or Ramon de Cardona. These two generals, the Pope's new Captain and the Viceroy of Naples, were linked at the other side of the Po. But Lorenzo de' Medici, the Pope's nephew, who had succeeded the Pope's brother Giuliano, was utterly unreliable

as an ally. Giuliano, who was dying, was not wholly unworthy of
the tomb Michelangelo would consecrate to him, but this young
Lorenzo was the scut of the original Medici. He had secretly
assured Francis that he would bark but not bite, and Cardona, who
had learned of this message, barked in chorus. He had not had
the slightest intention of being deserted by the Pope and nipped
between Francis and the Venetians.

Hence, with the Swiss boiling in Milan, the French could camp
within striking distance. Their rear-guard was at Melegnano, ten
miles out, which the French called Marignan. Francis was encamped at Santa Brigida with the main host. Bourbon was still
nearer with the vanguard, while la Trémoïlle was at the gates,
watching the mouth of the bee-hive.

At Rome Leo X attended nervously. Would it be Florence's turn
next? He had sought to win Francis by secret messages. At the
same time, being a prudent man, he bestowed the cardinal's hat on
Wolsey. He had no convictions to guide him, only the desire to
make his nephew Lorenzo a great prince, and to use Spain to trip
France, and France to block Spain.

18

On the morning of September 13 Francis was still in suspense,
not knowing which way the Swiss would decide. So far, as
Guicciardini put it, he had not allowed his judgment to give way
to his indignation. Lautrec was treating for him, and he was prepared. The dandyish San Severino had brought him his new suit
of armour, German made, so well joined that one could not have
wounded him with a pin or a needle. This he intended to try on in
the afternoon.

Meanwhile, inside the city of Milan, the Swiss were seething. The
French proposals, as the King had hoped, induced one great section
to cry quits while the main body felt their wrath rising and shouted
to give battle. All was diversity, rancour and confusion. Their pikes
bristled, their tongues clattered, the heat of argument steamed from
them in the sultry air, until the alarm summoned all of them to the
great square outside the Franciscan convent. A tremendous force
of martial humanity, fresh youth ranked with wiry veterans, their

bodies proud as those of antique Romans, they came to the debate flaming with excitement.

The Cardinal of Sion, Matthias Schinner, got up on a chair. He was "the worst Frenchman that ever was." These were no easy men to sway, truculent and fearless, but Schinner was a pastor. He distrusted and despised the French. Raising his powerful voice he went to the point in words that vibrated with life and death. He poured out a strong, terse appeal to these tawny legionaries surging round him, recalling Novara, contemptuously arraigning the enemy, depicting their awkward encampment amid dykes and canals, sneering at the effeminate nobles, goading Swiss manhood and virility, describing the glory, the profit of a victory now well within their grasp.

Schinner's words could not move Albert von Stein. He was in French pay. He was anti-imperial. He was going back to Berne with his contingents. But the Cardinal so enflamed the others that hardly had he finished before their cornets blew their mother tongue, and within a few minutes they began to pour from the Roman gate, firm rank on rank, bare-headed, bare-throated, unencumbered, an endless column of muscled, dauntless men aching to plunge their pikes into the enemy. Some Milanese cavalry rode with them. They had companies of firearms, and they dragged a few great cannon. A cloud of dust rose as they strode onward, "sans bonnets et sans souliers et sans armeures," crying no quarter, their brows beaded in the sun, creamy dust flaking the creases of their golden skin.

Francis was in his tent, patiently standing to have his new armour adjusted, when Fleurange burst into his presence.

"You are armed?" Francis turned his gay head. "But we expect peace to-day."

"Sire," exploded Fleurange, "we need fool ourselves no longer about peace. You may arm, just as well as I. You may order the alarm. To-day you'll have battle or I don't know the nation you are dealing with."

Francis jumped. He ordered Fleurange to sound the alarm. All ready save for his plumed helmet, he mounted his war horse, galloped forward at once to the vanguard, where Bourbon and la

Palice were already stirring. For the time he had forgotten to summon the Venetians, to recall Lautrec or to advise his captain at Pavia.

All Francis had imagined of warfare in his childhood, all he had dreamed of chivalry and prowess, now sank beneath the business of instant decisions. But he was camped on ground he had deliberately chosen. He had a preponderance of force. He had seventy-four pieces of artillery where the Swiss had half a dozen. Bourbon was in place. Briefly urging the vanguard to fight "virillement," "au nom de Dieu et de Monsieur Saint Denis," he wheeled round to take up his own position.

Just before the clash the landsknecht captains came to Francis. They put it to him that their men must have a third of the booty in Milan. Francis did not want a Milan that had been plundered. "This is the thirteenth of the month," he told them frankly. "You shall now get a full month's pay. We begin a new month from to-morrow." This appeased them. Meanwhile, the Swiss were advancing. The landsknechts posted in front, to take the shock of the attack, were not braced by the good news. They yielded ground. The Swiss came on with the utmost fury, straight for the artillery. They gained the first trenches. Bourbon was flung aside, and the three great detachments of the Swiss, a hundred abreast, their pikes interlaced, pushed forward with ferocious impetuosity.

In the dense dust that billowed from the plain Francis could glimpse glints of steel. His foot were being driven back by the onrush of the Swiss. The mêlée was thick. The sun was setting. So far his artillery had not scored. Commanding two hundred of his gendarmes, Francis himself led a charge into the flank of the Swiss. They recoiled. He smote them "assez rudement." His French infantry supported, and the Swiss gave ground. Already it was dusk. Seeing a great body in action nearby, the King's forces cried, "France," whereat a whole host of pikes bristled at them, the enemy charging. At this point Francis was driven back on his artillery. Rallying a new force of landsknechts, he stood against the oncoming Swiss. Meanwhile Bourbon charged from the other side, cutting "five or six thousand" to pieces. Whereupon, his artillery safe, Francis renewed his advance, driving them over the canal.

And so, between three and eleven, he counted thirty charges, most of them in the dusk, or by the hazard moon. By eleven, when the moon went under the clouds, the forces on both sides had become so broken, so mingled and worn out, that a tacit pax was admitted, men flinging themselves down among the butchered dying and the dead, or clustering with their comrades, alert, wary, hushed, straining to find in what shape this battle stood, swathed in marshy mist, tense in hostility.

In this obscurity of the plain, amid groaning heaps, the cornet pierced the dark. Then a French trumpet rang out. Stealthily, creeping in the peopled void, units that had lost form and place, dumbly sorted themselves out. The moon stayed hidden as this movement stole on. Lights that had been incautiously struck for comfort were instantly quenched, to shield the murderous vigil.

Francis himself had come to the limit of his strength. He had sweated inside his armour, chafed and ached. Twice he had been stunned, and many times battered. Thirst tormented him. He asked for a drink. His trumpeter went to a canal and brought him back a mouthful. It was mingled with blood. Francis swallowed it, but it made him vomit. Then he threw himself on a gun carriage, clad in his armour, under the hooded moon.

Before dawn the Swiss were reassembling, and out of tents that they had pitched at some distance, nourished by food that Schinner had sent out from Milan, they moved forward in solid ranks, with the same magnificent temerity as in the afternoon. But this time the adroit Genouillac had found their range. Francis saw the Swiss recoil. Before the sun was up the fight was raging on every side, the Swiss withstood by Francis's battle in the centre but attempting a flank movement. So desperately did they advance that certain nobles fled, and camp-followers ran toward the baggage trains shouting all was over. All was far from over. Alençon arrested the flank movement. Bourbon swung in. Francis struck forward. At eight o'clock in the morning word flashed that the Venetians were approaching. Alviano, with his light horse, had rushed all night from near Lodi. The Swiss tried to dig themselves in, seizing a wood and occupying Bourbon's headquarters in the line of retreat. These quarters were set on fire and some Swiss roasted to death. Their grip was loosened. Still combative and grim, their faces threatening, they began to withdraw by the Roman road. By noon all was over. They had receded to Milan.

It was not twenty-four hours since Matthias Schinner had exhorted them to "exalt the name of the Swiss above that of the Romans."

"It was a marvel," said Prato, "to see the routed Swiss return to Milan—one had lost an arm, another a leg, a third was maimed by the cannon. They carried one another tenderly: and seemed like the sinners whom Dante pictures in the ninth circle of the Inferno. As fast as they came they were directed to the hospital, which was filled in half an hour, and all the neighbouring porches were strewn with straw for the wounded, whom many Milanese, moved with compassion, tenderly succoured."

On the field of battle, under the ruthless sun, there lay almost uncountable dead. Huge ditches were dug for them. In the afternoon between 16,000 and 17,000 were piled into these holes. About two Swiss, the French said, to each one of their own combatants.

The tension under which Francis had fought, the responsibility that had weighed him down, the effort that had bent his spirit since he left Lyon in July, now gave way to wild joy in which thankfulness to God mingled with boyish exaltation.

The fight, as Francis saw it, began clearly enough but soon lost semblance to reality. The forces that opposed him swelled into legions, and in the thick twilight on the plain, where the Swiss, wearing white crosses mingled with the French wearing white crosses, it had certainly been impossible to form any true notion of loss or gain. Francis knew that he and his gendarmes had plunged into the flank, and he reckoned that four thousand Swiss had recoiled from this encounter. The flood and ebb took on for him fantastic volume, great companies of men looming into vision, then reversed and overwhelmed in triumph. That he and his nobles hurled themselves repeatedly on advancing hosts was the main fact he could attest. He was deep in the mêlée. But in a brain already half-drowned in sensation, men under his horse's hoofs, men gutted, decapitated, cloven in two, his impressions smote twice on the flickering brain. He had lost his bodyguard, never slackening his attack, back and forth between the stream and his artillery. But his final illusion, that thirty thousand had been slain, marked the inevitable divorce between the hallucinations of excited blood and the fixity of facts that can be measured. All he said afterwards, and all he wrote to his mother, was perfectly plausible. Like a hot spring to the unfamiliar observer, it was so lucid and unmoved that it seemed evidently and temptingly cool. Put to the test, he had reached one of those points in excitement where the whole of a recent experience is so closely embraced that possession has the air of self-possession. And this marvellous exaltation ran like a current through them all. Hardened Trivulzio blazed with it. The battle, he said, had been a combat of giants! Ravenna and all the other eighteen battles of his life had been child's play to it. This was the feeling throughout the French camp. It was victory so uncertain in the balance, so desperately contested, so well earned, so complete, that human feelings could scarcely hold it. Francis told his mother that Bourbon and his companions had no more thought of them-selves than maddened boars, sangliers échauffés. "Not for two thousand years," he burst out to her, "has there been seen so spirited and bloody a battle, une si fière ni si cruelle." Not a word against the Swiss. A dip of the ensign to Humbercourt and Amboise, whom he knew to be dead. Great glee that his nobles could no longer be called "hares in armour." And, at the last, schoolboy de-light that Lautrec had been cheated out of the show. "Thank God heartily, Madame, throughout the kingdom for the victory He has been pleased to give us. And Madame, you will have a good laugh at Messieurs Lautrec and Lescun. They missed the battle! They were kept negotiating by the Swiss, and the Swiss were pulling their legs."

The retreating Swiss were shepherded to the gates of Milan by Bonnivet. Meanwhile, on the emptied field, Francis encountered Bayard with a shout of joy.

"Bayard, my friend, I wish this day to be knighted at your hands."

"But Sire," said Bayard, "he who is crowned and anointed by the oil from heaven is the chevalier of chevaliers."

"Bayard, hurry up. Don't go into laws and canons, steel or bronze or iron. Do as you are told if you wish to be my friend."

"Well, Sire, since you wish it, unworthy as I am, I'll do as you command."

He took his sword and, as Francis knelt to him, named him knight by the honoured formula.

"The first king I ever knighted," said Bayard.

He raised his sword and spoke to it. "You are blessed this day to have given knighthood to so fine a prince!" He flourished it, lifting his voice. "Yes, my good sword, you shall be treasured and honoured as a relic and never drawn again except against Turk, Saracen or Moor." With that he sprang twice into the air, pointing his sword to heaven, and then returned it to his scabbard.

At this moment the King sighted Fleurange, coming back from the retreat of the Swiss.

"How is this, my friend," Francis shouted, "they told me you were dead."

"Not dead, Sire, and I won't die so long as I can serve you."

"I have just been knighted," cried Francis, "and I pray you that you accept knighthood at my hand."

When this honour had been bestowed on Fleurange, the King withdrew to his "logis." He had been twenty-eight hours in the saddle, helmet on head, without eating or drinking. But before the day was over he poured out the whole story to his mother. On that very day she had made pilgrimage on foot to Our Lady of the Fountains, outside Amboise, recommending to Our Lady "him whom I love better than myself, my boy, glorious and triumphant Cæsar, subjugator of the Swiss."

Schinner had not been so far off when he proclaimed the noble French "orgueilleux et glorieux et triumphans."

19

"They came to chastise a prince," chuckled Francis: the hole pierced through his vizor proved it. But now the Swiss were broken. Maximilian Sforza still held the citadel of Milan, but the victors pooh-poohed him. Pedro Navarro would root him out. Meanwhile the field was clearing. The Swiss were already streaming home. Schinner was hurrying to the Emperor.

The cock was tempted to crow. These Swiss were insolent rogues, "a wicked little nation." But why pursue them? Cardona had withdrawn. To mop up the rest of Lombardy, to take Cremona and

Brescia and Verona, was a matter of time. The real victory had
been scored. And now for the Pope. Forgetting their ally Venice,
the French promptly drafted terms in their own exclusive interest,
and with these in his pouch Canossa rushed to Rome. The next
thing was to lay hands on Parma and Piacenza. This would take the
front window out of a Tuscan duchy. It would stir Leo in his
marrow.

Francis's figure was wreathed in triumph. Marignano presaged
the future. He had Europe at his feet. After his all-night battle, his
review of the Venetian troops, his long letter to his mother, his
council of war, he still had need to celebrate the victory: he had
supped horrors and drunk blood: he needed solace, escape, a touch
of humanity. But if, as the legend said, he spent the night with a
beautiful Milanese, he clearly did not dally with her. In the next
few days he was constantly alert. Not till the Vatican sent its
answer could he take himself to Pavia in exhilaration.

20

Marignano was a triumph, and Marignano was a disappointment.

Henry VIII took it hard. He and Wolsey believed that Francis
would come a cropper, and, in the event of his coming a cropper,
Henry was building a galley. It was a stupendous galley. It carried two hundred and seven pieces of artillery. It boarded one
thousand fighting men. It was christened by Mary Tudor and, as a
memorial to Louis XII, was called *The Virgin Mary*. What use was
to have been made of this galley, had Francis crashed, was naturally
not proclaimed at St. Paul's. But when Louise complained that it
was disloyal to make war without giving warning, Henry and his
council thought her words "very harsh and unpleasant."

At Rome the disappointment was almost instantaneous. There
had been a premature burst of joy when a Swiss victory was reported. This had been based on the gains of September 13. The
next morning the latest news came. While Leo was still half-
dressed, the exultant Venetian ambassador forced his way in. Leo,
fat, flaccid, dishevelled, looked in dismay at his informant. The
French back in Milan. "What is to become of us?" he asked with

loose lip. Then a quick thought, an Italian thought, shot through him. "And what is to become of *you?*" His mind raced round the trap until he came to the priestly exit. He lifted his plump hands. "We will throw ourselves into the arms of the Most Christian King and beg his mercy." That was the moment, one might almost say, in which Catherine de' Medici was conceived. Leo was thinking of intimidated Florence, of his dying brother, of treacherous Urbino. He was thinking of the Medici. And his mind raced through his assets. His brother's marriage to Francis's aunt had begun a process. His nephew Lorenzo remained. This was the line. In the meantime, how to keep the barbarian from Rome?

21

But Pope Julius II had educated the French not to advance rashly. And this was the vendange. The young barbarian was at Pavia, with vine leaves in his hair.

One often sees a village in Normandy that turns its back to the public street. To enter each house there is a small door, but the façade is otherwise closed. Everything that expresses the house— the lights, the flowers, the curtains, the open lodge, the glint of an interior—is offered only to the trusted visitor, to privacy and intimacy. And what the Normans do with their life in community is what many a French woman does with her inner life. She presents a chalky façade. She understands the subtleties of intimacy. To seem bleak and tight, even if the eyes are liquid with intelligence, is her way of protecting her intricate self.

Very far from this art of self-protection was the habit of that Milan of which Bonnivet had been telling Francis for years. The southern sun brought into these façades a glow of invitation. The bony flange of the jaw, the long flat cheek, the jutting nose, all those features that record a difficult adjustment, could be seen converted into an oval at once shapely and sympathetic, suave and serene. Nature had moulded these Milanese, giving them form as the Italian hills have form, and yet investing them with a strange emotional receptivity, a subtle bloom. In the north, irregular as the weather, an apple-tree declares its struggle. Here in Italy full-bodied fruit hangs brilliant among sharp-cut leaves. A quality of decoration, of decisive balance, gave the women a new coherence, the gift of an enveloping sun.

And when Francis saw within his reach these women of the sun, these women in whose dawn and twilight there was enigma, he found in himself that Latin nostalgia which struggled in him against the savage Gaul. The woman at home who is a conscious artist in her sex he compared to these women desirable by the ordering of nature, existing to attract their kind. The suavity of this transition could not awaken romance in him, but it moved his love of beauty, it stirred his veins.

A soldier would have seen that the duchy of Milan was far from conquered. Any man who had lived long enough to admit the plodding accountancy of life might have hesitated to call his victory secure. But Francis was impatient. His senses were keen. His knowledge of his capacities was still buoyant. He had, against his own nature, advanced step by step, soberly and calculatingly, to his supreme trial of strength against the Swiss. He had not presumed on fortune by pursuing them, since he wanted to reconcile them, and he had not plunged into Milan. But he had dislodged forces that had oppressed his imagination, in a battle fought to the limit of endurance. He had stored in his nerves the whole terrible and marvellous phantasmagoria of this encounter in which eye had flashed into eye and hand been raised against hand. He had been more powerful, quicker, more cunning, than his adversaries, and gone out of himself into those rare regions where man dances with death. Now he was surcharged with victory, and while the news of it widened over Europe, to return to himself, he looked about him in that delicious avidity where, for the first time, the world chimes in with the audacities of imagination.

Those audacities were princely. He saw Pavia with dilated eyes. He heard of Leonardo da Vinci with dilated interest. Italy, in this triumphant September, spread its harvest before him, the harvest of a renaissance that till now had been a name. He studied it with emulative eagerness. He saw it in terms of France, which must shape and assimilate it. He was flooded with impressions. And as he moved among them the Italians saw the prince in him. He struck everyone by his coarse yet vivid expression, his bold and masterful bearing.

22

The soldiers kept busy. Bourbon and Navarro put their minds on blowing up Sforza in his citadel. Fleurange tackled Cremona, roaring with delight when the fop San Severino fell into the moat at the bang of a loud gun. Trivulzio was lent to the Venetians, to help them recover Brescia and Verona. La Trémoïlle and the others made plans for crossing the Po. But Francis had proved his worth and now proposed to have a good time. He kept busy with embassies and delegations. The Milanese, the imperials, Lorenzo de' Medici, the Swiss, the papacy—he had to see all of them, including his allies the Venetians and his own people who had to organize Milan. His ideas were shrewd. This was the time to buy off the Swiss, to pension Sforza, to press home an agreement with the Pope. His mind was active and his tongue voluble. But this was his first sight of Italy and it stimulated him on every side. He could not look at the Chartreuse of Pavia without a desire to have it in France, or something like it. His nature placed him in the flower, not the vegetable, garden.

Pedro Navarro did his dangerous job, blew Sforza out of the citadel, and that dejected gentleman came to Pavia to say he was Francis's "serviteur." He was rueful about the Swiss. "When I was Duke of Milan," he said, "I was not duke but valet." Francis was lordly, promised him a pension of 36,000 ducats a year and despatched him to his mother in France.

The entry into Milan, "merveilleusement belle et triomphante," was gay with hautboys and trumpets and clarions. Out of the 2,500 gendarmes, 1,800 could parade. Out of the 40,000 foot that combated at Marignono, 24,000 were in the line of march. The new master had arrived in Milan, and the citizens handed over 300,000 ducats to prove they understood.

Francis was royally fêted. He shifted from the dismantled palace in a night, but he stayed to enjoy banquets and masquerades and festivals. He took as valet a peculiarly smooth and slippery Venetian, who came from a city where there were, in 1509, 11,654 prostitutes, and this Coppo showed Francis the town. But the town needed a wash. Plague, which was death suddenly became ravenous, broke out overnight. Leaving Bourbon and Duprat to settle the details of government, Francis withdrew to Vigevano. There the Montferrats, the marchioness being Alençon's sister, surrounded him with great Italian ladies. There he celebrated his first baby, Louise.

He was in high spirits. He went hunting with his hosts. The game of palla he loved and he played it to win, giving and taking blows in the scuffle, knocking over his courtiers and, while everyone laughed, colliding violently with big Federico of Bozzolo. The ducats that war provided were flowing at the card-table, but Francis made time for his Italians. A graceful young man of the world, Federico Gonzaga, presented himself in place of his ailing mother, Isabella d'Este, and Francis made him write home at once for a wax doll clad exactly, robe and vest and sleeves, as the ladies wore at Mantua, even to the hair, "so that the French ladies might be able to copy them." And this amused curiosity he did not confine to wax dolls. He heard of Isabella's lovely maid of honour, Brognina, whom the Cardinal of Gurk and Ramon de Cardona had disputed, and who was now locked in a convent.

A beauty in a convent! Francis was diverted. To get hold of her a scheme was devised worthy of Bonnivet. Francis had a papal brief concocted, and sent the Bishop of Nice with it to Goito, to decoy Brognina. It was far from amusing to the young gentlewoman, and a band of chivalric Spaniards came to her rescue and beat off the bishop.

This was subaltern sport. But there were greater decoys in view. Pope Leo was willing to meet Francis, and Bonnivet was hurried to Rome.

"He'll fool you," warned the Venetians.

Francis smiled. "I am persuaded that I shall fool him."

23

Not at Rome, Leo decided. Not at Florence, since the Medici were unstable in Florence. So they had to meet at Bologna, a town that detested the Papacy.

Leo X set out for Bologna by way of his native city. It was the first time that the son of Lorenzo il Magnifico had appeared among his fellow-citizens as Pope, and nothing could have surpassed his reception. Raphael came with him. A wooden façade, made to look like marble, gave enchantment to the Duomo. Genius poured itself out in every form of gracious salutation. San Gallo, Andrea del Sarto, Sansovino, celebrated the arrival of this exalted Medici. Leo gazed about him in ecstasy, half-standing, his heart open. He knelt by his father's tomb, and wept.

At Bologna he had a sour reception, but he took it philosophically, and waited for Francis. "Remember, don't put your hand to your biretta," admonished the master of ceremonies. That was the awful mistake that Alexander VI had made.

Francis arrived four days later, and even the Pope had to peep out of the window to see this grand figure in a cloak of gold brocade, with rich Zibelina furs, astride his ramping horse.

The crowd was astonished at the archers of the guard. They "looked like bargees, with dirty faces and greasy, threadbare coats." They had neither style nor order, and they shoved every one about, rude and haughty, rough even with the Italian nobles and the Pope's servants.

The Pope kept his hand from his biretta. Some say Francis kissed his foot and then his hand. Others say that Francis tried to kiss his foot but was drawn up by Leo, and then they kissed on the mouth. Others say that Leo kissed him on one cheek, then on the other. The greeting, in any event, was in a great hall of the public palace so packed with cardinals and French grandees that the floor sagged under them, while it overflowed with the magnanimity that swells in those who, under dramatic circumstances, find one another human.

Francis was deeply reverential to the Pope, gracious to Bibbiena, and soon perfectly at home with the Cardinals. He spoke in French and was answered in Latin.

The Pope, sweltering in a cope and bowed under his tiara, had to listen to an implacable Latin oration from Duprat. In reply he said a few charming words, greeted the nobles, rose up, seized Francis by the hand, and took him to the ante-room. He withdrew to shed his tiara and his cope. Then for two hours they were closeted together. It was the first of four days' interviews.

If the Pope was supple and astute, he was supremely anxious, and

Francis, boyish and high-handed as he was, had every reason to make terms with him. Everything favoured an understanding. It was the Medici whom Francis approached rather than the Pope. They talked over Italy in detail, even the papal salt from Cervia, and a Schinner prisoner at Rome. Francis, as victor, was not too shy to ask for the Laocoön. Leo made many concessions, pleaded the Emperor and Ferdinand, tried to save his face, conjured up the Turk, exposed his burdens. He was adamant on Francis's ally, the Duke of Urbino. Francis gave up Urbino. Felice della Rovere had come to see him, and won him by her charm, but Pope Leo was resolute: he would chastise Urbino.

Francis was devout at Mass, Bourbon acting as altar-boy to the Pope. And when the Pope was about to give Communion to the French nobles an extraordinary effusion of sentiment that had been smouldering since the wars against Pope Julius burst out without premeditation. Disregarding Francis's presence, one noble begged for absolution, then another, then a chorus of nobles. Francis took his cue promptly and urged absolution, but saying, "We had no enemy so terrible as he, for Julius II was indeed a most capable general, and far better suited to be such than to be Pope."

This touched the sore point of Louis XII's revolt against the Church. It was easy for Francis and the Pope to agree about concubinage in the French Church. Francis was correct on concubinage. But the old arrangement of the Pragmatic Sanction gave to the French clergy the right to choose their own prelates, to decide certain ecclesiastical issues, and to refuse annates. The Vatican wanted a new arrangement to obviate schism, and neither Francis nor Duprat was loth. Duprat would agree to annates but the monarch must take from the chapters the right to name his archbishops, bishops, abbots, and priors. This was a very long step in the direction of absolute monarchy. It would hand over the entire patronage of the upper hierarchy to the Crown. Pope Leo assented. In addition Francis gained the tithes for three years, 400,000 ducats, in the name of a crusade. He also managed to get a cardinal's hat for Bonnivet's brother.

Such was the Concordat. It decided French policy with the Vatican for many a crucial year.

Leo had brought Francis a present. It was a gold cross, thick with

Cardinal Ascanio Sforza's jewels, worth 15,000 ducats. Thus Sforza paid for celebrating the victory.

Bologna was amazed to see Francis walk the streets, making his way through the crowds, during the four days he spent with Pope Leo. But this lack of ceremony did not prevent Francis's pleasure in meeting Baldassare Castiglione. He urged him warmly to publish "The Perfect Courtier."

At last the King and the Pope parted with the utmost cordiality. It had, in essence, been a meeting between princes who had booty to divide and alliances to knit, within a system that professed loyalty and brandished force.

It was just eighteen months before Martin Luther was to upheave in Germany. But he would not upheave in France. The King was going home laden with abbeys and priories, archbishoprics and bishoprics. The King had no need for Reformation.

This booty might not anchor him to the faith, since his real faith was monarchy. But they anchored him, and they anchored the Valois, to the Vatican.

And when Francis swaggered away from Bologna the Pope's retainers darted angry little glances after him. His tips had been shabby.

24

The road that crosses the icy Alps from Susa runs to Sisteron in Dauphiny. In January, 1516, a long troop of cavalry came down this road. Perhaps their horses slouched along, lances sloping as they would, the valets and the pages loaded with armour and the pack-horses head down with burdens. As they neared Sisteron the tempo changed. The company in furred cloaks, handsomely mounted, flashed into animation once again, fife and tambour playing. And while villagers cheered and children stared they swung to the point where two women waved in ecstasy. Francis answered. He was greeting Marguerite and Louise.

Louise did not hide her emotions.

"God knows," she bursts out long after, "I was overjoyed to see my son safe and whole after all the violences he had suffered and endured to serve the commonweal."

This moment has found little chronicle. We must imagine the sparkle, the glow, the grand confusion of this scene, with Francis bathed in glances, and young Federico Gonzaga, and Bonnivet, and Alençon. Perhaps it was raining. Their kisses may have mingled rain and tears. Or perhaps the mayor broke in with an address. No history seems to record the actual meeting. They were only soldiers returning from the war, caressed by welcome.

Marguerite had been wildly anxious before Marignano. Her honest soul never doubted her hero. Hers was the love that consecrates its object, incapable of question: and now he was restored to her, handsome, gallant, gay. She flowed with delight. Intensely serious, yet bubbling with laughter, she was full of the subdued radiance of her warm and eager temperament. Her good sense, and she abounded in it, made her, for all her friendly family, loyal to any genuineness against stiff tradition and brutal power. But her king came first. Perhaps because Francis was arranging the Concordat she found herself urgent to set the monasteries to rights. She had just been visiting a disordered convent at Hyères, where the young nuns had been confusing sacred and profane love. But this desire to reform them did not spring from a harsh nature. Here at Sisteron, meeting the three men who most absorbed her, she was no model of repression. Alençon was tame and timid but her brother she worshipped and Bonnivet had the fatal power to quicken her. He would have watched her with guarded avidity while she, the regulator of nuns, tingled with his attention. She invited it, as Francis did his own forms of violence, by the way she suffered and endured it.

At this isolated town, deliciously remote, these young men could feel themselves in France. Brutal experiences buried in their souls, they now felt a strange assuaging sympathy. Some of them had sniffed the violets at Parma, but this had the essence of that nostalgic perfume. The words that had greeted Leo X in Rome, "Mars has reigned: Pallas has followed: but the reign of Venus will never end," could better be the legend of these Frenchmen. Grace and gaiety now cleansed their swords, Marignano took on lustre. Down toward Marseille they filed, Bonnivet alive with wit, Marguerite sparkling. They were leaving the winter hills and nearing the suave sea.

25

The vibrant town of Marseille gave Francis a rousing reception. It had the Southern brio that really stirred him. The bands played. Noises rained on him from land and sea. Two thousand children came out in white to meet him. The authorities gave him the keys of their city, and to his huge amusement, the orators forgot their Latin. There were the usual laboured classic tableaux, with St. Louis thrown in. A battle with oranges was in season. In Italy he had avoided oranges, for fear of being poisoned. Now they skimmed and plopped, turning war to comedy.

The slow voyage up the Rhône was halted for receptions and pilgrimages. At Avignon the Jews came out and danced for him. He prayed before the body of Mary Magdalene, at Saint Baume. Now he gave thanks before the winding sheet of the Saviour. This was with his mother, at Chambéry.

His eye was still on Italy. He remained at Lyon for months, while his conquest of Milan was being tested.

The first military test was by Maximilian. Furtively encouraged by the Pope, and supported by the Swiss whom Henry VIII was secretly financing, Maximilian arrived as early as March. He had a big army. His section of it would have been at his own expense if he had been able to pay for it. The other section was rewarded with ready money that he craved. This twin force advanced right up to Milan. Bourbon prepared for it by destroying the dwellings of thousands of poor people, outside the walls. He then sent Maximilian an insulting invitation to lunch inside the walls. The attack was inevitable. But Maximilian was short of cash, he was not sure of the Swiss, he had bad dreams, he was at loggerheads with Henry VIII's paymaster, he was less anxious to draw blood than to draw blood-money. With a few followers he disappeared. His ride took him as far as Trent. His landsknechts, foiled by his desertion, ripped their way home through Lombardy. And Cardinal Schinner and Richard Pace, who had come in his train, nearly died of exasperation.

This feint was happy news for Francis on the Rhône. No one was ready to challenge him. Now was his chance to organize European supremacy.

But supremacy even in the Milanese was easier to win than to organize. Maximilian still had Brescia and Verona. The Pope itched to recover Parma and Piacenza. The Swiss were holding on to Locarno and Lugano and Bellinzona. And how about Milan itself? Valentina Visconti had indeed been Francis's great-grandmother. The Milanese admitted it. They resigned themselves to Bourbon. When he left the city, they resigned themselves to the dispute between gruff Lautrec and weathered Trivulzio. They especially resigned themselves to French artillery. But artillery cannot grow wheat or weave silk or make cheese. Conquest ruined commerce. Lautrec's expeditions to recover towns for Venice were further waste and derangement. It was singularly unsettled, miserably uneconomic, quivering with unrest. The citizens could not contest the notion of proprietorship on which Francis based his claim, but they found it a high price to pay on account of a great-grandmother.

But Francis left it to his captains. The military lustre he had acquired was indisputable. He now yearned for Amboise.

26

Francis's return to Amboise, in August, 1516, was his debut as a renaissance prince. He had brought France out of the slough. He had turned shabbiness into brilliance. And he was now in the full flush of success, where the sun could get at him.

Being a politician by profession, he naturally could not resign from the direction of his affairs. The egoism of his sovereignty would not allow it. But at the same time, like a private gentleman who has rounded out his property, he proposed to enjoy life. There was no keen pleasure, no epicurean surprise, that he did not look forward to. He had the gusto of a Gascon but the nerves of an Orléans. Jean Clouet's pencil was not more delicate than some of his intuitions. He had befriended Clément Marot's father, neglected by Louis XII, and he had made a place for the young poet as well. There was no minor art that did not interest him: the exquisite touch of a Jean Grolier would delight him, and his eyes could suffuse with pleasure as he fondled an Italian binding.

He had brought one proud trophy from Italy: Leonardo da Vinci. A gentleman could not paint, it was too manual, but he could be ravished by the painting of a genius. Francis sorrowed because he could not take the *Last Supper* from Milan. The *Mona Lisa* he acquired. Did he see in it the fleeting question which at times inquieted Marguerite, that look in which one may read both the garden and the serpent? He paid for it munificently, at least, and Louise gave the venerable master a mansion at Amboise.

But before Francis could really let himself go, before he could actually settle in Amboise, he had to lay the tracks of his policy.

27

He could not himself go to Noyon, to beguile Charles, but that young King would soon be in Spain, since Ferdinand had just died, so Francis needed to get his young signature to a treaty.

There was no nonsense about goodwill in this treaty of Noyon that Boisy and Chièvres schemed out between them. It was a rather dreadful treaty.

"Mon vassal" was now to take the baby Louise as his 1516 fiancée. He was to acknowledge all the claims in dispute, to open Navarre to the Albrets, to dole out 50,000 crowns a year until Louise bore him a son, and 100,000 crowns a year "rent" for Naples. Charles stood for it like an obedient "son" and Maximilian soon concurred, taking 200,000 ducats for Verona. Neither side, of course, had the illusion that these bargains would hold, but meanwhile his mother proposed to make a nest-egg of the money from Naples. The treaty, in addition, brought England into line. Wolsey, weary of Maximilian, veered toward "universal peace."

This suited Francis. No man had less Messianic delusion, but if he could hold England and the Pope he might pull off the grand coup of the Empire. This was going back to Philippe le Bel, but it was a young, bold, zestful conception, and Louise encouraged it with hard resolution. She had heard of Charlemagne.

Francis as Holy Roman Emperor became plausible because Charles was to find Spain heavy going. No sooner was Ferdinand dead than all Spain's magnificent powers of dispersal began to manifest themselves, until anarchy threatened. Charles landed with his Flemings in the summer of 1517, and every special interest in a land of fiercely special interests at once surged around him. He was bewildered. But the very fierceness of these disparate forces gave the youth a chance to survive since they would not unite to down him. He stuck grimly to the saddle, unhappy but intent, learning his lesson.

It was the young Archbishop of Mainz who opened up the imperial business with Francis. He was an Elector who might be induced to support the victor of Marignano.

A more direct customer was Franz von Sickingen. He was a needy knight who privately employed landsknechts on a large scale, the disbanded soldiers from Italy and elsewhere. Whenever two German communities began to wrangle, the one that first hired Sickingen was likely to win. He understood frightfulness. And Fleurange, fascinated by this post-war adventurer, was not happy till he brought him to Amboise.

He was a great talker, Franz von Sickingen, "le plus beau langageur" that ever was heard. He found France so "schön." The mode of living was wonderful. The ladies at the court were adorable and adoring. Francis did not wholly trust him, but he affably hung a gold chain on his neck and gave him 3,000 francs a year as a retainer.

"I know what's afoot," Sickingen nodded to Fleurange. He had detected Francis's desire to become Emperor. He went away an ally, granted that his own line of business be not impaired.

The Archbishop of Trèves was as good as a Frenchman. That was one electoral vote out of seven. But the Hohenzollerns were really pressing. When Francis decided to circle the north of France in 1517, to reinforce his fortresses against England, he was able to negotiate without scandal. At Abbeville Joachim of Brandenburg got in touch with Duprat, and made his proposal. All he wanted was Renée with a dot of 150,000 crowns, plus an annuity, plus a deal about landsknechts. To this Francis agreed. Then Brandenburg's young brother the archbishop, who had already organized the sale of indulgences with the Fuggers, sent Ulrich von Hutten to take his vote to market. He too did well. And then Louis of Bavaria sniffed the wind and looked wistful.

Francis thought the Germans very mercenary, but in order to have the money to satisfy this mercenary spirit he had to clash with parlement over the concordat.

FRANCIS I

From a Painting by Clouet in the Louvre

It had been hard enough to push the concordat through the Lateran Council, but to have it held up in France, where the patronage was quite indispensable to the crown, tried Francis's temper. So the young soldier proposed to hold open the beaks of parlement while Duprat rammed down the concordat without flinching. Half the parlement, after all, was clerical.

28

In February, 1517, Francis had to forget Amboise. Surrounded by his dignitaries, he demanded in person that the concordat be registered. He expected resistance from his high court of parliament, and he did not mince his words. His legislators feared slavery to the crown. They believed they could match his brutality by an appeal to opinion. They asked for an ecclesiastical convocation. This brought out vehement "displeasure and indignation." Francis would soon perceive the worthlessness of representative institutions.

For months the parlement dodged a decision. But when its delegates were summoned north to excuse these delays, Francis broke out like a stern master talking to bad servants.

"There are some men in the parlement who are all right," he said, "but there are others who are only fools." He knew this batch of fools, who owed everything to his House, but he was just as much a king as his predecessors, and he would be obeyed by them. He would send his uncle to hear the excuses of parlement. The protests against this method made Francis turn on his heel, leaving his visitors to back out as best they could.

Parlement plucked up courage to tell the Bastard of Savoy that there must be a convocation of the clergy. Francis thereupon requested another delegation to confirm this. The delegates whom they appointed tried to get out of it but at Amboise, nearly a year after Francis's initial demands, they arrived trembling to see his Majesty. They were compelled to put their arguments in writing, the full arguments of a Gallican autonomy. It took some courage to do it. Duprat met these arguments in a long, close, specious, ingenious answer. Then Francis sent for the two parlementarians.

They asked to see the answer to their memorandum. This enraged their young King.

"There will be only one King in France," he shouted. "What was done in Italy shall not be undone in France. I'll take good care that France will not have another senate like Venice. Look after your administering justice, which is just as bad now as it was a hundred years ago."

If parlement did not attend to its proper business, he assured them, he'd make it trot after him, as he did his own Council.

The delegates stood their ground. At last Francis burst out, "Allez, partez demain," "Get out! Get out the first thing to-morrow morning."

They left muttering their complaints. The Loire was in flood! Boisy came to them and declared that if they had not departed by six a.m. the King would undoubtedly send a dozen archers to sling them in a dungeon.

They departed.

Some months later parlement felicitated them on their courage, but again Francis sent angry messages, this time by la Trémoïlle, and his menaces left no doubt that if he were not obeyed he would constitute a more compliant body. On what, against this truculence, could the parlement fall back? Making every protest that moral respectability demanded, they registered the concordat.

This triumph of violence over the legislators of France cleared the way for a monarchical church. But the Sorbonne remained, a stronghold of the Catholic tradition, to oppose a monarchical theology.

29

These struggles with parlement, these intrigues with the Germans, were only the underside of Francis's mood as a renaissance monarch.

Anne of France still lived, a woman nearing sixty, and the earlier France survived with her, with its clear æsthetic simplicity and serenity. It had been an epoch in poise. Those whose tastes were formed in it knew an art that had flowed from religion. Their sculptors had "drunk the milk of paradise." But just because this epoch had matured, it was catholic only on its own hearth and on its own terms. It had become inflexible. The very quality that made it appear durable to its own generation made it unendurable to the next. Healthy youth may just as well strive to build up an order that its fathers broke down as to break down an isolation its fathers laboriously built up. But it must not stand still. It is compelled to destroy poise and test somnolent peace. It wants whatever is strange, brilliantly expressive or the very reverse, a thirst for the palpably unfamiliar.

Francis had peregrinated his imagination through Pavia and Milan and Bologna. He had transplanted Leonardo da Vinci and he would make a place for Andrea del Sarto. This showed how Italy had impressed him. He had seen those towns that men of passionate sensibility had fashioned, towns in which the stones spoke of an existence at once beautifully resourceful and perfectly contained. Something in him responded to this spirit. He could feel in stone. He knew the validity of this beauty that Italy had revealed to him. His fingers tingled with the desire to remodel the form of royal splendour. He had made terms with Rome, where a luxuriant connoisseur of the arts was enthroned in the Vatican, and what he desired on his return to France was a liberation of energies that had been too faithful to an idiom. He favoured change. He drank in the beauty that had allured Charles VIII. He had bold preferences, a clear love of splendour and the vast courage of inexperience.

It was not merely the stimulus of Italy that counted. His predecessor had known the renaissance for twenty years, had seen more of it than Francis. Louis XII had seen Milan while the blossom was on the branch. He had lived with Cesare Borgia when Leonardo was in Cesare's employ. He had fired a salvo across the lagoons. But Louis was no magnifico. Francis owed to his mother that Midi refreshment of the blood which gave him a sparkling curiosity and a positive energy. Gone were the shades of the gouty Louis and his wife in her Breton cloak. Anne's portable altar had disappeared. A great breeze of secularization swept through French nobility.

Francis chose Amboise. Paris would have poked its Gothic nose into the liberty he sought. He wanted seclusion and he wanted space. Already he was moving beyond Jeanne le Coq to more courtly experiences. What he loved was the Loire with the endless hunting in its forests, its tall skies, its ordered distances and terraced views. He gained much from having brought the ageing Leonardo with him. Leonardo made pensive sketches of Amboise that have in them a ghostly memory of Florence and Francis listened to him with respect, dimly conscious of his genius. But he and Louise employed the genius, first of all, to devise canals at Romorantin. And Francis looked for builders, executive Italians who could think in terms of Touraine, French contractors who could work with the Italians. Grandiose conceptions were shaping in his head, and he demanded men to embody them.

Where was the money to come from? He had enriched his Gouffiers and his Foix. He was giving Marguerite the duchy of Berry. Issoudun had gone to Sforza. Mary Tudor had the revenues of Saintonge. The Swiss had to be bought. The Venetians cost money. So did Urbino and Ferrare. He wanted to buy back Tournai. He wanted at least quarter of the national revenue for his expenditures. He must give his ladies jewels and brocades. When the Parisians, egged on by the Sorbonne, called Louise naughty names, Mère Sotte, and said she had peeled every one, it gave a serious hint. Francis was already passing sumptuary laws while dazzling the world in silk. The cost of living was rising. But he was a gentleman, and a gentleman's right hand does not know what his left hand is spending. He left these things to Semblançay.

The true symbol of this confident politics was soon seen on the margin of the Loire. Italy was germinating in France, and out of it sprang princely constructions framed for a European dominance.

Who designed Chambord it is difficult to say, but there can be little doubt that the design fulfilled Francis's superb intentions. It was a building that would cost as much as a campaign. To create it would cramp him. But he had the impulse to crown the earth with one of those vast, sumptuous, regal experiments in line and volume which, giving body to a grandiose harmony, are yet balanced in restraint. The restraint in this case affirmed itself in a low extended line. Chambord is a wave rolling in on a shallow

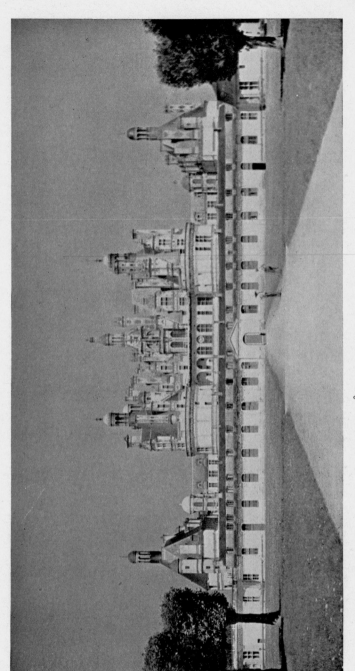

THE CHÂTEAU DE CHAMBORD
From a Photograph by Mr. Bertram Park

beach. Considering the flat country in which this isolated château was to stand there was every chance for it to inhabit it insipidly. But Chambord is at once severe and multitudinous. It frankly refuses to ascend. It rolls out of the plain subordinate to the long horizon. But no more does it submit humbly to the earth. At either end it rounds into a massiveness capped by a point, while in the centre, stabilized by twin towers, it mounts into a froth of detail that has the lantern for its peak, the wave caught at that spontaneous moment when it has broken into foam. This movement at the centre is an effervescence of old France, sportive, complex, vivacious, a scherzo in stone. It has something of that spirited improvization which makes the staircase at Blois a happy affront to tradition, a winding gesture of defiance.

Francis began this enterprise in hope. In a well-ordered state the supreme chief would operate by plan, achieving conquest by foresight, attention to detail, application, hard work. Not simply in business but in good government it is the man who has character, with perhaps a sprinkling of inspiration, who fulfils his mission. So are great roads builded, and mighty aqueducts, and sewers. But the crow seems to fly by one law and the swallow dart by another. In Francis there was little of that straightforward onwardness that distinguishes the crow. He was not a routine housekeeper, like the crow, who is a bourgeois among birds. Francis was lavish and disorderly. He took it into his drunken head to plant this imposing and useless structure of Chambord on a spot where great cavalcades could go and come at ease, where hunting could be combined with ceremony, and royalty impress elegance. Here privacy would envelop privilege without contracting its grand gesture or its naughty caprice. Chambord had no excuse except that it really represented the scale of indulgence at which Francis aimed. It was, in short, to be a true domicile of absolute monarchy, of a size and a seclusion that later was held desirable for lunatic asylums. But it had a vigorous enjoyment of the inordinate problem it sought to solve. This imperial palace is a passionately personal palace. It stands like a symphony. Even in the widowhood of unemployment it is a witness to creative impulse, on terms assuredly royal.

30

One person Francis hardly imagined at Chambord, which she was never to see completed. That was Claude. Francis's wife was indeed to share his blaze of glory. In 1517 she had a belated coronation. But her part in the reign was very much under the medieval shadow. "As regards the individual nature," says the great Aquinas, "woman is defective and misbegotten, for the active force, the male seed, tends to the production of a perfect likeness in the masculine sex: while the production of woman comes from defect in the active force or from some material indisposition, or even from some external influence: such as that of the south wind, when it is moist, as the Philosopher observes."

Claude's destiny was a simple and exclusive one. She existed to provide heirs, and within five months of Francis's return Louise was able to state with happy proprietorship: "On the seventh of June my daughter Claude, at la Tour Dupin in Dauphiny, commenced to feel in her belly the first movement of my daughter Charlotte." That was Claude's function. Already in 1515 she had given birth to Louise. Charlotte arrived in October, 1516. By this time it was rhythm. She repeated the familiar duty in 1518, in 1519, in 1520, in 1522 and again in 1523. Then she died.

A wife who undertakes these labours is not always amusing to her husband. "This prince," as Marguerite confessed, "was a man somewhat enslaved to pleasure, having great delight in hunting, games and women, as his youth led him, but having to wife one of a peevish disposition, to whom none of her husband's contentments were pleasing." And she added with a smile, "he would always have his sister with him, for she was of a most joyous nature, and a good and honourable woman withal."

A peevish wife, occupied with the restless Charlotte, and a husband somewhat enslaved to pleasure. Three months before Charlotte arrived, and three months after it, he was at home at Amboise. Claude, daughter of Anne of Brittany, had not her mother's authority. The Angoulêmes were too much for her. Rumours rose to her, words slipped, moods evaded her. Her husband was finding a distraction near home.

He was not one of those men who remain virtuous till nine-and-twenty. He could not walk down a path, ride a street, enter a church or a room, without seeing beauty and reading invitation. His mood was incurably gallant. Later on the thin calf of his leg, the pump melon in front, would give him the comic touch that accentuates lubricity, the benignant satyr. But now, before he had lost his freshness, he was keen, deferential, absorbed, intensely personal. With men he was usually on guard. A certain reserve is noticeable. With them he was the prince. But beauty conscripted him for "la guerre amoureuse."

Lautrec and Lescun had a sister. She was perhaps of Francis's age or a little younger. She was especially recommended to the Queen because her husband's family, the Lavals, had given Anne of Brittany her governess. It was an old family, royally acceptable, its pride blazoned in the fact that the head of it was Guy XVII. The husband of Lautrec's sister was not the head of the family. He was Jean Laval de Châteaubriant, destined to the melancholy fame of giving matrimonial background to a beauty.

This beauty, Françoise de Foix, would leave most husbands in the shade. She was one of those women whom a court ensconces. Her style was stately in form, her youth clear and resplendent, with vivid glance and glowing flesh. And, so far, she had a reputation as good as her complexion.

Lautrec had been one of Francis's favourites from the beginning, and his brothers were not forgotten. This disposed Françoise to a rather extravagant gratitude. Her brother Lautrec's reputation, though he knew no Spanish, was that of a superb person who came from Guyenne with the gravity of a Spaniard. In Françoise this weightiness became fervour. She turned her great eyes on Francis to no small account and when, with a signal kindness, he sent her a handsome present of brocade she could reveal how she really approved of him.

Her first letter to him is rather breathless. She was not able to thank him sufficiently. She pledged herself to him. She included Lautrec and of course her husband, expressing their perpetual servitude and obligation, in fact that of all her house, present and to come. "What do you want of me?" she asked. "To satisfy it would be the perfection of my desire." To wish him "longue and bonne vie," seemed too plain. She wished him "bonne vie en

longueur très heureuse." And she remained his very humble and
very obedient subject and servant.

This formula her monarch expected. Marguerite could not
address her brother as other than Sire or Monseigneur, nor sign
herself other than his "very humble and very obedient subject and
sister." It assured Francis that the sun had risen that morning. But
his answer to Françoise took the amorous formula. He moved at
once from the statesmanship of prose into the finer courtesy and
gallantry of verse. There with a measure still lordly but admitting
his "douce ardeur," he showed himself honourably tentative, wor-
shipping her beauty but mingling gratitude to the Creator of it,
declaring "la guerre amoureuse," but "licite seullement." They are
the verses of a royal hand, stiff from the sceptre, but conveying a
definite prayer for her favour, and asserting that it is not to have
pleasure of her that he wishes but to gain a just idea of Paradise
through so sublime a human object, and to augment her good
reputation.

The care for her reputation that Francis expressed, and the
délicatesse, moved Françoise to a lyric. That his beautiful white
hand should have written her a letter, that such exceeding sweetness should have come from his mouth, made her heart "weep for
joy." Before this, she said, she had been charmed by him: now she
was captured, nothing could efface his great beauty for ever. "What
do you wish me to do?" If he endeavours to see her frequently, as
he says, he may know that there is no hour or minute that she
would not go anywhere to look for him, if she dared, so much
she loves him. She says this to him, feeling "tant d'honneur et de
sense" in him. He can trust her to death, but "guard my honour,
for I give you my love and my heart."

This outright declaration took the King's position into account,
no less than her own. She stood in convenient relation with his
wife. She was sufficiently of his world, sufficiently accepted, to
become his matron of honour, as well as Claude's. Louise of Savoy
looked with favour on Lautrec. Francis was choosing his mistress
from a clan she approved of.

So Francis must have hoped. But while his mother might be
friendly to Lautrec her woman's eye did not approve of this
opulent lady. As for Marguerite, she seemed to concur with her

FRANÇOISE DE FOIX, DAME DE CHATEAUBRIANT

From a Drawing attributed to Clouet in the Bibliothèque
Nationale

(From the Photograph in Sir Robert Witt's Library)

mother. Françoise de Foix would have a difficult rôle. Her explicit first poem, addressing Francis as "tu" and spelling out her honour, did not promise the deference that could make her the good friend of a mother and a sister. Louise and Marguerite had been rather spoiled by Jeanne de Polignac, who had never been possessive.

But Françoise was beautiful and she could satisfy her prince. This she knew. "Ce beau corps," murmured Francis as he gazed on the wife of Châteaubriant. He saw her, to stroke with the eye, of a rank to which he had not yet attained in mistresses. His love of beauty was tender, voluptuous, rapturous, unfeigned. He could be simple and gentle. And between them began that duet which, in its ecstasy, is almost a union. He was King of France. She was a Venus, her limbs rounded by a divine hand and warmed in an antique sun, her white shoulder suddenly discovered. Would not any prince love "de l'antique Vénus le superbe fantôme"?

31

And at the beginning, how tentative he was. One day she sent him word that she was to visit friends "en ville": the King arranged to arrive at the same house, for the joy of encountering her. She was not there. He waited in vain. She did not come, and no word from her. But here, instead of anger, there was a light reproof in verse. She had broken faith, he gaily upbraided her. And "qual infamia major che romper fede?"

A lover so gentle she could answer in kind. In measured verses and tapestried gestures they interchanged their sentiment. Their "ympuisante escrypture" swathed their actual emotions. But the circumspect verses marked each stage of an attraction that had one classic obstacle: the husband. In one muffled phrase Françoise provokes her lover. She confesses that when she is alone with her husband he will not utter a syllable to her. And this admission, made in ceremonious monotone, arouses the galantuomo.

She must have defied her husband, with the truculence of a Foix. That equally truculent Breton, fuming at her defiance, posted himself outside her door to defend his honour with the sword. The lithe Francis, "très débonnaire," mounted the staircase to keep his rendezvous, his sword by his side, blood bounding with excite-

ment. He saw Châteaubriant. With one leap he had him by the
throat, threatening to cut his head off if he lifted a finger or made
a stir. There and then Châteaubriant had his choice to make—to
defy his king or cede his wife. He heaved with fury, but left the
entrance free. Francis closed the door.

The brother of Guy XVII could not leave court without a
scandal. He stayed. His anger earned him the name of an "insensate
beast," an uncouth husband. But Francis gave him his douceur,
and even found him useful as a Breton. He sent him to urge the
Bretons that they must pay hearth-money.

32

He was only twenty-four, at the beginning of this affair with
Françoise de Foix, and through these joyous months the court was
at its gayest. When she wrote long poems in after years Marguerite
dwelt on these marvellous days when Amboise was in triumphal
state, with coming and going, rich and poor, mean and wise, bold
and timid, one pacing, another galloping—she watching the
pageant with delight. Francis had cleared the formal garden to
make a place for tilting, just as he had walled off a space for a
fight between a lion and three savage dogs. But these young
brutalities were not noted by his sister who, gazing about her in
ecstasy, said to herself: "This is the Court."

She opened her eyes to take in everything: tourneys where lances
were shivered and knights thrown: the best man carrying off the
prize to the cry of heralds and the long blare of trumpets. The
spectacle of a great feast was not lost on her: the delicacies that
incite the gourmands: the good wine, subtle and suave, making
even the satiated drink: and then the company swaying from their
surfeit to join the dance. A daze of entertainment, sometimes
masques and mummeries, farces and comedies, would begin in a
cloud of talk that drowned the hautboys. And then the fine ladies,
great beauties, would rise to dance to their own soft singing, the
sounds of it shivering Marguerite's heart. Amid this loveliness of
the damsels her keen eye detected the young courtiers, touching
up their looks, polishing their speech, learning to dance well, to
play the lute, to ride a horse, to carry arms: and so, with naughty

intention, summoning tears, looking up to heaven, showing the whites of their eyes as if in amorous transport, pretending to suffer with hand on heart. With kind irony Marguerite noted the eternal comedy, for her own belief was in true love, "surety of true and loyal love that is more than royal glory, for to be great and powerful on the earth without to be loved and to love, ce n'est rien."

She was already a matron of more than eight years, married to Alençon, the male version of Claude, who had no power to quicken or satisfy her life: and she was coming to the height of her charm, quivering with that expectancy of nerve and sense which draws life taut, filling it with sweet and mad vibrations that tremble never to be answered. Surrounded by the court, meeting Francis's favourites, while the parade of ambassadors and councillors, churchmen and secretaries, trooped through her days, she was at once amused and stimulated and allured. And it did not lessen her enjoyment that Bonnivet, who had pursued her since she was fourteen, should still secretly yearn for her. His mother was a Montmorency, and old Montmorency was Marguerite's staunchest friend. Bonnivet held her imagination in leash, the imagination of a princess who was a humanist, a passionate woman who was a coquette. And yet she held him off. She knew—she knew not.

Her brother's career she was watching with protective care. He was high-handed, she admitted, but he won her by his knowledge, his confession of weaknesses. She asked no more, and saw only benevolence in her despot. But the outer world, deprived of these endearing admissions, cannot see beyond the despotism.

There was no open scandal about Bourbon's withdrawal from Milan, though his pensions now began to be unpaid (55,000 francs a year). When his heir was born in 1517, to the vast joy of the Bourbon family, Francis did go to Moulins for the christening, since the boy was to bear his name. But Bourbon's successor in Milan, Lautrec, was quarrelling with Trivulzio. The occasion of this quarrel, as Bibbiena suggested to Rome in 1518, was a cynical epigram that the Italian had uttered. "Milan built up Château Meillan," he said referring to Amboise's gains, "and Châteaubriant will pull down Milan." This delicate reference to Lautrec's advancement, through his sister, was bitterly resented. Lautrec was not the sort of man who could take any joke. When he had acted

as escort to the rump council of Pisa some years before he had
fumed at being called "the priest's handyman." His services to
Francis antedated his sister's, and he broke out so vigorously that
old Trivulzio hurried back to France to lay his case before the
King.

But Francis was forewarned. He refused to see Trivulzio. The
old man, unable to walk, had his litter planted in Francis's path
at Vendôme.

"Sire," he begged, "deign to give audience to a man who fought
for you in nineteen battles."

Francis ignored him.

The old man was carried to his house at Chartres, where his
fatigue and illnesses confined him to his room. Francis then relented
and sent a messenger to him, but Trivulzio shook his head.

"I am well aware of the King's kindness—but too well aware of
his harshness. There's no more to be done now." And so the
veteran died.

Francis had not intended to be cruel, but his first impulse was
to smite anyone who crossed him, and to scorn the notion of compromise.

Franz von Sickingen was soon a case in point. In the course of
his occupation as a hired Captain he had held up some Milanese
merchants to the tune of 25,000 francs. Francis hotly resented this
ruthless pillage of his subjects. His reprimand could not be tolerated
by the equally headstrong German. It broke his golden chain.

Germany at the moment, in 1517 and 1518, was in the worst
possible confusion, social and moral. Guelderland was devastating
Holland to the north. Sickingen was intimidating Lorraine. Life
was everywhere unsafe, farming impossible, trade upset, private
warfare bestially cruel. The advent of Martin Luther was favoured
by the acute nationalism which surged under so much suffering
and unhappiness. And even Sickingen and Hutten were not the
least symptoms of a shocking political maladjustment. That Francis
could come in on top of this, to ride national forces which were
churning from the depths, was one of the strangest aberrations of
the century. Even Fleurange's father, la Marck of Sedan, called
for better management than Francis or Louise could give him.
His pensions were not paid. His gendarmes were broken and "five

or six" ordered to be killed by Francis—and this largely because la Marck had been friendly with Anne of Brittany and was resented by Louise. The irritation might have been allayed, since his son Fleurange stayed loyal, had not Francis promised a cardinal's hat to Erard de la Marck, bishop of Liége, at the moment when Louise of Savoy was demanding the same hat for Antoine Bohier. Someone at Rome despatched the proofs of this double-dealing to Liége. Bohier got the hat. Erard de la Marck threw up the bishopric of Chartres, broke with France for ever, and was eagerly welcomed by Charles V.

These setbacks would have been nothing to a methodic statesman, but Francis wanted both the fruits of goodwill and the luxury of pride. In the same way he still owed for war while playing the renaissance prince. Duprat accepted the problem. He knew that the renaissance court was one method of controlling the nobility and he thought he could get revenue by creating tariffs. A great new scheme for erecting a tariff wall had been elaborated, but most of the towns protested: their answers were rammed into a leather trunk, and high tariffs with them. Francis, undismayed, gambled on the Empire. Slyly borrowing from Italians in London, he was offering thousands, hundreds of thousands, to the Germans.

33

The conquest of Naples would be immensely aided by Francis's securing the Empire. Pope Leo knew this, and he never could afford to be a Frenchman.

He loved music, Pope Leo. He would lean back, his eyes half-closed, his lips smiling, as he kept time with his finger. He loved music as he loved Raphael. He was a Florentine, brought up by his father Lorenzo in the idiom of the fine arts and giving the Vatican a strange flavour of the epicurean.

Not that he was building up the Medici at the expense of the papacy, but with the aid of the papacy. Maximilian and Francis had spoken of partitioning the north of Italy between themselves, but Pope Leo was too powerfully in the way. He had Florence. He aimed at Parma and Piacenza. He planned to ally Siena in spite of a Petrucci, and to confiscate Urbino.

To the furious resentment of Cardinal Petrucci, he did gain Siena. Urbino was a harder nut to crack. It cost 700,000 ducats to drive Francesco della Rovere out of his patrimony, the cost of a crusade, but at last his nephew Lorenzo was Duke of Urbino.

Francis had to stand by while Leo carried on this princely warfare. It was an odd occupation, the year Martin Luther was emerging, but his aggression in Siena was rather more unfortunate since it brought crime into the recesses of the Vatican.

The outraged Siennese, Cardinal Petrucci, conceived the plan of having Leo's fistula poisoned by a physician. He planned it with Cardinal Riario, who approved of it, as did Cardinal Adrian de Corneto, the man who had entertained Pope Alexander VI at his last supper. This conspiracy was still in cartoon when it was exposed to the Pope. His anger was drastic. Petrucci was arrested, tried by his college, found guilty and strangled in his cell. Riario, who was extremely wealthy and deeply penitent, was allowed to pay a fine of 150,000 ducats. He died the next year. Adrian fled. The physician was fiercely tortured and executed. On the top of this, pressed for money because of Urbino, determined to dilute the cardinalate in order to weaken its power, Leo appointed thirty-one new cardinals. He made a Bourbon cardinal to please Francis, and Adrian of Utrecht to please Charles. He raked in huge sums for the hats he sold to wealthy Romans. And he named a number of devout and serious men for the sake of those who still connected the cardinalate with religion.

Francis learned very soon that this assiduous prince was no ally. He retorted by secretly helping the ousted duke of Urbino and by strengthening his own alliance with Ferrara. This buttered no parsnips, so at last came a new marital arrangement between the Medici and France. Giuliano had died, but Lorenzo could have Madeleine de Boulogne, a Bourbon.

It went hard with the French aristocracy to see a Bourbon given to this Medici upstart. They murmured that he was a coward. His campaign against Urbino was inglorious. "He is only a simpleton who plays at being a captain and a great man," Francis himself had sneered, "and boasts of these conquests that have not cost him a single man or a drop of blood, and wishes to make himself lord of all Italy! But if he has any sense he will be content with this one state of Urbino. I doubt myself if he will ever manage to keep it for, remember after all, he is only a merchant."

There spoke the heart. And when Francis had to yield to dire circumstance and bring this merchant into his family, he still infuriated his nobles by the contamination. The Duke of Lorraine, himself married to a Bourbon, went home rather than be put on a level with him.

The French nobles had watched Cesare Borgia with ire. They watched Lorenzo with contempt. Laden with treasure, Lorenzo arrived at Amboise in the spring of 1518, but he came slowly, Fleurange noted, because he had "bien fort la grosse vérolle, et de fresche memoire."

Banquets and dances and junkets preceded the wedding, and then the damsel married her Duke of Urbino. But "elle ne l'espousa pas seul, car elle espousa le grosse vérolle quant et quant."

They hated him. And there were more suppers and dances and carols, a glorious sham battle, the finest Fleurange had ever seen, the nearest to the "naturel" of war, but, as he chuckles with baronial humour, the pastime did not please everyone since there were "beaucoup de tués et affolés."

And so Lorenzo de' Medici took home his bride. Within a year he was dead—"of the spleen," as the Papal historians put it. His young wife died in childbirth within five days of him. And the offspring was Caterina de' Medici. She would become Francis's daughter-in-law, and Queen of France.

34

But these compromises, which made Francis sigh, went with his adventurous policy. He hated them, but he went hunting, risked his neck, and came home cheery. He was extremely resilient. And then Françoise de Foix was his maîtresse en titre. It came naturally to him to have his mistress in full view. He was upholding a family institution. Henry VIII did not acknowledge Elizabeth Blount, which was a different system. Soon Claude could compare notes with Katherine of Aragon. The French system made Francis amiable. He had danced gaily at Rouen, where they had given Marguerite a silver statue of Saint Francis, and he was inordinately happy when he returned to Amboise early in 1518, to glory in his first son, François, the dauphin.

Marguerite was with him in these rejoicings. And when the festivities were at their height, for the Medici wedding and the Dauphin's christening, perhaps she went with him when he condescended to visit Neuville and Oiron.

Bonnivet's château was a fine and well-ordered establishment, as good as that of the richest noble in the land. And no one was more delighted to welcome them.

Francis and the queen were lodged in one wing, Marguerite opposite to them. Bonnivet's mother had the chamber under Marguerite's, but since she had a cough she gave up her bedroom to her son. In this way Marguerite's aspirant found himself, either by chance or by design, lodged directly beneath her. Every circumstance encouraged him to think of her. Francis and he were chasing stags in the intoxication of the spring. Their feasts at noon did full honour to the royal guests and Bonnivet's talk, heightened by the laughing approval of Marguerite, was as brave and graceful as his person. The King's mistress may have been in the company, since in this inmost circle the god of huntsmen was Pan. And in the evening, when the venerable hostess brought Marguerite sweetmeats before her couchée, Bonnivet was at his mother's side, lingering in the room as she undressed, till the very last moment, which added fuel to his flame.

Between her bed and the wall there was thick matting, and under this matting a trap-door. Its existence was unknown to Marguerite. She drowsily saw Bonnivet leave her room with her attendants, and was already just asleep when suddenly, without paying attention to her rank, without by-your-leave, without even bending his knee to her, a man was in bed with her, and she in his arms. She only knew that his shirt was finely scented, and his night-cap "of surpassing device," which she apparently saw in the dark.

"She, being strong," as she says in her account of it, "got from between his hands, and having required of him who he was, fell to beating, biting and scratching with such hearty good will that, for fear of her calling out, he would have stopped her mouth with the blanket."

The gentleman "spared none of his resources to rob her of her

GUILLAUME GOUFFIER, SEIGNEUR DE BONNIVET
From the Drawing attributed to Clouet in the Musée Condé, Chantilly

(From the Photograph in Sir Robert Witt's Library)

honour" and she "spared none of hers to defend it." She called at
the top of her voice for Madame Châtillon, her matron. This excellent lady, clad only in a nightdress, came running to help her
mistress. The visitor promptly slid out and disappeared.

"A man!" cried Marguerite, searching everywhere. "It could be
no one but the lord of this place, you may be sure," she blazed at
Madame Châtillon, "and in the morning I will put it to my brother
so that his head shall be witness to my chastity."

Seeing her tremble with anger her matron began to soothe.
"Quite right, my lady, his death ought to be the price, attacking
your honour out of his overpowering love of you. But you may
hurt your honour in trying to help it. My lady, I beg of you, tell
me the real truth of this affair."

Marguerite, from her embattled bed, still flamed in anger, but
Châtillon was a very old friend and she told her everything.

"Do you really assure me that he had nothing from you but only
scratches and poundings?"

"I do assure you, not another thing, and if he does not find a
good surgeon he will bear the marks of it tomorrow."

"But you may thank God, my lady. And if you wish to punish
him, leave him to his love and his shame: they will torment him
more than you can. What a humiliation for him! But if you accuse,
you will tell everybody, and he will never tell anybody. And if
Monseigneur does what you ask and this poor gentleman goes
out to die, why, my lady, nearly everyone will say he did what he
wanted to, and could not have attempted it without great encouragement. Everyone will say it hasn't been without fault on
your side. And high as your honour is, it will be questioned everywhere."

Marguerite listened to this straight talk intently.

"But what ought I to *do?*" she asked her matron.

"Since you are good enough to ask me, my lady," purred
Madame Châtillon, "you ought to be enchanted that the hand-
somest, most attractive gentleman I have ever seen has—has not
been able, either by love or by force, to turn you from the path of
righteousness."

Marguerite said nothing.

"And, my dear lady, you may thank God more than yourself

because many a sterner woman has been led astray by many a greater scallywag. But offers of 'friendship,' you ought to avoid them. Many give in the second time. Remember, my lady, love is blind. Just when it seems safest, the path is most slippery."

With these shrewd shots, Madame Châtillon prepared to depart. "Bit by bit," she said earnestly, "cool off your favour to him. It is too dangerous. And be content with the victory God gave you, without insisting on punishing him. And God give you grace, my lady."

With this little sermon, the matron left. And Marguerite thought of the poor gentleman below examining his bites and scratches, or her bites and scratches, before the mirror, and saying: "Now look what I have done! And I deserve it. I should not have tried to take that chaste body by assault. I should have tried to gain her favour, till by patience and long service my love gained the victory. For without it, all the merit and power of man are worth nothing."

So she imagined him putting her own thoughts in words. But Bonnivet was too Bonnivet to moralize.

He sent out word he was ill. He let his King go away without putting in an appearance. He hid in his room until his wounds were healed. And when he next encountered Marguerite he blushed. He could not look her in the eye. Little by little she cut him off, but not too subtly. And he took his punishment.

What Bonnivet could not understand was this woman who aroused him and then denied him. She knew, as she undressed before him, that each lift of her arms would speak to him, but when this drove him to the point she was impregnable. Was it her chastity that made her fight tooth and nail against the man she had attracted? Did she seek desire, the man's and her own, within a more sensitive scheme? Or was she a divided woman who, for all her strong intelligence and love of freedom, was inextricably caught in a contradiction? The citadel of this personality, an honest self that asked to be respected, could not be taken by assault, though she was passionate. What withheld her? What was it that would always make her the friend of the friendless, against the Church, against the Sorbonne, against parlement? What possessed, not her body, but her imagination?

The supreme loyalty was to Francis. The only form of power

that would always be too strong for her was the State, which was Francis. Women who love work within the limitations of those they love, and Marguerite, of a higher stature than her brother, could never quarrel with him. It was not in her to combat his power, since her love of him corrupted her will. She had helped to bring him up. She would match her step to his. She would walk hand in hand with her young brother.

The court that he was creating would take its shape around emotions like these, assailing them, inflecting them, even corrupting them: and its ultimate care would be its privilege. Marguerite, high in aspiration, deep in humanity, would rush her whole life to work out another solution, only to be pulled up short by her attachment to her brother. And he, with royal complaisance, would count on his mignonne.

Whatever held this woman to her brother, her sympathies never narrowed down to her own lot in life. She remained accessible, quick, open-hearted. She spared neither body nor spirit in the response she made to her kind. As the struggle intensified, as black passions thronged round her, her spirit mounted. Rabelais watched that quivering, climbing flame, and could only say, "Esprit abstraict, ravy et ecstatic." Planted on this earth, Rabelais refused to look for a vast compassion. Marguerite, locked within a contradiction from the beginning, always yearned for compassion and found the earth a prison.

Francis had no subtlety to match hers, but he knew the part that women could play at the court, by virtue of intelligence as well as beauty. Besides his natural tenderness for women, he had to draw into his system the nobility that was ceasing to be feudal. He had to entertain, literally and figuratively, the aristocratic order, to make them at home with him, loyal to him, intimate with him, and this by the aid and with the art of women. The court became the supreme centre of his power. To house it meant immense palaces. To move it from place to place meant a vast locomotion. And if Francis was lavish with his mignons it invested him with glamour, drew his nobles out of fighting him into courting him. But to have them around him, these hot-blooded men, without "la guerre amoureuse" was impossible. Anne of Brittany had sought to arrive at amenity by the discipline of the seminary, and Claude was like her. This was not the creed of Cognac. Francis instinctively desired the sportive freedom of both sexes, conducted in courtly fashion, with pleasantness, with measure.

The medieval baron took some handling. Francis's confederate the duke of Würtemberg could sit astride his wife booted and spurred, and could go bawling for another woman to the point of murdering her husband. This brutality could never be reconciled with a courtly dispensation. When he visited a château the young king hoped to have his eye alight on a beautiful greyhound, a beautiful horse, a beautiful woman. He saw all three with the same kind eye, but it was far from the raw meat of feudal baronage. A sudden brawl and a swift murder could still take place within Amboise, but Pompérant would have to flee. Francis frowned on the fierce manners of the fortress. He sought amenity, and he heightened the prestige of women.

The French were too close to nature to hide physical love. The transition at Francis's court would be from the spine to the brain, from the coarseness of Louis XI's bucolic badinage to the bold wit of the Heptameron. There would be more real curiosity about give and take, finer shades of meaning, greater play of the intelligence. The result was still libertine but it brought the soldier from the fille de joie to the maid of honour, and so the court glittered for the provinces.

But the barbarian was not yet tame. How to keep up the tent when the Christian pole was taken away, was the real difficulty for court manners. A Cortès could carve to empire through a hundred thousand naked Aztecs, but that was remote. The difficulty came with homicide as a domestic habit. The Italians who were breeding the Perfect Courtier had to combine him with the condottiere, and so domesticate an irate husband who dug out a lover's eyes, or a captain who, taking his method from the Turks at Otranto, sawed an enemy in half and exposed him on a stall. That was the underlying impulse. Once the Pope had become a prince, and once soldiering was the norm of princely society, it was hard to set limits to behaviour. The sacredness of life might be reiterated by Utopians like Erasmus and Thomas More, but Lautrec, Bonnivet, Fleurange, Montmorency were fresh from the camp, and the camp was unbridled.

Françoise de Foix, the exuberant sister of three soldiers, could also play with fire. She saw Francis flag in his attentions, while Bonnivet, who had failed with Francis's subtle sister, could gallantly attend on Francis's mistress.

Brantôme, who was not born till 1535, and who wrote down gossip at the end of the century, but whose grandmother was Madame Châtillon, did not hesitate to report Françoise's badinage.

"He thinks himself so handsome, the good Bonnivet," she said, to pique Francis, "and the more I tell him he is, the more he believes it. I make the greatest fun of him and so I pass the time, but he is most agreeable and says the funniest things. One never stops laughing with him, he talks so well." And here, no doubt, Brantôme could hear the abundant woman laugh, her bright eyes dancing, her bright teeth gleaming.

As by right Francis knocked loud on his mistress's door and sailed in without ceremony. One day he arrived too soon. Bonnivet was in his shirt, and had barely time to dive into the fireplace, crouching behind the leafy boughs that filled it. Francis was blithely unaware, all absorbed in his mignonne. He made love to Françoise and then, with the simplicity of the campaigner, freely made water into the fireplace.

Françoise could not stop him. Neither could Bonnivet. She could only help him when Francis had departed.

"Tout femme varie," Francis would later trace on a windowpane at Chambord. Not Bonnivet but Françoise would be blamed. For even to a man who varies, it always comes as a surprise.

Yet in Francis there was no concentrated heat. He had no murderous moral pretensions or homicidal fury. He had made his voyage to Cythera. It was coming to an end.

But she cared. And fairly soon he could hear that estranging, that desolate cry, a hunger and a loneliness, piercing through her exile from the court, as plaintive and as surprised as the cry of a wounded animal.

35

But this was not for several years. In 1518 she was still part of the pageant of the court, and public life did not cease because

Bonnivet was pursuing Francis's old mistress or Francis was veering to a new one. The negotiations with Wolsey were coming to a head. Bonnivet was sent to London with an embassy in the autumn of 1518. It was, perhaps, the high point of his diplomatic career. Though the ship sank that was carrying everything for the joust he and his nobles dazed London by their magnificence. Henry VIII was affable. Wolsey did the honours at Hampton Court in almost regal style. And the French gave some diversion by riding on their mules all over London. It was a gay and successful visit. Francis had told Bonnivet to "warm up those cold ladies" in the North, and Bonnivet smiled at acting proxy for the infant Dauphin, slipping a tiny ring on the new Mary Tudor's finger. A return visit was then ordained, and Francis came up to Paris for it in December.

It was an essential part of his task to win these visitors, and no one did it with more presence. A great power must rise to the occasion, must resort to dignified devices that impress both savages and reflective human beings—the blaze of gold, the stab of silver, the flash of silk, the imprisoned sunshine of the fabrics, the reverberation of old names, the pomp of priests, the ache of standing at attention and bending the knee and bobbing the head, music and wine, food and dance, and some ritual reference to the Deity. Then, if it goes well, stag hunts, boar hunts, mellowing acquaintance, and a truce to tribal animosity.

Francis followed with scruple every genial act and every liberal entertainment of which Henry had set the example in England. The idiom differed, but the cordial value was rigorously the same.

For the public audience the Palais de Justice served admirably, with a stage on the floor, a platform on the stage, and a royal dais on the platform. The eye followed a purple velvet carpet up to the canopied chair where France was enthroned in its young king, a beret cocked on his head, his athletic form in cloth of gold, an exquisite robe draping it, cloth of silver lined with herons' feathers from Spain. Around him, beside his own princes, were significant guests—the boy King of Navarre, Bibbiena from the Vatican, the Duke of Ferrara, Luneberg from Germany. And immediately behind him, hardly less significant, Boisy, Bonnivet, and Madame

Châteaubriant's brother Lescun. The royal ladies sat on a little screened platform in the corner.

The ambassadors were escorted into the hall by the older courtiers, René of Savoy, Châtillon, and the rest, while two hundred noble gendarmes, battle-axes in their hands, made an avenue of honour.

The routine was familiar. The ambassadors presented their letters. Duprat mumbled through them and, at Francis's request, asked the purpose of the visit. West rose to explain in a Latin oration. Duprat responded for the King. The English then stood up, Francis descended from his height, mingled with them and greeted them, chatting with old friends and embracing each of the gold-chained noblemen, thirty embraces. So ended the audience.

At Notre Dame he knelt on a silver-brocaded prie-dieu with a gold canopy. He wore a cape of gold tissue lined with silver brocade. Bonnivet's brother chanted Mass. And later, on solid gold plate, the ambassadors dined with Francis at the Bishop's palace.

The great celebration took place at the Bastille. There had been gay jousting in the afternoon, with bright edgeless swords used as scimitars. After sunset a canopy of waxed canvas was drawn over the Gothic courtyard. This canopy was blue, spangled with stars and hung with gold balls. It was lit up from below by chandeliers thick with big wax candles, and hundreds of torches shone around the hall. On each side wooden galleries had been built in three tiers, like balconies in a square theatre. The walls were hung in white and tawny stripes, Francis's colours, and the wooden floor was covered in the same colours. In each corner was a high cupboard loaded with gold or silver vessels. The whole room was therefore sparklingly bright, with a high blue sky. And in this artificial sunniness, on a brocaded platform, with festoon of flowers and box and ivy behind them, sat Francis with Marguerite by his side. The Queen and Louise sat apart in the lowest gallery, Claude ablaze with jewels. But this evening it was brother and sister.

Along a covered street decorated with box and laurel the guests arrived at the Bastille. When they had passed into the hall, some to the floor, some to the stage, others to the platform and the galleries, the doors were closed as fife and trumpet sounded for the dancing. On the walls were mottoes which no doubt corresponded with the devices of the dancers. But this was merely a distraction while tables were noiselessly brought in, a horseshoe table on the high platform for the royal company, straight tables on the stage below, and more on the floor. The total number for the banquet would be two hundred and fifty. And when the tables had been set, and Francis had washed his hands, the music struck up for supper. The trumpeters in a row, eight of them, swung in and wheeled in front of Francis. A company of archers, the leader with a wand, followed in unison. Five blazoned heralds came after them, making deep obeisance to the king, then the seneschals and the Lord Steward. So arrived the first of nine courses, four-and-twenty pages with dishes that danced in flame. These served the horseshoe table. The other guests were attended by two hundred archers. In two hours the nine courses were carried through, and Francis, according to custom, gave two large silver dishes to the heralds, which luckily went off without a brawl.

When the tables were whisked away without confusion it was to make way for the masques and dances. In the lilt of the blood that everything had excited, with tongues as quick as flame and eyes as brilliant, the whole company swam into that light and proud delirium in which the bud opens to a rose.

Madame de Châteaubriant had been near Francis at the supper. She had watched him afterwards, as the young ladies of the court came among the company, and later, as the pretty custom was, offering confections and sweetmeats.

One of these girls, a blonde with curling hair, had been followed by Francis's eyes, and Françoise did not conceal her knowing it. He had previously told her that this meant nothing. He had given her his heart: God would not allow him to have any other emotion. If his glance were ever "deranged," it was as if an alien hand had moved the needle of the compass. It might alter the needle, he said in a poem, but not the compass of the heart.

Now he moved about, "in a long gown, fitting close, both behind and before, of white satin, embroidered all over in gold, with certain compasses and dials, concerning which various interpretations were given."

Clément Marot, a dry-humoured observer of the court, could not look at the flashing Françoise without crediting her bon savoir, her prompt intelligence. Now she watched Francis's compass and where it was pointing.

Under the canvas sky, with its pasteboard stars and its gilded planets, Francis was the centre of these women to whom he was more than monarch—his mother, his wife, his sister, his present mistress, his mistress-to-be. To their dilated imaginations he was a Roi Soleil. The canvas heaven was like one that Leonardo da Vinci had long ago devised for Ludovico Sforza. Had Leonardo stood in the Bastille, that evening, to see this luminous canopy installed? He had built bathrooms, made toys, invented lions that opened their hearts to show them full of lilies, and this dainty pageant was Italianate, a seedling from Milan. The venerable exile may have lent it his genius, with a gesture of his practised left hand. He knew how to bring his greatest gifts to little excellences, and to give lovely patterns to the princes.

36

The first six months of 1519 saw the final tussle for the Empire. Maximilian had lived into the new age as a kind of sprightly anachronism. It was a long time ago, in another world, when he had ridden out of the East to claim his bride, and begun his court-ship according to ritual, groping for a flower in her bosom. So was the heiress of Charles the Bold linked with the son of the Emperor, and so were the Netherlands brought to the Habsburgs and to Spain. The inconsequential, impecunious Maximilian had never become stable anywhere, and yet out of his incessant mobility, his quicksilver fluidity, had sprung an amazing amalgam. This man with winged sandals, a volatile thief, had been a messenger of the gods for his Habsburgs. He was barely sixty when, at Welz in Austria, he fell mortally ill in January 1519. He ordered his attendants not to cry over so natural an event as death. He wanted all his teeth pulled when he was considered to be dead, perhaps to make sure there was no mistake, and then he directed them to bury him next his "real spouse," Mary of Burgundy. It was a last surge of his romanticism.

37

Maximilian's death made the imperial election actual. It was set for June 28, 1519, and now the final struggle to capture the Electors began in earnest.

Only seven princelings, four lay ones and three in the church, were destined to name the Emperor. But beneath these seven traditional Electors was the immense complex of German territorial nobility. Germany, in effect, was composed like a cauliflower, spouting from a common stalk into innumerable subheads, each as complete and separate as possible. The territorial noble is pushed to self-sufficiency, rounding himself as naturally as does an isolated tree and making this tree into a family one. The ferocious isolation of marks, palatinates, counties, duchies, kingdoms, was the danger and the distinction of Germany. Men were at once lordly and rude, vulnerable and incorrigible. Compelled to stand by themselves, they made squirearchy into sovereignty, but sovereignty on a scale that sometimes gave a broadsword to a dwarf or set a giant on a pony. It favoured character, but not cohesion or proportion, and the cities in turn became knobby and spiky with character, so that the noble met his match in the burgher, no less vehement and intractable. And since so much positive will in the leaders flattens out the followers docility and subservience marked the underlying population.

But by 1519 Luther had emerged. He was not yet a European fact. He had not been excommunicated by the Pope. But he was the supreme fact in Germany.

When the young Hohenzollern, Albrecht of Brandenburg, acquired his three bishoprics in a hurry, he had had to square Pope Leo by paying him 10,000 ducats to overlook the irregularity in addition to 13,000 ducats, as the regular fee. This was in 1515. It was more cash than he could advance, so Jacob Fugger, the genial Augsburg banker, advanced it for him. To repay Fugger the Pope granted the Archbishop of Mainz a "crusade," which meant the despatch of a trained religious agitator in 1517 with the power to sell indulgences. These were not indulgences to commit sin, merely a remission of the punishments incurred by the sinner, provided he confessed and was contrite. Such certificates were rather costly, graded according to income, and naturally presupposing expert knowledge of divine penology. The Fuggers sent their representative to the "crusade." He took the cash. Part of it was forwarded to the Pope. The rest of it was credited to the archbishop with the Fuggers, minus a percentage with Maximilian getting a rake-off. The Dominican agitator, whose methods were hot and whose arguments were crude, received good pickings and first-class expenses for his conduct of the drive. The whole device worked well so long as no strong-minded priest dwelt on the traffic as a spiritual transaction. But was it good for the faithful to buy these certificates? Could the cash they paid over to the Fuggers really procure for them the immunity certified? And were they clear that they were not buying absolution for reserved sins, regardless of their state of soul? These were the bitter questions that stirred Martin Luther. They were the questions he nailed on the door of his little university church in October, 1517, and, of course, he questioned also the whole doctrine of grace, and the authority of the Church behind it.

Early in 1518 Pope Leo, stirred up by the young Hohenzollern, decided to remonstrate with Luther. The Dominicans, smarting under the attack on their agitator, advised the Curia to summon Luther to Rome. He retorted by pronouncements on excommunication and large appeals to the Bible. The Pope's representative at the Diet of Augsburg pressed the Elector of Saxony to yield up Luther but Frederick, his sovereign, and patron of Wittenberg, positively refused.

The Imperial Election was now too near for the Pope to antagonize Frederick of Saxony. Luther's personal interviews with the Papal nuncio ended in a fatherly warning. And a young dove flew from the ark at Rome with a golden rose for Frederick, and an olive branch for Martin. Little more could be said until an emperor was elected and an imperial mandate issued against Luther.

But Germany, coming up to the Election, was in a state of extraordinary ferment, mental and political. The Electors were jealous of their sovereignty, yet confronted by two types of noble adventurers, Sickingen armed with the lance and Hutten with the

pen. The young humanists, in addition, had taken the yeast of
their ideas from Erasmus, siding with Reuchlin against the repres-
sive Dominicans and brazenly aware of the corrupt bishops on
top and the troops of illiterate, undisciplined, swarming monks
and priests underneath. To swell the tumult in which the nation
was swaying there were grievances among the peasants and the
artisans that swept them like a hurricane in the forest, so that life
roared, with restlessness and confusion, the princes demanding
obedience, the knights predatory, the citizens knotted into protective leagues and walled cities, the poor starving and glowering
into revolt. It was a Germany at once sublime and chaotic, violent
and incompetent, inviting revolution and meat for the demagogue.
And deep in their recesses, serious men like Martin Luther were
shaping a polity in the mould of their own agonized lives. He was
a theologian, delving in the sacred entrails of the Bible, demanding
the spiritual guidance that was denied him by Medicean Rome. A
man prostrating himself before God, counting himself as nothing,
abandoned to the mercy of his Creator, he could in the same
instant turn on the Papacy and blaze with fury and wrath. And
his anger, first provoked on the indulgence issue, which stirred the
whole people, gave his own prince, the Elector of Saxony, a grievance against the encroaching Hohenzollerns.

It was into this half-insane turmoil that Francis interjected his
candidacy for the Empire. And as between himself and his "son"
Charles he argued there was no personal conflict. It was still "la
guerre amoureuse." The Empire was a mistress, he gallantly put
it, for whose hand they were both contesting. They could rival
one another for her hand in all friendliness and chivalry.

The means, of course, were not pretty. Francis regretted that
they were squalid, but he gracefully indicated his position.

"If we had to deal with upright men or men seeming upright,"
he explained, "our method would be straightforward. But in times
like these, anyone who wants anything, the Papacy or the Empire
or anything else, must get them by force and fraud, and those one
has to deal with do not make a small matter either."

But the end was not on a level with the means. "The end I am
striving for," Francis added with royal gravity, "is neither pernicious nor naughty, for I am not moved by greed or ambition or

the lust to dominate, but solely by the object of facilitating as much as possible the war I am to make on the Turk."

This same object he expressed to Sir Thomas Boleyn. Seizing the English ambassador by the hand, gazing fervently down at him, and laying the other white hand on his heart, Francis declared: "Three years from the election I'll be in Constantinople, or a dead man."

The formula of a holy war had just reached him from Rome. Pope Leo had decided to favour him for the Empire largely because Charles's Neapolitan territory was within forty miles of the Vatican. So the Turk was providing Francis with all his window-dressing. But behind this comedy of high purpose there was no comedy in method. He had sent agents as far as Poland, disguised as pilgrims. He had poured agents into Germany. Wherever there was a point of internal friction the French accumulated their forces. Anything that could give leverage on any of the Electors was considered commendable. If private war was the best way to menace opinion, war was immediately stimulated. The Pope promised cardinals' hats in writing, and offered to make the Archbishop of Mainz his permanent legate. Had Francis kept his grip on Sickingen the game looked as though it might have been easier. But Würtemberg, with 15,000 Swiss to help him, was not afraid to tackle the Swabian League with Francis's encouragement, and Francis was not afraid to send out a proclamation repudiating the fatuity of such perfidy.

The lord high negotiator was Bonnivet. He went to Germany himself to get on the inside of the intrigue, and he kept in daily touch with Francis. He appealed as a fellow-soldier to Sickingen. He made up to the archbishops. He hid behind the tapestry as Henry VIII's agent falsified Henry's promises given to Francis. Bonnivet was not himself deterred by any scruples, and he itched to see the Electors intimidated by war. He disguised himself as a Captain Jacob to creep near Frankfort as the fateful day arrived. His joy in trapdoors and hiding-places and false names and disguises gave comic relief to an episode heavy with consequences. To him it was not a conflict with an inner meaning. It was a game, an intrigue, a seduction. He judged it by the means he was employing, and he forgot the Holy War.

Of the seven Electors with whom he was dealing only one was

thinking of Germany. Frederick of Saxony was a sober and prudent prince. He could no more give scandal in the matter of this election than he could tolerate it in the matter of the indulgences. He had stood by Martin Luther. He had convictions as a prince. He took the Holy Ghost seriously enough to cast his vote on principle.

The Archbishop of Trèves was as good as a Frenchman, and his vote was not in the market. But of the other five, four had pledged themselves to Francis even in Maximilian's lifetime, while all five had equally pledged themselves to his opponent. In short, they were auctioning their votes. The old Emperor had gone up to 500,000 florins in his preliminary guarantees. Francis was ready to spend three million. So the first five months of 1519 were filled with frantic marketing.

Charles could not leave Spain to look out for himself. He had hard work extracting subsidies from the Spaniards, and it was with the greatest reluctance that he had forwarded cash to Maximilian for the first douceurs at Augsburg. But if he was out of it himself, his Aunt Margaret of Austria had her supreme chance in this election to wipe off her old score against the French. For her it was the House of Habsburg against the House of France. She was absolutely convinced of "the great and inveterate enmity that the French bear to this House." She threw herself into the campaign. Her agents swarmed among the Electors, keen and nimble men, the most capable and the most conversant she could find.

At one moment, in her determination to win, it came over her that the young Ferdinand might be a better Germanic candidate than Charles. This she and her nobles ventured to put to her nephew in Spain. His answer flamed out of hot dark ambition. He knew he was not clever. He knew he was not experienced. But he was shocked that he, the acknowledged Head of the House, should be displaced even during a flicker of the imagination. His young brother he would provide for. But his alone was the claim to the Empire, it was a French trick to weaken his power by dividing it, and he held to his Plus Ultra with invincible tenacity. No one could doubt the Flemish grit he put into this incensed reply. Margaret hastened to make amends. She was plunging with the Fuggers in the first of those transactions that would enslave the young prince to his bankers and finally interest at eighteen per cent. She dealt for him with the English, the Pope, the Swiss. She won Franz von Sickingen to her side. And each of the Electors was chivvied by her agents.

If the Fuggers refused to give Francis letters of credit, eight hundred mules jogged into Lorraine with 400,000 ducats in leather sacks. But though every inordinate request made by the Brandenburgs was agreed to by Francis, and though Joachim gave his written "parole de prince" to vote for him, there was one obstacle to the goods that the French were buying, and that was the impossibility of having them delivered. By April it was clear, even to the Archbishop of Mainz, that he simply could not vote for a Frenchman. The mere suspicion that he was a Frenchman physically endangered Pace's movements. It was bad enough for Charles to be an Austrian by birth and a Burgundian by affinity. But he was Germanic. Francis might war against the Turks, and even safeguard the Eastern frontiers, yet his very power and wealth marked him as dangerous. He had bribed right and left, he had financed internal war, and the resentments he had stirred were homicidal. The fact that the Pope had backed him was another outrage on the German nation. Francis had not a chance. He might not understand this. He might blame the Electors for betraying him. But they had essentially been using him. His eagerness had not purchased them. It had simply made them more expensive to his rival.

The Election of June 28 saw a feeble attempt to find a third candidate. Frederick of Saxony grunted his declination. And then Charles was unanimously elected.

Bonnivet, according to Fleurange, thought it much better not to go straight home. So he took the cure at a watering-place until Francis had a chance to recover his temper.

38

Francis had played for high stakes in Germany. He had plunged recklessly, gone the limit, gone it blind. And now at Poissy on July 3 he learned that he had lost and young Charles V would be Emperor.

He burst out in temper. He was furious especially with the German princes who had sworn to vote for him. His precious money had gone in useless bribes. Bonnivet was lucky not to be present. But Francis was essentially incapable of dwelling on any disagreeable situation that he could evade. It was the hunting season. He departed for Fontainebleau to relieve himself by prolonged and violent exercise.

In a great organization like France there was all the material for an amended policy and renewed decision. Duprat, Semblançay, Robertet were at hand. The du Bellays were beginning to be serviceable. Old Montmorency was close to Marguerite and Louise. But Louise was tight-minded as well as strong-willed, and Francis had to be reckoned with. In the lull that succeeded the election a veteran would have prepared for the difficult future, but Francis was emotionally stunned and politically numb. He had tried by a brilliant stroke to cut through his complexities. This had failed. He needed distraction.

It was, in reality, the first serious rebuff that life had given him since he came to the throne. From 1515 to 1519 he had enjoyed the benefits of Marignano. His whole policy had been smoothened by that dashing victory, by the decline of Ferdinand and Maximilian and the adolescence of Charles. He had Lombardy. He had kept the road open to Navarre and Naples. Even up to the end the prospects of being Emperor had allured him, and as Emperor he would have solved the advancement of France by the subordination of the continent. To lose such a gamble angered him, since so far his career had been crowned with glory. He had revelled in it, as soldier, as diplomat, as patron of the arts, prince of the renaissance, dionysiac, lover. He had enriched his family, gratified his friends, created his court. All he had required was the final prestige of Emperor. But instead he had carried the fight into the heart of Germany, artillery massed behind it, and this had crystallized his rivalry with Charles. At the last moment the Pope had said: "It is no use dashing yourself against the wall." Luther could have had a cardinal's hat, in the June of 1519. But Francis had not listened to the banker-pope. He had gone on. He had followed up the supposed weakenings of Maximilian.

Maximilian, odd combination of fantasy and wile, had opened his old turkey eye on the conflict that he took to be innate in Europe, and he had rounded off his career by electing Charles. It was a

Habsburg calculation. Brittany and Burgundy had been lost, but Milan and Naples could be disputed. That was the real meaning of this election. And Francis stood up from the gamble, stiff and a little unhinged, scuppered by the old man's ghost and by Margaret of Austria, reading huge losses in the unsympathetic dawn.

So passed his juvenile glory. He was five-and-twenty, still an adolescent by medieval reckoning, but now saying good-bye to radiant Marignano, and facing a duel. It is not pleasant when change is brought home to a young champion, when the heart that beat lightly is suddenly squeezed by a brutal grip of circumstance. But Francis took this with him to Fontainebleau. His proprietorship was not at stake, but its aggrandisement was challenged. France was surrounded, the encirclement complete but for England, the Swiss, the Papacy. It was no longer châteaux on the Loire and wedding-bells for the Medici. The Emperor, it is true, having been engaged to Claude and Renée and Louise, was now in a new pew. He was engaged to Charlotte. But this was only a jury-rig. Charlotte was not as many months as he was years.

And in May, 1519, as if to mark the closing of Francis's first flight, three men had died.

Boisy had fallen ill at Montpensier, in the midst of new negotiations with the pliant Chièvres. Each of them was gouty, but Boisy went first, and it ended their four years of useful connivance. It was, in its way, a windfall for Francis. He took a "loan" of all the gold and silver at Chinon belonging to Boisy, about 132,000 crowns. It was set aside for war.

The death of young Lorenzo de' Medici snapped the sole personal link with the Pope. Leo, indeed, persisted in alliance. He would never let the same man be Emperor and hold Naples. But this was like Francis's saying, "the Catholic King will think three times before he tackles us." It was a hope. They were marking time.

The third death, which occurred in the exile of Amboise, was that of Leonardo da Vinci. By dying in a strange country Leonardo had only proved himself at home. He had always lived in a strange country. Technically illegitimate, he had never legitimatized himself in the consoling prejudices and easy folkways that make the earth fraternal and fratricidal. He hovered somewhere above the serviceable and beyond the immediate, unpunctual by the human clock, obedient to a true rhythm in the universe which ran through sex, art, science, religion, and took the span of time. He wished water to run up mountains. He saw man at home under the sea and in the air. He lived not in the small enigma of a fugitive smile but in the large enigma of a fugitive life, gripping eternity with a human hand. This man gravely interrogated the universe. A certain inhumanity seemed to invade him because he dared to employ his exact intellect at the command of an indomitable and arduous imagination. But this ceaseless experiment opened doors to him that no man had ever tried, and by unfaltering inquiry brought the illimitable within reach. Benign as Prospero, the earth was his Caliban. And if the legend were untrue that he died in Francis's arms, at least Francis had led him to the Loire and often stood enchanted within the range of his discourse. There is something, after all, in the divine right of kings. But with this king's death the renaissance lost a star, and Francis closed an honourable extravagance as magnifico.

39

One of Francis's first visitors in the late summer of 1519 was Sebastian Giustinian. That sage Venetian was cordially received. Francis was peculiarly anxious to discover England's attitude. Giustinian assured him that England stood for peace, which greatly relieved him. But he was insistent on questioning the old ambassador, who had had four years in England, about the real character of Henry VIII. Only a few months before, as Francis knew well, all the gay companions who had French polish had been banished by Wolsey, on the eve of the Imperial Election: it was the epoch of Elizabeth Blount, and Giustinian, pressed hard for his opinion, at last admitted that Henry devoted himself to "pleasure and solace" leaving the care of state to Cardinal Wolsey.

"By my faith," rapped out Francis, "the Cardinal must bear his King light good will, for it is not the office of a good servant to filch his master's honour."

Giustinian did not demur. And then he obediently followed Francis to see a sight that Henry VIII could not have shown him, two small boys, the Dauphin and his younger brother. The little one, Henri, was a few months old. Claude had borne him in the spring. Marguerite had held him at the font, with Thomas Boleyn, since the child was named for Henry VIII. The proud parent no doubt recounted this as they watched the children. And the Venetian could not say, "Yes, the sole fear of the English people is lest they should pass into the power of the French through this marriage."

But he said it to the Signory in October. He extolled the universal popularity of Claude in France. He added that Francis and his mother "were more unpopular all over France than words could express." The reason was hard times. He stressed Louise's miserly reputation. "She is supposed to have invested much capital throughout the country, and is intent on hoarding, for the purpose, it is said, of aiding the King in the event of any sudden need."

From Fontainebleau he returned to Blois for more hunting, and in September, galloping through the woods, he was struck between the eyes by a low bough. This was all in the game, so far as he was concerned, but it was simply horror for his mother. She had no trust in the universe. Her whole nature, now that she was in power, was to build up defences and gather resources. Like so many people whose anxieties have grooved their brains, Louise remained avid for security, raising the parapet of gold. She was the mother of a king, but she still cradled him in her mind, gouty from sheer worry, sharp-tongued, hard-bitten, suspicious.

Yet she wanted him to buoy up his spirits in the conflict that was crowding on him. She gathered her family around her, Claude at last on her feet, Marguerite recovering from a grave illness, Francis in need of a fillip. She took them on their first great visit in state to their own Angoumois. It was to be as joyous as every artifice and every fancy could make it. Genouillac was sending all the wine of his vintage to make his King rejoice. Lautrec, on the eve of his marriage with an Albret, was coming up from Milan. His brother Lescun was being named Marshal. Bonnivet in his great château at Neuville would receive them. And Bourbon would welcome them at Châtellerault.

"And what do you think of it?" Francis asked Bourbon, showing him the great château built by Bonnivet.

"I think, Sire," replied Bourbon, "the cage is too big for the bird."

It was Francis's bird. "You are jealous!"

"Can your Majesty believe I am jealous of a gentleman whose ancestors were squires of mine?"

This bitter speech, if it were ever really uttered, gave Francis a clue to Bourbon's grievance. But he had not come for grievances.

With gay voices and fluting praise around them, with pageants and receptions, with masques on the river and hilarious pantomime, with vigorous sham battles, with music and spraying colour and carnival mirth, Francis and Marguerite and Louise were lifted into cordiality, pressed to the bosom of the Midi. Where now was the frown of grave news, the long face? They returned to confidence. The meeting with Henry VIII was definitely arranged for June, the Field of the Cloth of Gold. Messengers went to Wolsey and came from Wolsey. Francis was growing his beard until he met his English compere, letting his ringlets run over his collar, and he believed that over there, where England huddled in fog and the mysteries of the north, Henry was growing equally hairy, until they should fall into one another's arms. So eager was he to meet Henry, he willingly agreed to meet no one else, in the meantime. By this Wolsey was able to secure for Henry a private interview with Charles V, so that he could arrive in France with Charles's terms in his pouch.

Francis was counting on the Pope. He was persuading himself that Charles V was still under the thumb of his Flemish advisers, the lord of dispersed countries with poor revenues, inexperienced in government and the cost of war. "Those who have been at it a long time," he said sagely, "know what it costs." "Fault avoir infini argent et ung gros trésor." As for those arrangements made when Charles was a minor, Francis held fast. He did not propose to concede one point or yield one inch. He was abandoning nothing and softening no contention. He was sure Charles would be "prince de foy et d'honneur."

Charles said nothing. Spain threw him like a bronco, and he picked himself up and remounted. He went from province to province, always meeting the same recalcitrance, always hanging on to his request for cash, always taking demands under advisement and making demands under pressure. He knew how to stick to his point. He also knew how to dissemble. Promising to employ no foreigners in Spain, he left Adrian of Utrecht as his viceroy. But by that time he was sailing to his rendezvous with Henry VIII.

40

The French were desperately hard up. That was the gnawing reality. They were planning the Field of the Cloth of Gold, but where was the money for it, let alone money for a war? Boisy's gold and silver were a help. Charles's 100,000 crowns from Naples was a nest-egg. But the Election drained the King, and bankers were querulous. It took some skill to borrow 200,000 livres at Lyon to pay for the coming celebrations. The people were grumbling. The treasury was unhappy. And yet Wolsey kept urging, "magnificence," "gold," "magnificence."

41

But the meeting would seem perfect opulence, would glitter into history as the Field of the Cloth of Gold.

It was actually a broad field at Guines, on the apron of Calais, and consequently an English possession. By consenting to meet on conquered ground Francis gave the key to this interview: he was personally courting his ally and royal "brother." He wanted Henry as friend.

The 200,000 livres had started the silkmakers at Tours and the carpenters in Picardy. It was convened that thousands of tents should be erected in the plain, and Francis ordered his to be cloth of gold, with apples of gold to crown them, and a gold St. Michael to dominate them all. In addition a Roman theatre was built of wood, and some temporary buildings at Ardres.

There were sturdy men on both sides who bristled at the dangers of this encounter. It brought dark memories of Burgundian days, of treachery and assassination. No one was more contemptuous of these animal suspicions than Francis himself. He was coming with Claude and Marguerite, with his mother, with Françoise de Foix: and Henry was bringing his Queen and Mary Tudor. The whole occasion was resolutely amicable. It had been planned to unite not two nations but two courts, to entwine knighthoods and branches

of chivalry. Francis saw it as a natural sequence to the superb
embassies of 1518, when Wolsey had thrown open Hampton Court
and he himself had responded in Paris. But that was in winter, by
candelabra. This was by the candelabra of the sun. Both sovereigns
were stalwart, gorgeous, proud. Both had learned the lesson of Italy,
the joys of parade and pageant, tourneys, banquets, music, and
novelty of setting. No form of courtly interchange could be omitted
in this three weeks together. The place itself was designed for it,
organized with the skill of war with war tents festive and radiant.
And while the nobility played, diplomacy could work alliance. It
was an attempt to melt the political mood.

The English astounded everyone by their workmanlike prepara-
tion. They had constructed a capacious windowed palace in England, on four sides of a square, shipped it to France, in sections, and
assembled it in a flash. It was covered with canvas, painted to look
like stone, a replica of the Guildhall at Calais. And this building,
with wine-spurting fountains in its courtyard, was hung with rich
tapestries and flooded with light. When it had served its purpose
it was returned to England, and, as du Bellay put it, nothing lost
but the carriage.

Judged as artisans, the French proved less impressive. They had
frugally used the Bastille equipment in their Roman theatre, but it
hardly suited the occasion. They set up a huge tent for the royal
reception, sixty feet square, but this was blown about by the high
wind. They managed, however, to improvise a hall for the "festin"
which was amply successful, and their entertainments, and their
"caves," were not less royal than the English. There was something
indefinably right about their use of fabric and the elegance of their
women.

Every detail was a matter of written treaty. Henry and Wolsey
arrived at Calais the same day that Francis reached Ardres. That
was in the contract. And not until the last dot had been put in the
treaty did the two kings meet. Wolsey had himself gone to Ardres
to finish the arrangements with. Francis. And, having had several
fresh ideas during the night, he hurried back the next morning to
insert them in the plans. Then the political treaty had to be drafted.
Francis chafed at all these intolerable formalities. He had uncovered

his head to Wolsey and embraced him. He had made much of him. But his eye was on Henry.

Francis had known a considerable number of political cardinals already. Amboise in his boyhood, Bibbiena quite recently, not to speak of his own creations, Bohier and Gouffier and little Bourbon. And Schinner and Lang and Gurk were also cardinals he had parried. But, having handled Pope Leo to his own satisfaction, he no doubt felt capable of handling Wolsey. It was Henry who did not sit square to his vision.

Yet this interview was Wolsey's, not Henry's. It had been first mooted long before, and when Bonnivet was knitting the alliance with Wolsey in October, 1518, it had again been revived, while Francis was gracious and triumphant. The Imperial Election was still in the future, and Wolsey had agreed. But he was far too brilliant a showman not to seize on the outcome of the election. "Really," one despairing continental would say of him, "that fellow is too wonderful. He wants to interfere in everything and do all himself. There's no holding him." And the advent of Charles had gone to his head. Here at last was a calculable presence, no chamois like Maximilian but the nephew of Margaret of Austria, the nephew of Queen Catherine. Wolsey had met the grave young Emperor at Dover on May 26. During three days he and Henry had made great progress. England had now two strings to its bow. This was very different from dealing with a gracious and triumphant Francis.

There were details to regulate, schemes to propose. Wolsey knew, for one thing, that until Francis repaid the imperial bribes that he had borrowed from Lombard Street, Lombard Street could not meet its obligations to Henry. To ask Francis to pay Henry direct pleased the Frescobaldi, and Francis agreed. This was one practical item that Semblançay could arrange with the Cardinal. But when it came to a large understanding, based on real friendship, Wolsey had already killed it. The conference died at Canterbury before it was born at Guines.

The kings, beautifully apparelled, rode through the barriers in the late afternoon of June 7, embraced as well as their restless steeds would permit, dismounted, and walked arm-in-arm into a golden pavilion. With them went Bonnivet and Bourbon, Norfolk and Suffolk. This was the beginning of many graceful ceremonies, equally studied, equally symmetric. It was rubbing noses, but rubbing noses very politely, with a pane of glass between.

Marguerite tried to break through. She called Wolsey her "father," and he called her his "daughter." Bourbon did his best. He rode on a horse that jumped its own height, and when Henry admired this courser Bourbon made him a present of it. Francis himself made the bravest effort to extricate the conference from Wolsey's ordinances. Much as he hated to rise early, he came down one morning before the court was astir, took the first noble and the first page he happened on, and cantered over to Guines. At the gate he was challenged, but he made his way to Henry's chamber, knocked on the door and walked in.

When Henry really looked up he could not believe the sight of his eyes. There was Francis beaming at him.

"To-day," said Francis, "you are my prisoner."

Henry at this period was under thirty, big but surging with vitality, with golden hair and blue astonished eyes. As he sat up in bed, a precious collar gleaming around his neck, he stammered out: "My God, but this *is* a surprise." He really liked it. "My brother, you show the greatest trust in me. From this hour I am your prisoner." With that he whipped off his collar, and said: "Take this, for love of your prisoner."

Francis slipped off his bracelet, even twice as valuable, with the same impulse. And then, whisking Henry's shirt from the hands of his attendant, he said, holding it to the fire, "To-day you'll have no valet but myself."

"You must stay to dine."

"Ah, I have arranged to joust." But they talked and came near one another, their natures intersecting. And then, in the highest spirits, Francis rode back to Ardres.

On the outskirts he met a company of his own people, all flurried and pop-eyed, his friend Fleurange with them.

"My master," burst out Fleurange, "you are a madman to have done what you have done. I am greatly relieved to see you again. And the devil take whoever advised you to do this."

"No one advised me," answered Francis. "I know well there isn't a soul in my kingdom who would have advised it," and then, his

QUEEN CLAUDE, ABOUT 1520

From the Drawing attributed to Clouet in the Musée Condé, Chantilly

eyes dancing, he recounted his adventure, delighted with Henry and himself.

For once, at any rate, something natural, something spontaneous, had happened. But not only for once. Henry had triumphed at archery, and he and Francis were taking their wine together, in their royal pavilion. There had been talk of wrestlers and wrestling. "My brother," exclaimed Henry, throwing his arm around Francis's neck, "I wish to wrestle with you."

Before Francis knew it, Henry got a strong grip of him. But it was an old game for him. He gave his adversary a twist and threw him flat. Henry got up. "Come on," he said. The whole party tingled with apprehension. A feminine voice said, "It is time for supper."

This was a spark to tinderwood. Everyone was nervous. The tourneys went off amicably but Louise actually shuddered when Alençon's tent took fire. The conference had become a mockery to her. Ardres was "a forbidding, an iniquitous place." She watched with acute impatience the last embraces of Henry and her Cæsar. She knew that this vast expense, what du Bellay called "la grande despence superflue," was to no purpose. They were riding to Gravelines to meet the Emperor again. And Wolsey had only just celebrated High Mass, with Richard Pace conveying the plenary indulgences, and the Host soaring, by thin wires, in the air.

There was one thing, at any rate, that Semblançay had not forgotten to do for her. He had kept all the trimmings that were left over from the decorations and the costumes, all the snippets of cloth of silver and cloth of gold. Louise crisped her fingers for these pickings.

42

Wolsey rode away satisfied from Guines. The Field of the Cloth of Gold was a political failure but a diplomatic success. Since 1515 he had been baffled by the French. The Treaty of Noyon had been a defeat for him. Chièvres had blocked him in Flanders and through French connivance, he had been meanly exasperated as Bishop of Tournai. But he was still one of those inexhaustible men who become political brokers by sheer persistence. He knew the French were short of money, and short of allies, and his object was to widen the division between France and the Empire in order to insert England as honest broker. To this use he had turned the conference at Guines. England had shown itself royal and puissant. He had plumbed Francis's anxiety. He had imposed himself less as ally than as arbiter, elbowing the Pope out of the picture. By this means both sides must count him and so, by a sort of capillary movement, he might work into the Papacy. It was a prospect that invigorated him.

He was at Henry's side, on the way to Gravelines, and they were going to offer Mary Tudor, the Dauphin's bride-elect, to the Emperor. It was bold. It was perfidious. But so "universal peace" would be manipulated.

The young Emperor, who had been waiting in the wings until the great festival closed, went on with the English from Gravelines to Calais. Only illness kept Erasmus from being in his train. Chièvres was with him, and his young brother Ferdinand.

Those of his Flemings who had been with Charles in Spain, and watched him through the Election, knew that for a troubled young man he was uncommonly wary. Of slighter build and paler hue than the two older princes, he spoke thickly, dressed modestly and said little. By cutting himself off from gay companions and lively moods, he could easily seem lacking in temperament, and where his Aunt Margaret wrote poetry and loved objets d'art, Charles was clearly subordinating his amusements. He had æsthetic responses but all his responses he passed through the auditing department. Even at twenty he was grudgingly careful with his brother and managerial with his sisters. He took his rank as Emperor extremely seriously. But the really vicious combination he represented, the combination of autocracy and mediocrity, was still hidden under his nominal freedom from vice. And while a priest of Wolsey's type could never really gain his confidence, he could gain Wolsey's confidence just by burning low. So Wolsey made his plans for "arbitration."

43

Francis was profoundly uneasy. Some of his nobles, franked by their English friends, had gone masked to the ball at which Henry was entertaining the Emperor at Calais, and he himself, hovering as near as Boulogne, had done his best to be invited to a three-cornered conference. He had offered to come without ceremony, but Wolsey had given him no encouragement. He would later retort by beginning to fortify Ardres, but when the English took issue he stopped fortifying Ardres and he stopped exciting Scotland. He was anxious to give no excuse for a quarrel. He believed that so long as he was paying for Tournai and pensioning Mary Tudor and delivering an annuity by treaty, the English were unlikely to break with him. But he could not quite penetrate the sham neutrality that England was fabricating. The Pope he could reckon on for some time. Bibbiena had written his mother that the Pope "would live and die in true union and amity with Francis and herself." That was hopeful. But if he broke neutrality to attack Charles he lost the English, and if he waited to attack Charles he lost the tide. He was in a hard predicament, and what made it worse was lack of money.

These were tense months after Guines. When the "trinity" were closeted together, Francis and Marguerite and Louise, they could only admit that the conference had been a fiasco.

It was only six years since Louis XII had been in a dreadful predicament, and now his successor saw grey waters ahead. He was unprepared for it.

By the way he hunted and amused himself he seemed quite indifferent to his fate, but this was disquiet, not indifference. He needed something direct and palpitant to deal with, and the deer and the boar, the goshawk and the falcon, were able to meet his surface mood. Or were they? He gave no visible clue to his emotions.

Claude was occupied with her new baby, born in August. Alençon was mainly engaged with his mother's retiring to a convent. Françoise de Foix had begun to see the end, the "grief and martyrdom" that would come when she lost Francis, but neither Louise nor her daughter had any sympathy for her. They had seen her playing fast and loose with Francis. "When she was elevated into favour," they said in a quatrain, "she did not know how to appreciate her fortune."

An obscure demoralization seemed to overcome Francis. Buoyant by nature, he had gone to the Field of the Cloth of Gold in his effervescent spirit, full of the loyalty and courage, the faith and confidence, that his situation required. And now the world was insecure, if not inimical and faithless. He was in danger. He wanted someone to lean on. He turned to his mother and Marguerite.

Marguerite was not a statesman. Had she possessed the firm detachment of an Anne of France, had she been willing to disregard human impulse and drive to a solution, she could have offset her brother's defects. But this was Louise's rôle. Marguerite's whole concern was with the precious claims of human nature and the defencelessness her brother exhibited. If her desire for emotional satisfaction led her in the end to mysticism, it was mysticism that joined Boccaccio to Santa Caterina de Siena. It was mysticism wholly alive to the comedy of human behaviour. And that aliveness, that amazing catholicity, showed the capacity of heart as well as brain. She would have to accommodate within that heart her own hard-mouthed mother, her dreary husband, her drearier sister-in-law, the soldiers like Bonnivet, the priests like Briçonnet, men as varied as Rabelais and Calvin, women as varied as Châteaubriant and Francis's later mistress, Diane de Poitiers and Catherine de' Medici. She had Francis's children to include, the intelligentsia in all its oddity, hot-headed and hot-hearted Marot and his rivals, men who camped on her, men on the run. And while making a place within her heart for all these incompatible subjects, she still had to remain Marguerite de France, her brother's partisan, accomplice and even champion. A more tangible heritage might have been bequeathed by a hard-headed woman, but Marguerite's achievement was in that special domain that writes no documents. She wanted to sustain her brother. In her whole life, so far, there had been no complete emotion. Bonnivet had hurt her. Alençon she held at arm's length, and she had no children so far. The only man who really mattered to her was her brother. The precise nature of her feelings toward him could hardly be defined through the shimmering light in which he stood for her, but there was in her that yielding, that surrendering tenderness which almost demands immolation. He was, after all, toweringly masculine, this gallant brother of hers, whose courage had glamour for her and whose generosity melted her. It was not, of course, very correct to be absorbed in him, but Marguerite belonged to a generation that was above everything incorrect. Its religion was no longer the solid orthodoxy of old France, the unquestioning confidence, the blind fidelity, of the Annes and the Jeannes. That belonged to the fifteenth century and Marguerite was a child of the new century. Hers was a belief that had strayed from the acquiescence of her Bourbon cousins into a region somewhere between land and sea where the heart could swing out of itself into a radiant mist and there, by its passionate need to risk itself, find ultimate comprehension. Sincere, poignant, tremulous, she beheld her hero helpless without her, and her quivering eagerness of heart referred her, not to the Church, but to a God of Love beyond and outside the Church, a sublimity before which she was inculpated and through which she was redeemed. To add to all this moral and emotional turbulence came Francis's need to be sustained by her. She was older and wiser and subtler, and at the same time aching to be dependent. In this double need she bestowed on him the whole devotion of her sheltering personality, the full caress of her solicitude. Since he came to the throne, he had been a devoted brother. He had brought her husband forward. He had given her great wealth, assuring parlement that it was still the kingdom's, and he had kept her at his side, to comfort and delight him, an only sister that was his "mignonne."

While he flung himself into continuous amusement, unable to command his will, Marguerite went to Argentan in October, to see her mother-in-law, a gentle and loving elderly lady, give up all her worldly goods and go into a convent. For some reason, no doubt to help Francis, Marguerite was asking for her dot and accumulating all the money she could. In what state of mind she was, or in what state of mind he was, no one was likely to know. She was a loyal aunt to all his children, and the whole top of her life could be peopled by birthdays, christenings, teethings, mumps and measles. But underneath she could only have been passionately concerned with this cornered brother of hers, who could not find his way out.

Suddenly he seems to have made some extraordinary demand of her. If she loved him, she who gave him every indulgence, every irrevocable assurance, why could she not save him by proving her love. He asked some proof of it that brought her to her knees.

The year was coming to an end. With whatever urgency, in whatever form, Francis had appealed to his sister, she sat down to write him a letter that was meant to be burned. It was, perhaps, to answer a cry of despair, and to urge him to let her see him, to dissuade him. The letter is wilfully obscure, veiled and enigmatic. Its wording is ceremonial, as all letters to her King would always be ceremonial. But the woman palpitates in it as if her heart beat to suffocation.

"To the King, my Sovereign Lord,

"Sire, What it pleased you to write to me, that by persevering you would make me understand, has made me persevere and, moreover, made me hope that you would not leave your straight path to fly those who, for their chief happiness, wish to see you. Still, from bad to worse, let my intention be over-ruled, if you will never have need of the faithful and honest service that I have devoted and do devote to your happy Good Grace. And if the perfect imperfection of a hundred thousand faults makes you disdain my fealty, at least, Sire, do me enough honour and kindness not to add to my deplorable misery by demanding proof of surrender, there where you know me powerless without your help, as will witness the token [poem?] that I am sending you, not petitioning you to end my troubles and begin New Year unless it please you that I be in some small way what you are infinitely to me and shall be in my mind unceasingly. In awaiting the pleasure of being able to see you and talk with you, Sire, my desire for it forces me very humbly to beg you that, if it does not trouble you, to let me hear by this messenger, and I shall leave on the instant, pretending some other reason. And there is no weather so vile or road so bad that would not be made pleasant and agreeable by this. And you will deeply oblige me, and more than that, if you will bury my letters in the fire and my words in silence. Or else you will render:

> "*Worse than death my sorry fate*
> *Living in you, my sole reliance,*
> *This knowledge I do meditate,*
> *And cannot set you at defiance.*
> *And do I weakly supplicate,*
> *Your Grace will pardon a nescience*

"Worse than death.
And thus to you I dedicate
My will, my strength, my entire fate.
Take it, and my true alliance
Never shall end; or is my state
Worse than death."

"Your very humble and very obedient more than subject and servant."

The signature is cut away. But the writing is hers.

She seems to have written this highly tortuous letter as the messenger stood waiting for it, and she expected him to bring back word that she was to come to her brother. It seems to have been written in feverish haste. It is almost incoherent. Marguerite cannot conceal that she is in conflict with her brother. He wishes her to understand something that she cannot assent to, and she hopes that he will not abandon the straight road, the road that "they" want him to abandon. Who are "they"? Why have "they" a singular verb? Marguerite gives no clue. She speaks of her own "intention" being proscribed. And she speaks of her deplorable unhappiness, to which Francis will only add by demanding "expérience pour défaite." But in opposing her brother she does not oppose him out of disloyalty. She fills her letter with protestations of passionate loyalty. Her life, her will, her strength, her everything is his. She makes it clear that she is nothing without him. She is wax in his hands. She will fly to him at a word, and the worst winter roads will be joyous and easy if she is on her way to him. Her love for him is the love described in Thomas à Kempis, immolation in the will of the beloved.

What is at issue between them? It is impossible to be certain from the letter alone. All we see is this passionately devoted woman torn between the contradiction of Francis's unmentioned demand and her own infinite submission to him. He is her God, and yet his demand is resisted by her. Hence she suffers the agony of a division in her own soul, a division that is worse than death, a division in which she sides against herself with her sovereign lord at the very moment that she begs him not to press her to the sacrifice.

Anyone with imagination, studying this strange letter, must

wonder what Francis and Marguerite were really thinking of. Her letter is beyond any doubt of the most passionate character. And at the very moment that she is protesting her love for him, her complete surrender to his will, her absolute self-abnegation, she is also begging to be spared the proof of love that he asks for, and she is counselling him to follow the "straight path" as against those who want to undo him. She is ready to fly to him, at a word's notice, to "talk to him." She has no dread of an interview with him. On the contrary, she burns to have an interview with him, to discuss this very proposal in which he perseveres.

Could she be so eager to see him and talk to him, if he was proposing physical surrender to himself? It seems improbable. Her undoubted eagerness to see him points to a complete innocence as between herself and himself. Between herself and himself, "Ce n'est qu' ung cœur." That she has said to him in a rondeau, and her mother has also said it to him in another rondeau. Mother and daughter have exactly the same idiom with him, in fact, use the same extravagant protestations, the same passionate words. The mother says, "Ce n'est qu' ung cœur, ung vouloir, ung penser." Two souls with but a single thought, the eternal platitude of devotion, two hearts that beat as one. The question of incest between Francis and Louise of Savoy could possibly be raised as well. An interesting supposition. But Marguerite's love for Francis is illimitable, and it is this very unreserved devotion which makes her letter painfully intense. What has her brother asked of her? What proof? What service? What sacrifice?

No one can say. But if "they" are involved, the service and the sacrifice which he requires of her are no longer secretly personal. He wants political service and sacrifice. So much seems evident. He is trying to leave the path of righteousness, and Marguerite urges him, on his own account, not on her account, to resist "them."

What is the brother asking his devoted sister to do? To sacrifice herself in what way?

Possibly Bourbon is surmised a widower, and Francis sees that if Marguerite would marry him all would be well.

But Marguerite is married to Alençon? Yes, fruitlessly married. The marriage could be annulled. And then she and Bourbon could be united to save him.

The letter remains enigmatic. But those who think it points to incest forget the other shameful requests that can be made by a cornered prince.

44

Sometimes, when a man is so cornered, he has an accident. The New Year had come for Francis. He was at Romorantin. And he had three accidents.

In the first he escaped lightly. He rode on the frozen ground without proper horseshoes, and he was thrown.

Being twenty-seven years old and a King he might have been expected to have the deportment of a Dead March, but of course he had nothing of the kind. After the banquets of Christmas, with a savage hilarity that comes in certain moods, he wanted to risk his neck. And the second accident, in which he was hidden in a hamper that was set on fire, recalled the royal catastrophe in which, in another reign, a half a dozen had been burned to death in just this fashion. But he escaped, for the second time in the day. And still he wanted excitement.

At this stage he and his mignons nearly always had a sham battle, and it was less sham than battle. One side held a fortress against the other. The defenders armed themselves with snowballs, apples, potatoes, eggs. The attackers did the same. And the game was hot. Francis, wild as a madman, led the attackers against the fortress. He gained the door. One exuberant youth above saw that the day was lost unless he struck boldly, so he seized the first weapon handy, a log of firewood and crashed it down. It hit the King on the top of the head. He fell unconscious. In the appalling hush that ends such a game he was carried indoors. At first they thought him done for. Word leaped abroad that he was killed. They shaved his head to dress the wound, thus making short hair fashionable, and, after some days' anxiety, he began to mend. But for two months he was invalid at Romorantin. And, as Louise naïvely remarked, if anything had really happened to him, she was "femme perdue."

Who threw the log? Louise was revengeful, but Francis did not care to know. It was all in the game, he said. "I must take what comes if I want to play the fool!"

During those two months at Romorantin, nominally invalid, Francis prepared his war against Charles. As he convalesced, he applied his mind to the most artful subterfuge by which he could suddenly seize and throw his antagonist. Charles was embroiled in Germany with Luther, while a revolution had broken out in Spain. To take swift advantage of these disorders was the only way in which France, depleted in revenue, could snatch a decision.

And the schemes were ingenious. The first was worthy of Fleurange, the second of the Foix contingent. The lord of Sedan, a border lord of diabolic reputation, was to defy Charles and start the offensive on the Meuse. The French would equip him but the responsibility must be his own.

Navarre was to be the second objective. Lesparre, the brother of Lautrec and Lescun, was to lead a grand incursion into Navarre. And the French official policy would be to fold its arms and disown. This it must do since England was pledged to side against whichever nation first broke the peace.

Fleurange's father took his instructions from Francis in March, 1521. He went home aggressive. But Charles V welcomed the break. Evard, the future cardinal, stood by the Emperor against his brother. Nassau took the field and forced de la Marck to make submission. It was a speedy débâcle. Lesparre was equally inept. In spite of such unrelenting Basque opponents as Ignatius Loyola (the future Saint), he did cut through Navarre into the Spain of caballero and communero. But by arriving too late to help the rebels and by proclaiming himself their champion he brought on himself an inflamed caballero resentment. His paymasters had weakened his own side by peculation, so that his troops had no tenacity and no fidelity. He was crumpled up at Logroño, temporarily blinded and taken prisoner. And Navarre slipped from French hands for ever.

45

While Francis was organizing these offensives Charles was deep in his German education. In October he went to Aix to be crowned, and from there he went to Worms. It was at Worms, in March, 1521, that he was confronted with Martin Luther. There it was laid bare to the young Emperor that two prime working conceptions in Germany were no longer reconciled. He did not himself know German, any more than he knew Spanish, and the religion that Martin Luther was disrupting he conceived as a necessity of his Empire, a binder of princedoms. He was inflexibly anti-Lutheran.

Martin Luther, German on his lips, hunger in his soul, fire in his heart, could not repress the revolt of his nature. Little as he expressed it, there was something in him of the great nostalgia of the renaissance, the nostalgia for an individual life, a reconciliation between the sinful creature and the merciful Creator. He broke away from the circumscription of the parental system in which he had been slaving, and reached out to a horizon where the unsullied truth abides. This vision, which so many of the German princes chose to share, was for Charles a glaring fallacy. He saw Luther as a heretic against both Church and prince. Thus Germany became the arena of a struggle which wrenched its political standards from this or that theology. The sacraments became political banners. The doctrine of grace and the theory of transubstantiation became cornets and bugles. It announced a peculiarly bloodthirsty and wholeheartedly murderous squabble that would go on for some hundred years.

Erasmus had been watching it germinate since 1517. At first he sympathized with Luther. But in these months he had concluded that the outcome could only be bellicose and intolerant and, under brutal pressure from both sides, he became a non-combatant.

Even in 1520, while Charles V was heading toward Germany and the Diet of Worms, a tremendous tension had been generated. A condemnation and menace was issued by the Pope in May, while Luther, backed by Hutten and Sickingen, poured out pamphlets and defiances, inviting the German people to wash their hands in Roman blood. He wrote a powerful appeal to the German nobility. Frederick of Saxony rejected the Papal demands and in December, after Charles's arrival in Germany, Luther solemnly retorted to the pronouncements against him by publicly burning the Papal Bull. Aleandro, the nuncio, felt every confidence that Charles would prove a good Papist, but he reported from Worms that "all Germany was in a state of religious sedition, and nine-tenths of the people were adherents of Luther."

Hutten and Sickingen were a distinct menace to the young Emperor, but he had discreetly given Hutten a pension and seeing the attitude of the princes had reluctantly decided to give Luther a hearing.

This duel between the Habsburg and the excommunicated monk lacked nothing of the dramatic. Their first encounter was in a small hall, under a low ceiling, when Martin stood in front of the Emperor, moving his head in a queer rotary movement and mumbling a demand for postponement. It was granted. "This man," growled young Charles, "will never make me a Lutheran." But the next day, in a larger hall, and with a greater audience, incoherence yielded to a bold, strong utterance, first in Latin, and then in the people's German. Luther did not recant. His defiance rang clear. And when Charles would hear no more the rugged monk, his arm straight in the air with the gesture of a victorious landsknecht, walked out of the hall unflinchingly. What he had said rolled through the Germanies and reverberated in the Seven Hills.

The next day Charles stood up in his Diet with a single sheet of paper in his hand. In his own French, he read his own defiance, the bright Aleandro glistening at his side.

Thus Charles parted with Lutheranism and ranged himself with Rome.

Pope Leo was committed to France. But the imperial mandate was now essential to his campaign against Luther. Under the table, so to speak, he grasped Charles's hand. Charles promised to recognize his claim to Naples. And, since he also pledged himself to capture Parma and Piacenza for the Medici and to restore Francesco Sforza to Milan, the Pope made common cause with him to oust the French from Lombardy.

Charles could only thank God that the failures of Sedan and Lesparre should be visited on Francis just when he was losing the Pope and about to suffer Wolsey as arbiter.

"O God," he exclaimed, "I praise Thee that this war has not been begun by me, and that this King of France seeks to make me greater than I am! Thanks be to Thee always that Thou hast given me the means to defend myself. I hope shortly either I shall be a poor Emperor or he a poor King of France."

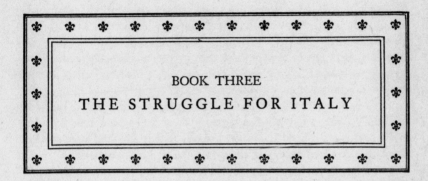

BOOK THREE

THE STRUGGLE FOR ITALY

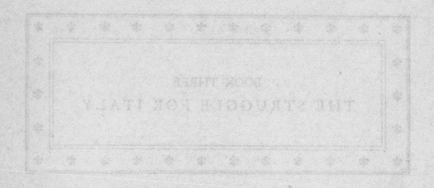

❖ ❖ ❖ ❖ ❖ ❖ ❖ ❖ ❖ ❖ ❖ ❖ ❖

THE STRUGGLE FOR ITALY

Now Francis was in for it. It would be a European War, lasting four years. France would be "encircled." It would receive what it had invited, in the person of its King.

It was almost a nightmare for the young King and his mother, at the beginning of the crisis. Enemies rolled up, and the means by which they could be combated were lacking. If the Emperor had been alone, it would have been easy, he could have been withstood. But Pope Leo went over to the side of the Emperor. England went over to the side of the Emperor. Francis saw himself cornered. The conflagration ran round the frontiers, from Flanders down to Italy and over to Spain. Everywhere, before it would finish, the test of war would be applied to France—in France itself, up to the environs of Paris, hard against the walls of Marseille. But these foreign invasions would scarcely be so injurious as the fiscal expedients that had to be practised within, expedients which grew out of the very nature of Francis's sovereignty.

Young as he was, only twenty-seven when the war began, he should have been sufficiently experienced and responsible to judge the cost of the course he was pursuing. A good general picks his battleground not only for victory but for retreat. He does not stake everything on a single stroke. He does not say "after me the funeral." But in actual fact Francis was neither experienced nor responsible. He had been so indulged by the women who loved him, so favoured by fortune, so lulled by the sirens, that he never came down to the hard facts of his struggle for Italy, or made true estimate for the war he had invited.

He started with his object: he wanted Milan. Nothing is so admirably stimulating as the goal of an ambition, and Francis had this definite one: he wanted it as a soldier and as dynast. But such an ambition costs a price. There would be an intangible price that could be passed on to his children and his grandchildren—the dreadful price in blood that would have to be paid by non-combatants, in broken bodies and broken lives, the scrapping of homes, the loss of creative industry. These things, done in the name of "government," would ferment intolerable difficulties for a "government" that had gouged the people. But Francis could ignore remote consequences. What he could not ignore, what would hang him over the brink of ruin, was the immediate cost of war. Ambition would not ask of him his state of soul. The black-browed goddess does not require "soul" of the men she urges to exceed themselves. But ambition would demand: what generals have you chosen? How do you propose to sustain your people's morale? Are you healthy? What money have you? If you play for great stakes, can you dig into your pouches? If the price is blood, can you spurt blood? Are you truly gallant?

The answer during this four-years' European War would be anything but fluent.

Francis's generals would be his younger men, Lautrec and Bonnivet. These were not chosen because they were of the first eminence as soldiers, but because they suited their facile master. One was the brother of his mistress, the other his boon companion. He could count on them to serve his purposes, just as Henry VIII could count on Suffolk to serve his purposes. They were, in fact, the natural spawn of his absolutism. Bourbon was a greater soldier than either of them, as would be proved in the field, but Bourbon was audacious enough to lift his head in the presence of Francis, and he soon was to be marked down, by very reason of wealth and eminence.

Impoverishment would force Francis to take perilous steps within the next few years. To put Bourbon in the wrong, his greatest vassal, would be no less a temptation to him than to denude Semblançay and the other bourgeois treasurers whom he had elevated on coming to the throne. These two sacrifices, Bourbon and Semblançay, would be the most shameless of his career. His mother would countenance and even encourage him. Her Cæsar had proved incapable of dull housekeeping and was driven to recoup himself by ugly deeds. She assented. Bourbon and Semblançay were war casualties. They made the mistake of being both rich and politically objectionable. It was a mistake that Buckingham and Cromwell made in England.

And the price might have seemed reasonable. Had the technique of war remained gentlemanly and amateurish in Italy, Francis might have triumphed again on the buoyant terms of Marignano. But Mary Tudor's husband as general in the north would be an easier nut to crack than Vittoria Colonna's husband in the south. This Spanish Italian soldier, Pescara, one of the best soldiers Charles V ever had, would test the metal of Lautrec and Bonnivet. Pescara would serve under the sagacious Prospero Colonna, if he could have been said to serve under any one. And with him would be the one formidable soldier the Medici ever produced, Giovanni de' Medici, a true condottiere. They would later take opposite sides, Pescara and Giovanni of the Black Bands, but they stood for a new type of soldiering in Italy that surpassed the blunt-minded art of Lautrec or the flashy art of Bonnivet.

Yet Lautrec and Bonnivet should not be maligned: they were both to suffer from lack of support. They led expeditionary forces that were pampered to begin with, and starved in the end.

Francis had his own troubles, trying to support his generals. Money was hard to come by. He had lived beyond his means. And in order to procure money he had to face other troubles. The Reformation was in full swing in Germany, while Pope Leo and Pope Adrian were to make things difficult for France. It was thus necessary for him to toy with theology.

So much for his handicaps. A less defined handicap may be summed up in a word. It was now said in Europe that Francis was suffering from syphilis. Between 1521 and 1525 there are certain references to his state of health which might support this assumption, and the abscess that broke under dramatic circumstances in 1526 might corroborate it. But it remains a surmise. Whether the long confinement at the beginning of 1521 was due to his Christmas accident, or whether it was due to the beginning of the dire malady then so widespread, cannot be plainly known. It cannot be positively asserted, "Francis now had syphilis."

2

Once he came back into the open, recovered from his wound, Francis was much his old self. He had not left everything to the raids by Fleurange's father and Lautrec's brother. He went building ships, collecting troops, consulting his captains. By the time de la Marck had failed and there was truce in the Ardennes, Francis was preparing for war on the grand scale. All the nobles who had rallied for Marignano were once more ordered to recruit, but this time there would have to be three armies instead of one. Lautrec would wage war in Lombardy. Bonnivet would carry war into Spain. Francis himself would meet invasion from the east. It was the full sequel to the Imperial Election.

It was more than that. This war, which would last Francis's lifetime, would be waged in terms of church, as well as state. Out of it would come the subjection of Italy, the incursions of Luther, the bitter fruit of Calvinism, the Council of Trent. Red Indians would dig silver for it out of the mines of Potosí. The Turk would join hands with Francis in it. The Netherlands would be shaped by it. And religious wars would be fomented by that sallow youth who had just had his leg smashed at Pampeluna, that youth on a mule who was giving up his light loves and aching for crusade, Ignatius Loyola. War and asceticism, the twin extravagances: and no one to laugh at them, no one except a Frenchman called Rabelais who still was reading Greek, until his books would be snatched from him by the Sorbonne, as part of war dementia.

3

A shrewd young Englishman, William Fitzwilliam, could report that war was afoot by putting bits of information together. Francis had resumed hunting in the spring, and he chatted about hunting with Fitzwilliam.

"By the faith of a gentleman," he exclaimed (a foy day gentelhommes, as Fitzwilliam spelled it), "no man living I love better than Henry." Henry was his brother, and he would like to see his brother again. He would like a "new, secret, loving and familiar interview."

Such cordiality meant that Francis was in need of England. He was soon admonished from England that he need not break the peace. He vigorously retorted by calling the Emperor aggressive; and he doubled his friendliness.

Underneath, however, there was the grim reality: he had no money. Not until war was declared could he anticipate the taille for 1522, yet Navarre, Milan, the Swiss required actual cash. He suffered. Acutely he suffered.

It was probably the worst period that Louise had yet endured, but with confident exigence she turned to the treasurer. His master was in need, she told Semblançay. I count on you, she said. Without you, he must suffer. "Do as the one who, in such an extremity, is my last hope."

The old treasurer did not hesitate. He sent the King everything he controlled, the Naples fund of 300,000 crowns, Louise's savings, 107,000 livres. Two millions were needed, and if they were under his hand he would have produced them.

Francis knew that Burgundy was Charles V's political goal. He established himself at Dijon. There he proceeded to put the Burgundians through the wringer.

"Here be the greatest shift made for money that hath been seen," Fitzwilliam wrote home, "for the King borrows of every man that hath any, and if any man refuse to lend he shall be so punished that all other shall take ensample of him." Every fiscal expedient was used. "A man would pity to see how the duchy of Burgundy is pilled." And Fitzwilliam was not given to pity. "They eat up all they have, to their shirts."

It surprised Fitzwilliam to detect French nervousness. He "never saw men more afraid of war than they be, nor gladder they be when they hear any comfort." And they needed comfort from an

Englishman, since, for some strange reason, "they have the King our Master in doubt."

It was, in fact, a crisis in which, for all his insouciance, Francis had reason to be afraid. What if England went in with the Emperor? Before he was prepared?

4

At this crucial moment, with enemies and debts pressing on him from every side, Francis received startling news. Suzanne de Bourbon was dead, the wife of the Constable, Charles de Bourbon.

It was not unexpected but it was of the gravest political import. For five years the Bourbons had been estranged from the throne. Now, with Suzanne's elimination, would come a trial of strength.

The fate of the Bourbonnais had hung on her existence. So long as Suzanne might have children (and she bore not only a son but twins) there could be no excuse for opening up the intricacies of succession. But Suzanne's children had no stamina. Her own body was malformed. Long before she followed them to the grave her sad end was in sight.

The death of this ailing woman, the richest heiress in France, now left Bourbon a childless widower. On this fact hinged two serious issues; the issue of his personal succession to the Bourbonnais; the issue of his re-marriage.

It seemed hardly possible that the first nobleman in France could, at this juncture, contemplate marrying into the Imperial family. Charles V was actually at war with France. An alliance with him would stab France in the back. Yet already Bourbon's re-marriage had been discussed while Suzanne was dying, and the bride suggested for him was Eleanor of Portugal, Charles V's elder sister. Such was the alarming project credited to Charles de Bourbon.

One evening after his return from the Field of the Cloth of Gold, it was soon revealed, Bourbon was walking with a friend in the garden of Moulins. The hour was pensive, and he discussed his possible re-marriage. It was not callous. Suzanne had not been of "those where one could take much pleasure," but Bourbon had been good. "Honestly and modestly" he had comported himself. Yet his fragile wife was visibly failing, and he mused aloud. He had been in treaty with the Emperor about his holdings in Naples, and he knew he could have the Emperor's sister Eleanor. His mind was brooding on the future of Bourbon, made dark by Louise's hostility.

If the duke were to make an imperial marriage, its consequences inside France would be incalculable. But Bourbon was too outraged to calculate them. He had that feudal heat which makes a secessionist. Francis had belittled him. He had never appointed him at the head of great missions or embassies. Bonnivet, an upstart, was constantly preferred to him. He had not been merely held at arm's length: he had been misunderstood; he had been cheated.

Anne of France held her fair regions without any favour of the Angoulêmes. In those regions the password was reverence. Moulins was a treasure house of beautiful things, and the Bourbonnais revolved in contentment. Anne of France's subjects had given her son-in-law an initial 100,000 livres with tears of gratitude. And when he had needed 80,000 livres to pay his expenses in the Genoa campaign, or 100,000 livres for his part at Agnadello, these well-treated subjects secreted with alacrity. All was gentle virtue and benignity in the duchy of Bourbon. Bourbon was faithful as a territorial lord, impeccable as a husband, tenderly dutiful as a son-in-law, an obedient son of the Church. And to see himself tamely stripped of his rights would not be in the range of human tolerance. His hand flew instinctively to his sword. He was not merely a lord of France but a vassal of the Empire.

At the same time, inflexible by pose, he was really hesitant and bewildered. To clear his title to the Bourbon inheritance Anne of France would have to acknowledge him as the surviving male heir. She would, in reality, have to abdicate. To admit her own elimination, before Suzanne died, would alone have cleared Bourbon's heritage. But the great lady could never do it of herself, and no one in her duchy could pluck up courage to tell her to do it. By maintaining her false title to the last, even while making Bourbon her heir, she was opening the way to endless disputation. That was the flaw in his position, certain to cause trouble when Suzanne disappeared.

By right the Bourbon inheritance should come to him. When

Auvergne was alienated from the Crown in 1400, by royal consent, the King had exacted that all the Bourbon possessions should revert to the Crown in case the male line became extinct. To this the Bourbons had willingly agreed. And it was this inexorable fact that had always confronted Anne of France as a married woman. Her husband was the last male of the elder branch. The younger branch of the family, the Montpensiers, was Bourbon's. Anne and her elderly husband should have had a son to keep the inheritance; they only had Suzanne.

Since the original arrangement with the Crown in 1400 there had of course been many deals inside the family, but these revisions, though they might give arguing points to lawyers, did not, and could not, touch the unimpaired claim that Bourbon had to the original inheritance. He was, in fact, allowed to offer homage to Louis XII, but rather than oust Anne of France, it seemed simpler not to challenge her but to merge all the Bourbon rights in a unit created by marrying Suzanne. So Charles de Montpensier became Charles de Bourbon.

But with the death of his wife, the Crown could plausibly contest the inheritance. Both Louise and Francis, the two persons most concerned, could put forward claims to the Bourbonnais. Louise was the daughter of Marguerite de Bourbon. She could assert a claim on female lines, while Francis could contend that the younger branch were not male heirs as devised in 1400; hence the original inheritance must revert to the Crown. Thus Louise and Francis would wholly disagree as between themselves, and yet would be in perfect accord that the Bourbonnais should be wrested from Bourbon.

Bourbon in France was no less prominent than Buckingham in England. But Buckingham had been violently indiscreet, he had uttered words of treason, and he was now being executed. Bourbon so far had made no overt act. His imperial marriage was only mused in a garden. He was still Constable.

Louise of Savoy, at her wits' end to get money, made the first move. A kinsman went to Bourbon with the intimation that Louise would marry him.

It is a Burgundian chronicler attached to the Croy family who narrates the scene. Presumably Bourbon had told Beaurain, and

Beaurain told his family chronicler. "When the Duke heard these tidings," Maquerieau reports, "for a long time he spake no word, but stood looking at the noble messenger, his brother-in-arms. And at length he said to him, 'Is it an act worthy of our friendship to bring me the offer of such a woman, the worst woman in the realm, the dread of all nations?' "

He did not spare Louise. Then he vehemently added, "I would not do this thing, no, not for the whole of Christendom."

The chronicler, who believes in satisfying human curiosity, tells how Louise received this answer, even to the rending of her garments. "The matter shall not rest here," she exclaimed, "for by the Creator of souls his words shall cost him dear." And she turned to Francis, "my son, you shall avenge me."

Maquerieau perhaps drew on his imagination, but Louise's offer was promptly reported abroad. Henry VIII gave the news to Charles V's ambassador. "There has been much discontent between the King Francis and the said Bourbon, since he has refused to marry Madame the Regent, who loves him very much."

The death of Suzanne came when Francis was in straits. Duprat was an Auvergnat. He saw at once the plausible case that could be urged against Bourbon's vast heritage. He was not slow to counsel the use of his own excellent tool, the parlement.

5

While Francis and his mother addressed themselves to despoiling Bourbon, the third member of the Trinity had nobler preoccupations. Marguerite was at this period in the deepest spiritual distress. So far, in her young life, she had found a supreme outlet in her devotion to her brother. As King she exalted him, and she loved him as errant man. She was two years older, so that while the Salic law made him her King, those two years bestowed him on her, in all the superiority of sex and rank and destiny. But the impulse that had driven them together could not satisfy a nature so much richer in human feeling than her brother's. Marguerite had reached a crisis in which she demanded the meaning of life. She reacted against her own former frivolity. She did not condemn Francis. She condemned herself. She blamed herself in relation to

her husband, to whom she now dutifully turned, and she yearned
for the only help strong enough to support her, the consolation of
religion. She needed a guide who could open gates to welcome the
self-accused, admitting her remorse without cutting off her love,
taking her town while leaving her the citadel.

Semblançay had nephews in the Church, the Briçonnets. One
was an abbé: another was bishop of Nîmes: another, bishop of
Meaux. They were of the family that had given Charles VIII his
supple counsellor. The one most in view, Guillaume, the bishop
of Meaux, was a soulful churchman who had ideas about reform,
and when Luther was facing Charles V the bishop of Meaux seems
to have come in touch with Marguerite, through his uncle
Semblançay. Marguerite sought in him her spiritual father, while
the bishop, in turn, wanted her to sponsor his rose-water reformation.

He imagined a French variant of the German revolution.

The significance of Luther had been brought home to all Europe
when he was formally excommunicated by the Pope. Nothing
could have done more to arouse curiosity—a simple monk denounced by a papal bull—and Luther rose to the occasion by pouring out pamphlet after pamphlet, the full-blooded defiance of an
institution with which every country in Europe had profound
reasons for being dissatisfied. His written word took the magic
wings of the printing press. Bales and bundles of his books flooded
the intellectual centres throughout Europe. They were carried
swiftly into France, from Lyon to Paris. A young noble from
Picardy, by name Louis Berquin, translated his most telling pamphlets into French. It was a new voice in Europe, a loud alarm
bell that woke up Louvain and Cologne, that fluttered St. Paul's
in London, stirred Henry VIII to royal anger, made the Sorbonne
growl incoherently and then rush to denounce the heretic who had
so foolishly supposed that the "liberty" of Gallicanism meant liberty of thinking.

Marguerite was not long in discovering the significance of
Luther. He was more than a theologian, he was a political factor
of the first importance. At the moment when Charles V and Leo X
were uniting against Francis, Luther was not only defying the
Emperor but breaking with Leo X and arousing the animosity of

Henry VIII. His was a moral offensive of the kind that at once
attracts and repels the astute: good because it is subversive, to be
watched with malicious sympathy but advocated with care.

Marguerite was genuinely attracted by his theology, but how
to use this explosive without injuring Francis? Francis's anger
with the Medici Pope flamed out in July, when Leo went over to
Charles. To reform the French Church from the inside, orienting
it by the Bible rather than by the papacy without at the same time
following Luther so far as to break with the papacy, would put
the strongest pressure on Rome while avoiding the vociferate
threats of excommunication.

Between 1521 and 1523 there suddenly began, and equally suddenly ended, this ardent "reform" activity in France. It had nothing to do with Luther himself. And it was touched with Marguerite's sincerity.

Like all variants on revolution, it was to be educational. It was
to be gradual. It was to be gentle. Light without heat. It was to
take the high explosives and work them into safety matches, thus
brightening the path back to primitive Christianity. And therefore
the emphasis of religion must be less on sin than on love, less on
the world than on the other world, less ritualistic than mystical.

Marguerite was precisely in the state of soul where she sought
this guidance from a priest. A princess in distress, she turned from
the sordid and squalid institution around her to the Kingdom of
Heaven within herself to which Guillaume Briçonnet had the keys.
She had faith in him, and a strained, pleading, wistful need of his
co-operation. The more Charles V, Leo X and Henry VIII combined against France, the more she desired to see religion become
evangelical. And when Briçonnet appealed to a conspicuous
humanist who was all religious, Lefèvre d'Etaples, Marguerite was
no less ready to welcome so sweet and serene a Christian. A tinge
of neoplatonism did not dismay her. She was exalted at the thought
of a great change in the French Church which, beginning at
Meaux, would be carried by trained preachers through every
diocese. Briçonnet saw the immense possibilities of this reform, and,
in between the lines of his rhapsodical letters to Marguerite, he
kept urging her to secure the practical help of her brother.

The great enemy of the reform, the Sorbonne (the theological faculty of the University), would think twice before it smote Francis directly.

Francis was not precisely a mystic. He put his gentlemanly impression of Luther very succinctly when he termed him a "triste personnage." But this "triste personnage" had transferred ecclesiastical authority from the Vatican to the Bible, and the Bible had become practical politics. Francis could appreciate the utility of making evangelism a royal concern. So very soon he and his formidable mother were joining Marguerite in singing psalms, and in listening to radical sermons. This would tell Rome that Francis could not be taken for granted.

The Bishop of Meaux was richly encouraged. He began preaching on quasi-Lutheran lines. The poor people in his diocese seized on the evangel with hungry appreciation. A number of young priests, under black looks from the Franciscans, flocked to the Cathedral at Meaux. The word began to spread. And Lefèvre d'Etaples, a fragile old man of pure spirit, worked with feverish delight at his commentaries and his Bible. All this took place within twenty miles of Paris, while Béda of the Sorbonne boiled with the rage of a chained watchdog.

A Dauphinois who could match the ferocious Béda, one Farel, had been attracted to Meaux. He was no temporizer. But the French movement from the start was wholly subordinate to the King. Briçonnet did not attack the Sorbonne: he strove, under the royal wing, to edge forward the news of the gospel. This was an apostolate that bore the same relation to Luther that a company union does to the class struggle. And the moment the venerable Semblançay got into trouble with his royal masters, the Sorbonne struck hard and there was no more of the mystical Briçonnet.

6

But Marguerite was not content to guide religious reform at the outset of the war. She and Louise were active at court. They saw Wolsey arrive in August for the conference of Calais, and they watched, through Duprat, the sham meditation from August to November.

This conference was Wolsey's bid for the papacy. He did not

know that the Holy Ghost was to inspire the choice of an honest man, the son of a carpenter, before going for ever Italian. He eagerly looked to Charles to secure the tiara for him, and when Charles called him to Bruges, saying, "You and I will do more in a day than my ambassadors will do in a month," the great arbiter ("a marvellous busybody and detestably arrogant") jogged over from Calais in all splendour. Charles and he struck their bargain, even discussing the partition of France. Wolsey found him "right cold and temperate in speech, with assured manner, couching his words right well, and to good purpose when he doth speak." The Cardinal then returned to renew his mediation at Calais, which was winnowing the wind. Henry VIII was fully committed to the Emperor.

The fighting on the east did not abate during the conference. Once Mouzon was captured by the Imperials, the war would press on to Mézières. Bayard would be a hero in the siege and Montmorency of "grand cœur." But meanwhile unfortified Ardres would be razed by the Imperials, and Tournai would be attacked. Francis himself departed for the army.

Already in July Marguerite had made friends with Fitzwilliam, the new English ambassador, and her talks with him were faithfully recounted.

"A strange thing," she said to him, "the House of France hath ever used a plain way without dissimulation," not of course referring to de la Marck, "and yet all princes are glad to hear of their loss!"

"The King my master," Fitzwilliam answered gallantly, "is not glad of the loss or dishonour of France."

"If so, there is one," Marguerite said laughing. "But no more!"

By September, however, the war was growing fierce, and Marguerite did not hide her vehement convictions.

"The King is now departed towards his journey," she said to him, on hearing of Ardres, "and I doubt not, by God's help, but he shall have good speed, for he goeth upon a good quarrel and deals justly with every prince, and yet all princes go about to deceive him!"

Fitzwilliam, looking the lady in the eye, observed, "My master is in the number of 'all princes,' but I trust you think he goeth not 'about to deceive him.'"

Marguerite did not recede. "See you not how the Cardinal is ever treating of peace almost to the day of battle? Our enemies come still upon us, and Ardres, which the King forbode to fortify at your master's request, Englishmen have now been present at the winning through, and helped to raze it. What say ye to that? And as for trust, that is past. The King will make himself strong, and trust in God."

Fitzwilliam was a "young man in years and choleric in complexion." He was not accustomed to stand argument from a woman. "As for the treaty," he coldly hit back, "my Lord Cardinal hath gone about in the name of my master, Madame. I made request to the King your brother for the same in the King my master's behalf, afore any war was begun, and at that time the Emperor was content and the King your brother would not be contented. And there is no *man* that shall say and prove it that either my master's or my Lord Cardinal's grace drives the time on so long, to do the King your brother any displeasure. The King my master is no dissimuler! No prince living——"

Marguerite recognized the tone, so at once began to "speak fair." She reckoned on Henry, she said, and would do so till she saw the contrary. But once she saw it, she would never trust man after.

And as they spoke Fitzwilliam was shrewd enough to catch sight of Louise. "This is a thing devised by my lady," he reported, "for she stood so nigh she heard every word."

7

Francis and the young Emperor were now actually at war. Neither was ready for it. Each of them sustained the appropriate manly and arrogant tone, but while their armies grappled on the Bidassoa, on the Adda and on the Meuse, the significant combat was being waged at Calais. Here three very able men, all to bear the title of cardinal, were arguing with pungency and heat.

Wolsey was the loud-voiced referee. Duprat had succeeded Boisy, and Mercurio Gattinara was successor to Chièvres who had recently died, befriending Charles by leaving 800,000 ducats available. Had Wolsey been honest, Duprat and Gattinara might have come closer to agreement, but since Wolsey was secretly pledged to be imperial Gattinara pushed his master's claim to Burgundy, one of those plausible and impossible demands that turn a conference into trench warfare. This Wolsey desired. He prolonged delays and dwelt on grievances, though fearful lest the Emperor should win too quickly and so dispense with England.

Francis's hopes of winning quickly had faded. He now considered peace, but he was forced to repulse Nassau and Sickingen, and came north with a grand army, along the Meuse.

On the eve of his departure for the front one person was certainly consumed with anxiety. That was Marguerite. She could not bear to think of her brother in danger. She wanted him to be a conqueror, since he alone was worthy to be a conqueror, but to have him risk his life was more than she could bear. She let him go, but her heart followed him, and she only lived to hear good news.

Marguerite's feelings were of an intensity. It was as though the rest of the world saw him from outside and she alone from the inside. The dull window they gazed on was, for her, luminous and alive. She yearned over him with the tenderness of Jacob for Joseph, of Magdalene for her Saviour. There was no boundary between this feeling she expressed and her religious emotion. She was consumed in a flame that his danger drove into white heat. He was, more than brother, more than friend, more than child. He was her ruler, her king, her Everything.

Into a long poem she poured her burning feelings, and they mounted into an almost intolerable desire to carry him through the dangers that surrounded him.

He was too occupied with his war to answer her ardour. All the action on the Meuse tended to shift north, where the Imperials had long been besieging Tournai. Francis, advancing from Reims with a superior army, soon avenged the capture of Mouzon. Bayard's glorious defence of Mézières was vindicated. "God has shown Himself a good Frenchman," exulted Louise. The Imperials withdrew, while Landrecies was also evacuated. The French themselves destroyed Bapaume. It was already October, and the two armies converged on Valenciennes, in the neighbourhood of Tournai. About 12,000 landsknechts were advancing from the east, with Charles himself in command, when Francis, who had up to 26,000 foot, was able to cross the river at Valenciennes before an attack could be delivered. He had given the vanguard to Alençon, instead of to Bourbon, and he himself commanded the "battle," keeping Bourbon close at his side. But on the morning of October 22 there was thick fog, and the forces of the enemy could not be estimated. Francis's captains, including Bourbon, hotly urged him to fight. He hesitated. And before he could change his mind Charles was in retreat. Heavy rains soon fell, to make further campaigning impossible.

"God delivered the enemy into our hands," lamented du Bellay, "and we would not accept it." But, at this moment, Francis was deliberating "un accord" or "une paix," and possibly he feared to stake his fortune on a battle. Charles's retreat seemed shameful enough. He asked for no more. And Marguerite's Te Deum was a transport of joy, a leap from hell to heaven. "Car mon Roy est vivant."

The prospects of peace, strangely enough, were injured by Bonnivet. He had won a triumph. His advance on Fuenterrabia was a series of zigzags and feints, highly characteristic, but at last he crossed the Bidassoa and eventually made an audacious attack and gained the fortress. It was his highest military achievement, mettlesome and swift. If the English had their foothold at Calais, the French now had as spectacular a foothold in the north-west of Spain.

Francis thereupon hardened his peace demands, but it was too soon! Lautrec was losing to Pope Leo.

Pope Leo combined the prince and the priest. Like any prince, he went to mass, and he learned the idiom of his office, but he encased the Pope's toe in hunting boots. He had flooded Rome with Florentines, and young artists in velvet slippers flaunted in the streets. He hunted and banqueted, flung away millions of ducats while permitting jobbery and place-seekers, and laughed with equable mirth through the witticism of his court, the antics of his clowns, the tartness of his poets. He sought an art in curves, leaving Michael Angelo at Carrara while Raphael mellowed his line. And yet, through this facility and levity, there swelled a strain of gross burlesque fleering obscene shapes behind normal instincts, revenging itself by grimace on decencies that no one held sincere. Yet the rich profusion of sensations that glutted Leo's life could sober when Tuscany was disputed. Francis had long angered him, and in July he gladly committed himself to the Emperor. Perhaps he felt that Luther and the Sultan could keep the Emperor from overpowering Italy. In any event the French goaded him in Lombardy, in Ferrara, in Urbino. He now tensed his will and showed cold resolution. He had revolted under the political usury of the French.

And he had revolted at just the right moment. Lautrec had said he would leave nothing of the Pope but his ears. And then came one French reverse after another. Faced by such admirable soldiers as Pescara, Antonio de Leyva, Giovanni de' Medici, with Prospero Colonna in command, Lautrec had turned out to be at once rash and hesitant. He asked for money. He needed money. He cried for it, and none arrived. Uncertain of his resources, he continually delayed and fumbled. Driven back on Milan, the "exiles" so stirred up the disaffected city that he dared not remain. The Imperial forces advanced on him. He abandoned Milan. Thus, in November 1521, the triumph of Marignano was cancelled.

With this came the fall of Tournai, after a siege of five months. And Wolsey wound up the hollow conference of Calais.

Francis went into winter quarters. The outlook was black. But suddenly a brilliant consolation flashed into his heart: Pope Leo was dead. In the midst of the Pope's rejoicing over Lautrec's defeat, in his delight at regaining the Parma that Francis had obstinately refused him, he expanded in his lavish mood, the windows restlessly opened, the damp night inhaled, his fat body perspiring. He returned to Rome from his hunting lodge with something like incipient pneumonia. Men said malaria and men said poison, but the truth seemed to be congestion following a chill. He seemed to gain ground and everyone felt assured but in the night of December 1st he flamed into fever. Fra Mariano, the glutton who so often had childishly amused him, was his last companion on earth. As the appropriate ministers were being summoned, the frightened buffoon attended him. He was unconscious, or dead, by the time the chaplains hurried in.

8

The loss of Milan was a heavy blow to Francis. It made him
want to throw everything on one side, to raise an army himself, and
cross the Alps for another Marignano. He sent René of Savoy to
raise 16,000 Swiss. But his own impetuousness, which had enabled
him to reverse the disasters of Louis XII at the beginning of his
reign, and which resentment and anger still could arouse in him,
was blurred by the knowledge that he could do nothing, move
nowhere, without dragging a ball and chain after him. He had
scorned the parsimony of Louis XII but the penury of the last few
months was desperate. He had lost Milan. He was threatened in
Picardy. He distrusted the English. And he was at his wits' end
for money.

There was a bright side to his news: he could count on Soderini
and other Italians to block the election of Giulio de' Medici as
Pope. He could count on della Rovere to regain Urbino. There
would be a new deal in Italy. He took heart. He warmly encouraged Lescun to expect the reinforcements he was arranging
for Lautrec. He engaged himself to enliven the Venetians.

His promises ignored the dearth of money. He racked his brains,
and Duprat and his mother racked their brains, to discover the
means that would enable him to renew the war.

To meet difficulties by sketching out the best solutions is notoriously exhausting, and after great efforts like these Francis had to
refresh himself. He diverted himself in hunting as often as he
could, but he was on the eve of a supreme struggle and incessantly
occupied. He went to le Havre to inspect his marvellous new ship.
He gave a little of his attention to Marguerite and her theologians.
He disdained the latest inspiration of the Holy Ghost, the election
of the Emperor's tutor to the Papacy. He would not call him
Adrian VI. He called him the Cardinal of Tortosa. He planned,
however, to have Soderini as close to the Dutchman as possible, and
he did his best to make a fresh treaty with Henry VIII. Francis
was much too alive to his danger not to shape his conduct for prolonged hostilities.

Yet his mind was oscillating with his fortune. At one moment
he announced he was joining Lautrec in Italy. Yet at the same

moment he was asking Venice to lend Lautrec as little as 25,000 crowns. Then the Imperial threat, "we are firmly resolved to obtain supremacy in Burgundy," made him alive to his responsibilities at home. Louise saw the dire complications of war. She appealed to Margaret of Austria and courted her by sending her fifty carts of good wine. Charles V, however, was going to England. Towards the end of May, Wolsey was seizing the Venetian galleys as a direct method of applying political pressure to a weaker power, and Henry and Charles were soon embracing each other for the space of two "miserere." By June Wolsey was giving a banquet. Forgetting Charles's broken promise to make him Pope, forgetting his own broken promise of "universal peace," he raised his voice in the verve of a new war, "Francis must be exterminated!"

9

Lautrec, in the meantime, was making a brave effort to recover Milan. He had retained a ring of towns about fifty miles from Milan, beyond the Adda and the Po, and the citadel was still impregnably French. His object was either to dislodge Prospero Colonna from Milan itself, co-operating with the citadel, or else secure a powerful foothold within striking radius.

Prospero Colonna had excellent lieutenants and a high degree of soldierly resolution. He had cut off the citadel by deep trenches and gun emplacements, so that when Lautrec advanced to the walls he could establish no connection. This failure in direct assault reduced the French to long-term manœuvres with short-pay mercenaries. Anne de Montmorency took Novara from Toriello who was reported as having opened his French prisoners' bellies to fill them with oats for famished horses—living horse-racks. Montmorency made savage reprisals, in the fond hope of terrorising the Spanish. But the campaign drew on in sodden marches that circled Milan. Lautrec prowled around, harassed and restless, a toreador to Prospero Colonna's bull. At last the bull advanced to Bicocca, a well-chosen hunting ground, where the French cavalry could not be deployed, and it was in this position that Lautrec's Swiss contingents demanded to join issue, sick of uncertainty, slow pay and bad weather.

They advanced against George von Frundsberg's landsknechts, Pescara's Spaniards and Colonna's Italians. The fight was cruel. The artillery slew the Swiss in their mad rush against steep ramparts, with Pescara enfilading them from cornfields. Anne de Montmorency, in the front rank with the Swiss, received scores of wounds. Lescun made headway on the other side, but by the time that the Swiss leaders were killed, with 3,000 of their men, the back of their aggressiveness was broken. The Venetians held aloof. Lautrec raged and pleaded for a renewal of the attack, but the Swiss were as stubborn one way as the other. Escorted to the foothills, they took home to the cantons the miserable story of Bicocca, where the pikemen smashed in vain against firearms. This defeat was final for Lautrec. He withdrew the remnants of his forces and crossed the Alps to Lyon.

10

Francis was at Lyon when Lautrec arrived in disguise. The defeated general was coming to defend himself.

A few years before, Lautrec needed no defence. He had displaced Bourbon as governor of Milan and superseded Trivulzio. He had squeezed the inhabitants for wealth and lavished money on ceremonial. The Venetians, the shrewdest courtiers in Europe, had thought well of giving him a single ruby worth 3,100 ducats, two massive gold basins, handsome Oriental carpets, table covers, perfumes, scents, and a picture by Titian. That was in 1516. But since then his own fortunes, his sister's and his brother's, had swiftly declined, and the time had come for explanations.

They would not be humble. One glance at Lautrec disclosed his character. He was short, square-cut, powerfully built, with the red signature of Ravenna on his welted face. By the rights of his seignorial catarrh he constantly spat, anywhere and everywhere. He was by nature curt and peremptory. And this man, surcharged with grievance, Francis refused to receive. An attendant, speeding the parting favourite, slammed the door on his heels. But this was premature. Jerking back the heavy door, Lautrec asked Rohan what he meant, smashed him in the face without waiting for an answer, and strode off fuming. He might not be a genius as a general but he was a born fighter.

Francis had his own grievance. He had been "marvellously angry" during the Lombardy campaigns. "All my men there," he exclaimed before the English envoy, "be worth nothing much." It went hard with him to see the soldier who had undone Marignano but at last he admitted Lautrec and opened his assault by saying roughly to his Gascon, "You threw away Milan!"

"It is your Majesty who threw away Milan, not I," retorted Lautrec furiously. "For eighteen months the gendarmes served without being paid a penny. The Swiss forced me to fight at a disadvantage. They would not have done it if they had been paid."

"But I sent you the money," shouted Francis.

"Your Majesty's letters I received. I never received the money."

This astounded the King. He could not comprehend it. He demanded Semblançay.

The thin, white-bearded treasurer arrived, still keen and supple. With Lautrec planted in front of him, Francis asked his "father" Semblançay if he had ever despatched the 400,000 crowns to Milan.

There are situations in life that refuse to conform to prearrangement. Semblançay was one of those delicately resilient men who endear themselves to their masters because they are shock-absorbers. It was his business to see much and not too much, to say much and not too much, to perform the miracle of the true majordomo, provide oil for the lamp, keep up the heat, assure the climate of confidence. He had always been an artist, expressing himself by subordinating himself, taking an interest in the small as well as the big things, managing the treasury, worrying about the Dauphin's mumps, knowing his place and indefatigably improving it. But here was a miracle he could not perform, a shock he could not possibly absorb. He had indeed received Francis's command to forward the money. He could not deny it. And he had had the money ready to send. But Madame the Regent, the King's mother, had taken the said sum of 400,000 crowns.

Francis, his face furious, strode to his mother's room. He would never have thought it of her, he burst out, like a boy, to withhold the money he had ordered to the army.

She faced her son boldly. She absolutely denied that the 400,000 crowns that she had taken from Semblançay were the moneys for

Milan. They were her own savings and the Naples fund that Semblançay had broached in 1521. These were to be restored, as everyone had agreed, and she had taken them.

Semblançay was called in. He stood firm. He insisted it was the Milan money. She insisted it was the Naples money. Francis stood dumbfounded between them.

He had utterly relied on Semblançay. The old man's father had served Louis XI on commercial missions and out of this Semblançay himself had worked into finance and administration, combining the public servant with the private adviser, the long robe with pantoufles. And he was brave as well as loyal. At Agnadello he had stuck so close to Louis XII under fire that he had been made a chevalier. He had always been helpful, responsive, far-sighted, sympathetic. And now he was at loggerheads with Francis's mother.

When the treasurer left Francis's presence—and he was indispensable for the approaching lawsuit with Bourbon—one man at court took heed of the brewing storm. That was the harsh realist Duprat. Semblançay and Duprat had been as naturally uncongenial as cat and dog. The feline success of Semblançay aroused the bristling resentment of Duprat. This hostility, veiled for years, had been animated by all the mean jealousies of acquisition. Both men were taking their rewards in visible form, advancing their families with a zeal that was as shrewd as it was shameless. This exposed their interests, and hence their nerves. So far Semblançay had never lost favour. Now he had come between Francis and Louise. Duprat asked no more.

II

Francis's loss of Milan brought England to the front. Toward the end of May Sir Thomas Cheyney presented himself to deliver an ultimatum that bristled with accusations.

With no one but Bonnivet by his side, Francis received the indictment with gravity and dignity. Going back no further than his personal meeting with Henry he declared with human warmth that after what had passed he would never trust living prince again. Bonnivet seconded him in scorning the suggestion of a truce. He would rather see his master in the tomb, Bonnivet said, than accepting dishonourable terms.

That settled it. In the afternoon of the same day, in the grand hall of the archbishop's palace, the whole court assembled after dinner to attend on Clarence, the herald-at-arms. Apparently it was a trying experience for Clarence, so far from home. According to Cheyney he did right well and substantially, "and as for audience, he lacked none." But Louise said he trembled with fear, and "my son" withered him with his icy rejoinder. Francis met each accusation without a moment's delay. He knew his lesson. He had never assisted de la Marck. He had never sent Albany to Scotland. He had withheld English pensions because he felt sure Henry was his enemy and he did not want his own money to be spent against himself. He would give the lie to any man who said he had not kept his promise. Everyone, said Louise, was delighted and at the same time astonished at his clear eloquence.

She herself was proposing a "general truce" in London, as late as June 7, but zero had come, and the war would be "vigorous and cruel."

12

By July the rougher side of it was felt by the mean citizens of Brittany and Picardy. Incursion and devastation, burning and looting—it was mainly a war of civil outrage.

At Noyon in 1522 there lived a small boy called John Calvin. The grey town knotted itself round the austere cathedral, and John's father tripped through the cloisters, a lay agent of the clerics. In 1521 he frugally secured a benefice for his son, having him tonsured and planning to make a priest of him. This boy of thirteen was meagre and sharp of feature, white-skinned, black-eyed, intensely intelligent. He lived in the war zone, deep in the rumours of war. The Swiss at Abbeville had refused to stay under arms. At Beauvais the ramparts were being cleared of houses and gardens. Doullens was gutted. Bapaume had been "rasée, bruslée et ruinée." Vendôme watched his own château go up in smoke. There was no peace in Picardy.

And as Noyon endured the war, with bread beyond price, the

priests could be seen speeding in white rochet through the streets, to the bedsides of the pestilent. A town of set faces and grim mouths, of tight hands and tighter privileges, it was breeding in the boy Calvin his own strange conception of the universe, a universe lacerated by strife, big with evil, heavy with predestination. And as the war went on, too ready to smite Noyon, the youngster was sent to Paris to attend the university. There he would enter the college that Erasmus so piteously described, a barrack filthy, bleak, inhospitable, reeking with the foullest smells, clotted with dirt, brayed with noises, where the dinner would be stale bread and half a herring. Here, at four in the morning, a small wretch of fourteen would begin his lessons. With short breaks they would go on to seven in the evening, larded with mass, with religious exercises and with floggings. So was prepared an inexorable intellect strained to encompass human destiny. And at the same hour, in 1522, down at Fontenay-le-Comte, Rabelais, still a Franciscan frair, was studying Greek in happy company, translating Herodotus, proudly corresponding with Budé. Not for six months would the Sorbonne decide that Greek makes a man a heretic and that a knowledge of Hebrew turns him into a Jew. But before the year was out it would make these crucial discoveries, and would tell Francis that his sister was a Lutheran.

13

The war was grinding Francis hard.

By August, in spite of his high words, he was ready to give up Milan, to pay tribute for Naples and to surrender Fuenterrabia. This for the dire reason that he was short of money.

How to raise money! A year before war was declared he had begun to alienate crown property. That was a trick worth knowing. But he needed 2,400,000 livres for Picardy alone, and there was no device he did not welcome if it gave him silver and gold. He had early revoked the pensions and surveyorships that he had granted too frivolously since 1515. He now looked around him for assets. Like the late Pope, he gratified the place-hunters. He sold offices. He borrowed hugely from his nobles. He sold titles of nobility. He collected salt-taxes for a whole year at a 25 per cent.

discount. He augmented the taille. He took the jewels from the cathedral at Reims and turned them into cash. He took the silver grille from around St. Martin of Tours, worth 60,000 francs, and stripped St. Martin of his jewels. Not realizing what would happen to St. Thomas of Canterbury, Wolsey threw up his hands. "He has molten the garnishing of St. Martin's corpse, and founded the twelve apostles, with other jewels and sacred ornaments." But he went further. The towns bought privileges from him. Abbeys and cathedrals paid him to ratify their purchases of land. And still he peered everywhere, in Dauphiny, in Provence, in Burgundy, in Normandy, in Brittany, to see what taxes he could levy or what domains he could release. He bitterly needed money.

His mother and he turned their eyes on Bourbon. They had begun their lawsuit in April, laying claim to his immense territories, counter-claims that were curiously related. Louise protested that she did not want to make any claims she could not uphold. She desired the proceedings to be honourable and discreet, for the discharge of her conscience and the preservation of her rights. But as parlement actually went about fulfilling these laudable intentions, the legal points magnificently argued and Bourbon having entirely the better of it, Louise was not content until a stealthy order was issued during a recess, giving her the right to sequestrate the Bourbon property. Bourbon, in part, was to share the fate of Saint Martin.

But the pressure on parlement was quite secret. And Francis was a dutiful figure in these months of suspended war. He personally replaced a sacred Host that a Lutheran had violated. And in October, when his mother had a bad attack of gout, he sat up all night with her.

She was grateful for this loving devotion, and for his loyalty about the monks and the Sorbonne. "My son and I," she noted grimly, "begin, by the grace of God, to recognize the hypocrites, white, black, grey, smoky and all colours, from whom may God in His infinite goodness and mercy preserve and defend us, for, unless Jesus Christ is a liar, there is no more dangerous tribe in all humankind."

The fight was on. Briçonnet was advising Marguerite to "hide the fire," and a Sorbonnard said that God smote Madame with gout "to punish her." The condemnation of Erasmus, Berquin and Lefèvre would be delivered in some months. The King was in serious emergency.

14

The lawsuit against Bourbon was animated by Louise. That Bourbon had spoken in 1516 of displacing Alençon as heir to the throne—that alone made him suspect, if it had ever been said. But Francis was too aware of Parisian opinion and noble opinion, of the army and the Sorbonne and of opinion in parlement, to pursue Bourbon with outspoken zeal. He stalked him, but cautiously. It was an enmity that might shatter the kingdom.

In the midst of the lawsuit old Anne of France was known to be dying. But the work of her life was now assailed by Louise, and it was not in her blood to yield to an assault. She rallied her strength to overwhelm the Angoulêmes.

Anne's had never been the Angoulêmes' France. It had been the kingdom of her father, of her own regency, of her brother. To that kingdom Louis XI had added Burgundy and she had riveted Brittany. But she was not herself without the vehement passion that had made her father a rebel. She could not conceive of disrupting France, yet under this provocation she could use Emperor and King and Pope to wrest France from the Angoulêmes. Bourbon would secede, not to betray Francis but to dislodge him from the throne. So could she consecrate a traitor and hallow treason.

"My son," the dying woman said, "the House of Bourbon has been allied to the House of Burgundy, and during that alliance has always flourished and prospered. I pray and commend you to enter into alliance with the Emperor. Promise me to do it as quickly as possible, and I shall die more content."

From Languedoc, at the beginning of 1522, Bourbon had opened negotiations with the Emperor. These he renewed through an agent in Flanders, in the summer. While the lawsuit was still undecided, and while Francis and Louise were doing their best to keep him on good terms, Henry VIII was sounded as well as the Emperor. It was Bourbon's plan to "reform and redress the insolent demeanours of the said King," and to marry the Emperor's sister. He was to join 500 gendarmes and 10,000 foot to the enemy's forces, within ten days of their entering France, and so to "reform and redress" Francis.

The grave obstacle to his alliance with England was Wolsey's formula that Henry VIII was entitled to France and "meant to possess himself of it." Not until Bourbon pledged allegiance would Henry willingly touch him.

In the midst of these subtle negotiations Bourbon did not hesitate to come to court. He waited on his partisan Queen Claude as she was dining alone, when Francis, who had finished dining by himself, entered the room. Bourbon started to rise but Francis bade him remain seated.

"Seigneur," the King addressed him abruptly, "it is showed us that you be, or shall be, married. Is it true?"

Bourbon said, "It is not true."

Francis flatly contradicted him. He said he knew it was true, "and you will remember it." And he knew of his traffic with the Emperor, "and you will remember it."

Bourbon stood up. "Sir, then you menace and threaten me! I have deserved no such treatment."

He thereupon withdrew. Many nobles immediately crowded to him. He rode at once to his hôtel, "and all the noblemen of the court with him."

This episode came close to Anne of France's death on November 14.

15

By showing his impatience to Bourbon without taking any action, Francis revealed weakness, but this was not so much in his nature as in his circumstances. The year 1522 had been appalling. It began with the Emperor naming his own tutor as Pope. Tournai, for which he still owed 400,000 crowns, was captured. Lautrec had been driven from Milan. Henry VIII had declared war. Picardy had been harried. The treasury had only been filled by devices that outraged the people, and the Sorbonne, like the parlement, was simply waiting to take the aggressive. It was an accumulation of difficulties which would drive most men to distraction, and some explosive behaviour was highly natural.

But Francis was one of those men who soon rise to the surface

of their troubles. Marguerite might go on pondering good and
evil, calling herself an "imperfaicte, mal ronde et toute contre-
faicte perle," but he accepted himself more easily.

A year before a gulf had opened and he was in dreadful dismay,
but he had managed to scrape through 1522 without signal
catastrophe, and that was the essential thing for a man of his
temperament. He did not take life dogmatically. He took it prag-
matically. He only asked to have it grouped round him in comfortable or plausible order, and then he could display all the classic
virtues of measure, proportion, moderation.

The speed with which he regained his poise indicated his faith
that man's first duty is to survive. The natural recuperation of
France indicated his good sense. But in any event he was seldom
exposed to the raw air. Louise comforted him and succoured him.
Marguerite bathed him in reassurance. By holding his officers to
strict account without giving them any true chance to do their
work, he would have to produce crises, but a run of luck could
always enable these officers to put a good face on their story, and
so the game could go on. He had had a wretched year, but by fair
means and foul he had amassed the funds for renewing the war
on an adequate scale. Bonnivet, triumphant from Fuenterrabia,
would now be his general in Lombardy, while Lautrec could try
his hand in north-western Spain. The English and the Flemish
did not frighten him. Many of his soldiers would be wretched
underfed men, without footgear of any kind, but à la guerre comme
à la guerre, they could be shod by Lombardy. Semblançay he
turned over to a commission of inquiry, and a new treasurer,
Babou by name, would now save him from depredation and in-
efficiency. When he was perfectly secure he would deal with Bourbon and the Sorbonne, but no man can stretch to do everything.

There is usually some cruel person who breaks through the
charmed circle to force a man to face consequences, and that person was Lautrec's sister. But she herself was too vulnerable to
chastise her lover.

Françoise was by no means subtle in her jealousy. She knew
that her successor was in view and her reproaches were outspoken.
You are reputed to be loyal in private friendship, she attacked him
in verse, but in my case you change soon. Frizzy hair has taken

your fancy. You have shown little perseverance with me. I desired to be your lady of honour all the days of my life but "honneur se varie." And then, in lighter tone, she attacked the rival blonde. You are clerbrun, she told Francis, and blondes are unsuitable to "us." Blondes are cold, and what is cold is contrary to nature.

Francis replied in verse, but he soon dropped banter for recrimination. The lady was holding him to account, and he would not stand being chided by anyone. I have been badly repaid for my long constancy to you, he said, and you always regarded me as inconstant. You want to cashier me. You are "ingrate," with no cause or reason. I have gained nothing by loving you, except to learn that one cannot rely much on a dark woman. No, I will commit myself to no one, blonde or brunette. I assure you that what I have learned about you does not attach me to you. I have nothing to reproach myself with, except that I valued you too highly. And so, for the time I spent with you, I can well say, R.I.P.

This harsh adieu could only mean that he knew of his mistress's behaviour. She was formally dethroned, and her place would not stay empty.

And Louise and Marguerite had no pity for the handsome black-browed woman who was now to be sent from court and restored to her husband. "When the woman was raised to happiness," they wrote in a quatrain, "she did not know her good fortune. So to her great unhappiness has she been coupled with the insensate beast and despatched with him into the country."

16

The "blonde" who incensed Françoise de Foix was a quite young girl, whose stepmother was a Laval. She was attached as a maid of honour to Louise's household, and could hardly be more than fifteen. She was, in fact, born the year before John Calvin and in the same part of the country, which seems to prove that geography is not everything. Her father was a noble whose family name, Pisseleu, "pis que loup," worse than wolf, had in it a strong reminiscence of savage feudality, though he himself did nothing more untoward than have three wives and thirty children. This daughter of his, Anne de Heilly, came of the middle marriage. She was brought up by her stepmother, moving from one of their châteaux to another until the time came for her to seek her fortune at the court.

A slim blonde, confident, intelligent, level-headed, she was to attract Francis just as Anne Boleyn was to fillip Henry VIII. But there was never a prospect for Anne de Heilly to be Queen of France. This was adamantine. Though Claude of France was lamentably unwell, after seven childbirths in eight years, a noble-woman could no more be Queen than she could be Pope. Claude indeed had never imposed herself on Francis as a person. By accident a Queen might be a person but in reality she existed to produce heirs, just as the Pope's castrati existed to produce high notes, at no matter what cost to human nature. In France, for that reason, the King would have to practice open polygamy. When Luther put it in so many words the whole Catholic world shook as if palsied, but this was tactical indignation. The sacrament of marriage for a French King was known to comprise one official wife, to bear him children, and one official mistress to bear him company. Without this polygamy he would have had to marry outside the stud-book, and the inconveniences of this romantic behaviour would have compelled him, as it compelled Henry VIII, to get divorces with a sword. That procedure offended a sense of order in the French. It worked better for their man to have two women, to portion out honour to one and affection to the other, with occasional kindly transpositions. It would, of course, base Francis's convenience on an injustice to one woman or the other, but the arrangement was above board, and what girl at court could suppose herself vilely treated to be chosen as his mistress? If she had any such prejudice she would scarcely be at court.

The young Anne de Heilly was evidently without prejudice. A rival's eye could read her at once. Françoise scorned her coldness, but it was precisely this northern clarity that seemed to stir Francis's imagination. Little did he know the firm character he would have to deal with. He only saw that she was indefinably fresh, that her hair curled, and that she had blue eyes.

But in 1523 the germ could hardly have been more than implanted before he had a despatch that a great surprise offensive was promised by his generals in Picardy. He had been hunting hard, from Blois and Chambord, but he departed in all haste, rushing 80 leagues from Chambord to La Fère, not to be deprived of an adventure. His generals did not thank him: the clatter of his departure and arrival ruined the surprise.

It was not in the north, however, that he looked for victory. He was going to Italy. He hurried Montmorency into Switzerland to hire an army, and Bonnivet was to cross the Alps, stopping to see Bourbon at Moulins. It was much the same formula as in 1515 except that Bourbon was not recruiting for him and Bourbon was at home. But in August Francis engaged himself to link up with his chief vassal, on his way to Lyon.

17

Bourbon was ill. That had been his trite excuse for not joining Francis. But the truth was otherwise. He had followed the royal lawsuit against him with feelings of wild resentment and under cover of this illness, real or feigned, he had been treating with the King's enemies to make common cause with them. The negotiations with the Emperor had come to a point a month before Francis started for Lyon. The arrangements with the English had still to be concluded. John Russell would not reach Bourbon for some weeks.

So long as Bourbon had been merely flirting with the enemy, he could indulge his violent resentment of Francis's and Louise's legal assault on him. But while still toying with the idea of revenge, and plotting to strike Francis in Burgundy, in Normandy, in Picardy, in Auvergne, the enemy was much too receptive, much too eager to commit him, to let the conspiracy remain in the air. Charles V was actually sending his chamberlain Beaurain to Montbrison. And Henry VIII, who had blown hot and cold, was also sending Dr. Knight to Montbrison. By that moral chemistry which nothing seems to stop, the liquid words were hardening into fact, and Bourbon making irrevocable decision.

A small group of nobles were meeting Bourbon at Montbrison early in July. Most of them were from the Bourbonnais, young bloods of local fervour. One of them bore a famous name: the father of Diane de Poitiers, Lord of Saint Vallier. There were two important bishops, one the brother of the venerable marshal, la Palice, and the other a Hurault, a link with parlement. And young René de Brosse was fresh from a hot encounter with Francis. His estates in Brittany had been conferred on Bonnivet. He sought the King but his protests were answered by flippancy. When at last he burst out that he would ally himself with the King's enemies, Francis merely laughed at him. "You can do whatever you like."

They all had grievances, but their indignation was not cased in brains. Machiavelli must have permitted himself a smile when he heard the details of the conspiracy. Bourbon was half Gonzaga, but his methods were Gothic. After dinner, on this evening of July 10th, he took his old friend Saint Vallier into a private room and, closing themselves in, said in a hushed voice that he valued Saint Vallier more than anyone in the world, that he had something to say to him, and that he wanted him to take his oath, on the fragment of the True Cross that was in the locket on his neck, never to breathe a word of what he was about to reveal.

When Saint Vallier was telling this, three months later, he narrated just how he had sworn on the relic. And if he had not told the "boot" would have crunched his shins.

So he swore secrecy. Then Bourbon went into his grievances against Francis and Louise—his pensions unpaid, his services refused, the lawsuit, his enforced loans.

Saint Vallier barely listened. He had his own grievances. He claimed a dukedom in vain. His huge loans were not repaid. And he had been known to threaten to kill Francis, saying Francis had deflowered his young daughter Diane. But many a man who is hot about his own wrongs is cool about his friend's. "My Lord," he said, "if the King and Madame have treated you badly, you too are at fault. You do not make yourself understood to the King as you should."

"But, cousin, you are as badly treated as I am."

"My lord, let us leave that aside."

"Cousin, will you swear on this fragment of the True Cross never to tell what I am about to tell you?"

"Yes, my lord." And he laid his hand on the holy relic.

Then Bourbon said the Emperor was offering him a great match, with his sister Eleanor and 200,000 crowns for a dot. He recounted all the terms.

"My lord," the veteran inquired, "are you sure you can trust all these promises?"

The Constable nodded. "You will see the lord Beaurain, who is coming this evening. I'll send for you when he arrives. You will hear what he has to say."

So they went to supper and then the old gentleman, no doubt sighing heavily, said bonsoir to his host and took himself to his quarters.

They had no meat for supper, so it must have been a Friday or Saturday. And about 11 p.m. the Constable sent for him. He took him into a room where Adrien de Croy, Lord of Beaurain, warmly greeted him.

"He is one of the best friends I have," said Bourbon. So Beaurain embraced Saint Vallier.

Then the elegant Beaurain produced a short, simple letter of introduction from Charles V, addressing Bourbon as "mon cousin," asking him to credit his chamberlain as if he were his "cousin and friend Charles."

He was a fine talker, Beaurain, and he conveyed that the Emperor upheld Bourbon in his grievances and would make him "one of the greatest men in Christendom."

He was not obliged to show his instructions, but he would willingly disclose them. He thereupon unrolled a great sheet of paper with the Emperor's seal on it. Saint Vallier would have read the paper if he had had his glasses. But he could not read it without his glasses. Its contents, however, were given to him. It covered everything, about the projected marriage, and the invasion of France by the Emperor from the Pyrenees with 18,000 Spanish, 10,000 landsknechts, 2,000 gendarmes and so on. Henry was likewise to invade the same day with 15,000 English. Margaret was to send 5,000 men from Hainault. The Emperor was to add 3,000 landsknechts for Henry. All this was to happen once Francis left Lyon; and the Constable was to receive 100,000 crowns from each sovereign to pay for the 10,000 landsknechts who were awaiting his command to invade Burgundy.

There was another paper in Beaurain's roll, signed by Henry VIII. He had himself seen Henry in London and told him what Bourbon was to have. "And I," said Henry to him, "what am I to have?" "Sire," said Beaurain, "you will be King of France." And Henry said, "There will be much to do to have Bourbon obey me!"

After dinner the next day, before Bourbon had signed anything, Saint Vallier went to see his host.

"My lord," he said, "you really trust me? You consider me your very humble servant?"

"Cousin, I assure you I trust and love you so much that if my own brother were alive this day I could not love him more than I do you."

Saint Vallier humbly expressed his thanks and then went on, "All this night, my lord, I have been pondering and going over the many things you told me yesterday so that I was unable to sleep, and I wish God would give me the grace to know how to speak to you according to God, right reason and conscience. My lord, you told me yesterday and I observe that, by this alliance they are offering you, you would be the cause that the Emperor and the King of England, the Germans, the Spanish and the English, are to come into France.

"Think and reflect on the great trouble and calamity that must flow from this, the shedding of human blood, the destruction of towns, and big houses and churches, the violation of women, and all the other evils that come from war. And consider that you sprung from the House of France and are one of the leading princes in France today, so loved and esteemed by everyone that everyone rejoices to look on you. And if you come to be the cause and occasion of the ruin and downfall of this Kingdom, you will be the most reviled person that ever was, and the curses that are heaped on you will last for a thousand years after your death. Moreover, do you not realise the great treason it will be if after the King leaves the Kingdom and turns his back to go to Italy, leaving you in France and trusting himself to you, you repay him in this manner and destroy him and his Kingdom? I beg you for the honour of God to think of all this. And if you have no regard for the King and Madame his mother, who you say have wronged you, at least have regard to the Queen and the children and do not seek to bring ruin on this Kingdom. For after you have brought in the enemy, out they will drive you, themselves."

"But, cousin," answered the Constable, "what do you want me to do? The King and Madame wish me ill and never will rest until they destroy me. They have already taken the best part of what I have, and they would do me to death."

"My lord," the older man said, "I beg you, give up all these wicked plots and commend yourself to God and resolve to talk outspokenly to the King, and you will see what he will say to you."

Bourbon then began to weep, and so Saint Vallier was moved to tears.

"I give you my word, cousin," pledged Bourbon, "that I will do nothing, and I will act as you suggest, and I beg you to remember your oath and keep everything secret, and divulge nothing."

Saint Vallier gave his word. Then he said, "My lord, no more of this. Let us have a game."

And then Bourbon and Saint Vallier found one of the squires and one of the bishops, and all four sat down to a game of Flux.

18

How genuine Saint Vallier sounds, and how clear his first-hand evidence. But his mind had been tormented at Loches how to think up the best story. He had *not* dissuaded Bourbon from signing. The imperial chamberlain, as he well knew, had gone off with Bourbon's name to the treaty.

But Bourbon was satisfied. He now had "two strings to his bow." He dispatched his messengers in every direction, to Normandy, Picardy, Burgundy, Spain, to knit his union with the invaders. As for himself, he talked of a pilgrimage to Puy-de-Dôme, and when at last he had to see Bonnivet, who assured him that Francis would make him "greater than ever," he was intent on his conspiracy.

But it was a nation-wide secret. "He who conspires," wrote Machiavelli ten years before, "cannot act alone, nor can he take a companion except from those whom he believes to be malcontents, and as soon as you have opened your mind to a malcontent you have given him the material with which to content himself, for by

denouncing you he can look for every advantage." This was the
danger. Francis kept receiving hints. But the real damage was done
by two young Normans who took Bourbon's proposals as dishonourable. Since they were sworn to secrecy they went to the bishop
of Lisieux to lay their predicament before him and he did not
scruple to take their story to the seneschal of Normandy. Louis
de Brézé was a solid Norman, devoted to his master, wholly unaware of his father-in-law's complicity. He wrote a guarded,
weighty warning, and despatched two couriers, each with a copy,
to Francis, by way of Louise. And this news overtook Francis as
he was nearing Moulins.

It was more precise than any that had yet reached him, and it
came in good time. He had meant to go to Moulins with a light
guard of honour and he might have been carried off to a fortress
in the hills. The letter forewarned him. His instant feeling, or at
any rate his dominant feeling, was that of a shrewd hunter who is
biding his time, and his first concern was to be unconcerned. He
gave a hint that he had hurt his leg and could not take the saddle
for a day or two. He then sent Genouillac to secure the road from
Moulins to Lyon against ambush, while he delayed for Richard
de la Pole, the "White Rose," leading his 4,000 landsknechts.
Escorted by this English exile—who, indeed, was another Bourbon,
a traitor duke, but on the right side—Francis went on to Bourbon's capital.

The strain had unstrung Bourbon. He was in bed. Francis had
his physicians look him over, and they reported that he was gravely
ill. They said that he would die if moved. The King waited overnight, his soldiers everywhere. He then went to the sick room. His
cousin's face was greatly changed, and the illness no pretence. He
might have confronted Bourbon with the rumours he had received
or he might have made him a real offer—the hand of Renée, the
restoration of his lands—but the lawsuit and the conspiracy were
both afoot, and Francis could not close a conflict in which his
mother was engaged. He asked Bourbon to come with him to Italy.
This the invalid said he "marvellously desired," and pledged his
word that as soon as he could bear to be carried in a litter he
would take the road, probably within a week. So Francis left for
Lyon.

From there he wrote a long letter to his mother begging her "very humbly" not to worry in the least, that he was taking every precaution to safeguard Burgundy and that Bourbon could do no harm. That was all. He was disturbed, but not gravely. His mind was set on Italy, and he wanted, without giving anything away, to have Bourbon at his side. He had left Perault de Warthy (Perrot de Warty) to escort the convalescent from Moulins.

Bourbon was more high-strung and more in danger. He had a rendezvous with Sir John Russell for September 6th, and at the same time Francis was urgent. He was much better, he told Warty to inform the King, he would start for Lyon in two days.

Warty arrived late. Next morning he gave the good word to Francis as soon as his curtains were drawn. Francis was delighted. But five days passed, and no Bourbon. Warty returned. He found his man coming by slow stages, but as they proceeded the Constable developed another bad attack. His own physicians pulled very long faces. They could not terrify him by taking his pulse. His urine was the very worst they had ever seen. He could no longer go forward, he had to return to his "air naturel." Warty listened and Warty understood. He rushed to Lyon.

He arrived at midnight and woke the King. That day the King had entertained Saint Vallier at dinner. He now (September 5th) ordered his arrest, and when he saw his prisoner he had an access of fury. He would have killed him, it was reported, but for the guards. The bishop of Puy and Aimar de Prie were also arrested. Then Francis ordered a heavy military force to advance on Chantelle. Warty was speeded back, this time as a decoy.

Bourbon was not waiting for him. The interview with Sir John Russell had been snatched at a wayside village, and then the invalid had ridden to Chantelle. He smiled when Warty caught up with him. He stuck to it that he was being falsely accused. He knew the military were coming, and in spite of Warty's disavowals he knew of Francis's fury. He detained Warty until he had held a council of war. After five hours he handed him an open letter for the King. Letters to Claude, to Louise, to Marguerite, to his "Bourbonnien" Robertet were going by Hurault. These were to keep up the fiction that he was loyal, assuring the King on his honour that he would never fail him, telling each lady that he was pained to be in the King's bad grace and begging her to intercede for him. And then, dressed in black velvet, with 240 followers, he started for Spain. They had 30,000 gold crowns in their saddle pouches, and his body-servant carried his jewels in a box. Too unwell to make an effort, he rode on a mule.

Behind him he left the Moulins of Anne of France, with its magnificent palace, its lovely gardens, its forests, its fountains, and "every sort of elegance worthy of a prince." In that great park he had cast his princedom over nature, with francolins and partridges and turkeys and parrots, his subjects in the empire of the air.

And now, after hearing mass at dawn, he was turning his back on Moulins. His mind was in turmoil. After one day with his troop he formed new and secret plans. Leaving his adherents to fend for themselves, he narrowed his company to five, and later there was but himself, Pompérant and his servant.

For Pompérant, a wiry soldier, this was a keen adventure. He agreed to take the master's rôle, and Bourbon to act the valet. But this poor valet, in black linen coat and black hat perched on a red toque, found it no easy experience. At Ruines, not far from Saint-Flour, Pompérant had a house and there they went under cover for three days. They had encountered a great band of soldiers on their way to Lautrec at Bayonne, and this made them reshape their plans. They would swing over to the Rhône. Taking by-paths to elude pursuit, they passed by Serverette into the mountains, a desolate region where monotonous pastures widen in treeless melancholy, with chains of forbidding hills swept by the autumnal winds. Bourbon was not hardened to solitude. He had often hunted the stag, and now he was himself the hunted animal in a world as friendless as these hills. They neared Vienne. At one small place, tired and lame, they had stopped for the night, only to renew their journey to avoid the King's post. At the next place they had to borrow a mule, to ease a foundered horse. When they sighted the Rhône at dawn the duke hid behind a house while Pompérant accosted a butcher on the road, and said he was a king's archer on the hunt for Bourbon and searching for his company. The butcher said that he would find companions across the river, so they dared not risk the bridge. They took a ferry lower down, but a dozen soldiers haled them back, and piled in with them. On the way over

Romme foubs qui trembloit iadis la terre, e' l'onde,
De cet Heros francois fut la proye, e' l'honneur:
Et fans la dure Mort qui borna fon bonheur
Le Monde eftoit â luy, ayant le chef du Monde.

Tho. de leu fe. P.A.

CHARLES DE BOURBON, CONSTABLE OF
FRANCE

From a Contemporary Engraving in the British Museum

the river, to Bourbon's consternation, several of them cheerfully saluted Pompérant by name, the friend of all the world. They meant no harm. So when they landed, Pompérant waved them good-bye, as if going to Italy, turning for Chambéry when out of sight. The next day, again, the widow woman who kept their inn greeted this lively captain.

"You are not one of those who are playing the fool with Monsieur de Bourbon?" she asked.

"No," he answered slyly, "but I would give everything I have to be in his company."

Then someone remarked that the King's provost had passed, only an hour before, hot on the trail. Bourbon was for starting to flee, but Pompérant made him sit still. He took him into the mountains, for a respite, and to shun the endless bands of troops that were streaming through Dauphiny to Italy. They turned north, for Savoy, and, by October 3rd, Bourbon was safe at Besançon. Once more he was a duke, with his case of jewels and an escort. He went to Trent, to the Emperor's brother, and then to his cousins at Mantua.

19

Bourbon's flight made the open break that Francis had evaded. He tried a final appeal, urging liberal offers, but Bourbon rejected them as "too late." He said "victory or death" and stood with the enemy.

Francis did not dare to leave Lyon. He remained there till November, wary about Burgundy, while Bonnivet was to command the Italian campaign.

The autumn of 1523 shook the kingdom to its foundations. Henry VIII landed a great army, for whose maintenance he had been compelled to summon parliament, and this army, under Suffolk's command, ravaged the defenceless country up to the Somme, burning Bray and Roye and Montdidier. From Compiègne the citizens fled to Paris. The landsknechts had previously harassed Champagne. In the south-west the Emperor's army crossed the Pyrenees. Lautrec, however, held Bayonne against desperate onslaught, and this invasion Charles V was too impoverished to continue. Not till next year was Fuenterrabia yielded to Charles V himself, under conditions that enraged Francis and would be expiated on the scaffold.

But no one could afford this European war. If Francis felt the dearth of funds, so did England and so did the Emperor. It was all very well for Venice to have deserted France, and for the Pope to have come down on the side of the Emperor. But the imperial cardinals who hung over the Pope's deathbed shouting, "Where have you hidden your money?" could not extract a ducat for the struggle. Pope Adrian had hidden nothing.

This faithful Christian had come to Rome as an apostle of peace. He had doled out a ducat every morning for the day's expenses, and his old Flemish housekeeper had cooked his veal and served his beer, while he grimly spoke of a linen tiara. Against insidious beauty he was protected by a barbican of Dutchmen—Wilhelm van Enkevoirt, Dietrich von Heeze, Johann Ingenwinkel, Johann Winkler. From the land of Van Eyck and of the Imitatio he had brought his true religious feeling, and he had thought of no enemy but the Turk. When the Turk captured Rhodes, in 1522, he had cried salt tears, and yet gradually he had been compelled to take into his white hands the dirty hand of tradition, and to stoop to the level of the Medici. Inflexible as he was, he learned the hard lesson that man is a habit-forming animal and that it takes time to reform his habits. Soderini, his adviser, was a Florentine of old and slyly conniving with the French for revolt in Sicily. The indignant Pope sent him to his tower. The vituperations of Duprat did not mend matters. The French were impossible to work with. Before he ended his reign the good Dutchman was sitting with Giulio de' Medici and had eaten of the tree of knowledge. He ended by allying himself with the Emperor and hiring an army with Peter's pence. He had touched Italian politics, and it killed him.

This was in September, 1523. Wolsey felt strong enough to cope with Italy, but it was Giulio de' Medici who won the tiara. And if Leo X's policy could be related to his myopia, it was ominous that the new Pope Clement VII was cross-eyed. Even as an Imperial candidate, Francis had managed to communicate with him.

But while Europe bore down on Francis, the thing that occupied him was his security inside the realm. He was not to blame for the invasions. He was surrounded by wicked enemies. And he had obeyed Briçonnet by much public worship before he started on this campaign, even going to the extraordinary length of a personal confession in public. What now engaged him was to root out conspiracy. He had not wanted to provoke his greatest noble in the middle of a war. An accident of death had forced the lawsuit and the lawsuit had bred the conspiracy. But even if he must remain in Lyon, taking the pulse of Europe, he did not relax his vigilance at home. He promptly appointed a judicial commission and impatiently demanded results from the beginning.

He had used his scholar Guillaume Budé in the preliminary investigations, just as he had used Merlin de Saint-Gelais in the Semblançay case. He made good use of brains. But Jean de Selve headed the judicial inquiry, with three subordinates, and it was this tribunal he hurried.

The confessions were soon extracted. They revealed no vast plot. The conspiracy had grown so naturally out of the lawsuit that no member of the parlement needed a magnifying-glass. It had taken enormous pressure for parlement to help the crown in the lawsuit. It would take even more pressure to make it act in the conspiracy. Francis might flog them but they lowered their heads and stiffened their muscles and refused to budge. It was no wild display of courage, but a superb display of those less martial powers by which the humbler beasts regulate their hours of labour, or refuse to drink.

Francis demanded no laboured proof of Bourbon's guilt. He wanted the names of those who were to have given Boulogne and Thérouanne to the English. He wanted prompt condemnations. He wanted to hang and quarter the wicked culprits, to "make an example." No delays. Torture if necessary. Saint Vallier has fever? He found no reason to delay his condemnation. His tribunal must proceed not coldly, but "virilement et vertueusement" and not spare those who had been "so wicked, so cowardly, so disloyal, so perfidious and so traitorous as to have known what was afoot and not revealed it to us."

The English were dangerously close to the capital by the end of October, and yet these commissioners were urgent to refer the matter to parlement as a whole. Francis utterly disagreed.

"We do not find it good, seeing what the times and the circumstances are, that you ask us to refer the whole matter to our parlement. And such words as 'by this method everyone will learn Bourbon's culpability' must no longer be used to us, for it is too evident and established. If anyone wishes to ignore it, one must suppose he is either devoid of intelligence or is in communication with him."

The pusillanimous commissioners were unmoved. Bourbon indeed was no longer a chevalier of the Order. He had sent word that his collar of the Order would be found under his pillow at Chantelle. But Saint Vallier was of the Order, and the commissioners thought it was due to his rank that he should be solemnly judged. So they kept thwarting the King.

20

In this emergency Francis had blustered. He could not hide, even from himself, that his position was often untenable. He could not melt the gold apostles of Laon without forcing the common people to look to his notorious extravagance. He was putting Semblançay on trial, which incensed many members of parlement, and he was finding himself at loggerheads with the Sorbonne. Public safety had suffered terribly through the war. Rumours of pillage, of larceny, of rape, of murder, were flooding into Paris, these roving gangs of bandits being altogether apart from the straightforward invaders who were drowning hundreds of non-combatants in the Somme. If Francis, under these circumstances, could throw on parlement the odium of punishing the Bourbon adherents, he would still remain the "gentil prince" he aimed to be, especially in his own order, where the Guise family and Saint Pol and Vendôme were naturally concerned with the fate of the Constable, not to speak of Louis de Brézé and la Palice and the Hurault connection. But if parlement failed him, if his bluster did not work, he did not lose sight of his main object, his own dominance. He was by now a seasoned politician and well capable of using his wits.

He daubed Bourbon in telling colours. Chabot de Brion addressed parlement for him in November, loudly declaring that Bourbon had threatened to make Francis and his children into meat pasties —the good Francis, who would sacrifice himself for "la chouse publique." Were Paris in danger, cried Chabot, the King would rush to it. "Sooner than lose Paris, our liege lord would sacrifice his life, and all that is dear to him. He is ready to defend you. He is determined to live and die with you. As he cannot be amongst you himself, he has resolved to send his wife, his children, his mother, all that he has, as pledges of his presence; for he is convinced that if he should lose all, and save Paris—Paris safe—all will be saved."

The truth was, he had become anything but well at Lyon, and as soon as he was better he went directly to Blois.

21

And at Blois, from the end of November till the end of February, he refreshed his spirit. His wife, Claude, was ill from before Christmas, and his small boy Charles was unwell. But Francis, indefatigable and irrepressible, left Paris to stew in its own juice and had a few weeks' glorious hunting. He could not resist it. At the end of January he and Chabot were at it for two whole days, in the saddle till ten at night and arriving home drenched and satiated.

But this craving for the chase went with that other keenness of the blood which, at thirty, had made Anne de Heilly thrive with him in her absence. He came to her again with that sting of delight, that feeling of appointment, which proved it was a true attraction. He pursued her. But the driving appetite that made him a hunter passed from rude vigour into a fine pursuit, a wooing warm and insinuant. Startled though she might be, she was wise in expectancy. She could match her tiptoe hunter, for all his skill.

They stood together at dawn, looking out a window of the château. And, as the sun swam up, with the girl's gaze lost in it, Francis's gaze lost itself in the girl. "Go back to your sky, heavenly god," he said softly, "for her beauty darkens you." And just as he was speaking a cloud hid the sun. His heart, to his own astonishment, melted within him. He had defeated a rival. It amused him, though lost in love, to see how he had wished to fend off a rival who could stand in his way. Even with the glorious dawn he could be jealous, saying, "her beauty worsens you!" So he knew he was in love.

22

But if in love Francis thus cocked an eye, he was no less alert in politics. He kept up hard pressure on parlement until Saint Vallier was condemned to death. Then he had his trump card. The whole Bourbon clan was bound to save Saint Vallier. Saint Vallier kept up the most piteous appeals. Much against his will, the loyal Louis de Brézé made his humble plea to the King. Francis remained obdurate. He had been conspired against. Vendôme, it is true, had been sent to Paris to associate himself with Chabot de Brion's propaganda. But Francis had been conspired against and he spared Diane's father nothing. This was no longer the "gentil prince." It was the master. He knew the new Pope was striving for peace. He knew England was sick of the war. He knew the Emperor had drained his resources. He began to smell his way out of the dark morass of 1523, and he would "make an example."

On February 17th, the enfevered Saint Vallier, who had been brought in December, from Loches, lay in his cell in the Conciergerie. He was first of all to be degraded from the Order of St. Michael, then to have his last revelations squeezed out of him by torture, and finally to be executed. The Duke of Luxembourg was to take away his Order, and Duprat to superintend the rest.

Saint Vallier had no collar of St. Michael. He had lost it when battling in Italy. But another was attached to his neck despite his resistance, to be formally wrenched off. Then he was propped up, to be examined. But the old man had already confessed everything he knew. He lamented the desertion of his friends. He had been in high fever for weeks, had gone through violent emotions and now seemed to be at the end of his reserves. Even Duprat could not bark the sixteen judges into torturing him. A sort of elementary human decency made the judges spare themselves this shame. He made his confession and the confessor was allowed to divulge what he had said. Then he was brought to the Palais de Justice to hear his condemnation read from the platform.

With a robe lined with fox thrown over his shoulders, his hands tied behind his back, he was lifted to a horse, an archer sitting behind him to hold him upright. He wore no cap. People noted that his hair had turned white since his imprisonment. One of the

executioners led this burdened horse through the mob, with the
curé on a mule beside him, and the guards thrusting ahead to push
an avenue open.

At the place de Grève he mounted a platform. He was roughly
undressed by the executioners, made to kneel down and say his
prayers. Then came a pause. The kneeling man supplicated the
headsman to do his work, but he was ignored. An hour limped
by, the crowd lining the streets and ranging the windows and
filling the roofs, gazing at the tiny stage in the centre, with the
kneeling puppet, who was going to give them their pang of excitement, the masked headsman, with folded arms, the black dot of the
curé, the rows of guards.

Hola! Hola!

Cassez! Cassez!

"The King's reprieve!" A horseman, waving a parchment, was
clearing the crowd.

The old man bowed his head to kiss the boards on which he
knelt, and repeatedly he crossed himself. The terms of the reprieve
could only have droned meaninglessly in his ears. He was to be
walled up, fed through a little hole, in perpetuity—the merciful
formula of the Inquisition. But life, he had life, the thing he loved,
for which he had shed tears.

And Bourbon would not forget him when the time came. Saint
Vallier would leave Loches, see sunlight in his Dauphiny again,
marry a Polignac, stay far from court and live for many years.

23

If Francis had reprieved Saint Vallier, he was far from finished
with the conspiracy. He had hardly reached Paris at the beginning
of March before bad news hit him. Bonnivet, who had been hammered all winter, was being driven back. And since the death of
Prospero Colonna the Emperor had given the high command to
Bourbon. Bourbon, who had not yet been condemned by parlement, whose goods had not yet been confiscated, was now animating
the war with passion, was in fact its mainspring. Francis's temper
rose to boiling-point. He determined to give parlement the benefit of
his mind.

With Alençon and Vendôme in attendance, Montmorency, la Trémoïlle, Brézé, Chabot, and the requisite bishops, he raised his voice to his high court without the slightest compunction. He went back to the resistance that had been offered him on the Concordat. He said that the impeding of the sale of offices had "cost him Milan." The parlement derived its authority from himself, he told them. "It was not a Roman senate." And if it did not condemn the conspirators, he would take the matter out of its hands.

He did not stop with hectoring parlement. He followed on foot a solemn religious procession to Notre Dame, where the preacher begged God to save the imperilled army. Some months before a dozen priests had been sent through the country to preach the Catholic faith, "to lay low and annihilate the heresies of Luther." Francis was soothing the Sorbonne and propitiating the Deity. He was preparing to woo the Pope and raise a new army. And he could thank the city for a loan of 300,000 crowns.

Then he hurried to Blois, where everyone was ill.

24

So dragged on this four years' European War. It was a season of trouble. The frosts, even, had destroyed lettuces, cabbages, turnips, sorrel, leeks, spinach, parsley, and the wheat under the ground. Little Charles d'Angoulême, a child with a temperament, had not been at all well. Marguerite, who had "no gift for being ill," had herself been under the weather. And her mother, worried about Claude, worried about Charles, cruelly exasperated by the news from the front, was suddenly threatened with pleurisy, which brought Francis to her side.

Marguerite stood with him, her quizzical humour lost in her solicitude. There was no one else to look after his family since Claude had become an invalid, and her mission seemed always to help.

Everyone in trouble appealed to her, and hers was a peculiarly difficult position. Her mother on one side, Francis on the other, committed her to actions that she was too feeble to influence and too loyal to question. When the Bishop of Autun was arrested and the Huraults appealed to her, she could remind them that their worth was proved, the best advocate for their brother. But when Semblançay struggled in the net and called out to her, she could only tell him not to worry, that her mother would always be "bonne maistresse." Marguerite could not afford to know differently. In her distress of spirit, with Berquin and Michel d'Amande and Caroli and Roussel carrying her liberal views across the border into a defiance of the Sorbonne, she turned with actual plaintive wail to her spiritual adviser, Briçonnet.

What a man! When once she concluded a letter by saying she was "sharing her cake" with him, this moral gymnast responded with a dissertation on cake. "Understand, Madame, there is in this world a cake of tribulation that you should share with your 'inutile fils'," himself. This cake made from prolific tares, ground in the mill of weariness, kneaded in cold water in the trough of faithless and disobedient presumption, cooked in the oven of self-love, whose devouring has been a fig poisoning the makers and their offspring, till the flour without leaven has been put in the pot of human nature —this remarkable cake Briçonnet grinds and kneads and bakes and eats until anyone but Marguerite would have yielded to delirious laughter. But Marguerite humble and distracted, craving someone to lean on, could not escape from this wordmonger until her troubles grew too big for words.

And when Francis went north, once his mother was on her feet, it was again Marguerite who would look after her young aunt Filiberte, who was to die in a few weeks.

25

Did Francis see Pont-Remy when he went north? For through this noble, secret negotiations had begun with England.

Wolsey was receptive. The expenses of the war were heavy. Charles V had not repaid his loans. Charles V was veering from his English bride to Isabella, rich daughter of the grocer-king of Portugal. And Charles V had not made Wolsey Pope. The English policy was still to devise the peace, but this war was costly, unprofitable, interminable. And Francis at last saw a prospect of freeing his hand. He wanted to grapple with Bourbon and re-enter Italy. When he learned that Bonnivet's forces were utterly broken, that Bonnivet himself was seriously wounded, that Montmorency had pestilence, that la Palice's brother was killed and that the incomparable Bayard also had been killed (April 30) while covering the retreat, the thing that dismayed him was the loss of Bayard. For the rest, if England did not invade him, he would smite Bourbon himself and carry on to the reconquest of Milan.

Bourbon was inspired by exactly the same motive. All he wanted was the help of Henry VIII. He was ready to invade France, to take Lyon and go on to Paris. And Henry might pluck out his two eyes, if he was not in Paris by All Saints' Day.

He foresaw, of course, a great rising throughout France when he made an appearance. He had his friends in parlement. He had "12,000 gentlemen" who would take arms all through the country. He begged Henry VIII and Charles V only to join with him in this invasion and he would crown Henry at Reims.

Yes, said the good Wolsey in the driest of letters, and "for the helping whereof ye desire me to lay my Cardinal's hat, crosses and maces, and myself, in pledge at this time." Bourbon could scarcely swallow his pride enough to take an oath of allegiance to Henri Deux de France. As for being Henri's vassal, no!

Limp promises and lame preparations were made by the Constable's allies. But the way was clear for him to cross the Alps, go to Nice and then penetrate to Aix and Marseille.

No one could say that Francis was indolent in face of this approaching invasion. His intelligence was received well in advance, and a month before Bourbon crossed the Var (July 1st) Francis had sent his keenest lieutenants to Marseille. Their preparations were vigorous, drastic and foresighted. It was easy enough for Bourbon and Pescara to take Vence, Cagnes, Cannes, Grasse, and all the other plump little towns that gave such marvellous loot to the Spaniards and Germans. The mayor of Aix opened the gates, and Bourbon happily pronounced himself Count of Provence. It was part of his heritage, and if only Henry VIII and Charles V were to help him with something beside 200,000 crowns he could still be in Paris before parlement punished his adherents.

Francis gathered his army as swiftly as possible, but as he receded from Paris he bombarded parlement with letters demanding the punishment of the conspirators, still preserved from sentence by the recalcitrant parlement. Neither parlement nor the Sorbonne could be effectively bullied unless the master came in person.

A cloud hung over the family parting at Bourges. Claude was dying, and the "trinity" seemed at last to realize that this woman was good. Francis wept. "If I thought I could redeem her with my own life," he said to Marguerite, "I would do it with a willing heart." They tried to comfort him. The doctors said she would last three months, but he sighed. "I never should have thought," he said, "that the bond of marriage was so hard and difficult to sever." And they parted in tears.

A few miles from Blois, at Herbault, word reached Louise and Marguerite that the Queen was dead. Louise was overpowered. Worn out by her journeying, depressed by Francis's departure, and broken by this news, she collapsed in a crisis of emotion, bleeding "par tous endroits." Marguerite feared she could not survive but hoped the Lord would fortify her and help her to rest, body and spirit.

Claude died on July 26. Francis was already moving south with Henri de Navarre, Francis de Lorraine, Richard de la Pole. He sighed for his dead wife, but life goes on. Within a week of her death he was restored to high spirits. "I am notifying you," he wrote Montmorency from Vienne on August 11, "that I set out to-morrow from this city to go straight to my camp, which I am pitching within three leagues of Avignon. And since I know not whether they are speaking of the war at Blois, or wherever you are, I wish to let you know quite straight that there is great talk of it here and it seems to me that if you want to have your part in it, you will do well to hurry up."

At Blois, no doubt, they were also speaking of war, and possibly of Claude. But she had been dead a fortnight, and war goes on.

26

The Count of Provence wanted his Marseillais to receive him, and they repelled him irresistibly with pike and cannon-shot, steel and stone. The siege lasted forty days, while Francis gathered and shaped his army at Caderousse, near Avignon.

Pescara watched September slide away and saw the landsknechts

refuse to fling their lives against impregnable ramparts. He called
his Spaniards.

"Enfants, the Marseillais have spread a fine feast for their visitors.
If you are aching to sup in Paradise to-day, go forward. If, like
myself, you have no such craving, then follow me to Italy. It is
stripped of soldiers and is going to be attacked."

Pescara was notoriously difficult to work with. He had hard
military vision while politics and passion were bubbling in Bourbon's head. Francis was edging forward, and October was almost
upon them. Possibly a great soldier and certainly a thorough professional, Pescara made no bones about abandoning a siege. He had
fought sieges before. He knew firearms. He thought this enterprise
hopeless and dangerous. He was leaving. Bourbon might stay. He
was leaving.

And Bourbon had also to leave.

27

Close on Bourbon's heels pressed Montmorency. From Marseille
to the Var, a rugged route, and from Nice across the Tenda pass
to Alba, the Imperial troops plugged along with bleeding feet,
shedding artillery, baggage, arms, their eyes glued to the horizon.
They resented the pace, but Pescara cracked the whip: he burned
the barn over drunken landsknechts who lingered. Forty miles
were covered in one day, while cautious Montmorency pricked
them on, causing "ennui et dommage," hunting them to the last
ounce of fortitude.

It was at the end of September that Bourbon left Marseille. It
would be well into October before Francis could campaign in Lombardy. At the thought of his wintering on that bitter plain both
Louise and Marguerite were alarmed for him. But he was at last
thoroughly aroused. The epicurean had given way to the soldier.
He was now a hunter in pursuit, collected, alert, sensible, with a
cheerful confidence in his lieutenants, and an overwhelming confidence in himself. Disentangling himself from the hands that would
restrain him, he urged his forces forward with the utmost rapidity.
He chafed at delays on the Durance. With the main army in two

great bodies, and his own household in a compact group, he set himself to reach Lombardy before Bourbon.

It was now nine years since Marignano. Against Maximilian and Ferdinand, two keen veterans, Francis had secured Milan for what it really was, the gage of political ascendancy in Europe. They were gone. The new adversary was unproved. Up to Marseille it had looked badly for Francis. He was assailed on his own ground, at a vital point, by his own Constable. But the salamander resists fire. He was shifting the battlefield to Italy. He had forty thousand men, as great an army as in 1515. He had funds in hand. The Emperor was harried in Spain and uneasy in Germany. Clement VII was looking both ways and Francis had a shrewd idea that his mother could buy off Wolsey in England. With little fear of disaster at home, with everything to induce the Pope to remain benevolent, he could not heed timid counsels. The time had come to strike. He was himself in poise—equable, genial, conciliatory. His despatches to Montmorency showed close calculation and a fixed preoccupation with the enemy. At Aix he stopped long enough to behead the mayor who had yielded the town to Bourbon. This was a placard. Then he carried forward without wasting a day: and stood against Milan by the middle of October.

The plague had been raging in Italy. In 1522 it had swept off Cardinal Schinner, among many another victim, and this same disease, never relenting except in winter, incubated in war-towns and possibly communicated by war-rats, now ran wild through Lombardy. Milan, which had survived Guelf and Ghibelline, French and Spanish, was yielding to the pestilence. Between thirty and forty thousand inhabitants, it was guessed, had died since 1523, and the city was not worth defending.

Bourbon passed through it to Lodi, just before the French arrived. They too saw it was useless to take contagion, even if they were presented with the keys, and in turn they went forward. They ignored Lodi, falsely reported to be braced for defence, and pushed on to Pavia. Much smaller than Milan, this town stood a boulder in the plain, strongly fortified and garrisoned by Antonio de Leyva. It was the point at which the Imperial army could best resist, but if Francis captured it, and he must capture it, Lombardy was at his feet. De Leyva refused to surrender. He showed Francis's herald the Germans, the Spaniards, the gendarmes, assembled in the square. And this gritty Spaniard who had been carried on a stretcher to and from Marseille, knotted with gout but inured to war, made no secret of his defiance.

The siege of Marseille had taken months. It had proved too much for Bourbon and Pescara. Now it was Francis's turn to batter a resolute town, against stout soldiers and loyal inhabitants.

He decided to rush it. He planted himself to the west, posted la Palice to the east, Montmorency on the river to the south, and Alençon in the walled estate on the north. He and la Palice bombarded for three days, made great breaches, poured in troops to meet the enemy hand to hand. These direct onslaughts cost several thousand lives. They were of no use. The arquebus was an improved implement of war, and the landsknechts, no less than the Spaniards, were tough, fiercely combative.

These rebuffs persuaded Francis that he must concert an attack from the south. The Ticino bifurcates before it reaches Pavia, one branch hugging the south wall, the other looping an island. Francis's engineers proposed to dam off the river above the island, to expose a dry river bed under the weak walls. A great force of labourers started building the dam, but the autumn descended, heavy rains swelled the rapid Ticino, swept away the works and restored its river to Pavia.

This set him back. A greater check on his progress was forged by Bourbon. No sooner was Lodi safe than he went north, to collect landsknechts at Nuremberg. To see Bourbon pawning his family jewels to hire Germans, linking himself with a roaring Lutheran like George von Frundsberg, a great fellow with heavy fists and an apoplectic mien, was part of his tragi-comedy as a dynast. Frundsberg had a son in Pavia. He was heir to Franz von Sickingen, another dealer in gun-fodder, and in short order he produced 10,000 fighting men. Another army was to be had in Würtemberg. With these ravenous fighters behind him, Bourbon would relieve Pavia.

But this could not arrive for some months. It was grim inside Pavia. During the December of 1524 and the January of 1525 it was relentlessly cold, the Alps breathing ice on naked Lombardy. Hard as it was to supply the royal camp, it was virtually impossible to supply the engirdled town. The ordinary food—bread, wine, cheese —was exhausted. Rations were slim. Even money, pledge of good times to come, was not in sight, and the mercenaries growled. Nothing but the frugality of de Leyva, his dry endurance long baked and smoked in war, his cunning, his audacity, could have kept the town keyed up, nourishing the hope of Bourbon's return and linking with Pescara.

28

Francis's multi-coloured army circled Pavia. It was several miles in circumference. Horse and foot, pioneers and artillery, it dug into trenches. The troops were shifted from time to time, as the offensive required, while near the walls there was constant menace and sally, taunt and rebuttal. Clarions, trumpets, drums, kept summoning men to their ensigns, Picards and Gascons, Germans and Swiss, Bretons, Italians. But as days drew into weeks, and weeks to months, only the fringe kept bubbling with activity. The outside quarters took on human kindness, bright with colour by day and by night alive with torch and bonfire. While Pavia burned its church beams to keep warm, and ate mules and horses, the French traded with fat Lombardy. Inside the park, at a distance from the walls, the siege lost all intensity. Stalls were set up for a market, pedlars and sutlers swarmed, the girls assembled, vagabonds throve, and eventually the host swelled to something like a hundred thousand. Wine tempered the sharp air. Laughter eased the war. The army life was still spiced by danger and hardship but the siege did not remain taut. The men could escape from their dug-outs, where they froze too readily. They were too polyglot to control and the lax spirit that pervaded the men merged with festivity above. Food began to be dear. Francis's nobles were glad to crowd into his warm kitchen and they paid loot-prices for a chicken. But he was making himself at home in the centre of the park, not without entertainment.

He believed himself intent on the war. He sent off negotiators. The nuncio Aleandro came to him from the Pope. He held council. He planned entrenchments. But in reality his spirit yawned while he waited for Pavia to starve itself to death, and into that yawn, those hours of depression when he seemed not quite himself, Bonnivet poured amusement. It was Bonnivet who brought Clarice Visconti to the camp, the beauty who had enslaved old Prospero Colonna. It was Bonnivet who shared Aretino's witticisms with Francis, and kept Lescun away from Francis, and separated the old warring men, la Palice and la Trémoïlle, from the patron whom they wanted to be a soldier.

Bonnivet, piquant and convivial, arrogant and truculent, had always played up to the "gentil prince" who favoured him. What attracted Francis in warfare was the prowess it demanded, the personal courage, the proof of royal will, the fulfillment of his pledge to his mistress, the defeat of his enemies. He took a telling attitude, in which Bonnivet sustained him, but he naturally abhorred the drudgery that captaincy involved. He could sustain an attitude better than his thinking. Work was not his delight. The grimness of the soldier, his capacity for analysis, for organization, for matching wits and for single-minded devotion, he converted into the mood of the connoisseur. He was refining on reality. He was surrounded, after all, by the walls of a park, and by a society no less formal, no less excluding. His courtiers were encaging him in a world of his own, where he ate amid dearth, was warm in iciness, clean in filth, laughed, drank, was cajoled, while the true soldiers muttered in undertones.

Pescara was a man who had moulded war while Francis was moulding a court. Ever since Ravenna he had been shaping a new technique. He had seen the limitations of armour and the possibilities of the musket. He had studied the conservative Swiss. Bonnivet described him to Francis and Francis said, "exquis!" But Pescara was on the other side. Who could match him? Only an Italian, Giovanni de' Medici.

Giovanni de' Medici. Giovanni, the Great Devil, was the true son of Caterina Sforza. She had stood on the ramparts against Cesare Borgia, and when Giovanni's murder was threatened—the small boy was a hostage—her answer was to lift her skirts and proclaim that she was still fecund. The son of this woman, the cub of this primitive breed, was a soldier. It was his gift. He gave his life to it, as Michael Angelo to his chisel. It did not concern him that he had cropped hair and broken finger-nails. He existed to unite his Tuscans to the arquebus and the nag, and to mill conflict into victory. He staked his life on outwitting his enemy, wily or reckless as the occasion decreed, his brain a bold servant of immeasurable ferocity. He studied, plotted, developed his craft, asked no quarter, gave no quarter, but by economy and dexterity, by whole-hearted delight in it, attained something magnificent and expressive. Death was his pigment and he made masterpieces. It was this useful man that Francis needed.

Giovanni's Black Bands wore mourning for Pope Leo. Now Giovanni was Clement VII's servant. He was willing, with the Pope's consent, to take French pay, but he gave back Francis's glorified bribes with a grin, and returned him the Order of St. Michael. He was an expert, not a partisan. Friend of the Aretino, amused observer of Machiavelli, he watched Francis reposing on a multiplicity of counsel as his escape from an effort of will. "Your Highness has more need of deeds than advice," was his frank conclusion.

Furious with de Leyva for tricking some of his men into death, he laid a trap for the tricksters in Pavia. They fell into it. Walking away from this triumph, blood-spattered, fuming, gleaming, he encountered Bonnivet. The artist in him made him flash out his success. Bonnivet, warm with admiration, took him back to the sight. And there a last Spaniard, a bruised wasp, shot at the two men, hit the wrong one, breaking Giovanni's heel. So Francis lost his hired hero.

The King had come saying, "I want nothing less than the State of Milan and the Kingdom of Naples." Now an army was sent south to Naples, to create a diversion. But the long blockade was weakening Francis's army. Bourbon was coming from the Tyrol with 12,000 landsknechts. The crisis was approaching.

29

Francis still counted on victory. He was pulling wires all over Europe. He had made a secret treaty with the Pope, won back Venice and worked Wolsey deep into negotiation. In Germany, on the eve of the Peasant War, he believed the Emperor fatally handicapped. Italy was courting him, and the wise men everywhere were debating his chances, most of them expecting his triumph.

Early in February he wrote grand letters to his mother. Pescara and Bourbon had come on from Lodi but had no stomach for a battle. A handful of cavalry had headed these men off, made them "turn their noses." They shirked fight! And just as he was dictating this letter, the alarm sounded, and Francis snatched his sword. He was, in truth, far from believing that his enemy shirked battle. They were camped to the north of his park. He could hear their distant drums, and his infantry were tasting Spanish skill with the culverin.

He was now camped on the edge of the park of Mirabello, sandwiched between de Leyva in the town and Pescara outside the park. His loose army was becoming restless under pinpricks. His Grisons, some thousands of them, had bolted home to save their own territory. Reinforcements from Marseille were smashed up. The Black Bands dissolved. His position was becoming increasingly uncomfortable.

What to do? His veteran generals did not like the situation. They began to suggest that discretion would be the better part. In another month, these elders said, the hungry landsknechts must revolt for their pay, the Imperialists having far less money than the French, and then would be the time to land on them. They counselled Francis to withdraw to Binasco, to refresh his army and let time work for him.

But this advice revolted the younger captains. They had invested four months in the siege. They could not endure to put themselves in the same humiliating position as Bourbon after Marseille. They appealed to Francis's pride, his sense of honour, his chivalry, his love of glory. They knew he would wear his mistress's scarf on his arm.

Francis could not make up his mind. He had pledged himself to take Pavia or die in the attempt. He had as good infantry as the enemy, better cavalry, better artillery. After all, he was a gentleman. Foi de gentilhomme, he was ready to meet them.

This decision of Francis's, to hold his ground rather than retreat to Binasco, was a natural outcome of his whole campaign. It was in the mood of Marignano that he had gone into Italy with his great army, and the resistance of Pavia had sapped his strength without undermining his intentions. He still wanted to join issue as he had done so gloriously before. The older men might propose a retreat, but that meant keeping his allies glued together with promises, keeping his army glued together with liquid money, keeping himself in the saddle. He had stood with his army through the whole devouring winter, and he had reached that stage of nervous fatigue at which, for an ardent man of action, further postponement becomes poison. He had not been famously well, and his temperament chimed with Bonnivet's in preferring the brilliant assault to the slow, sinewy, methodic action which makes a man the slave of calculation.

Ever since 1521 Francis had been stretched on the rack. It had been a weary struggle to niggle with Wolsey, to lose him, to stand an English invasion, and then to nurse Wolsey into complaisance. The disaffection of Bourbon had been an ordeal, even if that disloyal prince had been driven from France under the whip of Montmorency. As for Rome, Francis had survived the enmity of Pope Leo and the defection of Pope Adrian, but it had cost him great pains to lure Clement VII to his side. Meanwhile there had been the fruitless operations in Flanders and on the Bidassoa. If all these exhausting and complicated entanglements could now be solved as swiftly at Pavia as they had once been forestalled at Marignano, then Francis could ride home wreathed in triumph in the entrancing tenderness of spring. Then could he expand in happiness, master of Milan, conqueror of Naples, dictator of Italy. He could cup the Papacy in his hand. He could for ever safeguard his Burgundian domain and assuage himself in the Netherlands. France could blossom in palaces, thronged with creative art. The new era would not be noisome with the "triste personnage" of Luther. It would glow with the magnificence of the earlier epoch, but rising above the distraction of heresy, amusing in its play of mind, enhanced throughout the world by the tangible reward of military prowess, and benignly dominant by force of arms.

This would depend on winning Pavia. Wise Italians assured Francis that victory was certain.

30

It was early dawn, February 24. In the camp opposed to Francis there thronged a strange ragged assemblage, of many habits and mixed minds. Pescara, whose keen face bespoke confidence, had marshalled flying corps equipped with small arms, a new branch of military endeavour. Lannoy, the Flemish viceroy of Naples, a reflective man, by no means so naturally confident, had gloomily grouped his own detachments of mounted Spaniards. With these trained veterans there marched landsknechts that grim Bourbon was leading, and the other landsknechts commanded by Salm and Frundsberg. These were tough Lutherans, animated by a fierce spirit and hardened by rough usage in a native school. They had come far and lived hard. So had Pescara's lithe adventurers, many of whom he had reprieved from death at Marseille. They had endured lean winter in Lombardy, and now were actually famished. "I cannot feed you, my boys," Pescara told them with sharp humour, "but before you lies the camp where there is bread in plenty, and meat, and wine."

And beyond that luscious camp lay the encircled town that cooped up more Germans and more Spaniards. De Leyva had exalted every heart by his sustained defence of that girdled city. To break his bonds would crown the attack on Francis. Brother would link with brother, and father would embrace son.

To reach Pavia the forces that opposed Francis had to broach the great park of Mirabello, in which Francis himself had been encamped before he removed the wall on the side near Pavia and withdrew his encampment to the slopes, closer to the town.

This vast park now squarely blocked the approach of the Imperial army, and to pierce its high walls was necessary. The operation was commenced by sappers in the February midnight, the men wearing white shirts to make known their identity as three big openings began to widen in the walls.

So slow were these walls to give way, that Francis had ample time in which to marshal his whole army, save a certain number that were to contain de Leyva inside Pavia; and this assembled French army now spread out in formation for a pitched battle.

As the day dawned, in the cold purity of February, the great French host ranged itself between the city and the wide park into which the Imperials had swarmed. It would be a pitched battle. No general staff would direct it, since Francis already had concerted action with his principal captains. These included the elder heroes of Italian wars—la Palice and la Trémoïlle. An Englishman commanded the Germans from Guelderland: he was the rebel Duke of Suffolk, the "White Rose," Richard de la Pole. The Regent's brother, René de Savoy, was in the field. So was Lescun, brother of Francis's discarded mistress. The handsome Galeazzo san Severino, who once had galloped in gleaming white to take messages to Beatrice d'Este, now stood groomed for the conqueror's service. And near Francis ranged the trusted comrades of his early play days, Fleurange, Chabot de Brion, Montmorency, above all Bonnivet. They were now soldiers in their thirties, each of them commanding his own section of the field and this battle would test their young generation. With them was Marguerite's dull husband Alençon. Armoured like knights for a gallant tourney, they comprehended how grim this tourney would be. Through chilly hours of waiting they had braced themselves, heated by morning wine and yet quivering with icy tremors of anticipation, their nerves taut, their eyes burning away the dark.

Francis's army comprised sixteen companies of gendarmes, five thousand Germans from Guelderland, eight thousand Swiss, seven thousand French foot and perhaps six thousand Italians. He himself commanded his idolised "hares in armour," the noble corps whose repeated charges had broken the Swiss at Marignano.

Through the delicate pellucidity of the dawn, faintly rosy in the distance, the French could at last detect a creeping movement in the park. It gradually defined itself as the stealthy approach of several thousands of the Spanish arquebusiers. They and the light horse were streaming across the foreground, to cut their way round to reach Pavia. Behind them, in the looming light, there moved duskier masses through far trees, dim battalions of landsknechts.

The same Gascon who had so brilliantly directed the artillery at Marignano, Galliot de Genouillac, now stood ready to open fire. Within a few instants, his guns roared out. He caught the vanguard of arquebusiers as it crossed his range. Their ranks were visibly torn in ribbons, arms and legs and heads seen flying in the air. The oncomers were shaken, and they promptly recoiled, taking cover in a fold of ground.

In this grey light of six a.m. Francis's own squinting gaze could descry the enemy's recoil, and excited word came to him that Spanish arquebusiers had already been intercepted by Alençon and Brion. He at once decided to move down into the open, seeking level ground for his darling gendarmes. Surging with excitement as he saw the enemy ploughed by his artillery, he decided to unleash his nerves. Without a qualm, in the assurance of rapid victory, he gave orders to advance, forgetting that this precipitate advance would mask his artillery.

The great bulk of the gendarmes were told to come after him, steadily and deliberately. Meanwhile he set in motion his own three picked companies of shock cavalry, urging them to hold their lives cheap.

On his great charger, in cloth of silver over his mail, with plumed helmet, he towered among his host. It was a fiercely exultant moment. On his road, as he said himself, he expelled fear from his heart. The enemy was fleeing. He was riding to victory.

Through the opposing side, at this moment of interlocking, there ran a trepidation which almost warranted Francis's assurance. The prudent Lannoy, forced to lead his men across the deadly artillery fire, had made the sign of the cross, saying, "There is no help but in God's mercy! Do as you see me do." But Lannoy had not foreseen that Francis would mask his own artillery fire. The landsknechts came safely after Lannoy, a hundred deep. And then Pescara rapidly reinforced them, with his mingled lances and firearms.

By the time Francis's gendarmes had ridden into the shattered arquebusiers, the Imperial advance had been effected. The French King found his advance pounded back by these blunt waves of Germans. Four to one, it seemed to him, the landsknechts came at him. Pikes, lances, light horse, arquebusiers—they poured around his impeded gendarmes.

Savage as this onslaught was, the French repelled it. Overjoyed by their proud resistance, Francis swept his gaze around the frantic broken sea of conflict, reading white fear in the faces beneath his charger.

But while his own vanguard dominated the centre, in the clearing light of the morning, Frundsberg had pushed forward on the wing with his two stout battalions of Germans. To withstand them on the French side there ranged the hardy bands from Guelderland commanded by Suffolk, with Fleurange linking these Teutons to the Swiss. The Swiss pikemen were the first to crumple. Then the battalion from Guelderland lowered their heads, worked doggedly into Frundsberg's ferocious ranks and took their fatal punishment.

This disaster on the wing was unknown to Francis. Still persuaded he had won the day, he swung about to view the general advance. "My God," he cried, "what's this?" His Swiss were recoiling. Alençon, his brother-in-law, was not advancing.

By this time Pescara's small arms were beginning to score against the heavy cavalry. Prancing and careering in the mêlée, Francis strove to rally his men. He was caught in a receding flood. Seeing battalions in panic, "deserting without honour," throwing away a victory he had held certain, Suffolk's men pouring out their lives to cover the impotent rearguard, he felt wild rage and despair. He wheeled in the turmoil. Torn with outraged hope, aware that de Leyva must be sallying out, he fought a long time with his sword, having broken his lance at the very beginning, when he killed an Albanian, the last heir of the "Athlete of Christendom." Only a few of his own people were near him. Then a stab or a shot went home: his horse quailed under him and fell.

He was now on his feet, slaying to right and left, maddened soldiers determined to seize him as booty, to earn his gorgeous equipment. In this last stand Francis seemed doomed. The enemy engulfed him; no Frenchman could break through the turmoil to save him. But unexpected aid flashed to him from the hands of an enemy. Pompérant, that saucy comrade who had ridden with Bourbon in his flight from France, espied his King, the King whom he had deserted, caught in the murderous swirl of the battle. He plunged toward Francis, bidding his own men stand aside. Elbow to elbow with the King, he warded off murder until Lannoy came in sight.

There Francis stood, encircled, gasping, bewildered, shaken, his hand pierced, his cheek bleeding. Already his helmet was off, the gallant plumes wrenched away. Then Lannoy reached him.

The Flemish viceroy of Naples knelt to the defeated King. He kissed Francis's sword hand, took his sword from him, gave him his own. Francis was his prisoner.

Through the maddened field the news ran like fire. Francis stood in his cap, his face ashen with the shock. And soon the whole air rang with clarion, trumpet, shout and rolling drum, "Vittoria, Vittoria, España, España!" Francis saw the wild landsknechts about him: he asked not to be taken into Pavia.

This was shortly after nine, and already his captains had paid the price. Suffolk had died with his Germans. Old la Trémoïlle, a soldier since Brittany, had met his end. La Palice, disputed by two savages, had been murdered. Louise's brother, René of Savoy, was mortally wounded. So was Lescun. The dandy Galeazzo san Severino had died gloriously, and so had two of the Amboise clan, Francis de Lorraine and Saint-Mesme who had worn away Henry VIII's costume from London. The youngsters, the elders, the gay, the sober—they had thronged about their King to meet capture or "honest death." And "nothing was done by us contrary to honour."

The man who had most encouraged Francis to risk this battle was Bonnivet. Early in the fight he had grasped the weakness in the French front, in time to fling himself into the fray. He had striven desperately to rally the Swiss, he and Fleurange. Then it broke into his brain that the battle was lost. He had staked everything on Pavia. Nothing was left except the life with which he had always gambled. He goaded his horse, shouting, "fault aller mourir dans la mêlée."

As Francis was led off the field, the Abbot of Najera bent over the fallen Bonnivet, holding up his head. That handsome head lolled against the Abbot. There would be no more adventures for him. He was finished.

The slaughter continued until from seven thousand to ten thousand were accounted for. Immense booty fell into the victors' hands. Everywhere roaring mercenaries held prisoners to ransom: Fleurange, Henri de Navarre, Montmorency, Brion, Bonneval, Lorges, Annebault, Saint-Pol, Louis de Nevers, Guillaume du Bellay. And the papal nuncio and Clément Marot, the poet.

The imperial army wallowed in delight. Hard-bitten men secured fortunes that had stalked in gilded armour. Pavia, its shackles fallen, drank the wine of liberty. For several days the hard ground lay sheathed in blood, but the earth slowly imbibed its sinister libation, and joy flamed in the triumphant.

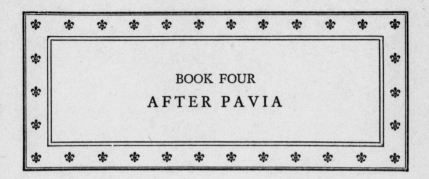

BOOK FOUR

AFTER PAVIA

AFTER PAVIA

Iᴛ ᴡᴀs between nine and ten in the morning that Francis was captured and for some time paraded to and fro, to show the battle was over. With this humiliating exhibition of him the catastrophe became news. By noon it had reached Milan. Quickly it ran to Genoa and Venice, and so, in rings of time, rounded out to China and Peru.

Francis had foreseen no calamity. He had left important papers (especially important to the Pope) lying loose in his camp. Now disaster had overwhelmed him. He stood in the bare armour he was captured in. He had no purse. He had to borrow a hundred ducats from his captor. He had to secure a valet, to find a comb. His only jewel was his ring, but this he kept to send with a message. For the rest, stunned and shaken, he was entrusted to Alarcon, a Spanish commander who was as tactful as he was vigilant, bound to protect him from the unpaid mercenaries as much as to guard him from escape.

The battle was on a Friday and the defeated man fasted. That night he was hidden at the monastery of Saint Paul. His wounds scalded and were dressed, and he tried to sleep. But the situation into which he was plunged had such manifold, such tragic meaning, not only for himself but for his mother, his sister, his children,

297

his people, that no matter how he sought to avert his mind it could not escape that steady and sombre reiteration which drums calamity into the tissues of the brain. He could not unburden it to a friend. He was no longer his master. The walls of his garden had been broken down and he was exposed not only to the hard present but to the accusatory past. Fatigue gave him snatches of sleep, but only to fling him with fresh surges of memory into the merciless brightness of his own perception. He had been defeated and captured in the full view of Europe. He had lost his army. His troops had fled. Throughout the night he fought his battle over, and told himself he had stood the test. To this he held. Below the edge of his mind there trooped the men who had lost their lives, the lamentable dead, but these he could not name or think of. Perhaps he wept. Yet gradually he forced himself to make his plans for the future. Would he, like Jean d'Angoulême, be a prisoner for thirty years? He brought himself to the presence of the Emperor. And his busy mind began shaping his retreat.

The next day he was removed to the east, to the strong fortress of Pizzighittone, and there he was allowed to write to his mother and Charles V. These two letters would be carried by the same messenger.

"Madame," he wrote to his mother, straight from his heart, "to let you know the state of my misfortune, not a thing remains to me but my honour and my life, which is secure. And since in your trouble this news may be a little comfort to you, I have begged to be let write this letter, which has been freely accorded. I implore you not to take it too hard, using your customary sagacity, for I have confidence that in the end God will not desert me. Commending to you your little children, and mine, and begging you to despatch this messenger on his journey to Spain and back, for he is on his way to the Emperor to learn how he wishes me to be treated, and with this humbly commending himself to your good grace, your very humble and very obedient son, Francis."

So he phrased the loose words that would be made pithy by his reporters, "all lost save honour."

To Charles he sent a note almost equally terse. He addressed him persuasively as a fellow-sovereign and a human being. I have no other comfort in my plight, he said, but my estimate of your goodness, by which you will use me fairly in the course of victory. I have firm confidence that your virtue will keep you from imposing anything that is not fair. I beg you to decide in your own heart what you be pleased to do with me, sure that the pleasure of such a prince as you are can only be linked with honour and magnanimity. If you are pleased to have this reasonable pity, to provide the security that the person of a King of France merits, which renders one a friend in place of a desperate man, you can be sure to have a benefit instead of a useless prisoner, and so make a King "your slave for ever." And so may it please you to name him, in place of prisoner, your good brother and friend.

It was a wholly submissive and even penitent appeal yet a bid for reasonable terms. I am in your power, Francis truly acknowledged, but on the way in which you use your power depends our future. Use me fairly (the word "honnête" occurs three times) and I am yours for ever, "votre esclave." Use me hardly, and I am desperate. That was the gist of this calculated appeal to goodwill.

What he employed was his natural tone, the dependent tone in which he courted his mistress or his Deity, and it conveyed the docile spirit in which he proposed to make his peace. Pavia was decisive and he did not hide it. He was defeated. He had lost Milan. But his defeat was, in military fact, confined to the Italian adventure. And whether the Emperor he had never met, his rival in Spain and Germany, could take an imaginative view of his plight had still to be discovered. Could Charles V use his victory with tolerance? Was he a bully or a pedant or a gentleman? That was the question Francis framed. And in his own soul, to wipe out his admitted follies, he was resolved to pay any price, anything, life imprisonment, anything, rather than see his follies visited on France.

He was, unfortunately, requesting goodwill of a man to whom he had never shown it. When the shoe had been on the other foot he had been blithely callous. Did it pinch at Noyon? La, la. Let Charles pay for Naples, "mon vassal." There had been no great goodwill about the Imperial Election, a powerful King elbowing a weaker one out of position. De la Marck and Lesparre had been unleashed like wolves. Now the weak was strong, and Francis besought honnêteté, honour, magnanimity. Was it shameless, or was it only human?

And his ring was slipped from his finger, to be carried as a token of friendship to the Turk. So must he provide against any pusillanimity in Charles, and so guard against his own fervour and impetuosity as a gentleman.

But sustained tragedy was not in Francis's character. No sooner was he installed at Pizzighittone than he began to flirt with Niobe. He was disarmed and disarming. He handed over his gauntlets. He was willing to see Bourbon. He desired to see Pescara. His mind was still fighting the battle and he needed urgently to talk it over, to expatiate, to decant his pain. So, in the fraternity that loosens men's tongues after a struggle, he held easy court in his prison, with Alarcon respectful through black bars and himself voluble and vibrant. This was no Roman hero. Nothing was more natural for him than to hold a court, accustomed to talk from levée to couchée, to be garrulous in his nightshirt. He liked visitors in his bedroom. Bourbon's conduct he deemed iniquitous but he could accept his obéissance and take his towel from him. He could talk to him as one prince to another. Pescara waited on him in sympathetically sombre garb, a perfect little gentleman, all in black. This charmed Francis utterly. He wrote to his mistress that Pescara was "exquis en paix comme en guerre." And in those who greeted him there were surprises. "You seem like a Frenchman?" he said to one man who bowed the knee. It was a gentleman named Montpezat who had been taken prisoner. Francis instantly saw he was trustworthy. He paid his ransom and sent him with despatches, the first step in a great career. In his misfortune the King found the warmth of human responses. On the battlefield, even, a Spaniard had given him a little lump of metal. "That was a golden bullet with which I had meant to shoot you!" And Francis took the souvenir.

But these deep impulses of human kindness had no way of showing themselves as between prince and prince. They did not alter the terrible fact that he was a prisoner, nor that he was at the mercy of Charles V.

And Charles, the whole of the Mediterranean and half of Spain between himself and the scene of action, was still bracing himself to hear he had lost Pavia, and was correspondingly furious with that traitor Pope Clement VII.

2

At midnight two horsemen pulled up at a bridge over the Rhône. The gate into Lyon was closed. They knocked imperiously: they had come from Pavia and were carrying messages for the Regent.

These wayworn men, Montpezat and his companion, had their news on their tongues: the army destroyed, Francis safe, the nobility shattered, Alençon in flight.

They knelt humbly to Louise, summoned from her bed with Marguerite at her side, and in the candlelight, in a group with little ceremony, they submitted their despatches.

Louise, grey-faced and frowning, questioned them with sharpness. The men had much to tell at first hand.

The news was more dreadful than the mind could grasp instantly, then at last, like a wheel of many knives, it cut through a life's defences and Louise broke into a flood of anguished tears, which stopped and recommenced, while she clung to her weeping daughter. Why had he not listened to her? Why had he not listened to la Trémoïlle, who might still be alive? If life had taught Louise anything, it had taught her prudence, and now her adored son, by his natural imprudence, was in the hands of his implacable enemy.

She and Marguerite, listening with desolated tension, drank in the full horror of Pavia. Through this town of Lyon Ludovico il Moro had ridden, with lowered head, to spend his long years in prison. Louise's father had been in prison. Jean d'Angoulême, Charles d'Orléans, prisoners for half their lives. King John, a broken victim. And, when the mind curved away from this cloud over Francis it met the sad troop of Bonnivet, la Palice, la Trémoïlle, with Lescun and her own brother René. And from the dead flying to the alive, it encountered Marguerite's husband.

Storms of grief assailed Louise. She was unstrung. An unnatural brightness began to enliven the hotel. Councillors were arriving, torches bobbing about. Duprat was by her side. Again there was a scene, great tears trembling in her eyes, spilling to her cheeks, while her words swam in lamentation.

The Auvergnat, far from well, listened with growing impatience. Marguerite reinforced her mother. Duprat squirmed unhappily. He could not stand it. Making very homelike remarks of a salutary character, full of plump discomfiture, he strove to impose calm on them, but neither Marguerite nor Louise could contain the overwhelming grief they felt. They cried forlornly and Duprat fidgeted. The landscape he saw, through the rain of these tears, was one that must occupy the Regent no less than himself. He wanted her to study it with him, to plan their action, to collect herself. It was, after all, he who must guide her to govern a threatened France, at the very moment when Semblançay's allies were seeking to destroy him. He could imagine ruin too clearly to dilute his will in tears.

Louise heroically conquered herself. Francis, after all, was alive and well. That was the basic fact. Her son had saved his life, and his honour.

3

Louise's first thought was to invoke every one in Europe who could possibly sway Charles as a person: his young brother Ferdinand in Austria, his aunt Margaret in the Netherlands, Nassau, everybody—everybody, that is, except those by whom Francis had harried the Empire, the de la Marcks and the Würtembergs, the Cleves and the Guelderlands.

These invocations would at once be despatched. And every one who received them would be prone to recollect the great conservative lesson of Louise's own life, the lesson of prudence. It was a tense moment in Europe. The Four Years' War was over. A deep adjustment was taking place. Could any one afford to indulge his imprudent charity? With a duenna like Louise every one must be punctilious. Every one would assure her that she could rely on the Emperor—very much as Marguerite had assured Semblançay that he could rely on Louise. It would be the guarded politeness of the neutral, not through indifference, through the caution of the little folk caught between two great powers.

Meanwhile Alençon limped home, and Louise, who sought pity for Francis, fell on him and flailed him with her tongue.

No one precisely knew what had happened at Pavia in that crucial hour. Fleurange held that the duke had behaved well. There was something about the baggage train cutting off his charge as Francis's charge had cut off the artillery fire. But to excuse was to accuse. He reached Lyon more and more unhappy, and whatever little shell he had managed to grow over his amour-propre was completely crushed by Louise. He was not strong enough for the Angoulêmes. He had, at any rate, been of no use, and he sat down before his uselessness in mournful contemplation. He coughed miserably. He was certainly no hero. And in a world where the weak need an ally he had no ally. He had failed Francis. Marguerite could not forgive him.

But at the sight of this wretchedness, Marguerite took compassion. He was actually unwell. She sent him to bed.

He was not very ill but she stayed by him, rather concerned. How clearly she remembered the way this illness turned!

"You promised me, Monsieur, to receive communion and you have not confessed!" He did get up, confess and take communion; then dined and chatted through dinner, and later lay down.

"Don't leave me," he said to Marguerite, "don't go out of reach, for I feel very much that my last hour is come." But later he asked for something to eat, got up again and walked around quite firmly, and again went to bed. He asked her to read the Passion to him. As she was doing this the doctors came in, five of them, and when she finished he went over each point, to their astonishment. Then he said, "O my God, I know that I have sinned and am of no worth. I am less than nothing. You have given me thirty-six years, and, I must say it, preserved my honour in war and peace, obeying, loving my sovereign Lord." He turned to Louise. "Madame, I am so distressed for you. Since the King went to prison I have had such misery, such grief, that it has killed me. I always feared death but now I find it happy and I am not afraid." He kissed her hand saying, "I ask your grace and commend her to you." He indicated Marguerite, who was standing behind him. "Do not leave me," he begged her. In spite of Louise, Marguerite embraced him, and showed him the crucifix. "Chandeniers!" he called. His chamberlain knelt to him. "Chandeniers, I do not want to make my officers and the poor servants break down. You'll speak to them, comrade, if you please. My wife could not bear to have to speak to them after my death. It seems to me you'd do it better than any one." To his doctor, Jean Goevrot, he said, "The end is here to-day. I beg you to look after her." Turning to Marguerite he presented the doctor, and then said what he wished done for his funeral and for his servants. The bishop of Lisieux arrived with the holy oils, and Alençon was anointed. Then, joining his hands, he accused himself of being weak, wicked, cowardly, and begged his sins to be wiped out by divine goodness. "I implore You not to wait till sunset," he prayed, "but while the sun shines to take me." His mind wandered to the war. "I feel my limbs grow cold. I die. I have no pain." He kissed Marguerite. "Good-bye for a little while." Then, in a feeble voice, looking upwards, he breathed, "I come to You." A ray of the spring sunshine glanced into the room and touched his pale face as he died.

4

Alençon's death made Marguerite a widow and left her completely free to devote herself to her brother. Her letters to him were saturated with religious feeling. She felt that he could only save himself in his extreme tribulation if he flung himself on God's mercy, and she sent him the Epistles of Saint Paul.

But Francis, much as he loved his mignonne and devoutly as he prayed and fasted, was thinking less of divine assistance than of making terms with the impenetrable Charles.

Charles V was perhaps the last person on earth whose heart would respond to Francis. He had been in Spain since 1522. In that year, rather reluctantly, he had ceded Austria to his brother and he had left Germany for a term that would last nearly a decade. He had chosen to stay west of the Rhine because of the rivalry that Francis had thrust on him. He was not unjust. He did not hate Francis. But he had accepted the conflict to which he had been born. In Lombardy it was reaching its climax. From there he would carry it to Burgundy, taking the aggressive. As to reconcilement he had few illusions.

At the beginning of 1525 Charles was anything but happy. He was willing to hispanize himself in the interests of the empire that Cortès and Pizarro were building for him. Spain was a reservoir of fighting men. The Spanish, with the landsknechts, were the stuff for war; reckless, ruthless, rapacious, and admirably led. Spain, in addition, was the key to Naples and a fair source of revenue, though in the end he would bleed the Netherlands for Spanish wars. Already he had weaned himself from his Flemish advisers, was working with a Spanish council and even learning some Spanish. But Italy, at the beginning of 1525, filled him with gloomy concern. Venice had slipped away from him. His English ally was limp. Wolsey, who still kept a French agent secreted in London, had recently spoken in brutal anger, calling him a liar, calling his aunt a "ribald," and actually laying hands on his diplomatic despatches. This could be put on the long finger, but what really stirred Charles V was the perfidy of his Pope. Clement VII, his own creature, had dared to make a secret treaty with France.

"His Holiness is well aware how, being a youth, and scarcely knowing what I was about, I entered on this war for him alone. I do not say for Pope Leo, but for him, for he ruled Pope Leo. Nor were the mutual injuries of the King of France and myself of such a nature as to preclude adjustment; but at his instigation I waged the war, and he has had very good proof how far the one and the other of us may be trusted."

Here the voice quivers because Charles, as against Francis, could persuade himself he could be trusted. He felt morally serious, and to feel morally serious results in a respectability that is half the battle. Charles, in fact, had the "calling" that Calvinism would later be supposed to have brought into Europe. To the State he gave his whole being, body as well as mind.

In point of fact, he could no more be trusted than Francis himself. At the moment he was in dire need of money. About 600,000 ducats were due to his mercenaries in Italy, and Fugger could not lend it to him out of chaotic Germany. He was thus about to break his word to England and to marry Isabella of Portugal, whose dot would be a million. He had been engaged to Claude, Renée, Louise, Charlotte and both Mary Tudors, but his breach of this last engagement was quite deliberate. Yet, while he might break a treaty, might not pay his soldiers, might not pay his debts, might promise Wolsey to write for the cardinals' votes and then hold up the letters at Barcelona, might very soon break faith with Bourbon about his fiancée Eleanor, these breaches of agreement proceeded from a different source than Francis's, and one far more respectable. He was not a prince of the Renaissance but a prince of the post-Renaissance. He let nothing, and certainly not his temperament, interfere with the pursuit of power. In this he could be relied on.

By being thus single-minded Charles gave the valuable impression of moral stability, and no less a moralist than Machiavelli had thoroughly recommended this stability. It makes a prince contemptible, he said, "to be considered fickle, frivolous, effeminate, mean-spirited, irresolute, from all of which a prince should guard himself as from a reef; and he should endeavour to show in his actions greatness, courage, gravity and fortitude."

There was no gay Bonnivet near Charles V. He did not write poetry. There were no frivolous evenings in Toledo, no lascivious lute. He did not mock, was not flippant, wore black wool. He might bully his sisters, show himself shrewdly suspicious of his great lieutenants, swallow up services as he swallowed up pastries, yet he never gave the impression of recklessness, flightiness or caprice. Even his illegitimate children he seemed to have conceived with gravity and fortitude.

In conflict with Francis, therefore, he would easily convince himself that the moral gravity was all on his side, when what was actually on his side was his gravity as a prince. In such character, as Machiavelli delighted to observe, Cesare Borgia was preëminent. So was Charles's slippery grandfather Ferdinand. And if Francis, projected into further generations, would indeed produce the utmost fickleness, frivolity and effeminacy, so would Charles intensify the gravity and fortitude that would pall on the world in his son Philip II.

A young man of this political weight, preternaturally solemn and apparently preternaturally sound, could hardly know himself well enough to know anyone else. He could only defeat his rival and then lay down the law. And Francis, of course, invited destruction.

5

"Sire," announced Lannoy's breathless envoy on March 15, "the battle has been waged at Pavia. Your Majesty's troops have gained victory. The King of France has been taken prisoner and is in Your Majesty's hands."

Charles stood stock-still. He had not heard the words. Then he said, very low, "The King of France my prisoner. The battle won by me." He turned and walked into an adjoining room where there was a little altar. There he trembled to his knees and surrendered his heart in prayer.

He could not exult. He had wavered in his faith. He asked for no rejoicing. Next day he put on his black cape to walk in a religious procession, and he ordered the preacher not to dilate on victory but to confine himself to the praise of the Almighty. Francis delivered into his hands! He could hardly grasp it. He quailed at this revelation of his intimate copartnership with God.

And in Spain, which was beginning to accept Charles, the news was triumphantly received. Round and about him there was intense political thinking. It was a land in the first ecstasy of colonial expansion, backed by a memory of holy war, fresh from a civil war, with hard judgments, class righteousness and intolerance. Navarra was still a sore point. The Moors in Valentia were just about to be scourged. Had Chièvres been alive, someone experienced and lenient and a little corrupt, perhaps the natural exigence of the Spaniard might have been tempered, as it was tempered by Lannoy to some degree. But there are mountains between France and Spain, and it was a stern race that had worked out soldiering with the Great Captain, that had bred lieutenants like Pescara, de Leyva, Pedro Navarro, not to speak of Alarcon and Ugo de Moncada at one end or Cortès and Pizarro at the other. These were doughty men. Ximines and Torquemada, Loyola and Teresa, there was in these natures something of the metal that was embowelled in Spain itself. They wanted from life the ultimate satisfaction of passion inexorably disciplined and hot blood invincibly obeyed. This was not the silver mud of Touraine, black interspersed with white, subtle indulgences and insinuations. This was black scored against white, the virulent sincerity of conviction, the steel-corseted brain. And Charles, with his own Flemish obduracy, was imbibing the absolute at the altitude of Madrid.

He soon wrote a dry word to "mon bon frère" at Pizzighittone telling him that his terms were on the way.

6

Francis had been willing to admit himself at fault. He too regarded Pavia as an expression of the will of God and he believed he had forfeited God's favour. He decided he would fast three times a week, and eat fish, though fish disagreed with him and though Louise and Marguerite implored him not to eat fish. He ordered a smoke-hued Lenten costume, and a robe lined with cheap furs, the equivalent of sackcloth and ashes. At the same time, forgetting the expressed will of the Deity, he slid his eye around to see if he could possibly escape.

Alarcon was there as if Francis were his magnet. He allowed the King to play la paume but there was no chance of deluding him. Fleurange might be released, on his word of honour that he would yield himself up to Margaret of Austria, which he did. But Alarcon's own fate depended on keeping Francis secure, and he was held tight as a drum.

Francis's mind did not occupy itself with the plight of France in his absence. He was self-absorbed. To Duprat and his mother he had resigned everything—parlement, the Sorbonne, taxes, the returned soldiers, the management of affairs with England and the Netherlands. These could not touch him in his inactivity. But he spent hours writing verses. He rhymed to his mistress about Pavia. He wrote melancholy rondeaux and a poem to the nymphs on the Loire. They were toneless, abstract, platitudinous verses of a dispirited classicism, distracting rather than embracing his mood. He was aroused by one important visitor. The Pope sent a messenger and, in a moment away from Alarcon, Francis begged for news of Albany and his expedition to Naples. Albany had never reached Naples: he had abandoned the attack and shipped his troops home. Francis gazed into the beyond. "Is it possible!"

At last Ugo de Moncada arrived with Charles's terms. The Emperor's advisers had paid no heed to Francis's early mood, though one Spanish bishop had warmly supported it. They proposed to reach a "good and sound peace" by the usual method. They first argued the need for Christian peace so that there could be Holy War. They then went back, not quite to Adam, but to Pope Zacharius and Pepin, to Boniface VIII and Philippe le Bel. No part of France really belonged to the French King. Having turned out the whole attic of historic myths and grievances, and having established French war guilt by showing that Charles had "inviolably observed" all treaties and that God, a just judge from whom all victory is derived, "recognizing our just cause and honest purpose," had added Francis's capture to a series of glorious victories, they thereupon came down with lingering slowness through the Count of Toulouse, the daughter of Louis Huton, the dauphin Humbert, until they arrived at the recent villainies of Louis XI. Here Charles's shadowed childhood came into play, intensified by the frustrations and injuries of Maximilian. Out of this soil sprang recrimination and revindication. Bourbon, of course, had to be reinstated, with his claim to Provence admitted. But it was not this claim or the claims in Flanders or in Italy that were put foremost. It was the demand for the restitution of Burgundy. Young Charles was proposing peace to his fallen enemy by encroaching on his kingdom and thus initiating a new war. And this he was doing in the familiar name of justice, the peace of Christendom, the will of God and the good of mankind.

7

"Impossible." So Francis wrote against the demand for Burgundy. He was still in the fortress of Pizzighittone and it was already late in the spring, but he would stay in prison all his life rather than give up Burgundy. He would give Bourbon to the Emperor, provided he never saw him again. He sought to marry the Emperor's sister, to keep Bourbon from having her. He would give up Milan, Naples, Genoa, Asti, Tournai, the vassalage of Artois and Hainault, Arras. He would pay 2,000,000 crowns as ransom. But Burgundy? "Impossible." In this Francis had been not fickle, not frivolous, not effeminate, but immovably resolute since he was captured. He had preferred honest prison to shameful flight, he told his nobles, and rather than infringe the liberty of France he would "spend all his life in prison."

8

The world was not standing still while Francis wrote "impossible." His mother was making frantic efforts to manipulate the world.

It would have gone hard with France if the allies had pushed forward, in the first hysterical months after Pavia. Bourbon demanded it. He wished to dismember France. But the victory had not filled empty war-chests, or built armies, or clarified war-aims. Wolsey did not propose to work for Bourbon's glory. Margaret of Austria did not propose to spend money to give Bologne to Henry VIII. The Pope, warmly congratulating the Emperor, was secretly conniving against him. Maximilian Sforza was now more afraid of Charles than he used to be of Francis. And all Italy yearned for a deliverer, a new Moses, not the symbolic Moses that Michael Angelo had so fervently chiselled.

While the brilliant, unscrupulous Morone began his plot for an independent Italy, with Pescara to be King of Naples, and while the French negotiators fostered division between Henry VIII and Charles V, there was a dreadful period for France—utterly distracted, wildly incompetent and vulnerable. Returned soldiers, unpaid and undisciplined, ravaged the towns crying "vive Bourbon!" The Church pushed its advantage to demand the arrest of heretics, the extension of censorship, the suppression of learning. Louise fumbled with a government in which Lautrec and Montmorency saw one way, Vendôme another. Louise was offering no front to the enemy. She took a compliant tone with parlement at first, yielded and conceded. Parlement, on the other hand, threw itself into the task of organizing a community in the gravest danger of disintegration. It diverted the vagrant soldiers to Lyon, to force Louise's hand. It addressed itself to the protection of the northern provinces. It strove, week by week, to mend the tissues that war had torn down. And it made the astonishing discovery, which Louise also noted, that it saved a great deal of money to have Francis in prison. It meant available revenues. The nation pitied him and cried for him, but his absence was a godsend. He could spend nothing at Pizzighittone.

Meanwhile these hard peace terms absorbed the Regent, Robertet, Jean de Selve, Duprat. At the conference of Calais Duprat had gone over all the historic arguments. He again attacked them with his merciless pertinacity and before he had finished with Charles's case he had reduced it to powder. In the wrangle between himself and Gattinara there would be no silly attempt at comprehension, but

clanging disagreement. Jean de Selve was to wear the robe, and
the fight would soon begin in Spain, but not until Wolsey had been
guaranteed a present of 100,000 crowns.

9

On May 18 Francis was to be taken to Genoa, and from there
shipped to Naples. This was the plan devised by Bourbon and
Pescara. Francis hated it. To spend the summer months in Naples
might mean his death. He managed to communicate with his
mother, and the daring plot was concocted to have his convoy
attacked and a rescue attempted. Better anything than the Château
Neuf.

But Lannoy, the man from Hainault who had charge of Francis,
made up his mind (undoubtedly with Charles's connivance) to take
on himself the odium of balking Pescara and Bourbon. He was
becalmed at Portofino for several days, and then changed his route.
By June 12 Francis was in Barcelona, under smiling skies.

The fury of Bourbon and Pescara was so unbounded that they
poured it into angry letters, brandishing their fists in Lannoy's
face. This was aimed at Charles but Charles was totally unmoved.
He had not wanted either Bourbon or Pescara to walk off with his
bird-cage.

The bird was safely in Spain, and Spain was wildly excited.
Francis's repute had travelled before him. He had been a hero at
Pavia. He was young, fascinating, dangerous, a devil with the
women, and a monarch in distress. Something genuinely kind and
passionate in Spanish attention was wholly captured by their visitor,
and Lannoy, with Charles's permission, gave it full play. The
progress from Barcelona to Madrid took two months, punctuated
by ducal hospitality, grand receptions, solemn bull-fights. Spain
fêted Francis, and Francis beamed on Spain.

His naughty attempt to kidnap Cardona's mistress, the year of
Marignano, had lost nothing in the telling. Now Cardona's widow
entertained him. He had been bottled up in Pizzighittone during
March, April and May. He had seen no women. Now, not free but
lured by freedom, he could walk through the crowd, sit enthroned

at mass, feel eyes dwell on him like black bees on a flower. It was life, and he savoured it. He made friends with the ducal family of Infantado. He forgot imprisonment. He again respired.

There had been a lively hour when his escort, unpaid by Lannoy, pursued their master with firearms. They shot at Lannoy through a window where Francis was standing, hitting the stonework, and then chasing their captain across the roofs. But the "majesty and graciousness" of Francis were such that he could help to appease these mercenaries.

Yet his spirit was extraordinarily troubled. He could meekly say, "I am treated too well for a prisoner." He was only sure of one thing, he wanted to leap over the formalities and intellectualities of his plight, to meet Charles, to present his case, to deal with him in person. He had never been isolated in his life before. He turned to his mother. In June he had written begging her to come to him. "Come soon, for never had I such longing to see you." This was out of the question. Louise was by no means well and she alone could withstand parlement through Duprat and buy high-priced peace from England. But Marguerite would go to her brother. She was free, and on her help might depend her brother's freedom. Louise's intentions were secret, but at last a rumour placed them; Marguerite's marriage either to the Emperor or to Bourbon! Marguerite herself had no desire for one marriage or the other. She said to Francis, "the road is long, and you know my strength." But there was nothing, literally nothing, she would not do for "the only one God has left me in this world, father, brother, husband." She would face anything—death, prison, calamity—and call it liberty, life, health, glory, honour. Her mother and her brother were her law. To them obedience was sweet. She would live and die in obedience to them.

And as the treaty with England drew to conclusion she prepared to sail for Spain. She would "throw the cinders of her bones to the winds" to do her brother service.

10

Francis's arrival at Madrid found his spirit greatly refreshed. He and Charles, after all, were both Catholic monarchs. He was still penitent. He knew he could win Charles if he met him. He was ready to confer with him, to lay his case before him, to demand absolution. He remembered from his meeting with Pope Leo how the floodgates had opened and the strain had sundered. He felt he only needed to see Charles.

A certain uneasiness came on him when he was firmly escorted to his first prison and then ensconced in the Alcazar. The music was over and the lights out: he was in a single chamber with an alcove, a hundred feet from the ground. The window in the alcove was doubly barred. The walls were thick. Down below stretched the arid country, baldly exposed to the naked eye of heaven, the Manzanares a serpent weaving through the thirsty stones.

Francis waited, expectant. Charles would come.

Charles did not come. And as the glow died out of his reception in Spain, as its memories wilted, Francis moved restlessly around his narrow room. He was a powerful man physically, with the urgent need to incinerate his energy, to rouse himself from indolence to excitement. But here his only exercise was to descend with the ever-present Spanish guard and trot on a mule with the guard hung about his neck, a chain of human beings. He looked at them. They were not human beings. They were implacable, impenetrable, blocks of discipline, solid as the walls. Again he was in his narrow room, with constant surveillance, a Spanish officer in the room with him, daylight outside, an oblong of glaring monotony, and his bed as lifeless and stupid as his meals. His mind was heavy. The whole world pressed on him, to stir his will and his spirit, but Charles made no move and sent no message. Charles kept him tortured by suspense, as if he knew all the laws of the novitiate and all the anguish of the Exercises. So Francis festered in prison, isolated and becalmed.

And he literally festered. There was a poison in his system that had possibly been responsible for his indolence between 1521 and 1523. It had perhaps reappeared in the lethargy before Pavia. His mother had been incessant in her inquiries about his health while he was at Pizzighittone, but the worry and derangement of prison, the horrible suspense in which Charles was holding him, at last found the weak spot and began to break him down. He fell ill. His disgust with life mounted to a fever, passed into torpor, returned in a misery of the nerves. He was indubitably ill. His jailors watched him suspiciously, then examined him, verified. He lay in bed, indifferent and half-unconscious, given over to the secret turbulence of fever. The Spaniards could not deny that he was in high fever. They sent word to Charles.

II

In the middle of September Charles was hunting near Segovia in the company of his grandees, when an urgent message interrupted him: his royal prisoner was sinking.

Though it was dusk and they had hunted all day, Charles and his nobles mounted horse at once and rode nearly thirty hard miles to Madrid, arriving about nine in the evening.

Montmorency came down into the courtyard to wait on the Emperor. Lannoy was with him. By torchlight they mounted the stone steps of the donjon and marched the long white corridor. The three Spanish dukes were left in the cold corridor. Then Montmorency raised a torch and the Emperor, followed by Lannoy, bent their heads in the arched doorway and stepped into the room.

It was the first time that the Emperor was to meet the King of France. This prison room, thick-walled and obscure, was very different from a Field of the Cloth of Gold. A fire flickered on the hearth. The walls were hung with an embroidery bearing the letter F and fleurs-de-lis. The air was heavy and confined.

The sick man lay inert, oblivious. Charles stood silent, attended by his torchbearer and his viceroy. At last Francis lifted his weary eyelids and saw the Emperor gazing at him. His courtesy stirred: he strove to rise. Charles strode forward to catch him and the two young men clung in an embrace.

"Sire," Francis murmured, "you see before you your prisoner and your slave."

"No, but my good brother and true friend, whom I consider free."

Francis mournfully repeated, "Your slave."

"My good brother," replied Charles vigorously in his Walloon accent, "and friend who will become free. I desire nothing more

powers, his kindness encouraged her to try her persuasiveness and do her best to reach a European settlement.

Charles came out to receive her as befitted a princess. He was at her disposal to confer with. For two hours, with Madame Châtillon on guard, she was quite alone with him. But to move that imperial will by appealing to the heart was to lap against a rock. No woman, and above all no Frenchwoman, could stir him. He was himself sparing of words and frugal of ideas, so that this flexible, rapid-minded, resourceful woman could merely make him suspicious. In her trouble he had melted, but he had early decided, with Gattinara to fortify him, that until Francis released Burgundy he would not release Francis, and on this conviction he had taken root. He had all the past behind him—Philip the Fair and Charles the Bold and Philip the Good, all the historic resources of a pre-determined man. He would be buried with his ancestors at Dijon. Had this been immediately possible it might have helped Marguerite. But to suggest Burgundy as Eleanor's dot, to frame a new "duchy of Burgundy," even to propose arbitration, could not make him shift his ground. He had closed his premiss.

It was, of course, a familiar dynastic method. Burgundy was a pillar of France and Charles wanted to pull down the pillar. Francis had pursued Navarra for a similar reason. He had supported the Duke of Würtemberg and the Lord of Sedan and the Duke of Guelderland and the Scottish earls for a similar reason. He wanted Milan for a similar reason. The historic unit would always conflict with the neighbour's unit—such was the principle Charles was obeying. And he still intended to force Francis to confer full sovereignty on Bourbon, in the centre of France.

Marguerite was futility itself. She went to Eleanor. Eleanor was dependent on her brother Charles. He had debarred her first love and bestowed her on an elderly Portuguese. Eleanor had served her time until the royal Portuguese had died. Marguerite wooed her for Francis. To depict Bourbon as an assassin, to show Francis as an enchanter, to describe Touraine in dazzling words to the parched widow from Portugal—it came naturally to Marguerite. But Charles knew his sister too well not to detect a strange note in her talk. He packed her off on a pilgrimage to Our Lady of Guadeloupe. Marguerite was at a loss. Lannoy intervened, to no purpose.

She felt Charles's fair speech was not in agreement with the imperialists' hard terms. She called it "dissimulation." She returned to her brother.

Brother and sister were torn. By gentle and firm resolution he might wear them down, and Marguerite's own nature inclined her to ideal patience. But his health, his realm, his future? They flung themselves from one desperate expedient to another. He would stay in prison for ever. He would abdicate. He would agree to cede Burgundy against national honour and would privately disavow against private honour. All these plans she and he revolved, under the double-barred window, she not guiding her brother but abetting him and yearning for him.

And then word came to them that one of his Spanish veterans could arrange relays of horses from Madrid to the border. Could Francis escape from his room? This daring possibility fired both of them. Marguerite cared nothing for the risk. She was prepared to stand by him and defy his guards and spend the rest of her life in a convent.

They devised their plan. He had to change places with someone who was broad-shouldered and tall, someone who came and went freely. The only one who had Francis's kingly stature and figure was the blackamoor who brought firewood. Then let the blackamoor play the King and let Francis play the slave. This coloured man would get into his bed and look regal, while Francis, smudged and humble, would carry the wood-basket out of the donjon. He would pass the dozen officers outside, the four hundred soldiers below, and walk out of Alcazar to the Arab horse awaiting him.

The plan was matured. But in Francis's entourage was Rochepot, Montmorency's brother, and in anger this feudal youth had hit a valet in the face. The valet could not hit back. He had no possible redress for this humiliation, as great to him as the loss of Burgundy to France. With raging heart he rode to Toledo and gave away his King's secret to Charles.

Charles did scarcely conceive that his royal brother would black his face and don vile clothes. But in this garb Francis was trapped, on the evening he stole from his room. And his Spanish captain was pounced on and arrested.

Marguerite's part was undeniable. She had to leave her brother.

14

When Marguerite departed she made a present to Francis of her little black dog, and this dog has not helped his reputation. One of his attendants wanted to buy a present for Brion. "I have found a beautiful young slave for Monsieur de Brion," he wrote, "that her mistress wishes to sell because she is too amorous." Later a historian found a letter saying that the "petite noyre" spent an hour in his bed every morning, which gave Francis pleasure: and the historian knew only of Brion's "petite noyre." He did not think of the pet dog.

But in the final stages of the struggle between Charles and Francis there is little chance to smile. So far Francis had based his self-respect in politics on "the faith of a gentleman." It was that which had carried him through Marignano and sustained him through Pavia. He carried his head high because he was a chevalier. He had overridden his parlement, overtaxed his people, overruled his council, since he stood in this proud relation to life, holding an aristocratic code of honour that lifted him above ordinary human assessment and gave him romantic validity. He vindicated war because he was a noble soldier, and a noble soldier was a gentleman. And having brought his realm to the verge of ruin by reason of this implicit faith of his, which had been indulged at Cognac and held against unadventurous Louis XII, he was now called on to prove what Gods he really lived by.

It was a cruelly hard predicament. And his pride had spoken from the beginning, in his manifestoes and in his letters. He would never yield. He resigned himself to a lifetime of imprisonment rather than a peace without honour. He would abdicate rather than yield. Or he would become ill and die, rather than yield. Anything but yield, since the loss of Burgundy meant the unthinkable weakening of his kingdom.

If any prince declares he cannot yield an inch of his territory, he must either have unconquerable armies, unconquerable lawyers, or unconquerable will. Under intolerable pressure from outside, if he is to keep his integrity, he must give up his life.

But Francis was not made for honourable suicide. What began to give way in him was the literal "foi de gentilhomme." He had no sword on which he could fall with naked breast. He held to his honour, as advised by his clergy, but he also held to his life. He had actually drawn up the papers for his abdication and entrusted them to Marguerite. For this cruel abdication he proposed to retain to himself a bare household of sixty attendants, including several men for the wine-cellar, a pastry-cook, an upholsterer, a man to play the "viscontin," a man to play the spinet and a man to play the lute.

The clearest thinker in the opposite camp was Pescara. Kept straight by his wife Vittoria Colonna, he had resisted the invitation to usurp the kingdom of Naples and had revealed this plot to Charles. Now, on the eve of his death, he declared to Charles his belief that Francis neither would nor could yield Burgundy. To make a treaty based on his surrender of Italy would be a great deed. This was the object Pescara urged. He was a mature soldier, quite able to imagine himself into Francis's position. But his advice was lost on Charles who, tutored by Adrian of Utrecht, thought far less of imagining the other man's position than of making an ideal treaty and enforcing it as holy writ. Gattinara strengthened Charles's Burgundian prejudices but urged harsher ways of enforcing it. Lannoy carefully inclined the other way. But Charles, believing that you can bruise human nature into the political mould that your interests dictate, set himself to secure a political bond he could enforce. Once he had his bond in writing, at the foot of his drastic treaty, he deemed his pound of flesh politically secure.

Francis went through many emotions. His honour was his true religion. But at last, urged by his mother and even by Marguerite that to remain long in prison would break up his kingdom, and unable to suggest any compromise that would tempt Charles to release him, he made up his mind that he would sign under protest.

So, at a secret meeting in his cell, he protested before God that he did not mean to do anything against the honour of God, or his own honour, or to the prejudice or hurt of his kingdom. He would sign the proposed treaty to avoid the evils and ill consequences that must come to France by force. He could not do anything contrary to the good of his crown. But, to put God and justice on his side, he would pay a ransom.

It was a very serious decision. At the point where Francis stood

MARGUERITE D'ANGOULÊME, QUEEN OF NAVARRE,
ABOUT 1525

From the Drawing attributed to Clouet in the Musée Condé, Chantilly

the morality of the state was intersecting Christian morality. The national state was a virile conception of self-assertion, each state a law unto itself. And Francis could not abandon it. But neither could he abandon without cost his conception of honour and fair dealing. Charles's savage intention of enforcing this peace drove him to duplicity. Francis made his secret declaration that he was signing "under duress" and then agreed to sign everything.

Charles was agreeably surprised to learn that Francis would sign. But to compel the Most Christian King to steep himself in lying, in case he was lying, he insisted on every sanctified formula—God, chivalry, high mass, as well as ribbon and sealing-wax.

Into all of these pledges and affirmations, hand-claspings, testifyings, Francis entered with hardihood and an alarming histrionic zest. At the same little altar in his prison room where he and Marguerite had worshipped, he pledged himself before God. He embraced his brother Charles V in public. They rode side by side into Madrid. They rode together in a litter. They visited Eleanor, and Francis, lifting her from her knee as she was about to kiss his hand, said, "It is not the hand I owe you, it is the mouth," and sealed his engagement.

This engagement had forced Charles to break his word to Bourbon who had been assured Eleanor since 1522. To give her to Francis was outrageous. But Lannoy, who detested Bourbon, persuaded Eleanor to say she did not want him. Charles thereupon became the humane brother who could never bully his sister, and, to compensate the angry Bourbon, dispossessed Sforza and give him Milan.

At the crossroads where the two kings parted, on the eve of the deliverance, they had a final word.

"My brother," said Charles, "you recollect the pact you have made with me."

"Assuredly," said Francis, who had a remarkable memory, "I could repeat it by heart."

"Give me your word that you will carry it out as faithfully on your side as I will on mine. For whichever of us fails the other will rightly be called a blackguard and a coward."

"I will fulfill it from the instant I enter my kingdom. Nothing can stop me."

"In our long war," Charles went on, "I have never hated you. But if you deceive me, especially in anything that touches the Queen your wife and my sister, I shall take it as so great an injury that I shall loathe you and do everything to draw down vengeance on you and hurt you in every possible way."

"I swear to you," responded Francis, "that I intend to carry out everything I have promised."

And then they said adieu.

Francis had hardened his heart. The Habsburg had formulated a peace to which he could never consent. In Italy and again in Spain he had been ready to make huge concessions, but Charles V wanted more than concessions. He wanted to cripple his rival's kingdom. Could Francis endure it? It destroyed the meeting of minds. It destroyed any form of working agreement. The only answer was to disregard oaths and incantations, bonds and sealing-wax. The integrity of his kingdom came before his faith as a gentle-man.

Yet his faith as a gentleman had been the thing he really lived by.

15

Meanwhile it was forced on Louise to decide if the dauphin should be the hostage to Spain. She did not dare strip France of its twelve principal noblemen, so she chose her grandchild, whom his little brother must accompany.

Marguerite had found the family unwell on her return. Her poor mother had had colic, "fort mal." The children had had measles. But in a few words she showed them convalescent to Francis. "Now they are all entirely cured and very well," she wrote. "M. le Dauphin is studying to perfection, mixing up 100,000 other jobs with it. No longer a question of irritability, but all virtuous! M. de Orléans is riveted to his book and says he wants to be wise. But M. d'Angoulême knows more than the others and does things to be taken as prophetic rather than childish, of which, Monseigneur, you would be amazed to hear. Little Margot resembles me in not liking to be ill. But they tell me she is extremely graceful and become prettier than ever was Mademoiselle d'Angoulême. Vela, Monseigneur, toute la vérité de vos enfans!"

And now, as the penalty of Pavia, these two small children were to be taken from Marguerite's brooding solicitude and transferred to a military confinement in Spain. At first it would not be intolerable, but before long they were to be deprived of every tenderness that could have been given to them by women. They had been lovingly reared. Now they were to be surrounded by soldiers and surveyed by gruff wardens whose sole concern would be their retention. They would live in cheerlessness, in neglect, in the shabby ineptitude of a male prison. It would be no worse than the fate of millions of poor European children, the everyday misfortune of those whom bestial war incarcerated in poverty. But these two small boys, François and Henri, were later to return to Europe, and to carry with them for ever the stigmata of those years in Spain when, as two unweeded little beings, they had huddled in a soiled room, dimly aware of a heavy cloud that had settled on their childhood, cutting off the light that dances in Touraine.

It was like their gay father to have loaded his burden on his children. He was not one of those men who could be cruel. He disliked cruelty. But always he had risen buoyantly above the consequences of his acts, the male whose supreme art is to win indulgence. So far he had met life with promissory smiles. Men could believe in him. But now there was a debit, and those who loved him would be privileged to pay. One of the subtlest degradations in human intimacy is the bland triumph of an inferior nature over the higher natures that bestow love. But Francis could not go outside himself to know he was degrading Marguerite and stealing childhood from his children. He had extracted himself from Spain by a fraud consecrated by his bishops. To see his children go into Spain would seem equally lamentable, and equally acceptable.

So, in the middle of the tranquil Bidassoa, on an anchored platform, Francis was to have one glimpse of François and Henri. While Lannoy was to accompany him to the middle of the bay, Lautrec would fetch the children from the other side. They were then to cross the float, Lautrec to return with his master, Lannoy to take the children into captivity. And it had been piously agreed, for everyone's sake, that Francis would no more than bless his children as he passed them.

The people had been kept from the bay for ten miles on either side. The military escort was limited to a thousand. There was nothing but to make the quiet exchange.

At seven in the morning the two boats set out from France and Spain. It was high tide. To Francis's left was the town that Bonnivet had captured for him, tawny Fuenterrabia on a height. Bonnivet, Pavia, the treaty—he turned from them as he turned his back on Spain. But from the opposite shore drew the boat that was bearing his boys, another reminder of Pavia.

The two bright, observant little princes saw their big father stride over to them, felt his strong hands clasp them, and in an instant were whisked into the craft that he had quitted. The father broke into tears and sat with his face buried in his hands. But soon he neared the French shore and glanced up expectantly. There stood his household cavalry, in glorious new uniforms. The boatmen shipped their oars, the boat gliding to the pebbles. He leaped into the shallow water, and ran up the slip. "I am a King!" he cried, "King once again!"

It was still early in the morning, March 17, and nowhere could the world have greeted Francis more benignly. It is a land where the Atlantic tempers the south, and while winds rush to it radiant from Africa, burnishing its skies, they soon melt in the softness of the ocean. There are moments in its springtime, green with young bracken, yellow with mimosa, red with the virgin leaves, so lovely that no heart could withstand them, and the Atlantic on which Francis had glanced rolled inland in long bars of lazy surf, crumbling to the flats where sea birds toss and swoop in freedom.

And to freedom he galloped. His road to St. Jean de Luz climbed rounded hills that billow from the Pyrenees. For a year and a half he had been away from France. For a year he had been in prison. It had been a period of inescapable pain, of humiliation, anxiety, illness, his nerves tortured and his senses starved. And it was over. His brave horse breasted the hill and there, the land unfolded, his Kingdom invited him. Beyond blue curves lay Bayonne, Bordeaux, Cognac, Blois. How serene the valley spread with forest, how suave the interlacing hills. "Comme grande est la joye presente!" So cried his heart. "By joy we are re-made!" So he would write in coming hours. One wave of joy surged through him on another. It was too much. He had not "force to sustain so much felicity."

FRANCIS, THE KING'S ELDEST SON, WHO DIED IN 1536

From the Portrait by Clouet in Antwerp

(Braun Photograph)

16

This Saturday was a fast-day. So at St. Jean de Luz they could only have fish. And they had fish—pike, salmon, codfish, lampreys, oysters, turbot, sword-fish, sturgeon, draine, allozes, gourneaux— a great deal of fish, with mustard and cress, and apple-tart and a flammèche. It was cooked by Francis's own cooks, with their own "batterie de la cuisine," white wine and claret to go with it. And after that, tuned for the day, he set out for Bayonne. The people had gathered, lining the road, cheering Francis home. With lifted chin, tall on a princely horse, he took their cheers: could he break up their kingdom?

Outside Bayonne the English ambassadors waited on him. At three he reached the town and straightway proceeded to the cathedral. His mother was with him. She was older. She had suffered. But she, and he, and Marguerite were together at last.

17

A loyal family conspires against the world, and these three remained a family. Louise had much to tell him, of Wolsey, of Italy, of the Pope. Duprat had aided her, armed her against the parlement. She solaced Francis on the iniquitous treaty. Now they could ask Burgundy to speak. She told him in her caustic intimacy of the encroaching Sorbonne, of truculent Paris refusing to ratify the English treaty and earlier inviting Vendôme to become regent. But his health, his contentment, his hopes—these were her passionate concern. She had nearly died in his absence and had once been a month without news of him. She now heard about Eleanor, his promised queen. To release the dauphin, Francis said, he would marry a mule. He told her of Charles. They spoke of the presents to Alarcon—gold vessels from himself, a gold chain from Louise, a present from Marguerite—in all, 5,000 ducats. To Alarcon was due much of his "good and reasonable treatment."

It was a surpassing hour. He made his nobles happy by filling the niches that Pavia had emptied. He made Chabot de Brion his admiral and Montmorency his grand maître and Fleurange his

marshal. These, with Montchenu, had been his boyhood companions. La Rochefoucauld of Barbesieux would soon command on the
seas. It was Cognac come of age.

And his mother had been considerate: she had brought Anne de
Heilly for him. This was the intimate consolation. He desired this
new intimacy that had lived in his imagination for two years. He
was still only half-cured from the old one and Anne could offer
him a new self. To be a placed experience in which the reefs and
sunken wrecks are taken on sufferance—that he had known. He
needed these fresh eyes, this clear profile and newly moulded throat,
this stealth of approbation. Yet Anne de Heilly would be no "belle
amourette." She had begun by winning Marguerite and Louise.
She would be saved: she believed in the trinity.

He was coming back to this new life, after living death. But
perhaps because he was no longer so sure of his panache he turned
to her the more eagerly. He had lost his proud brush in the hunt.
He needed sympathy, fresh indulgence, approbation.

18

Francis went to festive Cognac, ready to repudiate his treaty
with Charles V. He knew that the Lutheran princes had made
conspicuous gains in Germany and he knew that the Turk was
advancing in Hungary. He had every reason to hope that England
would eventually join him in the field. To give actual aid to Italy
at the moment was beyond him. He had no army. Peace with England would take two millions and he had no money. He would
have to find two more millions to be ready for the ransom of his
sons and his country had to be prepared for this possibility. But
while he would stiffen opinion to raise this ransom and to resist
Charles in Burgundy, he was more than willing to encourage the
Italians to spend their energy in attacking the Emperor. Clement's
league would become the League of Cognac, with Henry VIII
benevolently approving and Francis waving his bonnet.

Burgundy was induced to protest. The classic doctrines that
Philippe Pot had enunciated a generation before—"the common-
wealth is the people's," "kings were originally created by the votes

of the sovereign people"—could now be turned to a popular affirmation of Francis's will. And this was done in short order.

Charles V could not have foreseen this move, and Lannoy was disgusted. He knew that Francis could impose his will on Burgundy. But the Italians rejoiced at the resistance it declared. Italy alone could not throw off the Emperor. Pope Clement exonerated Francis from breaking his oaths to Charles. He greeted him as an ally and, despairing of Italian unity alone, proposed a Holy League to Francis.

By repudiating the Madrid treaty Francis seemed to take up a clear position. He seemed to appeal from the verdict of Pavia and to renew his great struggle with Charles.

So concluded the Italians. The Venetians were too close to Milan not to see how utterly demoralized were Bourbon's forces. He had no money. He was ignored by the Emperor and becoming hysterically desperate. But this was not the only feebleness that was exposed. All during 1526 the wiser Italians could see Charles's disadvantages everywhere. Solyman the Magnificent was advancing towards Mohács, where he would bring Charles's brother-in-law, Louis of Hungary, to his death. Pope Clement, fearsome and flittering, could see that the Turk and the Lutheran were working to free Italy. Guicciardini and Machiavelli, two Italian intellectuals of singular penetration, ached with the miserable urgency of the crisis. Here it was, ripe and ready, and everything playing into Francis's hands.

But an imprisonment has its sequelæ. Marignano had buoyed Francis's imagination. Pavia had left it wounded. This was a man who had suffered a moral catastrophe, had collided with the impossible. His triumphs in the exterior world had responded to his undaunted vigour as a youth. There had been no limit to his courage so long as there was no suspicion of his aptitude. He had been fully and gloriously employed, mind and body ardent. But this high-hearted man, careless of himself and callous for others, had been checked by forces outside and beyond him. He was the same man as in 1523 but he had learned, through his nerves, to dread precipitancy. Highly stimulated at home, working in plastic wills, induced to affirm himself, he had encountered another world in which the smile had died, and skies were leaden. His personality, aggrieved and bruised, shrank from any further struggle. It yearned for a luxurious nest, to curl itself within harsh circumstance.

So, while the Italians prayed for a liberator—a barbarian, that is to say, who would save them from the other barbarian—Francis gave them high promises, and sketched noble gestures, and devoted his real efforts to a saving alliance with England. He had suffered too great danger in 1522 and 1523 to go South until his North was protected. He could not dare to touch Italy until he was certain of Henry VIII. Meanwhile, Pope Clement and Ferrara and the Venetians must fend for themselves.

It revolted the Italians to see Francis so inert, and fresh from their own ascetic cities, they held up their hands at his laxity. Francis was frivolous. Francis was a pleasure-seeker. Francis was unable to muster his will.

He was indeed exhausted. To muster his forces he required to muster his will, and he was slack, for by repudiating Charles he was exposing himself to terrific reprisals and his first instinct was to build up energy.

Though Charles had left him for his joyous marriage to Isabella, his young bride soon saw her bilious husband wreathed in gloom, "full of dumps and solitary." Francis was wriggling from his hands. "He has not acted like a true chevalier," Charles acridly reproached the French envoy in June, "or like a true gentleman, but viciously and dishonestly." He even threatened a duel. "Please God we shall fight it out in person." He felt that his moderation and trustfulness had been cynically betrayed. He had not locked up Francis, as the English had locked up Francis's grandfather, or as the French had locked up, and ruined, Ludovico Sforza. And now, as Gattinara had foretold, not only was Burgundy withheld but Italy would once more be disputed with the Emperor.

Italy in 1526 had, in fact, come to the last stages of the crisis that Charles VIII had blithely started. For over thirty years, every day of Francis's life, the Italian nation had been struggling to centralize itself, and the papacy had always defeated that centralization. Each pope since Alexander VI, except Adrian VI, had been a prince, and a prince with territorial ambitions. At one end of the see-saw was Naples, at the other end was Milan, with the princely

Pope holding the balance. Julius II had done it by becoming a
soldier, and Leo X had done it by paying soldiers. But once Naples
had been gained by Spain through the shrewdness of Ferdinand,
once Leo confirmed Charles V in Naples, Italian independence
could only remain a possibility by keeping the French in Milan.
This Leo X had given up to aggrandize his family: hence Clement
VII's impotence. He could not see-saw if he and Francis together
did not counterbalance the Spaniard. With the Pope dethroned as
the centralizing force in Italy, the whole nation would wake up to
find itself at the mercy of Francis's conqueror, and the papacy would
cease to be European through the overpowering influence of Spain.

Those who loved Italy and who had large political conceptions
—Machiavelli and Guicciardini, even Contarini and Acciajuoli,
Canossa and Ghiberti—saw that the Emperor must be ousted. It
became more and more evident every week of 1526. Machiavelli
spoke of the Spaniards as "these wild beasts who have only the
faces and voices of men." Guicciardini looked with despair on his
own mad countrymen. "Murderers have been seen at large who had
played ball with their victims' heads in the public squares of Forli."
And later he exclaimed, "Oh God, what pain to behold so much
confusion." But he and Machiavelli agreed on one thing, "We must
not yield but resist with all our might."

The merchants of Venice had indeed hired an army. The Duke
of Urbino led his leonine army about Lombardy, keeping its mane
combed and its nails pared. It growled, but it kept discreetly out
of action. What was needed, to back up Giovanni de' Medici and
the Papal army, was a great contingent of veterans, steel-shod by
French determination, and a gold-shod war-chest to come after
them.

This was cryingly evident by the August of 1526, but by the
month of August the stags of Amboise, the stags of Chenonceaux,
and the stags of Chambord were in season. By August Francis was
joyous on the Loire. Impatient and censorious despatches left the
Loire for Italy. Francis seemed lazy, inconsequent, lascivious and
wicked, to the men who, at long last, realized the imminent danger
of Italian subjection. But the wise, hard-headed men spent no time
in blaming Francis. They were too Latin to be surprised that a

Frenchman should watch them drowning without lifting his hand. Italy was drowning because Italy had not learned to swim. All Machiavelli could do he did do. He urged plans for his militia. He and Pedro Navarro saw to repairing the walls of Florence.

The autumn went by in an apparent wastefulness of spirit. Marguerite persuaded Francis to give his mind to the terrible plight of Louis Berquin, about whom Erasmus had written. Francis rescued him from the Sorbonne. But he had made up his mind not to intervene in Italy except for his own sake, on his own terms. He saw to it that Queen Claude had an impressive public funeral, and he himself found time for several novenas that he had promised, and went reverentially to Saint Denis as the holy relics were restored to place. But he was neither able nor willing to obey pressure from Italy. From prison he had promised that he would in future devote himself to "la chouse publique." He would do strong, bold, devoted, magnificent things for his people. But he would do them in his own way. For as long as a fortnight at a time he hopped from château to château, hunting the stag, evading du Bellay and his other conscience-keepers. He clearly heard Pope Clement's screams for assistance, but he did not choose to heed them.

19

Pope Clement had been paying for the anger he had stirred in Charles V's veins. And to this anger Ugo de Moncada had given practical effect. Moncada understood the Pope's weakness. The simplest way to influence him was to terrorize him, and the best way to do that was first to disarm and then to punish him. He deftly seduced the Pope into a truce with the Colonnas. Clement relied on this truce and gladly disbanded his troops. Moncada then went to the rugged Cardinal Pompeo Colonna and prompted him to sack Rome. The elderly cardinal, who had missed becoming Pope because of Clement, was not unwilling. He poured his bandits into Rome. They stole over half a million ducats. They stole the tiara. They sacked St. Peter's. They were murderous, obscene and ribald. When the Pope had been sufficiently flailed, Ugo de Moncada reappeared and proposed a fresh treaty. He then wrote to the Catholic King Charles urging him to deprecate the raid.

Charles V was ready to deplore it, but he never forgave the vacillations of Pope Clement.

Francis was of course indignant at the outrage to the Holy Father. He sent Guillaume du Bellay to condole with him, and du Bellay brought a modest salve—3,000 ducats.

But while Clement was being urged to rejoin his own League, and while Francis was learning new dances, the military balance in Italy again shifted in the Emperor's favour.

The one considerable army that had been mustered in Lombardy was that for which Venice was paying. Its commander, Francesco della Rovere, Duke of Urbino, was Pope Julius's nephew. He had been spirited enough to murder Pope Julius's favourite, and he had fought brilliantly and bloodily for Urbino, when occasion arose. But now he was engaged to hold a watching brief. His masters in Venice told him not to risk his skin, to perambulate, to hang on the outskirts, to pick up trifles.

On these terms he had captured Lodi and Cremona, and refused to embroil himself with Bourbon.

Bourbon had not a ducat. He had served the Emperor's purpose up to Pavia but now he was rather a liability. He tortured the Milanese to get ducats. He released the conspirator Morone for a ransom (which Morone, with shameless effrontery, tried to procure by betraying Bourbon).

While these intrigues progressed a new army came down from the Tyrol. It was composed of Lutheran landsknechts, piping hot from killing the "canaille" at home. They were led by George von Frundsberg and they numbered 12,000. They were, with any luck, to be paid on arrival in Italy.

Only one soldier tried to take honest military action at this juncture. Giovanni de' Medici, at the head of his bands, went forward near Mantua to break Frundsberg. He was shot in the leg, had an amputation, and died.

On his death-bed his opponent, the Duke of Mantua, kissed him and asked, "What can I do for you?"

The dying soldier smiled. "Love me when I am dead."

His loss left Italy without a sword. And when Bourbon gave up Milan to join Frundsberg, the fate of Rome was already sealed. This was on January 2, 1527.

20

In the same month, January, 1527, Marguerite was offered a new way of showing how much she loved her brother. She was invited to re-marry.

Her first marriage had been political, thrust on her when she was not yet seventeen. It had been spiritually arid and it had lasted sixteen years. Another kind of woman would have refused a second such experience. Marguerite was in the same widowed state as both Margaret of Austria and Mary of Hungary, and these two devoted women had flatly refused to renew their political marriages. But Francis's sister was a captive. Through a strange sense of her own worthlessness, the self-guidance and self-assertion that would naturally have been hers were completely surrendered in the name of "the obedience that I owe Madame and the King." She was more sensitive, more subtle, more reflective, more unselfish than either her hardened mother or the man they both indulged. And yet Marguerite could not protect herself. This defencelessness, with other natures, would have been its own protection. But Madame and the King could not estimate the dreadful privations that Marguerite accepted. They were coarsely habituated to take whatever she offered as the natural bounty of a person as self-regarding as themselves. They now felt utterly free to scan the horizon to make the best of her. They were working in the mood for war. They welcomed the mood of sacrifice. Louise had indeed wrongly calculated on using her daughter with the Emperor. That had gone awry, and since Francis had captured Bourbon's bride it had not been necessary to tempt him with Marguerite. Henry VIII had been considered, since the rumour of divorce, but Henry was reserved for Anne Boleyn. The use that could be made of Marguerite was consequently narrowed. But Francis and Louise had inherited three feudal problems—Alençon, Bourbon and Navarre. Alençon was solved. The duke had left no heir. Bourbon was an enemy. But Navarre? Its heir was here at court, young Henri de Navarre, only nine years Marguerite's junior.

Navarre was important. If Francis undertook a Spanish offensive in 1527, the recapture of Navarre would be unwelcome unless subordinated to the Crown. He and his mother had never believed

HENRI D'ALBRET, KING OF NAVARRE, AND HUSBAND
OF MARGUERITE D'ANGOULÊME

From the Painting by Clouet in the Musée Condé, Chantilly

in Navarre as an independent kingdom. They had disregarded the frowns of Alain d'Albret at the beginning of the reign. They had legally annexed Armagnac, Castres and Gaure. And they had brought his good-looking boy, Henri de Navarre, to live at the court. It was Henri's sister who wed Cesare Borgia, and his brother the cardinal had recently died, leaving two bastards, eight bishoprics and a thousand debts. Henri de Navarre had his own gay style and would grow a gallant beard. Captured at Pavia, he had let himself down by a rope out of the fortress of Pavia and brilliantly escaped, thus saving his ransom of 100,000 crowns. This was the youth with whom Marguerite would renew her marital experience.

There was, indeed, the disparity in years. But Marguerite had only the regret that Nérac would be so far from Madame and the King. She accepted her young husband with an obliterating calm, writing to a friend on the eve of her marriage that the great thing was always to resign oneself to "the will of God."

21

Less resigned was her old friend Semblançay. While Francis was before Pavia his first trial had been concluded. He had been found guilty of nothing except failing to keep the Regent's accounts distinct from Francis's. But the Crown had not finished with him. A colleague, Jean Prévost, was ready to accuse him of irregularities that would expose him to paying a huge fine. And, in January, the old treasurer was arrested.

It was one of those legal pursuits which render a respectable family so desperate. His son, the archbishop of Tours, collapsed and died. His other son Guillaume managed, through an archer and a chaplain, to reach the incarcerated father and arrange for the destruction of dubious papers, the ante-dating of an assignment, and the signing of useful blanks. His own servants were all ready to help him to escape. The case against him, tried by a commission that Duprat had packed, was not very seriously compromising. He had received a bribe of two horses and fifteen yards of velours. He had given out that the treasury had no balance, in order to keep Francis from depleting it, and had made false entries to that effect, without touching any cash. This he and Jean Prévost had arranged

together. But enough irregularities were proved. The venerable
servant was sentenced to death, his property to be forfeited.

Bareheaded, in a tawny robe over a black jacket, and carrying
a wooden cross painted in red, the old man was taken to Mont-
faucon, saluting several acquaintances on his road. There was a
long delay, occupied by prayer, to see if Francis would send his
"father" a pardon. None came. Then he was hanged. And Marot,
who had himself so recently been in prison, had the gracious
courage to commemorate him:

> When Maillard, Judge from Hell, to death
> Led Semblançay at Montfaucon,
> Which of the two, in all good faith,
> Had prouder bearing, would you own?
> Maillard, if you can understand,
> Seemed him that death was taking; and
> Semblançay the firm old one
> Giving into the hangman's hand
> Judge Maillard at Montfaucon.

This cold-blooded execution gave Francis 900,000 crowns from
Semblançay's property and its revenues. And the rest of the treasurers paid big fines to escape Semblançay's fate—including another
Beaune, a Berthelot, a Hurault, a Bohier, a Ruzé, a Poncher. They
were swollen with commissions, out of their long administration
of national finance, and Francis squeezed their honey out of them.
Some of them he executed.

But it was Louise who had combined with Duprat to inculpate
Semblançay. And Semblançay's family struggled for rehabilitation,
succeeding in the next reign.

As Francis was speaking to a maid of honour, after the execution,
he called her "ma fille" repeatedly.

The moment she left him she put her hands to her face and
sobbed and sighed. The courtiers asked her "ce qu'elle avoit." "Alas,
the King called me 'ma fille.' Since he called Semblançay 'mon
père' and calls me 'ma fille,' I am dreadfully scared that the same
thing will happen to me."

They all laughed, since she was fooling. And Francis laughed.
But Louise sourly reprimanded her.

22

By breaking his word to Charles, no matter how well advised, Francis exposed his kingdom to danger. But by the spring of 1527 he had not suffered. On the contrary, he was making sure of English friendship, and his next move would be to send a great army into Italy.

He could not lead it himself. For one thing, he had a bad leg, but in any event his hands were full at home, with finance, with parlement, with Anne de Heilly. He would direct the war, when he had solved his problems of absolutism, and in the meanwhile he would conclude with Henry VIII.

It was the fashion to see "the judgment of God" in all unexpected happenings. God, then, had sent an angel to his rescue: her name was Anne Boleyn. Shy as Henry had been to commit himself to Francis, he now had no possible alternative. He desired an heir, and he was divorcing Catherine of Aragon. Wolsey was to procure him his divorce, and Wolsey must link him with the power that alone could smite the Emperor and bend Clement.

There was one awkwardness: Francis was engaged to Charles's sister. And the English were quite suspicious that at the time he negotiated with them he might also be making some underhand arrangement with the Emperor. The suspicion was not unjust, but Charles would not give up the children until he had his price, and Francis would not pay the price until he had his children. Francis at first put off the English. "I must do the things I said, as near as I can, without displeasure of God and reproach of the world." That meant, marry Eleanor and pay the ransom. Yet bit by bit he came round to the notion of marrying Mary Tudor, aged ten. "By my faith as a gentleman," he exclaimed, "I have long had a mind to marry my brother's daughter in England." She was small and thin and pale, but in four years she might be tall and blooming. Even Louise could see the advantages of a daughter-in-law who "would be loving and humble." To this Louise agreed, with tears in her eyes. At the age of eleven had she not herself been a wife, loving and humble?

Francis's roguish reputation was known in England, but Henry gave him a fatherly dig in the ribs, sending word that he "would have him now become and wax a good man." Henry thought the marriage actually possible. He would finance one-third of the war, and he only asked a pension of 50,000 crowns, and a quota of salt, worth 15,000 crowns. "I often lost as much at play," he said contemptuously.

It was a bargain. The French envoys went to Greenwich, and were sumptuously entertained. Henry led out his accomplished little daughter, with her pinched white face. Little Mary was a linguist. She could play the spinet. A rigid child, devoted to her mother, she would make a quaint bride for the gallant Frenchman.

The dutiful English sent over an embassy, to confirm the treaty of Notre Dame. Francis was affable though rather off-hand. He wore a purple velvet gown with sable trimmings, over white doublet and hose, and he still dined in solitary grandeur. But Lautrec and Montmorency leaned on the pommels of his chair, while he chatted merrily and familiarly to those around him. The ambassadors thought, it is not like that in royal England.

23

But Francis was soon staggered into seriousness by the news from Italy.

Bourbon had joined Frundsberg in the January of 1527. They were commanding penniless troops and these troops were tired of starvation. The landsknechts called out the old giant Frundsberg. They raged so savagely, his rebellious Lutherans, that he foamed into apoplectic death. They then turned to kill Bourbon. Bourbon, high-spirited with Francis and high-handed with Charles V, found himself surrounded by men wilder and more headstrong than he had ever been. He resolved to lead them by following them. They would have destroyed Florence but for enormous bribes. Whetted but not satiated, they blazed, "On to Rome." The desperate Bourbon could only say, "I will go with you." He was followed, at a safe distance, by the Venetian forces under the Duke of Urbino. And Urbino would not lift a finger to save the Pope. This sallow gentleman had been despoiled by the late Pope Leo X and he would never forgive the second Medici Pope, Clement VII.

The quailing Pope relied on the fact that Bourbon's troops had

no artillery. He did not try to negotiate. He believed that the Holy
City was inviolable.

On May 5 the Spaniards and the landsknechts rested for a day
after their march on Rome. They were a wild horde of famished
men, ragged, fierce and ravenous. On the next morning, in the
lingering fog, they swept over the outer walls. Some of them
stepped over their leader Bourbon, lying in the wet fog with a
cloak flung over him. His bowels had been ripped open by a gunshot. So ended Bourbon's proud rebellion.

To procure funds, in a final panic, Clement had named a number
of cardinals, including Duprat, the French chancellor. But it was
too late. Rome had been too poor to defend its liberty, just as Italy
had been too disputatious to make itself a nation. For the defence
of Rome a leading merchant had offered the Pope a contribution
of a hundred ducats. And now, with the Spaniards torturing the
householders to reveal their hidden treasure and with the landsknechts prodding and beating their prisoners, a golden rain began
to pour from these money-bags, merchants shedding 50,000 ducats,
cardinals shedding 50,000 ducats, until it was estimated by one of
them that between seven and eight million ducats were disgorged.
Since Bourbon's death the raid had no captain to control it. No
priest, no monk, no nun, no woman was respected. The raiders
flung themselves on everything that could stay their hunger or ease
their nerves. They destroyed for joy. They smashed the water-pipes.
Dead bodies rotted in the streets. They caroused in stale drunken-
ness, quarrelled over gains, slew in maudlin rage, stewed in filth,
staggered in delirium. Plague set in. St. Peter's had brooded over
horse-dung in its aisles, while its most venerated crucifix hung with
the rags of a landsknecht. And Alarcon, who had caged Francis for
the Emperor, now jailed the Holy Father.

The Sack of Rome brought Francis to his senses. Lautrec would
loll on his chair no longer. It was time to send his army into Italy.

The Italians, however, had misjudged Francis's quiescence. "It
is a pity," a Venetian had said, "that this King, who is so fond of
the chase, should not attend a little more to the imperial eagles and
a little less to the forest deer." He could not send his troops forward until they had their barrels of good English money. Much as
he liked to amuse himself, and deep as his political callousness

might be, he was genuinely alive to the necessities of absolutism. No sooner was Bourbon dead than he attacked parlement and forced his magistrates on the defensive. They tried to assert themselves, but no Bourbon party could strike back, and by July he and his peers laid down a definition of the powers and competence of parlement. During his imprisonment there had been defiance and encroachment. Now he carried the war into their camp. His magistrates might remonstrate with him, but his must be the word of law, his the will that must prevail. He publicly affirmed his supremacy over parlement.

Such a triumph was personal. Francis was astute enough to know how and when to assert himself at home. In this he was not dilettante.

24

It took until the middle of June for the Sack of Rome to become known at Valladolid. Charles was in the midst of celebrating the birth of the future Philip II, his heir to "universal dominion." At first the Catholic King was inclined to exult. The Pope had not been true to him. But the Spaniards were far too faithfully Christian not to be shocked and grieved. They had never respected Bourbon, a traitor to his King. They showed their disapproval, and Charles promptly changed his tone. His jailer, Alarcon, could not hold Clement without shame. Yet underneath, with his incorrigible phlegm, Charles felt it was a "judgment of God." He scorned his enemies' upbraidings, and at Clement himself he soon levelled the heaviest incriminations.

But the Sack of Rome had immediate political consequences. Lautrec could depart for Italy to "liberate" the Pope. He could carry the war to Naples, through help from the sea by the Genoese galleys of the famous seaman Andrea Doria. This was very different from Francis's ceding Burgundy to Charles V. He was apparently convalescing from the downfall of Pavia.

25

Wolsey arrived at Amiens. He came in full glory, to fulfil the alliance and to talk over the "secret matter" with Francis. Could

they wrench the papacy from Clement? Could Wolsey become the
acting Pope? He took it on himself to try how it felt by conferring
his cardinalate on Duprat.

He was, to all appearances, at his ripest and most powerful. "A
somewhat exaggerated and ostentatious pomp," said Acciajuoli, "yet
his talk, bearing and manner of transacting affairs show a truly
large and enterprising mind." He was, in truth, a superb politician.
But his young master had sent him on a fateful mission, to do or
die. The loyal priest must get rid of Catherine of Aragon. This
done, he could return to power. Thus fuddled, Anne Boleyn would
destroy him.

Divorce in itself would cause the Vatican no trouble. The
Marquis of Astorga had just divorced his wife in order to marry
a richer woman. Yet even this divorce could be rescinded, under
pressure from the Spaniards on the Emperor and pressure from
the Emperor on the Pope. All would depend on the army for
which Wolsey was bringing his money-barrels.

The English cardinal had an old friend in Louise. It was
rumoured that Suffolk had never got beyond Montdidier because
Louise and Wolsey had understood one another. And now the two
of them sat closeted with Francis, in the hot August afternoon, at
Amiens.

Francis lay on a couch, his swollen leg cocked up, and only a
white sheet over him. It was a frank and confidential talk, the
mother watching her promising child. He was easily persuaded to
allow his bride, Mary, to be transferred to his second son. Father
or son, what difference! But Clement VII was their topic. And
back it came to the soldier who could intimidate him. This time,
Francis was sure of victory. Charles VIII had failed in 1494. Louis
XII had failed in 1503. Francis himself had failed in 1525. But now
he would succeed. Now all would be well, and when Lautrec captured Naples, and the Emperor was wiped out, then the Pope
would know how to interpret Leviticus.

Such was the game they were playing. Religion, love, fatherhood,
motherhood—there was absolutely nothing that could not con-
tribute to the game, since, as Machiavelli said, the modern state is
to be arbitrated by arms.

26

That keen observer of the statecraft which was Francis's profession had just died in the plague that was sweeping Florence (June 22).

Machiavelli was poor, insignificant and rather obscure. Yet no one had watched the new Europe with more discernment, and Francis's place in it he had perfectly foreseen when, in 1513, he had sat down to describe the field on which the young hero was entering.

An unsentimental man, Machiavelli, he pitilessly encompassed the drama. Had he been a person of bold purpose himself, one whose powerful motives nestle in the warm darkness where plans germinate, he would have been a worldly success. As a cardinal, he would have been invaluable in the curia. But it was reserved for him to be a social pathologist. He was a remarkable example of the Catholic intellectual who, when faith has died, remains in the mould of the old system, his unshaded mind neither softened by loyalty nor dimmed by custom, envisaging a world of good and evil in which, however, grace has ceased to operate, and in which he takes the heart as a reservoir of vital lies and surprises its secrets because he remains terrifyingly detached. This detachment, which made him so free to understand, destroyed any career that demands illusions.

Yet in the chiaroscuro of medieval supernaturalism Machiavelli could see with the eyes of a cat. He discerned the modern state in the very act of being born. And he defined the laws by which the governors would be governed.

He was a true Florentine, urban, self-conscious, alert, ironic. But for him the æsthetic had become civic and the universal had passed into the international. For him, Savonarola unarmed was no match for the least of armed princelings. And, believing religious faith to be dead, he planted Europe at the dead centre of those sovereign realities that spring from animal instincts. He viewed the papacy as an instrument of worldly power. He was the first publicist in Europe to isolate the bacillus of national individuation. He called it the Prince. And, with something like ferocity, he urged its importance on Italy.

Fate had made him a minor secretary of state, an underling in a small diplomatic clique, doomed through the wariness of his superiors, who blinked at his brightness, to pass from an onerous occupation to no occupation at all.

When Francis came to power this perceptive man was living in a mean Tuscan villa, his five children about him, chained down by poverty, sitting stationary in the abundance of his faculty and powerless in the constant heightening of his own piercing observations. A man in the middle forties, check-reined and yet whipped by relentless ambition, he could find nothing better to do than set down his analysis of the Prince. The astonishing detachment of this performance is equalled only by the quivering lustre beneath its calm. It is a liquid eye set in an iron face. Machiavelli sits perfectly still, the teeth of the political trap faintly nibbling his shins, ready to spring if he makes one false move. It was not so long since the Medici had had him tortured, which to his surprise he had borne well. And now, with pellucid intellect, he turned his insight on the state, such as the dynasts were making it.

He saw Europe for himself. He denuded it of every ethical pretension, disclosing its mainspring as the insatiable ego. He did not, like the idealist Nicholas of Cusa, go back to the logarithms of celestial law. He took Man as he found him in Europe, Alexander VI, Ferdinand, Maximilian, Julius, Cesare Borgia, the Orsini, the Colonna, the Sforza, Louis XII. Within a few thousand words he encompassed the drama of the dynasts, the whole European episode of national sovereignty, and he narrowed it down to two objects, glory and riches, and to one supreme motive, the ever-growing appetite for power. The glitter, the caper, the tossing lance, the waving banner, the love-token in the helmet—all the gay distraction of the tournament and all the chivalry of a Bayard could not divert Machiavelli from the aboriginal reality of European politics. He had been at Blois. He had stood nose to nose with Georges d'Amboise. He had been on the inside. And, accepting it, he advised Italy, his patient, what the filthy medicine ought to be.

In offering this advice he did not pretend to be a Christian. He knew that Christianity was incompatible with the power state. He did not say, "the State is beyond good and evil." He dropped Sunday out of the picture. He said, men are *bad*. Yes, you must pretend to be merciful, faithful, humane, religious and upright—"all the things that the children are taught at their mothers' knee." "And to be so," he adds, "but with a mind so framed that should you require not to be so, you may be able and know how to change to the opposite," always remembering that in general men "are un-grateful, fickle, false, cowards, covetous, and as long as you succeed they are yours entirely; they will offer you their blood, property, life and children when the need is far distant; but when it ap-proaches they turn against you."

This was his philosophy. It was a tenable and consistent philoso-phy, not merely of politics but of human nature in general. It was Francis's philosophy, Clement VII's philosophy and Charles V's philosophy.

To reconcile European statecraft with Christian ethics he re-garded as farcical. He knocked the bottom out of consecration, either at Reims or at Chartres. He showed in its true light the valid French logic of Louis XII's attempt to drive Pope Julius out of the Vatican, and Maximilian's rival intention of wearing the tiara. Machiavelli did not suggest that formal religion be abandoned. He regarded religion as a foible of the common people that must not be ignored. But he turned God Save the King round about: the King must do his best to save God. Behind the scenes, however, he spilled God out of politics and reverted to the ruthless manliness of paganism, saying to Italy, "Deliverance is of no avail which does not depend upon yourself; those only are reliable, certain and dur-able that depend on yourself and your valour."

In an hour that demanded ruthless action he pressed his cold argument deep into the sybaritic Florentine flesh. Here it was not Christ he was renouncing so much as Boccaccio. Machiavelli was a patriot on unsentimental lines. When the high-minded young Italians slew tyrants they always draped themselves in the toga. But Machiavelli did not believe in martyrdom. He did not willingly see himself as the oppressed. He did not see himself crucified on principle, the stoic pattern in revolutionary politics. He was suffi-ciently steeped in hard Roman statecraft to pass to the positive rôle, to leave Savonarola and arrive at Cesare Borgia; to take the fasces, that is, and demand that an unethical power state be founded in Italy. It was this that made him concede reluctantly the triumphs of Pope Julius. It was this that made him admire the deliberate architectonics of Cesare Borgia. And this especially made him observe with flicking irony the essential feebleness of France in Italy.

Viewing France simply as a power, Machiavelli made three pertinent observations. One was of its political structure, another of its temperament, and the third of its policy.

For the French political structure, for its constitution, he had the fullest admiration. As an Italian drowning in diversity he envied the solid unification of France. Curiously enough, he took parlement as an implement of Roman importance, one which "could beat down the great and favour the lesser without reproach to the king," thus making for monarchial license and security. In this he was misled by Louise XII's technique with parlement, but he rightly saw the nobles as an ancient body acknowledged by their own subjects and fortified by privilege yet at the same time wisely submissive to the king, their younger sons cut off from the ancestral domain and bracing the army. The common people he described as gentle and docile, horribly exploited by the great lords and no good as infantry in consequence. The King, in fact, only lacked a strong national army to be invincible.

But the French national temperament was politically too frivolous to attract Machiavelli. These people, he concluded acidly, live in sensation. Their cupidity astonished him. They make a show of liberality but what they really want is to enjoy money, to eat it and drink it, to fling it around. They even spend money on the person they have robbed! When they have no intention of putting themselves out for you, they smother you in promises. If they do anything, they make a mountain of it. And when you ask them to do anything their first thought is to turn it to their own advantage. In war the Gascons are good fighters but bandits. The nobles, who make up the gendarmes, are impetuous—more than men in the first assault but easily and quickly discouraged, and then "worse than women." They are not adroit or stout fighters. But they are eloquent afterwards, with plenty to say about their prowess and turning their defeats into victories. They are insolent when on top and they can never be pinned down to keep their word.

With these impressions of the human-all-too-human French, nimble and greedy and tricky, Machiavelli combined a Roman judgment on Louis XII's attempts to secure his feudal heritage of Milan. He blamed Louis for not seriously settling in Milan if he really meant to keep it; for not building up a French colony in it; for failing to win the small neighbours that could not dispense with his aid; for helping the papacy; and for bringing Spain into Italy. The French do not understand statecraft, he told Georges d'Amboise, or they would not have allowed the papacy to reach such greatness. But in saying this, in the land of Bourges and Chartres and Reims and Notre Dame, Machiavelli forgot that the French, being far from the "infamous" court of Rome, could not echo him when he said, "We Italians are indebted to the Church and the clergy for the loss of our faith and the gain of wickedness."

Such were the criticisms made by the formidable Italian. He was a patriot because he wanted a powerful patria. He had the intuition that mankind is more anti-social than social. Beneath its obedience to law and order he saw vanity, murderous resentment, stark self-assertion, lust. The conception of the prince, and of the power state, could accommodate the glorious urgencies he acknowledged, and aristocracy for him was an allegiance to a system of manly pride and loyalty, scorn and animosity, which he genuinely shared. He did not resist the warping of religion to the true creed of the aristocrat, providing a strong state be the outcome. He would subordinate artists and scientists, poets and priests, to this establishment of the Prince: that is, the triumphant male ego; and the place of women must be similarly determined.

This was the road to which Machiavelli had pointed. And Francis was an exponent of the ideal, not doing too badly at home.

As for Wolsey, with whom he had been conniving, that troubled statesman returned to England full of French promises. "Many dishes, and little meat" had been his ungracious comment on a pompous dinner they gave him.

27

Lautrec's army revived French hopes immediately. It mopped up town after town in Lombardy. The siege of Pavia took a bare week, and Lautrec sacked it with savage joy, to punish it for its previous

resistance. Only Milan, held by Antonio de Leyva, remained in the
imperial hands. And Lautrec was free to go south for Clement's
"liberation."

But Clement was not to be liberated by the French. The imperial
forces still swarmed in the "stinking slaughter-pit." The plague
that had spread to Florence, killing 40,000 and that would kill
Lannoy and the Abbot of Najera in Rome and go on to Naples
and even endanger Anne Boleyn in London—this plague was
bringing the orgy to a conclusion. As Lautrec went down the
Adriatic coast, the Spaniards and landsknechts withdrew toward
Naples, leaving the villages they gutted, pillars of smoke, to mark
their passage. About forty out of every hundred had died or
deserted. They dragged themselves to retreat, trailing disease and
infamy.

Clement was afraid of being slain by them. He promised over
250,000 ducats to the Emperor. Then, on the night before official
release, dressed as a huckster, wearing a wide-brimmed hat, carrying a basket with a sack, he walked out of the Castello to a conveyance that was waiting for him. He could not carry away the
gold in which the papal gems had been embedded, but this gold
had been melted down by young Benvenuto Cellini, in the little
brick furnace that he had improvised. And Cellini had dug out the
jewels and wrapped them in bits of paper, so that they could be
sewn into the Pope's linings. With these valuables that could be
pawned, the Pontiff fled to Orvieto.

He arrived in the hill town with cruelly swollen feet. A handful
of cardinals reached his ruined palace, and there, in cold and dearth,
Clement drew a timid breath of liberty. His city of Florence had
been seized by the republicans. Rome was a shambles. He heard of
distant Lautrec through his sighs. He did not dare grant Henry
his divorce.

28

The month in which Clement fled from Rome, December, 1527,
Francis decided to risk assembling his Notables. He had not ventured to invoke public opinion or appeal for public funds until
there was some prospect of defeating the Emperor. But Lautrec
had revived French credit in Lombardy. The capture of Pavia had

been ostentatiously celebrated. The religious machine had been set in motion. A heretic, Pavanes, had been burned to death, without royal intervention. Francis could order a Te Deum. God was once more a Frenchman.

He did not leave his public appeal to the emphatic plebeian Duprat. He appeared in graceful person before his Notables. He was the father of two little children who were held in a Spanish donjon. He was himself prepared to go back to a donjon to keep his word, in place of those children, unless his loyal subjects could agree to his renouncing the treaty of Madrid. He made this alternative as poignant as possible, and few persons could be more persuasive, though a thousand troops could not have dragged him back to prison. His faithful supporters were ready to respond. The clergy, by the Cardinal de Bourbon, begged the privilege of presenting Francis with 1,300,000 livres, on condition that he release the Pope, restore the Gallican church and extirpate the heretics. Jean de Selve, on his knees, spoke for the commons. They promised 1,200,000 crowns. The nobles, through Vendôme, set no limit to their services. It was a magnificent response, and Francis took it with sweet and amiable words. He was seducing Paris.

This great oration was in December. And by February he began to realize the ambitions he had seriously in mind. They were architectural. The conquest of Naples was much to be desired but what he dreamed about were delightful palaces. The old Louvre was a frowning reminder of medieval power, walls brutally thick at the base. He was going to pull it down, to have new kitchens and a tilting yard and jeux de paumes, to build a light, free, gracious residence. He planned for water conduits into Paris. The castle at Fontainebleau was also medieval: he would make it over. And in the Bois de Boulogne he proposed to have a pleasant residence, to be called, perhaps ironically, Madrid. It would be a château in faience, and Girolamo della Robbia would come from Florence to Sèvres to make the plaques that would decorate its façade. The masonwork would cost 174,000 livres. But this was not all. He wanted another castle at St. Germain-en-Laye. These were the enterprises that had been twitching his imagination. He had been hunting near Paris from archaic buildings where he could not have his court, neither his ambassadors nor his council nor his bevy of ladies.

And he was starved for novelty. He wished to be near Mont-morency at Chantilly and Écouen. He wished to be near Duprat, at Nantouillet. The Loire had been the home of the Gouffiers: the Gouffiers were gone. Semblançay had lived in Tours; he was gone. Francis had shifted from Châteaubriant to Heilly. In March he announced that henceforward, for the most part, he would dwell in and near his good city of Paris. It would bring him closer to his parlement and his Sorbonne. The Sorbonne must report favourably on Henry's divorce. The clergy were contributing over a million livres. Francis was watching his clergy.

And he soon had a chance to show how deeply religious his feel-ings were. At a corner of the rue St. Antoine stood a shrine of the Blessed Virgin and the Bambino. Some evildoer decapitated the stone heads of the Virgin and the Child. The news stirred Francis. At first he raged and then shed tears. He ordered religious pro-cessions all over Paris. The mutilation of the statue aroused the people of the neighbourhood. Francis gave word that a silver statue of the Virgin should be made for him, and with his own hands he replaced the mutilated statue with his silver one, amid scenes of extraordinary devotion. It was not so tall as the gold ones of the Apostles that he had melted down five years before, and the grille that was to protect the silver Virgin was not like the silver grille he had taken from St. Martin, at Tours. The new statue, in point of fact, was a wooden one with a silver casing. But it showed faith. And the broken Virgin, carried in to the church opposite the shrine, was reported to be performing miracles.

The Sorbonne had gained ground. Louis Berquin, whose main offence was his translations of Luther and Erasmus, was again arrested by the Faculty of Theology. Marguerite was absent at Nérac. On November 16, 1528, her child, Jeanne d'Albret was born. This child would be the mother of Henri IV, who, like Francis, would think Paris "well worth a mass."

29

French success in Italy seemed once again assured. A fine chance of a pitched battle had been offered, such as Francis had refused at Valenciennes and had accepted at Pavia. Though the odds favoured Lautrec, and though he actually stood in battle array, he decided at the last moment not to risk his gendarmes. Another such defeat as Pavia would wipe out the nobility. He elected instead to close in on Naples and to win it by siege, since Andrea Doria's nephew would blockade it by sea. A naval battle followed in which the nephew gained a glorious victory, killing Ugo Moncada, a serious loss to be added to that of Bourbon and Lannoy. It was bad news for Charles V, and intensified his anger with Francis.

That anger had been revealed at the beginning of 1528. The joint heralds of France and England had come to him at gloomy Burgos to declare joint war, following Francis's success with his Notables. It was the open repudiation of the treaty of Madrid. Charles received it in the full dignity of his imperial court, and when he had heard the defiances from Guyenne and Clarence he indulged in vehement words. "The King your master," he put it in writing, "has behaved in a cowardly and treacherous way not to have kept his pledges, and if he wishes to say the contrary I will maintain what I say, man to man."

Here was Charles, the power politician, talking in personal terms, the terms of chivalry. But so angry was he at the turn that events had taken, he flung all the French envoys into prison. It was miserable at Burgos and for four months they were confined. The Venetian hated it. "We could not even send a servant out to pick a leaf of salad." But Charles was black with anger and no one could approach him.

Francis retorted in kind. He imprisoned the Emperor's ambassador, Granvelle. Then he summoned him to appear before his entire court and to take back a particularly rude message to Charles. Granvelle, removed as ambassador, could not undertake this delicate mission. But Francis was not to be baulked. He had been personally insulted. He sneered at Charles as a fighting man. "I do not remember ever to have seen or encountered him in any war where I have been." He had signed the treaty under duress. "If you say we did not behave as a gentleman should, you lie in your throat." He challenged Charles to name the day and the place. But no more, not another word from Charles, in answer to his retorts, simply the rendezvous.

"*He* is the liar," was Charles's violent answer. "I have said and will say without lying that you have behaved like a traitor and a coward." As for duress, that was the argument of a clerk, ill-versed and crafty. He chose as site for the duel the neutral Bidassoa. It was not quite clear whether it was to be an aquatic duel or to take place on a floating platform at high tide, in full view of the oysters on the ancient walls. Charles, at any rate, wanted a neutral spot where they could have at one another in knightly style. Francis was excellent with the two-handed sword and Charles won Spanish admiration for tilting at the rings. Francis was the taller but Charles was the younger. The fight began to make Europe smile. Everywhere, in spite of the war, there was amused excite-ment. Only Rabelais at Toulouse, however, could have done full justice to the "liar" challenging the "coward," the Most Christian defying The Catholic, insults hurled and fists brandished. But be-fore these two gentlemen met each other they were to be sobered.

30

Lautrec's campaign had not prospered. He had sat down before Naples, as Francis himself before Pavia, and the siege prolonged itself until disease began to eat into his army. His blockade could still succeed if he were helped from at home and if he could count on his naval ally. But Francis was building his castles and taking victory for granted. He was so flushed with confidence that he threw his naval ally away.

Andrea Doria was difficult. He made complaints about the way he was paid. He disputed the prisoners' ransoms with his master. He thought Francis ought to send him to Catalonia and he deemed it iniquitous that Savona should be favoured as against Genoa. In short, he was a contentious subordinate, such as Pescara had been with the Emperor. But Francis was high-handed, and Mont-morency, who acted for him, was even more high-handed. They forgot that Andrea Doria was essentially free. Semblançay could be condemned and no one could say Francis nay. The treasurer owed him his prestige, his rewards and his privileges. If not a parasite, he was, at any rate, a dependent. But Doria was no de-pendent. And when Montmorency, out of touch with a world not subdued to French authority, denied Doria's claims, he soon dis-

covered that he was dealing with a fiery nature. No sooner had this
Genoese veteran come to the end of his agreement with Francis
than he signed a new one with Charles, on excellent terms. His
goodwill had been flung away, in spite of frantic concessions at the
last minute, and now the Emperor could save Naples.

Lautrec was lying ill, in his plague-infested camp. Every day he
demanded news from his captains, doctors, valets. They dared not
confess that Vaudemont was sick, and Pedro Navarro, and many
another of his chiefs, while the common soldiers were dying by the
hundred. At last, suspecting cheerful news recited so cheerlessly,
Lautrec seized two pages who were alone in his quarters and declared he would have them flogged unless they told him the truth,
"de point en point." He frightened them and they revealed how
matters actually stood; everyone in danger of plague, hundreds
dead and hundreds dying, the whole camp in ruin. So much had the
sombre Lautrec feared. It was the final blow to the hopes of a lifetime. His spirit broke, and he died without rallying.

His death brought total demoralization. Vaudemont was dying.
So was Pedro Navarro. Those of the troops who could muster
strength began a wild retreat. They were pursued from Naples
and savagely punished. The straggling invalids were murdered by
the peasants. Of 25,000 only 7,000 survived.

31

The hideous catastrophe had scarcely dawned on Francis before
the imperial herald was admitted to him in Paris, to deliver the
Emperor's challenge.

It was again a state occasion, with the King on his throne addressed by the emblazoned herald.

"King-at-arms," demanded Francis, "do you bring me the rendezvous, answer me?"

"Yes, sire. Will your Majesty allow me to discharge my duty?"

"No, if you do not give me the rendezvous and nothing else, as
was arranged."

"Sire, the Sacred Majesty of the Emperor——"

"I tell you not to utter another word! I have nothing to do with
you. I have only to do with your master. When you give me his

challenge and name the place, I'll allow you to speak, not otherwise."

"Sire, he has directed me to read my message and then deliver it to you, if you be pleased."

Francis stood up and advanced a step, crying out furiously, "What's this! Your master wants to introduce new customs into my Kingdom? I'll not allow him to try his hypocritical twistings with me."

The herald did not flinch. "Sire, I am certain that the Emperor will always comport himself as a virtuous prince——"

Francis interrupted. Montmorency tried to quieten him, but he was not to be quietened. "No, no," he shouted, "I shall not permit it. You can go the way you came," he flamed at the herald. "Give it to him," he indicated the papers. And the audience closed.

Doria's defection, Lautrec's death, an army wiped out—and Francis and Charles gabbled of a duel. The real duel had been fought in Naples. Genoa would fall two days after this altercation, on Francis's birthday. It was the eve of the anniversary of Marignano; in twelve years Francis had contrived to lose Italy for ever.

32

Francis kept beating the tom-tom and even began noising fresh preparations; but there was one person heartily sick of the losing struggle, and that was his mother.

Louise had reached her fiftieth year when Francis was in prison, but the strain of her regency, the constant anxiety at home and the endless failures abroad that called for new effort and expedient, had changed her from the strong, confident, disputatious woman who had designed her son to be a Cæsar, an Emperor. In the early years of his reign she could flatter herself that he would be everglorious. In his worst days she had never hesitated to push him to extreme measures, as with Bourbon and Semblançay. Louise was not afraid of drastic action. But he was the child not only of herself but of Charles d'Angoulême, and the stuff of a Cæsar was not in him. Even before Pavia she had lost faith in the Italian adventure. At Tournon, when she was left alone in the autumn twilight to imagine him crossing the Alps, she had dared to tell him that "under colour of glory and a kind reception" in Italy, he was in "great danger of a very doubtful homecoming." She knew the men who urged him on, and she was astonished that these men who themselves could not be leaned on should let their desires blind them to "Kingdom, children, sister and grieving mother." This was too sincere for Francis's ears and she amended it at once, saying that between him and herself there was love without end, only one heart, one wish, one thought—that is to say, his.

But Lautrec's death closed a chapter in Louise's existence and she set her mind to the procuring of peace. She could scarcely approach Wolsey, but Margaret of Austria was a responsible woman of her own age, and with Margaret of Austria she insinuated the question of peace.

It would be tantamount to surrender, but on honourable terms. John Hackett, the English ambassador in Flanders, reported late in 1528, "the French King and Regent have a secret conveyance with Margaret to make peace with the Emperor, unknown to Wolsey." Hackett was right, though it took time for people to see it.

Charles himself could make no move. "How could I unsay what I said?" he asked in bewilderment, but his aunt, who had not the same obduracy, could unsay it for him. She could give up the demand for Burgundy and yet gain a magnificent victory over France. Charles could force his rival to desert his Italian allies and assent to the complete evacuation of Italy. And the Pope must resign his fate to Charles.

Francis could only acquiesce. He was beaten. His Italian allies would have to make the best of it. The Florentine Republic would have to sink or swim by itself. Venice and Milan and Ferrara— each representing a hope that had been bound up with the success of French arms—would now have to take what Charles would give them, because Francis could only pretend that he was looking out for them. He was exclusively occupied in looking out for himself.

And this is what Louis Berquin discovered. In the middle of April, when Francis was in Touraine, the Sorbonne was deft enough to obtain Berquin's conviction as a heretic. He was condemned to come before Notre Dame, bareheaded and barefooted, a torch in his hand, and cry for mercy to God and the Blessed Virgin: then to see his books burned at the place de Grève, where his

tongue would be pierced and the fleur de lys branded on his forehead: and then to be walled up for life. Twenty thousand Parisians
gathered to see this sentence carried out, but Berquin appealed. He
knew that Marguerite was his friend and would intercede for him.
But Francis had not yet received his 1,300,000 livres from the
clergy. He wanted peace with an Emperor who was fighting the
heretics. So parlement granted Berquin's appeal by ordering him to
be burned alive, and this order, delivered on the morning of
April 17, was carried out the same day. It was the triumph of a
pursuit that had gone on for six years. Twice Marguerite had saved
the man, and Erasmus had spoken for him, but the Sorbonne had
chosen its moment well. Marguerite could only bow her head.

33

Francis turned his back on Louis Berquin, not because he despised the modern mind but because the Sorbonne had exhausted
him. Berquin was a squire from Picardy who had sought the meaning of life within religion. He had welcomed Luther's early works
and put them into French. He had turned to Erasmus and corresponded with him and translated him. From the beginning the
Faculty of Theology had disputed his right to express himself, then
his right to think, and finally his right to live. Berquin had persisted with an amused disdain of the opposition he encountered.
And from the start he had had a friend in Marguerite. "Le povre
Berquin" seemed to her the type of human being who was precious
—sincere, disinterested, luminous. She had never forgotten to look
out for him. She had plucked Francis's sleeve to remind him of
this earnest man whom the Sorbonne wished to destroy. And
Francis had at first obeyed her and demanded Berquin as his own
prisoner, so that he could free him. But the Sorbonne detested Berquin. It was resolved to keep France Catholic, no matter what
censorship was necessary, no matter what prohibitions were required, no matter what cruelties were demanded. It had no personal accusation to level at Berquin. He was unselfish, serious, pure,
but his crime was to defy authority and to pursue an inner light.
He was not even afraid of arrest, or imprisonment or death, though
he believed in fighting by legal methods for his liberty.

Another monarch might have opened his imagination to this new view of life. Many princes in Germany had accepted it, and these princes were the Most Christian King's allies. He could well conceive of a new theology. But when the Sorbonne sought to destroy a radical, Francis would only intervene to punish the Papacy. As to Berquin's values, he washed his hands. He was a prince, and Berquin's values were not politics.

But Berquin's values were politics. It was this that Marguerite comprehended. In the state as her brother conceived it the Berquins were pawns, to win a square or lose a square, but inessential: the real object was to maintain authority. In the state as Marguerite conceived it there must be some place for those who are responding to change. She hated sterile authority, wilful authority, savage authority. She welcomed the Marots, the Nicole Bourbons, the Arandes and Carolis and Roussels, the Rabelais, the men who wished France to do something more than seek and provide security. The Sorbonne was the dead hand. Marguerite, whose charity sprang from her heart, had fought this ecclesiastical ob- scurantist for possession of Berquin's life. And she would have won if Francis, on the eve of making peace with the anti-Lutheran Emperor, had not deemed it wise to forget affection and pity. Berquin lost his life. But the victory that Francis gave to the Sorbonne would soon prove a costly one. The State could not allow French Protestantism to develop, yet by cutting it back there was formed the darkest, most stubborn, most inflexible of Christian creeds that civilization had ever to contend with. Francis's greatest frivolity was not his band of ladies or his châteaux in the woods: it was his orthodoxy. He was building a state that could not contain the growing intellect and burning conscience of his time, and could only adapt itself by revolution. This state, happy for the epicurean, gave no place to the responsive spiritual man. Erasmus, even Eras- mus, had been deemed intolerable to the Faculty of Theology, and his mild disciple Berquin had been delivered to execution. What prospect for John Calvin? Farel had already fled from France. It offered no shelter for religious evolution. The hunt had begun.

But meanwhile Francis deemed Berquin an acceptable forfeit. He did not pursue the Sorbonne. He wanted peace at any price.

In July the peace negotiations began at Cambrai. Francis was hunting in the neighbourhood, daunted by the loss of a final battle in Lombardy in June, and the long-promised arrival of the Emperor in Italy, following his prompt and lenient treaty with the Pope. To war with the Emperor so soon again was more easily said than done.

But the arrangement of peace was in good hands. His mother, Louise of Savoy, could only advance by slow stages yet she kept sending pleasant messages ahead of her. She was full of confidence. "Write boldly to her," she told Margaret's envoy, "that we must necessarily contend and argue but that I sincerely hope it will be without anger or ill-will." She could not, however, refrain from blackening the Pope. "He is no good to us, or to you, or to the Church itself."

The conjunction of these two women to devise the Ladies' Peace, was a proof of Europe's sodden infantility. Neither Louise of Savoy nor Margaret of Austria could be forgiven for their own predatory acts. Louise had pushed Francis to contest the Imperial Election, and Margaret had been guilty of proposing the ruin of Venice. But in the end, with the advance of years, the two women admitted the mad waste of a savage process that could never bring a peaceful solution. Rising above the deadlock in which their imbruted males were engaged, they lifted out of obscene pride into the daylight of an ordinary humanity. Europe was foul with war. They cried for fresh air and clean light. They had the honest impulse of nurses, of chambermaids, of nursery maids.

It was half a lifetime since these two princesses had met, though they had been children together at Amboise. Margaret's marriage to Louise's brother was now an almost forgotten event, and since then they had never seen one another (1503).

Margaret's life had been capably devoted to the Habsburgs but this last treaty she would recommend to Charles as subordinating "private hatred and revenge to the far nobler principle of the welfare of nations," and she approached it with the coolness of the Netherlands as against the hardness of Spain. She was now an elderly woman, "fat and replete," having had nearly as long a widowhood as Louise herself and having evoked almost as much curiosity as to how she had diverted herself. A sober, tactful, far-sighted woman, she was enough Maximilian's daughter to value the recovery of Hesdin, Lille, Douai, Arras, Tournai, and the abolition of French feudal rights in Artois and Hainault.

To relinquish Burgundy would cause her no immense pangs, since this peace of Cambrai would integrate the Netherlands and would crown her nephew as Emperor, though the Turk and the heretic must continue to threaten war.

Margaret and Louise interchanged frequent visits across the closed passages from the Hôtel St. Paul to the Abbaye de St. Aubert. Their treaty was signed at the beginning of August. It was, in effect the treaty of Madrid with Burgundy exempted and Bourbon eliminated and certain humiliations removed. The men could not have done it.

34

The peace of Cambrai was the last considerable act of Margaret of Austria's career. Next year, stepping out of bed, she had the misfortune to cut herself with a bit of broken glass that flew into her slipper when a lady in waiting let a tumbler fall. This cut became infected and her surgeons made up their minds to amputate. Fully prepared, Margaret set her affairs in order, but an overdose of opium killed her before the operation could take place.

Neither Francis nor his mother could resent her last negotiations. Francis was gracious enough to visit her, and was amiable about his fiancée, her niece. Margaret, on the other hand, wrote a kind letter to the Emperor asking that Francis's boys be better treated until their release the following spring. Ugly reports had arrived concerning the treatment of these isolated children, and they were still little more than babies, already forgetting their French.

35

But if Francis was gracious to the Ladies who had made peace, he resented the defeat that this peace coolly registered. It exacted the penalties of his failure in Italy, but instead of convincing him that his statesmanship might be at fault he felt inclined to blame the people who had failed him. And in this way his heart could be honourably constricted until it was so small and hard as to be invulnerable, in contrast to the expansiveness and generosity of his imprudent years.

It was highly unfortunate for Wolsey, to come to grief at such a moment. He had favoured Henry's divorce but not his marriage to Anne Boleyn, and this fatal opposition to Anne Boleyn was bringing him to ruin.

Henry VIII had begun to centre his life on Anne Boleyn. "This passion of the King's," the papal legate had said in February, "is a most extraordinary thing. He sees nothing, he thinks of nothing but his Anne: he cannot be without her for an hour, and it moves one to pity to see how the King's life, the stability and downfall of the whole country, hang upon this one question."

That sort of passion could never possibly grip Francis, and yet he was too good a politician not to understand that Henry was orientated by Anne. Wolsey had consequently become useless, and his annual 12,500 crowns a year—instalments of the promised 100,000 —would be so much money thrown away unless he recovered favour, which was unlikely.

The Frenchman on the spot, Jean du Bellay, was one of an inherently humane family, and he could not watch the downfall of Wolsey without a pang. He knew that two years before Wolsey had been Francis's "grand ami" and Louise's "fils et père." "I fully believe," he said, "that if Francis and Madame do not come to his relief in all diligence, he is in great danger." Du Bellay had gone to see him, and he was amazed at the Cardinal's broken will and his incoherence, "the worst rhetoric I ever heard." "Heart and words entirely failed him." But du Bellay was extremely moved. "He wept much, and prayed that the King and Madame would have pity upon him, if they had found that he had kept his promise to them of being their good servant, so far as his honour and ability would stretch." He was now without a friend. "He sees no means of safety, nor do I, except it should please the King and Madame to help him."

Francis and Louise had paid Wolsey hard cash for his being "a good servant." He, and his pain, were of no importance in themselves. Their eyes were on Henry, and they did not propose to let "affection and pity" interfere with their politics. Their hopes were now based on Henry's repudiating the Emperor's aunt. Francis had cared a great deal about his own "tribulation" when he was under the Emperor's heel, but Wolsey's "tribulation" did not touch his heart.

When one of the Boleyn faction came to get incriminatory evidence, Francis was naturally careful not to incriminate himself. He said "frankly" (with the "frankly" of diplomacy), "I shall tell you. When he was with me, I assure you, he would the divorce should go forth and take effect, for he loved not the Queen." But he gave a hint that Wolsey was not to be trusted. "Mine advice shall be to my good brother, that he shall have good regard, and not put so much trust in no man, whereby he may be deceived, as nigh as he can."

This was to show the infatuated Henry where Francis stood. So far from helping Wolsey, he gave him a vigorous shove on the downward path, and when at last the Cardinal had fallen, in spite of du Bellay's humane appeals, Francis gave another interview to Anne Boleyn's cousin Bryan. He spoke of Henry VIII's "faithful kindness" and he denounced Wolsey. He had always thought "that so pompous and ambitious a heart, sprung out of so vile a stock, would one day show forth the baseness of his nature." In fact, Wolsey "well merited either a life worse than death, or else of all deaths the most cruel."

This was cold-blooded, especially as Francis had long abused Henry's "faithful kindness" by bribing Wolsey. But that dog had served his turn, and the great thing was to win the Boleyn faction. Anne Boleyn, too, was of "base stock" and in due time it would be remembered, but Francis's snobbishness was not morbid. He could smudge Lorenzo de' Medici as of "base stock" and yet marry his son to Lorenzo's daughter. His own chancellor Duprat was denounced as the son of a "faiseur de sabots," yet Duprat was highly acceptable. The only thing that really galled Francis as an aristocat was to have base origin imputed to the royal line. When Luigi Alamanni read out from Dante that Hugues Capet had the same butcher ancestry as Wolsey ("Figlivol fui d'un beccaio de Parigi"), Francis flared out against Dante like a true blue. "Never let me hear this ridiculous author again!" And he proposed to have Dante put on the black list. Butchery with the sword, the spear and the arrow, butchery by way of justice, hands and ears and tongues cut off, but butchery as a trade? To be generated by a man who butchered in order to gain his living! No. It had forewarned him against Wolsey.

"Are you of noble extraction?" Francis would one day ask Duchâtel, the excellent man who tried to keep Francis from letting Étienne Dolet be butchered.

"Sire," said the bishop, "Noah had three sons in the Ark. I cannot tell you precisely from which of the three I am descended."

The King could smile at such a retort, but he held to his conception of nobility. He was selling titles in increasing numbers in order to maintain it.

36

"I am no longer needed in the world." In the melancholy that so often overcame her, that was the plaint of Louise of Savoy. She had seen her son through triumph and catastrophe, through affluence and penury. Her own heart, in this trying process, had become not dark but labyrinthine, and in the very centre of it was the weazened demon of the miser, hidden even from her children, fed on gold. Louise adored Francis and loved Marguerite, but somewhere, somehow, she had become an emotional starveling for the sake of this taloned god of hers, the one who holds out the promise of security, and already she had hoarded 1,500,000 crowns. Duprat, her companion in acquisitiveness, had also become notorious for this curious lust. It was Louise's lasting love affair, one that exacted a million and a half devotions.

In September, 1531, she and Francis parted on account of the plague in Paris. He went restlessly off to Chantilly, to visit his Grand Master Montmorency, while Marguerite was to take her mother from Fontainebleau to Touraine.

Louise had been seriously ailing, and it was impossible for her to continue her journey any further than a village named Gretz. She had been suffering for years from gravel and was in acute torment. Marguerite put her to bed, summoning the priest to bring her the sacrament. Her treasurer Babou, who had replaced Semblançay, bore the crucifix to her, and Marguerite was at her side.

It was the absence of her son that most afflicted her. "Oh, my child," she exclaimed, "I shall not see you. You will be needing me, my son, to the very end. Must I leave this earth without kissing you adieu." But she turned her dazed eyes upward. "It is for the best. Neither he nor I could have stood it. The love between us two was too great. But incline to him, Lord God, and help him in his great affairs. This death will be so terrible a grief to him!"

She spoke to her daughter. "Marguerite, my heart is still full of this love I bear you and my son." She was distressed. She wished to compose her spirit and sent her weeping daughter away. One of her servitors then stole to the bedside and begged her to speak a word, one single word, to console those whom she was leaving. The old spirit flared up. "Stop this idle talk!" she said, and Marguerite came to her rescue. "Leave her. Her mind is elsewhere."

"Well said, my dear. And so it is."

With the firmness that had marked her whole life this indomitable woman composed herself for the end. Marguerite glimpsed a half-smile, the smile of which the other half cannot be known, and so quietly did Louise go that the daughter did not know she had gone.

Louise was fifty-five. She had watched over her son for every day of his thirty-seven years. No union could have been more loyal. She had spoiled him, through her exclusive and unprincipled devotion to him. Even when she had come to disapprove of such aims as the Imperial Election or the pursuit of Bourbon into Italy, her opposition melted before his ardour. And this philanderer of a son, whose intimate personal accents would be so human if he had known how to convey them, showed time and again that he loved Madame. He walked by the side of her litter in that visit to Jarnac. He sat by her all night when she was ill. His warm eye, his amusing voice, his courtliness, his pleasant malice, engaged forever the adoration of this mother who trembled at the waves into which she had launched him and who braved the waves to rescue him when he was wrecked.

He never saw her again. But when the waxen image of her coffin caught his gaze in the church, he fainted dead away.

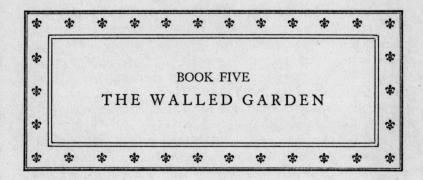

BOOK FIVE

THE WALLED GARDEN

THE WALLED GARDEN

The death of Francis's mother removed a central prop from his life. With eighteen years between them in age, she had always stood close to him from those early protective days at Cognac and Amboise. He had grown bravely in her nurture, sheltered by her incessant devotion and pushed by the vigour of her will. Louise of Savoy could deplore many rash acts in her son's life, but at any rate she could claim it had been a positive one. Between Marignano and the Imperial Election he had shown decisive energy, and from the Election to the Ladies' Peace he had maintained his heritage in a losing fight. She was much too loyal not to have reviled Charles V and contemned the Popes. She had in abundance that consoling by-product of feminine loyalty, scorn for the opponent. But in the tense days after Bourbon's defection and in the grim days after Pavia, the major aim of her policy had been to keep the territory of France intact, despite the ardour with which she had egged on Francis. She had repulsed every English tentative that envisaged Boulogne. She had held to Burgundy. For her the Bourbonnais had seemed as essential to the throne as Alençon or Navarre. Not Anne of France herself had done more to weave this feudal land into a seamless monarchy. Italy might pass to the Habsburgs, and the Popes go back to the confessional, that sentry-box on the frontiers of the Eternal. But the basic power of the dynasty reposed on the Kingdom, and Louise had never allowed her son to relax in his vigilance for this object, however urgent his duel with Charles V.

So far he would remain her true child. But from now to the end of his career he would never again develop any of that confident aggression with which his Savoy-Bourbon mother had informed his early policy and gingered his young temperament. If he had shown a strong preference for a certain type of Frenchman, Bonnivet, Lautrec, Lescun, Duprat, coarse-grained men who were ready to assert themselves, it was from his mother he drew this preference.

Now that she was gone, and himself approaching his fortieth year, he would tend to subside in this respect, and to aim at a balance between his own natural dilettante disposition and the urgencies of rivalry in Europe. He would poise himself between two forces, taking as little loss as possible, and extracting increased pleasure from his court. It would be a period of relative maturity and relaxation. He would ripen in taste. He would savour the sweetness that comes with over-ripeness. But he would do nothing that would cost him anything as Head of the House. His State would be his Ego, and any rival self-assertion would unfailingly chill him. Thus the amiable dilettante would close his imagination at the least sign of exaction. He ceased to be accessible, even to Marguerite, in anything really adventurous. He hardened his heart.

But this withdrawal to the Walled Garden, this dilettante resignation, did not mean that Francis's ambition had been frustrated. His hardness of heart no doubt went back to the failure of his central ambition, since men who act on conventional motives and think in set sentiments always meet frustration by hardening the heart.

He had been literally beaten out of Lombardy. Did he ever ask himself what had gone wrong with his Italian campaigns? Lautrec had failed. Bonnivet had failed. He had himself failed. And yet time after time he had despatched the same sort of military expedition into Italy, always bright to start with, always tarnished before the end, never equal to its problem.

The military mystery is a special one, and sometimes it is a question of helmets and sometimes of boots. Bad weather beats some generals and bad beef defeats others. The outsider knows nothing, except what he is told, which is as little as possible. But Francis did seem definitely anxious to hit the bull's eye in exactly the same way every time, while the enemy shifted the target in an unsportsmanlike manner. The great success was Marignano. In this, which was a pitched battle, his forces were still fresh. They encountered only one of three allies, and they had previously carried off the enemy's generalissimo. That type of battle was not repeated for ten years. In 1521, Lautrec had a long campaign in which he missed several chances of a decisive fight, and when he took his chance at Bicocca it was against his judgment. Bonnivet was weak in 1523 and driven back in 1524. Francis lost in 1525. Lautrec did well in 1527 against an enfeebled and impoverished opposition, but in 1528 he was afraid to risk a pitched battle, sure neither of cash nor reinforcements, and the fiasco before Naples was worse than Francis's before Pavia or Bonnivet's before Milan. The patterns in Italy had changed, yet the French patterns had not been revised to meet them. The army that was dispatched always had Marignano before its mind. Francis did not work out a new method of blockade. Improved defence by firearms made sieges difficult, and while Tournai did succumb and Florence would succumb, the expense of a siege was usually prohibitive, so that conquest flattened out before walled towns. Yet he had thrown away money in 1521-2, in 1523-4, in 1524-5, in 1527-8-9. His ineffective wars in Italy were horribly wasteful, steeped in almost the same noble ineptitude that had distinguished Azincourt. Francis's faith in his armoured knights had indeed been the fixed idea of a conservative. It had cost him Italy. And only reluctantly he began to consider a different type of war.

Yet if he turned away from the peace of Cambrai discontented with its inexorable verdict and recording the secret protest of the self-justified, this did not mean that he was resigning his struggle. He had worked steadily, under his mother's guidance, to become an absolute monarch. In this he had not failed, and he combined it with the airs and graces of a renaissance prince. His atrocious failure in Italy had used up his national income, year by year, had cost a great deal in goodwill, but had not seriously impaired his establishment. He could borrow from the municipality of Paris, but he was unable to roll up a national debt. He was unable to pass on the cost of his failures to the mortgaged unborn. If he ran a deficit for two years, the army simply oozed away and he had to hold a burial service and sign a truce. Yet no truce changed his point of view. After Cambrai, as before Cambrai, he craved Italian domination. His rights to Milan could be renounced, withdrawn, cancelled, abnegated. But they were embedded in his heart. He could never forget them. And this possessiveness, this clutch on property no matter what its function, was just as much his own characteristic as it was the characteristic of the man with whom he combated. He still wanted Milan, because it had come into his family through his great-grandmother. Such a right had no relation to use, or to cost, or to value. It was an instinct to assert it, a quite primitive instinct, but intolerably fierce, and backed by armies with banners. And through this instinct Francis felt he was King. To lose Milan was to lose something of his essence. He could order men's hands to be cut off, or their ears to be cropped. Every dog in a given village could be ordered to have one of its legs amputated, simply to preserve game. But what is a leg or a hand or an ear or a tongue compared to a duchy or a province? That duchy brimmed with lovelier promise than the daughters who had died in his absence, or the wife he had ignored, or the sons who were being warped in prison. Milan was worth incalculable price because instinct had coiled around it and had drawn it into the heart. There it nestled in the warmth of desire, richly nourished. What God became to Calvin, Milan became to Francis. If his mother had worshipped money and had been wholly unable to understand the innocence of Semblançay, her avidity was nothing compared to Francis's for Milan. This would remain ineradicable. He could not think of a crusade against the Turk except as a means of getting himself into Italy. He could never forgive Charles for ousting him, and he would consent to any arrangement that would promise him a footing in Lombardy. It was no part of a policy, though it was used to further a policy. It began with an instinct, this powerful acquisitiveness, and persisted against the verdict of long wars. It was now giving him a wife to whom he was perfectly indifferent. It had cost and would cost him millions. It would ally him with the Turk, with Henry VIII, with the Protestants. It made him ready to suppress books, to sanction executions, to sacrific sister and sons and daughters. Yet a deeper philosophy of the state was wholly incompatible with his upbringing. He only asked to acquire Milan, to assuage the ambition that had been frustrated. And for the rest he wished to distract himself like a Gentleman, to disport himself as King of France. Thus the Cæsarian notions that his mother had implanted in him continued to disturb him, but never to any vital extent. Life was too sweet in all its "menus plaisirs" for Milan to make him conscript. Hence he would continue as a lover of beauty who pursues a principality, and a prince who embellishes life.

2

This triviality in Francis's nature, baulked on the military plane, sets him at cross-purposes with his people, in whom the modern mind is visibly fermenting. He strives to impose a state, while France develops a civilization.

He can always count on France to defend itself. Behind him stands a great, resourceful, naturally abundant kingdom, full of "base stock," and out of its surplus he can always repulse the Spaniard, the Italian, the German. For whenever France believes itself threatened great reserves of energy can be released in self-defence. Otherwise it resents its despot. It grudges what it spends on Francis, and howls calamity, and opposes government. It knows too well the extravagance it must repress, and the limitless thirst for domination. It can be enrolled for war, and organized for the Kingdom, but never fully aroused except for self-defence. Then it is a unit, the most complete in Europe. The King's will becomes the people's.

But the national spirit is not really Francis's. Most of the French people take the meaning of life to be essentially that of which their priests have been telling them. They are born, marry and die in the Catholic Church. But a large number already question this Catholic Church. They begin with the institution. They note the utter insincerity of the wealthier clergy, the bestial ignorance of the monks, the superstitions that pullulate through France, the monstrous infidelity of one Holy Father after another, and out of this disillusionment with the institution they seek the direct message of the Bible. But some go beyond the Bible. It is an era of discoveries, and a few of those who set out for the Indies arrive at a new continent.

A friend in power like Marguerite reads the inner secret of the people, and, largely for Francis's sake, she guides the anti-clerical and encourages the study of the Bible. But this is only on the surface of that movement which changes France under its prince's feet. He commits his kingdom to war, through his relentless instinct. War breeds pestilence. The unsocial nature of war breeds human anguish. And, as the people writhe, there comes the collapse of France's renaissance. The Prince must breed the Saint, one extravagance produce its opposite, the Machiavellian hatch out the Utopian, and each become murderous in the end.

Of the Catholic stock spring Machiavelli and Erasmus, Luther and Rabelais, Loyola and Calvin. Three of them were monks, and Calvin a curé, son of an agent for collecting tithes. It is these men who speak with the voice of Europe. And these voices of Europe are deeper than any prince's. They are shaping the imagination of the present, the practice of the future. They summon into existence the forces that must annihilate Francis's progeny unless he give heed to them. Let Berquin die, and up climbs the flame of the imagination. The voices are never quietened by death.

Erasmus had spoken for Europe. Comfortably at home in Basel with a warm stove and good red wine, he had dared again and again to raise his voice against princely strife. Machiavelli's mouth was a locked door that said, no admittance, while Erasmus's mouth ripples with sensitive response, with quick retort, with amusement, with charity. One distrusts the universe: the other trusts it. Machiavelli runs the risk of hatred: Erasmus runs the risk of goodwill. Each is intelligent, one with grim exactitude, the other with vivid impressionableness. Machiavelli is the more detached of the two, but Erasmus has bestowed himself on Europe with infinitely larger spirit and an unremitting diligence. He is gold rather than steel, more valuable, not so hard, not so cutting.

Circumstances made Erasmus a theologian as it had made Machiavelli a diplomat. But Machiavelli had gone to school to the Romans, Erasmus to the Greeks. And Erasmus was a captain in that corps of the sensitive who act as pioneers of the good life. His small, nervous body was a sphygmograph that recorded every quiver and jerk of the world around him. Its currents and pangs and throbs and darts registered on his soul in acute recognition of pleasure and pain. His consciousness of God was lively enough, but the entire Holy Family seemed only another and more august household within the municipal boundaries of his sympathy. He took everyone in—popes, princes, messenger boys, scholars, dunces, saints, prostitutes, mariners, commercial travellers, patronesses, soldiers, queens. As a scholar he seemed much less interested in tessellating the awkward facts together with infinite and deferential patience than in rounding out his theology to include an unsubdued religion. What he began with, what always governed him, was his capacity for sympathy. He could not live without it and the meanest mortal was not indifferent to him. Anybody and everybody could hurt him but he was too strong to go into those by-paths of the defeated sympathetic—the megalomania, the hysteria, the persecution mania, the day-dreams, of those who must either have a social value or a nuisance value. Erasmus had comedy and self-criticism.

Through his letters we learn his weaknesses. He allowed his love to flow over the borders of ordinary reserve, as water could so easily overflow in his Holland. He could coo to his correspondents very sweetly and his begging letters are models for all literary men to study. He had his episodes in Paris with those whom priests are supposed only to meet in confession. But there was force in this pliant, fragile man. If earth and water mingled in him, something rose like the single spire in a Dutch flatness to proclaim that man is recalcitrant. Erasmus refused to limit himself by the pugnacity, the virulence of sect, the murderous intolerance of absolutism in one camp and indignation in the other. He was just as incapable as Machiavelli of merging himself with a mob to become a man of action. The task of the politician, as Machiavelli coolly intimated, is to enforce the unpalatable by the aid of the palatable. Erasmus knew that a humane appeal could not immediately work. But he saw the fundamental loss of honesty that is involved in organized religion. He would not be a demagogue of the Reformation any more than a demagogue of Rome. He had the motive of the educator; loyal to multitudinous disinterested arrangements which in sum make civilization.

To see scripture perverted incensed Erasmus, just as the raucous German innkeepers or the greedy English custom officials or the savage French university authorities incensed him. He hated the corruption of texts precisely as he hated the debasement of manners. He was revolted by Julius II as he was revolted by the English carters who stole his wine. He refused to sing in chorus with any institution, and when he sat down in Basel in 1513, at the same time that Machiavelli was thinking out the Prince, it was princely misuse of power that most of all stung him to expression. He did not counsel the Prince to mould a state. He counselled him to respect human nature. He was not less aware than Machiavelli of men's desire for kingdom. But he did not believe that man was bad. "Nature," he said, "or rather God hath shaped this creature, not to war but to friendship, not to destruction but to health, not to wrong but to kindness and benevolence." It was this creative faith in man that drove him to criticise the Prince, and on lines that went back to the Council of Basel, when the people disputed their church with the papacy.

"Wouldst not have princes fight for their right?" he hears someone ask; and he ironically asks, "Right?" And he goes on, "Let the citizens of Padua claim now in God's name the country of Troy for theirs, because Antenor was sometimes a Trojan." "The power and authority over men which be free by Nature, and over brute beasts, is not all one. What power and sovereignty soever you have, you have it by the consent of the people. And if I be not deceived, he that hath authority to give, hath authority to take away again."

Machiavelli would smile. The consent of the people! But because he goes beyond the state to the people Erasmus detests war. War was sent out of hell, he says passionately, and armour invented by craft of the devil.

"To strut up and down among the nobles of the court, and to be occupied in the king's business?" No, he does not plead for that, as Machiavelli does. He was forty-eight years old in 1513, not much older than Machiavelli, but power is not his God. He knows he is laughed at. "Many gross gentlemen nowadays laugh merrily at these things, as though they were the dreams and dotings of schoolmen." But he sees war with his eyes, he hears it with his ears, he smells, tastes, touches it. He has no more illusions than Machiavelli about righteousness in the state. He scorns the Christians who would war on the Turk. "Be the Turks never so wicked, yet they are men, for whose salvation Christ suffered death." Christ to him is more than the Church, and the hypocrisy of the Church stinks in his nostrils. "Unjust peace, for that matter, is far better than righteous war."

Motives are mixed, causes complicated, propaganda pernicious. And, his mind going back to his childhood when as a rather wistful illegitimate child he stood on the dunes in Holland: "when the sea is broken in, it passeth our power to restrain it within any bounds."

He thinks of man as he has loved him, "this most pleasant and reasonable creature, man." He thinks of tilled fields, the gardens and orchards, gay manors in the country, pleasures nourished, laws executed. And then he thinks of men in the trenches, "All the day long, be it hot or cold, wet or dry, stand in the open air, sleep in the bare ground, stand in their harness. They must suffer hunger, thirst, cold, heat, dust, showers." "There is no bondage so vile as the bondage of soldiers."

And it is the citizen who pays. "Peace may be got and obtained with the tenth part of the labours, cares, griefs, perils, expenses and spilling of blood, with which war is procured."

But power and glory and riches? The vulgar worship of glory, the sensuality of riches, the greed of power, Erasmus attacks because of this wanton and unfathomable suffering he has depicted. He attacks them because the Prince seems to him stupid and shallow and insatiable.

"Where is the kingdom of the devil, if it be not in war?"

"Why draw we Christ into war, with whom a brothel-house agreeth more than war?"

So Basel answered Florence, the humanist asserting values and the diplomat asserting methods, Erasmus asking to educate irrational man and Machiavelli telling how to manipulate him.

Erasmus had his adherents everywhere in Europe. Every prince, including the Pope, sought to enlist his pen. But how can such a man meet dogmatism—the dogmatism of the State, or of the Church, or of homicide? Though the sea of instinct had overflowed, he still was advising the refugees to cultivate their gardens. Idle advice once Luther had been driven to revolution and the dykes had broken.

And out of this flood rose Calvin. He was nineteen when he went to Orléans for a year. There he studied with merciless ascetic zeal. The year of the Ladies' Peace he spent at the University of Bourges, where the German who taught him Greek and Hebrew opened his mind to Luther. He was then twenty. The vibrant youth, bitterly serious, seared with a sense of sin, could only return to Noyon to harsh wrangles between his father and the clerics, feuds in which his father was excommunicated before he died. In Paris, again a student, Calvin found his lodgings with the adepts of the new religion, and these were hounded by Francis's lieutenant-criminal, a handyman who had served him in Spain. Calvin's first essay was on Tolerance. But the desire for the good life was soon swallowed in his desire for the good God. The young student, black-eyed, hollow-cheeked, pallid, bowed, intense, began to know God, to comprehend His system, to see why Rome had been dethroned. With his incessant intellect he milled the Bible, the Word of God the unquestioned Truth, and out of it he rolled blinding sheets of theory that he welded into a beautiful, inexorable, excruciating machine. Here was the French notary concerned, not with the trivial mathematics of this universe, but with the sines and cosines of eternity. To this he brought meticulous, unyielding reason, stridently controversial yet nobly fanatical, the man who must be absolute because he must never bend.

And at the same time, studying at Bordeaux, Toulouse, as well as Bourges and Orléans and Paris, came a buoyant friend of the instincts, François Rabelais. Did he meet Calvin? Did he meet Loyola? Not impossible. But here was someone who, like Machiavelli, asked wisdom from experience and, unlike Machiavelli, had no lust for power.

Rabelais was just as French as the sinewy absolutist from Picardy. That man Calvin with his metallic voice, his consuming gravity, his fierce appetite for abstraction and his cold appetite for power—he built on a book, not Das Kapital, only the Bible. He was moulding his absolute system, at twenty-four, carried from secret lodgings to secret lodgings, the body a black lantern for the burning brain. France would not parley with this celestial notary; it would drive him out. He was very strong, almost strong enough to defy the French state. But the head of the state opposed to Calvin a different type of absolutism.

Yet the renaissance, with its amelioration of the instincts, could not be consecrated to power without a laugh. The renaissance had freed something into life beside the desire for power. There was a desire to release energy into life within the terms of social reason, a desire to savour and to enjoy. It is supposed that in the year that Francis was born Rabelais was born. And Rabelais was a ringing voice of the sixteenth century, a voice as loud as joy bells, proclaiming an end and a beginning.

Rabelais, in his own way, is a Gothic cathedral. One sees, first of all, his gargoyles. How long the tongue of his devils, how broad his matrons, how sudden the shoot of his rain water, and how sly his imps. But in this cathedral that burst and ripples with laughter, this cathedral with a cacophonous choir and troops of monks who overflow in their stalls, the baptism font full of wine and the communion a gorgeous love feast, there is at times a quiet like the descent of a dove, and one is aware of a rose-window exalted and radiant, and of an altar with a new legend on its altar-cloth. The cement of the old cathedral was the devil. Its vaults were filled with hell. What Rabelais banishes is this dualism, and with it the consolations of repentance. Go as far as you like, and take the consequences! It is not scepticism. It is autonomy. It is a coming of age. And in it there is the exuberance of a new faith, a faith in science and a faith in mankind.

What Rabelais proclaimed, in his escape from the church, was the inalienable rights of man. Where the dogmatic theologian took his inventory of human nature for the sake of establishing a civil service, Rabelais made his inventory for the sake of informing the human householder what precisely he had come into the world with, what its use was, what its enjoyment was, and what could be done without a celestial civil service. The theologian said, discipline.

Rabelais said, responsibility. The theologian said, death and the next world. Rabelais, life and this world. Aquinas was a doctor of theology, Rabelais a doctor, *tout court*. With theologians he had no sympathy. He did not meet them on their own ground. He made loud, funny, obscene noises, because he took them, and knew them, as human beings. Under his hat he had more than brains, he had a tonsure. He was the apostate who had risen above the shame of impulse and the perversion of celibacy into an absolute, unconditional, hilarious acceptance of all that had become wistful and indecent. His own indecency was calculated and thorough. It turned the imagination inside out. It left no orifice from which the least secret could be extracted after him. The whole bag of biological tricks was emptied by him, under the nose of the theologian, saying to his reverence, "Here is your sense of sin." Without this bag of tricks there could be no confessional, and without the sense of sin there could be no church. Rabelais expiated for the whole world on this crucifix of candour. And nothing had ever been so straight a comment on the medieval experiment, or so buoyant, or so French.

It was in bad taste, since taste is another technique of power, whether "modern" or "classical." Rabelais's technique came from the street. It was that of the mountebank, "come up, come up." He plastered his booth against the old cathedral. He turned somersaults on the parvis. He made cartwheels in the vestibule. And this whole performance, unlike the performances in the cathedral, cost no one a penny. It was horrible, raucous, breath-taking, glorious and indispensable. Calvin, green in the face, would watch it sourly from the left bank of the theological Rubicon. But Rabelais was not a naked revolutionary. Rabelais was not Dolet. He was clothed in the asbestos of humour. He turned another handspring when Calvin frowned.

Down the hard Rabelais road could be seen Panurge, the vulgar cockcrow of humanity that abuses animal license, the braggart, the cheat, hungry for triumph, greedy for experience, thirsty for gold. And down the Calvin road was the theologian with talons, the spiritual usurer, the merciless accountant, the priest of power.

Between tendencies like these—the renaissance mind becoming fanatically idealistic, the renaissance mind becoming sanely scientific

—Francis had no inclusive conception of government. He was an opportunist prince, with his eye on Milan. To keep his way clear he must shut out Luther and Calvin, just as he must subordinate Erasmus and Rabelais. And so it works, since he has his army and can gather taxes and control parlement.

But as the century proceeds general ideas are winnowed by the powerful revolution in religion, in statecraft, in humanism and in æsthetic orientation. It is not for nothing that one says "renaissance and reformation." It is like saying of a cross-channel swim, "tide and current," or rather, "tide, temperature, wind and current." To reduce Francis simply to kingship would not explain him. There is a movement from Bourdichon to Cellini. There is a movement from diplomacy within the family to diplomacy with the Turk. There is a movement from the Council of Pisa to the Concordat and marriages with the Medici. There is a monarchy which must exclude Calvin and a court which must give to the Pleiade a footing it cannot go on giving to Rabelais. And underneath all this, there is the marriage of Castile to America, with a flow of gold which changes prices everywhere; and out of this golden foam will rise a new deity, Philip II. The half-century which Francis occupies is a half-century in which the equilibrium of the European household was destroyed, an equilibrium for which some people still have nostalgia. But it was not destroyed all at once, or all of it destroyed. The new orientations took place very unevenly, some patches of medievalism remaining perfectly untouched, as snow will last even after rain storms, in the crevices of mountains and the lee of the fields.

To watch Francis through this last epoch of his life is really to watch the Machiavellian prince flinging away the renaissance. The civilization is cramped into a court, and the prince becomes more and more a soldier. His wars have no more dignity than those that Rabelais has the audacity to mock, and yet Francis will be held less a person than Charles V because he was less a soldier. His real merit, to take life as a gift and make of it a thing of beauty, he dissolved in the foolishness of his wars. But Rabelais could not condemn his wars since they too spring from human nature. To embrace this comedy, that so easily loses its balance, that becomes cruel the moment it becomes fanatical, that is only redeemed by humility and knowledge and the tenderness of the physician—so the unsentimental Rabelais persisted. And the Sorbonne howled like a wolf on the outskirts of his gay hearth-fire, that it might prove the love of God by destroying him. If he could put good and evil in terms other than those of heaven and hell, he would rob the imaginative of their mystery. Not for this had Loyola dreamed of Jerusalem, or Calvin brooded on predestination. Rabelais was an animal, unlike Calvin or Loyola, and hence unworthy of the Absolute, where instinct is forgotten and charity must bow to dogma, the Idea triumphing over human nature and merciless in the end.

But there was one religious exaltation that exacted no inhumanity, and that was Marguerite's. As the reign advanced, clouded by a hundred misadventures, her spirit soared into the mystical experience which is as loyal to its own abstraction as Rabelais to concrete instinct. Hers seemed a contrary course to everything about her, as if the moon were sailing through a sky against a streaming pack of clouds. And as the cloud-floes swept over Marguerite, heavy with disillusion, she ever and again emerged in clearer spaces, the heavens in festival and this moon a queen. Her light had an amber warmth, brilliant with its own humble audacity, flushing even the obliterating clouds. Sometimes, when she was lost, there shone a little star, a silver islet in the black river between the banks, and this was her attendant poet, Clément Marot. But when this star was quenched she bloomed again. Through voluminous masses hurried through the years, Marguerite submerged and reappeared, bursting into vision with the gratuity of her beauty, an opulence that tinged with lovely colour even the oppressions that she sustained. At times she seemed conquered, seemed to dissolve like a great pearl and slide down the astounded sky. But she could never lose the glow of her spiritual existence. She was at once fleeting and illumined, beyond the world and of it. Her mysticism bestowed radiance on her, in a canopy of gloom.

These impulses within the soul of Europe—the lambent wisdom of Erasmus, the comedic sense of Rabelais, the drastic poignancy of Calvin and Loyola, the soaring abnegation of Marguerite—these were approaches to the European experiment for which a dynast

FRANCIS I

Portion of a Votive Picture on Limoges Enamel by Leonard
Limousin

(From a Photograph in the British Museum)

like Francis had no perceptive welcome. He could have exasperated or facilitated the experiment, as Erasmus and Calvin and Marguerite proposed. He chose, rather, to evade it. He was a Prince.

Perhaps within this evasiveness there lurked the germ of his fatal disease. For his last phase is one of powers slowly diminishing.

3

The Treaty of Cambrai had definitely cramped Francis's politics. "If you are not in the forefront of it," avowed Montmorency to the Florentines, "do not call me a man of honour: call me a traitor." But that was the usual bluff of the supposedly powerful. The Florentines could not get help from this treaty because it took all Francis's skill to help himself.

Or rather, Anne de Montmorency's. The Grand Master was now stepping into the place that Boisy had vacated, and he was ready to work on the same policy of appeasement even if the disadvantages were French this time, and not Imperial. Montmorency was perhaps the only one of Francis's early companions who was not reckless by nature. He preferred an alliance with the Emperor to any trifling with Henry VIII, or with upstarts like the Florentine Republicans. He believed in peace. But this would be peace on the terms of solid, accredited, authenticated persons and institutions. There was nothing yeasty about Anne de Montmorency. He could lend Margaret of Austria the royal rondeaux with a deprecating smile, if she really wanted them. "These little things promote friendship." But Montmorency would not take any chance with doubtful causes. The man who had prolonged his la Trémoïlle engagement for ten years and then nipped out of it to take the wealthy daughter of the Bastard of Savoy—he would always be proof against undue effusiveness. Perhaps he had made a mistake to pooh-pooh Henri de Navarre at Cambrai, as he had made the enormous mistake of being gruff and brutish with Andrea Doria. But Montmorency was a hard-working, strong-minded, stout, bullying nobleman who believed in summary methods with the weak, and sane co-operation with his equals. He despised the windy, wordy people. He respected and admired the Emperor, and for Francis, to whom he was loyal, he welcomed the Spanish marriage.

4

That was more than Francis did. He had seen Eleanor and she had left him cold. He was very much in love with Anne de Heilly. She had come to Cambrai as a maid of honour, and this treaty meant a sad interruption to their life. He could not quarrel with it, since he could not recover his sons without taking the admirable Eleanor: but the way of the transgressor is hard.

How would Anne de Heilly take it? When Clément Marot first saw her, he summed her up in a few lines:

> *Eighteen years I reckon you,*
> *Beautiful and sage,*
> *But so level-headed I*
> *Deem you twice that age.*

She would, indeed, suffer, and not in silence. But where Françoise de Foix had tried to hold Francis by hauling in the line, Anne de Heilly loved him enough to play it out. He had given up Françoise for her. He had pledged himself to her for the rest of his life, though from the first he had shown himself concerned about arranging a good marriage for her, finding the right husband, right for her, and right for him. Anne had not risen to this generous offer with great eagerness. She had her prince as a monopoly, and not until he married again would she need to arrange her own affairs as he tenderly suggested.

But the marriage was approaching, with the return of the children. To take care of the children, to become their official governess, would establish her at Eleanor's court and continue her nearness to Francis. That would be a natural arrangement. But her attitude toward the marriage? In this the young girl, now twenty-one and for three years Francis's mistress, showed a feeling that warmed her lover. When your wedding day comes, she said in verse, and when you are surrounded by great pomp in your triumphal honeymoon, with banquets and tournaments and great honours, served by lords and ladies, think then that the heart of your beloved desires no other triumph than to have you know that her love was always dutiful and that if she has had any fault in loving it is to have thought herself a true and loyal servant. If, through no fault of my own, she adds with intensity, I should lose the boon I have claimed, take for sure and certain truth this verse to be last sign of our love, by which I shall hold my poor spirit worthy to receive no other boon but death. All that you shall find out, for where life is dead to feeling, death is contented life.

This was Anne de Heilly's response to being called "cold" and "hard" and "ungrateful" and "disdainful." Such warmth inspired Francis and braced him for the unavoidable wedding.

5

The poor children could not come home until Francis produced 1,200,000 crowns in hard cash. His mother had more than that tucked away in her coffers, but the people of France, the clergy and the nobles had not yet yielded up the sums that had been promised. Occasion, as Jean de Selve had so wisely declared to the Spaniards, may have a bushy forelock and yet be bald behind. Francis had unfortunately begun at the wrong end, and once more he presented himself to his Notables to secure the needed ransom. This time it was better managed, and the necessary funds were forwarded to Bayonne. With them, in heartrending completeness, were assembled all the title deeds to the relinquished territories. These, as well as the coins, had to be exchanged, as against the children and the new spouse.

Montmorency superintended the ticklish business of seeing the treaty fulfilled. Bitterly as Chabot de Brion would criticize him at court, Montmorency was just the man for this arduous task, and Francis still had faith in him. The Spaniards were taken to a room in Bayonne and shown the bullion. It was to be packed into wooden boxes, 25,000 crowns in each box, and delivered to the Bidassoa on mules, each mule with half a dozen guards. But before this golden procession could start, were the crowns of perfect alloy? The experts took a crown. Horror! It was not everything it should be. An examination had to be made. No technique had been invented by which a transfer of these ducats could be made without bringing nationalism into play. The French had collected the actual coins with the greatest difficulty and they were anxious to hand them

over with the least fuss in order to bring the dauphin and his
brother home to the promised land. But now every coin had to be
bitten by a Spanish expert, so to speak, before it could be passed.
And no sooner was the scrutiny undertaken than it became clear
that the French had been cheating—a large proportion of the coins
were heavily alloyed. This discovery meant that the King of France
had been swindled by his own mints, but the Spanish saw good
reason for being suspicious. From the inspection of the money to
its being counted and nailed again into the small boxes and sealed
and transported by mule under escort, Spanish scowling at French
and French spying on Spanish, was a wearisome and exasperating
transaction that would have been bad enough under ordinary circumstances but in the hot weeks coming up to July, with rumours
spreading like poisonous gases and enmities generating like the
pest, the perfectly simple exchange of a fixed sum of money in
return for the release of two boy prisoners, in the company of their
future stepmother, became a tragi-comedy charged with wicked
human passions: all the good breeding of the Spaniard turned into
rigid and spiteful exactions of etiquette; and all the savoir-faire of
the French became a hot-tempered resentment of "those beasts,"
and a desire to thwart them. Not a single movement could be made
at Renteria that had not to be paralleled by a movement at St. Jean
de Luz. If a pawn was lifted from the board at Fuenterrabia, another had to be snapped off at Hendaye. The Constable of France
had his spies down as far as St. Sebastian. The Constable of Castile
was instantly told that a courier of his was held up for a few hours
at Bayonne. The French Constable glared back his excuses. The
Spanish Constable retorted by wanting acts of perfect contrition.
This international farce went on for several months until finally,
while the Constable of Castile was still lying in bed to perpetuate
delay, the French Constable jabbed him with a challenge to a duel.
This was the climax to a long transaction in which there was not
one solitary trace of tolerance or goodwill. Montmorency's fury did
sting the Constable of Castile into sullen acquiescence. The long
antagonistic dance, like that of two goats meeting on a mountain
path, was terminated by the first crack of the horns. The time for
the bride had dragged on from February. Nearly 9,000 pounds'
weight of gold, much of it coined since Charles V had sent a cur-

rency expert to France the year before, had been closely examined. It cost Francis more than 100,000 francs to meet the standard agreed on; and some of the mint officials would be sentenced to death.

But at last the inquisition was over. Montmorency came to Hendaye with his mules and his gold. The two small boys and their future stepmother were exchanged in a ceremony so symmetrical that two pages of equal age to François and Henri had to be carried to the raft for equipoise, and distrust had prescribed exactly when the first foot should step on to the raft on either side. But no mule stumbled, no boat foundered. The boys crossed the bay in the summer twilight. And Montpezat, who had brought Louise the news of Pavia to Lyon, was able, on July 2, to ride into Bordeaux with the marvellous announcement that all was well. He had travelled from St. Jean de Luz to Bordeaux in twelve hours. For this great day Francis had been living. The boys had been in Spain from March 17, 1526, to July 2, 1530. It had imprinted itself on them for ever.

The younger boy, the future Henri II, was only seven when he went into exile. He was now eleven, a year less than François. He had been an earnest, keen, charming boy. He came out overcast and dispirited.

When Francis at last saw his children restored to him, he could not utter a word for long minutes. His emotions as a father were simple and poignant, and he suddenly felt everything that prison had been for his own flesh and blood. The older boy had borne it better, but the sallow, dark child soon disquieted Francis. The imprisonment had bruised his spirit, and only Diane de Poitiers, now a woman over thirty, would be able to bring to him the delicacy and tenderness which would convert his childlike trusting gratitude into unshakable love. His father could not do it. He was too exigent, too brusque. He could be moved for a few minutes, but he was soon irritated with a boy who seemed alien and sullen.

The next duty to discharge was the marriage to Eleanor. She had asked to be met by four hundred horses, so she was coming for the duration, but Anne de Heilly was wrong about the wedding. Francis met his beloved Eleanor at Mont-de-Marsan, one of those hot sandy places that in the month of July seem to abase themselves in dejection on the flattened earth. There, late in the evening, in a neighbouring abbey, Francis was wedded quite casually to the kind, good, virtuous and sensible lady whose fault was to be a chattel.

6

A marriage so political as Francis's could not distract him from his real passion so, leaving his Spanish bride to her devices, he departed at once to chase the stag. Had Marguerite or Anne de Heilly been at the wedding, he might have resisted, but Anne de Heilly had held aloof and Marguerite was alone at Blois, enjoying its beauty, looking after the other royal children and herself expecting the son who soon gave her such joy, and caused such unnatural resignation when he died within six months.

The French people welcomed the new Queen. She was a herald of peace, and they yearned for peace. The court was divided about her. Chabot de Brion, who had been named admiral to succeed Bonnivet, was anything but a lover of peace, but Montmorency was Eleanor's courtier and her advocate. Had he been sent to Charles's coronation at Bologna, he would not have been so naggingly importunate as Chabot. On the contrary, he aimed at an understanding with Charles V.

Bologna still remembered Francis's meeting Pope Leo in 1515. The young Emperor Charles V now had his turn to treat with the Pope. He did not walk through the crowds with Francis's informality, or sit down to win the Pope in friendly chat. He appeared with great pomp and magnificence. If he could not be crowned in Rome, the whole Roman apparatus could be copied and on the anniversary of Pavia, his thirtieth birthday, he could be gorgeously crowned Emperor. And when he negotiated with Clement he did it with a slip of paper in his hand. Charles did not trust His Holiness, and never would. Hence he talked of a Church Council, where the papacy would arrange with the Lutherans and plan its thoroughgoing reform. This made Clement deeply uncomfortable. But Charles's growing political skill was shown in his schemes for placating the Italians. He allowed the humbled Sforza to remain in Milan. He wooed the Duke of Savoy with Asti. He made friends with Urbino. And when the heroic efforts of Florence to resist the Medici were defeated, he gave his extramatrimonial daughter Margaret to the half-African Alessandro de' Medici, the Pope's quasi-nephew. In the siege of Florence Michael Angelo had engineered for his Republic. Clement VII was magnanimous enough to employ him on the Medici tombs, and those tombs would be a tragic monument to a people's conquest, a mournful ode in marble.

Had Charles set out to crush Italy, Francis would have been served. But the Emperor appeared to have listened to Gattinara's pro-Italian advice, and against such wisdom Francis could do nothing. To have made the French renounce their old allies, indeed, was a futile clause in the Cambrai treaty. It merely compelled the multiplication of French secret agents. But no strong French party persisted in Italy. Francis could only think of Würtemberg and the Sultan. And soon Marguerite would have the intention of giving an Albret as bride to the anti-Habsburg Hungarian John Zapolya.

Meanwhile Charles's sister had to be crowned Queen of France. Clément Marot wrote verses of welcome, his poetry sluggard in the official canal, and Francis witnessed the reception sitting in an open window with Anne de Heilly for the space of two hours. The English ambassador was shocked. The wicked French King paraded his mistress, when Henry was labouring so royally to make his Anne a queen. Perhaps Eleanor was aggrieved but she had chosen Francis with open eyes, and it was some consolation to her that her Spanish costumes and Spanish dances were making a distinct impression. She was, moreover, not wholly isolated. Her competent sister Mary would succeed Margaret of Austria in the Netherlands. Her niece Christine of Denmark would soon be married to Sforza in Milan. And Mary Tudor, another niece, would be of pathetic interest in England. Had her new husband given inward consent to a European appeasement, she could have served its purposes. But Francis could no more espouse Eleanor than he had espoused Claude. He could be civil, even gracious and cordial, and Louise and Marguerite and Anne de Heilly would go further. But Marguerite was already so wedded to Navarre, in spite of the gnarled patois of Béarn, that she could not love Spain's sister. This drew her closer to Anne de Heilly, especially since Anne de Heilly was a linguist and aware of literature and the arts. She was even aware of theology, another bond with Marguerite.

It was the moment chosen for founding the royal chairs of litera-

ture out of which grew the Collège de France. It was no new
university in a grand sense, but Francis dipped his flag to Latin,
Hebrew and Greek. It was not a triumph for literature so much as
for freedom of thought. Literature was now to serve itself with the
languages that were opened to the Bible. Calvin's Latin "Institutio"
was made inestimably more important as literature when he turned
it from Latin into French. But the Faculty of Theology, called the
Sorbonne, was striving to narrow down the exercise of mind to a
class whose thinking it could control, and new non-theological
linguists were necessarily intellectual pioneers in France. Marguerite was the true "mère des lettres," but possibly the du Bellays
had their direct influence. It was a hard time for the Sorbonne.
Guillaume du Bellay softened Henry VIII's heart by offering to
range the French universities behind the divorce. A great jewel
called the fleur de lys that Henry had had in pawn for years was
shipped back to Spain because du Bellay could thus line up the pro-
fessors. And even Montmorency invited the gruff Noel Bèda to
Chantilly to ask him why he was not supporting the divorce.

Thus was the mind of Europe made flexible. But Francis was
open to anyone or anything that was anti-imperial. Sforza, his ally
for a while, gradually become "issu de basse condition et d'une
bastarde." To Charles asking for financial aid against the Turk he
replied tartly he was not a "banker." He would favour the Turk,
and oppose the Council, and back up the divorce, and treat with
the Pope—anything to counterbalance Charles. Yet war was
financially and politically out of the question. And even the Turk
could not be too openly favoured, since his incursion would frighten
Germany and throw both Catholics and Protestants into one camp.

7

The death of Francis's mother came soon after his new marriage.
Marguerite comprehended his grief and it made her the more
anxious to care for him. She began to idealize her mother, even to
descant on her chastity from the age of eighteen to fifty-five. That
very beautiful eye, so kind and so majestic, incited everyone to
chastity, said Marguerite, hardly remembering her brother. Perhaps it incited Marguerite, but when Montmorency wanted to break

his engagement with the innocent Jacqueline de Joinville and asked Louise how he could do it, that fine eye twinkled as she answered, "Insist on the child's being sent to this court." The la Trémoïlles, "sans reproche," quailed in holy horror at the prospect. Louise knew they would. She was by no means a reverend Mother, but Marguerite would enshrine her as a sort of abbess in the Heptameron, and her memory fondly went back to the early days, to herself and her mother embroidering every stitch of the Bucolics, and of Scipio Africanus. As for the strife stirred by Gié, Anne of Brittany, Bourbon, Semblançay, it was veiled for Marguerite in the opal benevolence of their past.

She and her brother were much together in the coming year. He was making a royal entry into Rouen with Eleanor, as he had done with Claude, and he was continuing to Argentan. But another visit was in his mind. He was going to Brittany, and his former mistress wanted him, expected him, to stay at Châteaubriant. To this he assented. Marguerite, Anne de Heilly, Françoise de Foix, were thus under the same roof in 1532.

8

The time had come for Brittany to be united to, and absorbed in, the Crown. So long as a second son inherited Brittany, the Duchy could be alienated. It was therefore necessary to induce the Estates of Brittany to make a voluntary request that the heir to the throne become their Duke. The master of Châteaubriant was the important person in this manœuvre, since Guy XVII was out of the picture, and when the Estates did as they should Jean de Laval would be appointed Governor of Brittany and named chevalier. This demanded the presence of all the court. For five weeks Francis stayed as Françoise's guest at Châteaubriant. Her brother Lesparre was still alive, but Lautrec and Lescun had both died for France, and he could scarcely have honoured any other house in Brittany.

It was a period of fond unions. He was joining Brittany to France. He was also joining a Breton to Anne de Heilly. By the death of Bonnivet it had been made simpler to restore Jean de Brosse to the estates that had been denied to his father, the Breton who had rushed into rebellion with Bourbon and had been killed at

Pavia. Jean de Brosse was the son of a rebel, which would normally have closed his career at court. But at Francis's court the careers were open to all the talents for pleasing, and this young nobleman could establish himself by marrying Anne de Heilly. In two years he would be the Count of Étampes and in two more years the Duke of Étampes. This would be his reward. He may not have accepted the rôle of cuckold knowingly, though this would have been strange, but he lived to be openly taunted with it by other courtiers, and his resentment burst into a recriminatory lawsuit in the bitter end. But until then any open resentment would scarcely have been healthy for the son of a rebel. His handicap made him an excellent choice for Anne de Heilly. There is a malign, perverse pleasure in forcing handicapped men to do something they could not want to do. Francis and his court delighted themselves at Nantes, for example, during the wedding festivals, by making two priests fight with open fists. This piquant entertainment was repeated later on.

It was, of course, a small affair to make the Breton priests box with open fists. But no affair is too small for amour-propre in France. When Vendôme's brother dared to call Francis "Monsieur," he was informed that to Vendôme the King was indeed "Monsieur," but to Saint-Pol he was "Monseigneur." So is the lawn rolled and watered, watered and rolled.

But in visiting Châteaubriant Francis did not callously inflict himself on his first mistress. His visit to her was her own lamentable delight. The sight and sound of the King had in them the exasperated joy of rending a wound. To have loved, to have lost, still to love—it was peculiarly dreadful for this exiled woman and yet she implored Francis not to forget her but to return. Her letters followed him when he went away. They had in them an aching emptiness, and in this void rang her unanswered cry, an unhappiness whose only solace was its echo, and yet whose echo was filled with his silence. To this misery she surrendered. She rhymed of death, but for her it was not literary death.

Perhaps it was on this visit that the younger woman, seeing the gold rings for which Marguerite had written clever devices, told Francis she would like to have them. Francis had not given many presents to his first mistress—some brocade, a few jewels, these gold rings. Françoise was not well, but sent word that she would return her lover's presents within a few days. They faithfully arrived, melted into an ingot. This defiance stirred Francis's admiration. "Who would have thought a woman would show such générosité de courage!" Even the sister of Lautrec and Lescun?

But he could not commend any defiance in Françoise's successor. Anne de Heilly was entering on her married life with a certain old-fashioned seriousness, and she conveyed to her master that "things could not be the same." "Cannot be the same?" said the outraged Francis. And he wrote her a rondeau. Who would have thought it, he gasped, such deception and treason hidden under such a face, when I had believed myself to have, on your emplacement, builded for the rest of my life! You wish to hate me? Who would have thought it! It is not the custom of the "honnête" to behave in this unthinkable way.

9

This was the tone of an amused and assured personality and Francis was gradually and snugly arranging his compromises and becoming assured. He had consciously fitted himself with Anne de Heilly for the rest of his days. He was reaching middle age. He sometimes had bouts of fever. He was rapidly ceasing to be adventurous, and his quite supple though limited intelligence was taking cool command of the ship. He had Marguerite on his left to favour Roussel and to shelter Calvin. He had Montmorency on his right. When Bèda put Marguerite's "Lamentations of a Sinner" on the black list, that truculent Norman was at last despatched to cool off at Mont St. Michel. Francis could play both sides. He could use Guillaume du Bellay, Jean du Bellay, Lazare de Baïf, to cultivate the German Protestants. Possibly the marriage of priests and communion in two kinds and a re-interpretation of mortal sin could be arranged through Melanchthon and the papacy, if politics made it feasible, but the main object would always be to circumvent the Emperor and to block his path to "universal dominion." On this main object he was alert and pertinacious, though the means would vary from month to month.

As for his inner life, the Flemish tapestries that Montmorency

was ordering, or the formal changes he had now decided to command at Villers-Cotterets, in addition to the buildings at Fontainebleau and Vitry and Madrid, would satisfy the most vivid of his
cravings, that and the moulding of his boys and girls. Everything
interested him, though nothing for very long. He liked novelties.
He could be excited by a contraption for cosmological phenomena,
fitted out by a needy Italian. But architecture engrossed him. Montmorency had just rebuilt Chantilly and this accounted in part for
his fascinated returns to it. Montmorency's great wealth was en-
abling him almost to rival Chambord. In these monuments to the
noble life Francis founded exalted pleasure. His hands moved to
touch them, to form them, to caress them. He could no more
imagine any treachery or treason in them than behind Anne de
Heilly's beautiful façade.

And with Anne de Heilly, as with Françoise, he delighted in
beauty. He was one of those Frenchmen who for some reason
seem less likely than an Englishman to enter with a woman into
that resolute effort to give all life the values of their amatory intensity. An Englishman, even Henry VIII, could become capable
of an extraordinary purgation of spirit. Nearly any English contemporary of Francis would strive to bring all his motives, as well
as all his conduct, into line with the conception he had formed of
his woman, and that woman would seem to him so high-minded,
so high-spirited, so disinterested, so lovely, so pure, that he could
never be "worthy" of her, continually as she would reassure and
absolve him. She would become, in a way, his goddess and he
would pour into his adoration of her all the anthropomorphic
aptitude of his steadfast and shamefaced nature. He would be at
once shy and sensuous, apologetic and flagrant, and by these devices
of the spirit he would reach a very high degree of amatory excitation. So would she. And their molten mood could be poured into
public moulds—a strange and in many ways beautiful outcome of a
quite humble instinct. But for some reason Francis did not seem
to be able to give this moralistic cast to his amorous life. He had
indeed a twinge, in his earliest love affair, of feeling unworthy, and
he was tempted to idealize the jeune fille. But he did not seem
to have at his disposal this almost illimitable fund of faith in the
goodness of his idol. It was her beauty that exalted him and allured

him. A kind of mysticism of beauty dominated his worship, and where the English goddess could conceivably be burlapped in her garden clothes, with stout shoes and a dibbler in her hand, the Frenchwoman never played Ceres. The rôle of motherhood, to which Elizabeth Blount could give herself with broad-hipped generosity, was reserved by Francis for the official wife. It was to an exclusive beauty he deliciously abandoned himself. Even if his brain remained relatively clear, even if he kept his account of the universe uncontaminated by his aspiration, even if he shook his head over the illusion that flooded it, he still resigned himself time after time to an attraction that was unconquerable, no less infinitely human because so simply animal. To guard the jeune fille against premature excitation seemed to him elementary good sense. And he probably had no argument against the reciprocation of a lifetime, if that tragic affinity should happen to occur. But heroic love is as rare as any other sort of heroism, and he was not capable of it. He was much too inflammable and he took fornication very lightly. But if he was far from the nobility of great lovers, since love has the quality of the human nature that is engaged in it, he seemed capable of sustaining a warm appreciation over very many years, and, as a lover of beauty, he had his own invincible integrity. He was building castles on earth while Calvin was building castles in heaven that had dungeons in hell. Poor Calvin, in whose household the domestics would insist on becoming pregnant, he could do little with that incorrigible instinct to which Francis gave the portico, the peristyle, the exterior and interior façade.

10

Philanderer as he was and always would be, Francis's heart was under control. He took women with the gallantry that offers amusement and sentiment but no tragic seriousness. To him it remained "la guerre amoureuse." But his brother Henry VIII had not controlled his heart. He was still resolved to marry Anne Boleyn, and he wanted an interview with Francis, at Boulogne. Francis had every reason to see Henry and even to pay court to Anne Boleyn, but neither he nor Marguerite was in favour of this unroyal marriage. Who was Anne Boleyn? Marguerite was now a Queen. Henry VIII had been proposed as her own bridegroom. To stoop to the level of Thomas Boleyn's daughter was technically beneath her. If Henry VIII brought his lady to France, before the divorce had been granted, Marguerite declined to see her. Who then would see her? The French could only offer someone whose tarnished reputation could not suffer.

The interview took place in October, 1532. Henry must have liked seeing Boulogne, which he always fancied acquiring. But in his present mood he wished to win Francis, and their meeting, fully ceremonious and admirably costly, was much more intimate than the splendid conference twelve years before. Henry was in full bloom, an abundant, energetic, capricious sovereign with a quick eye for realities and no fear of forcing himself into a position around which circumstances must group themselves. Francis lived amid circumstances infinitely more complex and was at heart more inclined to save himself trouble. The verve of a young adventurous race seemed to mount in Henry. With perhaps a fifth or a sixth of Francis's resources he was capable of great changes because capable of faith. Francis could make the best of his situation, too much an artist not to do it, and he was versatile enough to sign a treaty with the Protestants or ally himself with Solyman, but his faith in himself had been daunted at Pavia and had been humbled at Madrid. What was now operative was a disillusioned man, facile, even beautifully facile, with words, but less willing to depart from the consecrated path. He had no Messianic delusion. He could not take himself with the mystic-seriousness of Charles V but he could give convenient platitudes a sort of lustreless acceptance. He knew that Henry suspected him of putting his alliance with Pope Clement first, and he perjured himself with his practised extravagance in asserting the contrary. Francis lied so much, and so often, he should have done it better. But he was one of those naturally florid performers who put their hand on their heart. The very suggestion that this boy should marry a base-born Medici made him look at Henry VIII with mournful reproachfulness. It was a coarse thought!

This wedding, however, led him to Marseille within a year. On the way to meet the Pope, he met the Turk. This no doubt was another perfidy, since the Turk was the enemy of Christendom, the

wicked monster who inhabits the East, the Red Terror, the Yellow
Peril, the Black Hundred. But Francis encouraged the Turk and
would soon be his open ally on the principle of the balance of
power. "Monsieur l'ambassadeur," he would avow to a Venetian,
"I cannot deny that I earnestly desire to see the Turk very powerful and warlike—not for his own sake, since he is an infidel and
we, we are Christians, but to lessen the power of the Emperor, to
force him into heavy expenditure, to rally all the other governments against so great an enemy." This is what he said to the
Venetian. But with the Turk the crude word infidel was not men-
tioned.

He had wanted to meet Clement VII at Nice. The Duke of
Savoy (almost the King of Savoy since Charles became his friend)
refused Clement his palace, on grounds of hygiene, and Clement
had to take ship again to Marseille. There a street was covered
over to make a reception hall, and Francis waited on His Holiness
with the humblest religious manifestations.

Clement had let his grey beard grow after his imprisonment in
Castel Sant' Angelo. With his thin face, his slight squint, and his
cancerous misery, he was one of those patently inadequate men
whom responsibility undermines. The meagre soil had worn away.
The bare rock emerged. He had, indeed, given a prolonged interview to Charles at Bologna, following Charles's negotiations with
the Protestants and his successes against the Turk, and Henry
VIII's public espousal of Anne Boleyn had at last induced him to
commit himself to the rightful spouse Catherine of Aragon. But
the English envoy who said that two of the ladies who came with
little Catherine de' Medici were the Pope's mistresses must have
jumped to a partisan conclusion. This worn-out, meagre man had
no vitality for mistresses. What was killing him was the fatigue
of running with the hare and hunting with the hounds. He had
known from Campeggio that Henry VIII was a sanguine, headstrong man. To deal with an Englishman in that frame of mind
he must either have gratified him with a divorce or staggered him
with a refusal. He had nothing to gain by delay unless he meant
to poison Catherine of Aragon in all decency. But the Medici
Popes wanted to retain every one of their customers, at 20 per cent.
Clement could not even relinquish Florence for the Medici, which

tied him to the Emperor, much as he had suffered and bitterly as he had resented him.

Before Florence was recaptured by the Emperor for the Medici, this little creature born of Lorenzo Junior and Madeleine de la Tour d'Auvergne had been just as much a prisoner in her convent as Henri had been a prisoner in the Spanish stronghold. The two youngsters, each fourteen years of age, had been equally deprived of emotional sunshine in early years. The nuns had treated Catherine de' Medici with devotion, but her life was endangered during the troubled period, and this had left its grave impression. She came to France as a subdued, insignificant quasi-duchess, anxious to please. Her husband-in-trust, since the actual wedlock did not begin at fourteen, was already fixated on Diane de Poiters, aged 33. Diane and Catherine, however, were not so unevenly matched as would seem on the surface. Catherine de' Medici was half Bourbon—quite as Bourbon as Louise of Savoy.

The English came to Marseille and bullied Clement unmercifully. But this was spleen. The Pope had taken his stand, and even Francis was irritated by the roughness of his English allies. He could perfectly well keep his temper with Pope Clement, now that he was getting what he wanted. But everyone badgered Clement VII—the Emperor, the English, Montmorency. He was perhaps fortunate to have only one year more to live. And yet to the outside world, the world that Benvenuto Cellini led in papal procession because Clement had bestowed a sinecure on him, this was an awe-inspiring, beauty-loving, law-giving man. At the name Medici the goldsmith's heart chirped like the morning. Medici! Medals, jewels, coins, vases, bowls, sinecures, commissions, a cornucopia of patronage. Benvenuto had hurried from Florence when Michael Angelo was engineering the ramparts. For the decorative artist the word Republican meant wrangling committees, and grudging allowances. He had an art that needed Medici, Emperor, Magnifico. He was a carver, and they were his ivory.

II

Francis came away from seeing the Pope with a revived interest in Italy. He had discussed Milan and discovered that Clement was receptive. It was easy in return to oppose a general Church council. Clement did not want it and its postponement kept Germany torn by religious differences. And Francis was willing to pursue the heretics at home. He had failed to obtain consolation for Henry VIII that could avert schism in England, but that schism separated Henry from the Emperor.

There was much to do at home. His currency was in disorder. Prices were irregular. Finances were still disturbed. But these internal difficulties were chiefly of military importance to Francis. He was planning for the day when he would smite the Emperor.

The Emperor had gone back to Spain after a sobering experience in Germany. He had lost his old adviser Gattinara, but the lessons he had learned from him in regard to Italy and Savoy he had surprisingly learned. He was moderate and sagacious in Germany. Even Luther had been won by his capacity for suspending hostility in the interest if not of reconcilement yet of order. The Turk was the great danger. Charles was returning to Spain to attack him from the rear.

Francis could not oppose it. It was too gloriously in the tradition of the Crusades, and his own nobles were not less susceptible to this than the German Protestants. Charles could raise his banner and all of Spain would flock to it. Montmorency was not alone in seeing the glory and the valour of an attack on Solyman the Magnificent.

But Francis's ambassador to the Turk had already pointed out that Italy was the place where Charles would be weakest. And if the Turk did his part in Italy, Francis was prepared to second him. It was a policy peculiarly free from Christian prejudices, governed by the sense of Charles's disproportionate influence in Europe. It was, in its own way, another alliance with Cesare Borgia: and damn the consequences.

But Francis's supply of mercenaries was stopped in Guelderland and Switzerland. He needed a new type of army. Borrowing the plan from Machiavelli, he and his Council resolved to create seven provincial legions, each of six thousand, a formidable infantry. This was to have the same military code as the janissaries. The soldiers were not to brawl, not to fight duels, not to play cards or shoot dice. They were to avoid prostitutes. They were to be severely disciplined and to be specially honoured and rewarded for bravery.

A Venetian in the next generation would say of the French, "The French are almost obliged to have war with the Spanish. The nobility in France is very numerous, particularly in younger sons who have no way of enriching themselves or bettering their lot except through the army or the Church. Not all of them can or will be priests, and the army leads inevitably to war. But where to wage war? In Germany? No. That is too hard a nut to crack. In England? Not possible. The sea is too wide a ditch, and in naval warfare the English are much too strong. Against the Turk? But the religious ardour of the Crusades is past. Only the Spaniards remain, and to join issue with them, the convenience of attacking Flanders. As men always seek to wrap their actions in some appearance of reason, the pretensions of France in the Netherlands, in Milan and in Naples seem to offer a sufficiently legitimate excuse for war against the Spanish."

These same younger sons were anything but anxious to share the spoils with Francis's legionaries. It was soon obvious that the armed plebeian made just as good a soldier as the armed noble. The biological difference was nil, and the cultural difference very slight. But the French noble looked askance at this new brand of citizen. If it was now reckoned too dangerous to bring the Swiss mercenary into France, because he was spreading heresy, it was hardly less dangerous to arm the understrappers, who might spread another type of heresy. Fundamental as the new military system really was, it was just as instinctively opposed by the nobility as literature in the common tongue was opposed by the humanists. In each case a vested interest was endangered. But at the beginning Francis saw in it his great reservoir of cheap fighting men, the very thing he had so long needed for Italian warfare. And some of the best fighting men, the Blaise de Monlucs, were quick in their praise of these new legionaries.

12

The rakish nobles had their man in Chabot de Brion. An excellent soldier in defence of Marseille, a lively companion to Francis in the gloom of Spain, a resourceful diplomat, it came easy for him to clash with the Emperor or to intrigue with the German Protestants. And opposed to him, more and more, was the weightier Montmorency, who was as ready to crush heresy as he was to kill prisoners or to exterminate brigands.

No one had been more friendly with Montmorency than Marguerite. She called him her "nephew." Her trusted matron Madame de Châtillon was his aunt. Her best friend had been his father, to whom she wrote many playful and amiable letters. And she had had the most intimate obstetrical confidences with his wife. But Montmorency was just as naturally orthodox as Marguerite was open-minded. To take the royal post, spy into letters and then destroy them, seemed fair tactics to this noble handyman. It could never occur to him that the Lutheran revolution of 1517 had created a European problem of the first order, and that this problem could never be solved in France so long as the Sorbonne remained to give its religious policy to the government. Between 1517 and 1533 Francis had turned parlement to his own uses, but the Sorbonne was still more powerful than he, and when he said to his Grand Master that something must be done about the Lutherans, that blunt gentleman replied that he ought to begin with the Queen of Navarre. So it was repeated to Marguerite. It was impossible for her to keep her loyalties in separate compartments. Francis's faith in her was the first necessity of her life. She attacked Montmorency directly. She reminded him that he was the King's servitor and she the King's sister. The Grand Master went pale as death. But possibly his imperial policy, with its sacrifice of Navarre, had something to do with Marguerite's hostility. She was beginning to be dynastic on her own small account, the blight travelling from the sycamore to the rose.

13

Francis remained tolerant of her religious radicalism, and ready to uphold her against the Sorbonne. Her devoted Marot was even allowed, after a festival at Alençon, to draw a dagger and threaten to bury it in a nagging orthodox poet. But in October, 1534, the real blue-nose Reformers, fearing to be smothered by kindness, took it on themselves to prepare a placard against "ceste pompeuse et

orgueilleuse Messe Papale," a very long and passionate indictment
of the Mass, as well as "le Pape et toute sa vermine de cardinaux,
d'evesques et de prestres, de moines et autres caphards diseurs de
messe;" and this placard was not only displayed in Orléans, Tours,
Blois, but was smuggled into the heart of the renaissance kingdom,
and there, on the door of Francis's bedroom at Amboise, it was
pasted up.

Francis was not a man whose rest could be disturbed by a
crumpled roseleaf, but he liked to get up at leisure, to make his
toilet while receiving the news and stropping his wits, to take his
time adjusting himself to the world. To have this enormous thumb,
black with printer's ink, thrust invisibly into the sacred inwardness
of Amboise, and plant its imprint on his door, his bedroom door,
was something to make sleep a mockery and night an ambuscade.
Where were the archers? Where were the guards? A man with a
pastebrush slapping up a placard in the middle of the night, a
placard packed with words and reeking with heresy, was not a
simple intruder. He was a horned monster, a creature from the
abyss. Did Francis see the placard himself, in his nightshirt, or
was it peeled off for him? However it came to him, it was no
laughing matter. He read it with a revolt of all the feelings that
he had so far concealed. The Turk might well roll up in his
tens of thousands to Vienna, with the utmost contempt for Christians and everything sacred to Christians, and this attack Francis
could flick away with malice. Charles's brother-in-law had died at
Mohács. That was his Pavia. And it did not arouse the tiniest
sentiment of fellow-feeling in Francis. But here the long sincere
screed of one super-heated pastor from Neuchâtel, Marcourt, was
pasted on his door, and he felt as if the floors quivered with
irreverence and the walls shook with indignity. Christ had been
insulted, but Francis also had been insulted. Cursed! Abominable!
It stirred him to his depths. He saw that out of heresy could come
subversiveness, out of subversiveness could come the upheaval of
society. It shook him. He would act.

He did act. Marguerite departed at once for her home in the
south, where she was harbouring Calvin. This pastor of Neuchâtel
had released a spring that would prove uncontrollable. The passions
of the Sorbonne, so far compressed and congested by one free ex-

pression after another, were now ready to discharge themselves in black revenge.

Everywhere the queer people who had begun to think about religion and to read about it, the people who had been started by the Bishop of Meaux and Erasmus and Lefèvre, the merchants, the clerks, the workers, the asymmetric, the noble, the inquiring, the disordered, the disinterested, the sincere—drag them out, torture them, string them up, pull out their tongues, burn them alive, hang them, disembowel them, quarter them. It was painful to do it, but it had to be done. Christ had been insulted and Francis had been insulted. Lists of names, men, women, people who write books, people who are wicked and dangerous and subversive about private —private confession. People who never heard of Avignon and never heard of Pisa and yet dare to question the Papacy. Burn them alive. They are heretics. They attack His Holiness and la messe papale.

The total number of public executions was not very great. Forty or fifty. About the number that would follow a little military in-discipline in a town of the Midi. Forty, fifty. A paralytic, a great reader of books, who had been locked up before he had got out in 1533, he was burned alive. A draper from Noyon. A printer. A weaver. A mason. A bookseller. A schoolma'am. Then the rich merchant with whom Calvin had lodged. And so on, strung over months, until at last the new Pope said, "for God's sake, stop!"

The executions did stop, but Francis had in the meantime done away completely with the liberty of the Press. The imprimatur was now necessary.

14

Francis's defeat by the Sorbonne was of supreme importance in the history of France, in the history of culture, in the history of religion.

His defeat at Pavia left the nation intact: France was more France after Pavia than before it. But after the Placards France was no longer at one. The Sorbonne had triumphed over the Monarchy. And the consequences of this victory, due to Francis's evasiveness, would go on through the Huguenot episode up to, and beyond, the Revolution.

An English liberal might easily look back with gratification on the course that events took in England where the prince, in spite of his absolutism, paved the way for a settlement which had no such obstacle to it as the Sorbonne. Henry VIII grappled with the theologians, in the interest of Leviathan. And this brought religion into relation with parliamentarianism from the first. It eventually created "tolerance," which means the subordination of all enthusiasm to the working of representative institutions.

Francis, on the other hand, gave no serious thought to theology. It forced supreme decisions on the state but he did not grapple with them. His sense of order, perhaps, left these questions to the specialists. At any rate he unloaded on his children and on his children's children this capital question, along with the compound interest which always accumulates around a capital question which is not faced when it arises.

The Europe which passed from feudalism to national sovereignty through the furnace of the Reformation had no handy method for dealing with religious enthusiasm, any more than the national sovereign states to-day have a handy method for socializing industry. To reconcile the competitive principality with religious enthusiasm was too much for European statecraft. The Inquisition in Spain, the Wars of Religion in France, the persecutions in the British Isles going on to regicide and revolution, the upheavals in Germany going on to the Thirty Years' War, all indicate the stupendous complications that are presented to an inflexible statecraft by a popular ferment. The utter failure of absolutism to deal with this ferment is of all things the most significant, and yet the expedient tried by Francis I of yielding to the Sorbonne had its own lamentable price.

A vivid religious faith seems to seize on miserable and unhappy people with terrific force, and to be beyond political reasoning. The tendency in a religious majority is to become intolerant and in a minority to become insurrectionary. By the time of the Placards Francis was unavoidably aware of this tendency of the Reformers. He knew that in the long run they were prepared to collide with the state and, through the state, with the Sorbonne. It took no genius on his part to see the unenviable position of the state as buffer, and to see the desire for power becoming more and more accentuated in the leaders of the Reformation and the princes who were utilizing them.

So long as the common people had themselves no serious share in the responsibility of the state, so long as they were simply the raw material from which an aristocratic or monarchical state is fabricated, so much the more explosive must be a tempestuous religious emotion. The religious imagination, captured by a vision of earthly paradise and identifying its will with the will of God, is singularly revolted by the compromises of earthly politics. It refuses to be pedestrian. It flies to perfection. Once the spirit of reform begins to draw on the inexhaustible and scientifically uncontrollable resources of theology, the end can only be the state house or the madhouse, the throne or the scaffold. Such overwhelming emotions, always producing demagogues, split the unit with which a monarch has to deal.

Francis had struck a good bargain with the Catholic Church. His Concordat with Leo was one of those many contracts by which, since the council of Constance, Rome passed from empty universal claims to definite arrangements with national sovereignty. Having come to such an arrangement with the Church, Francis could use the Sectarians to keep the Church in place, but once they intruded on him, once they showed themselves to be insurrectionary, he was driven to exterminate them. In an absolute monarchy there is no safety valve for the insurrectionary.

But nothing excites the religious imagination so much as persecution. The French state was as thorough and as ruthless and as powerful as any absolute state could be. Its methods were drastic, though stealthy, and it had no vague liberal feeling about minorities. Calvin fled from France because Calvin knew France. His followers, who could not flee, had their tongues torn out by the roots and were tortured in precisely the manner most likely to strike terror into the crowd. But this brand of frightfulness, thoroughly understood by Francis's government and carried out with blood-curdling cruelty, only intensified the emotions of the Calvinists. And neutrals were shaken out of their prudent detachment. Every young legalist of first-rate intelligence was driven by these methods into furious thinking. The dark streak in French nature, the capacity for sombre and passionate conviction, the mixture of

invincible intelligence with a bleak and desolate but triumphantly
obdurate character, was bound to be developed by methods which
had themselves no human touch. Out of the sunshine, deep in the
shadow of death-in-life, in the valley of the eternal where every
flower is at once perpetual and sterile, where hope is immovable,
where its smile is fixed but dead, there loyalty to the state paled
into an illusion and men pressed their lips to the cold crucifix in
a frozen kiss.

The genial folk quality which pervades Rabelais, the good sense
which rises from him as waves of delicious warmth rise from the
old earth in spring, the pagan zest for life, amorous of wine, of
comradeship, of adventure, of women—all this liberality of instinct, saturated with humour and defiant of self-pity and sentiment,
goes down into a gulf of abnegation and despair when its inade-
quacy to exalt the imagination is combined with a sick body and
an avid mind. Calvin is just as French as Rabelais, and his antith-
esis. He is urban where Rabelais is rural. He is the child of
notaries where Rabelais is the child of farmers. Calvin is indoor,
Rabelais outdoor. Calvin is black, humourless, thin, seared, intense,
with a hardness which brings him at last to the icy lambency of
the diamond. Rabelais is the doctor, the man who accepts disease
and seeks to cure it, the tonic companion of Nature, indulgent and
yet sunnily indifferent, the foe of absolute ideas. Calvin is the
questing intellect, absorbed in absolute ideas, climbing from abysm
to heights canopied in a darkness that yet is peopled by stars.

In every nation there is the soul in solitude and the soul in
multitude; in France, owing to the pressure of those abstractions
which Calvin promulgated and to which the Sorbonne retorted,
the reconciling spirit of Rabelais could not hold its sway. The court
had not freed itself. Hence the rich vulgar gusto that in England
was to buoy up Shakespeare and to sustain his cloud-capp'd towers,
became in France a classic elegance divorced from the masses, refined in motive and exquisite in form. A conception of Taste was
thus developed in poetry, in prose, in art, in music, in architecture,
in sculpture, in manners and in eloquence, which sent the Rabe-
laisian impulse underground. Only in painting and in the novel
would the French eventually throw off their conservatism and reunite with nature. For the rest, their romantic liberty, the tilth out

of which lyrics spring as naturally as wild flowers, had been sacrificed by Francis's capitulation to the scholasticism of the Sorbonne.
What was in question was a people's spontaneity, working through
the freedom of the printing press. The Reformation, whatever its
doctrinal emphasis, was rich in popular spontaneity. Its suppression
in France gave little outlet for creativeness except in orthodox
terms, whether supervised by the court or supervised by the
Church. The joyous dawn that was filled with the clamour of
Rabelais soon settled into the sober midday of Montaigne. Montaigne is no more a Catholic than Rabelais but he is literally circumscribed by the classics. He has lost the folk quality. He is
bookish. He has entered into the solitude of the brain. The life of
the imagination in Montaigne had already been cut into partitions,
and his genius was not grand enough to englobe the national life
with a full sense of its adventure and its romance. Military and
intellectual adventure remained, to rise to great heights with the
Roi Soleil, but the huge kindness of life had found its last abundant
national expression in Rabelais.

15

Through streets hung with tapestries, guarded by archers with
white staves, an immense procession wended from the Louvre to
Notre Dame on January 21, 1535. A Venetian said that Paris was
just like Cairo on its days of fête, but on this day it was strictly
disciplined. All the most precious relics of a city rich in saints were
carried in expiatory solemnity. Sixteen bourgeois, wearing nothing
but their shirts, with garlands in their hair, bore the shrine of St.
Geneviève. The true cross, the crown of thorns, the iron of the
lance, the sponge, the robe of purple—most of them brought to
France by St. Louis—were allowed to be borne through the streets,
while all the officials marched with bare heads, carrying lighted
candles, and the Swiss guards, the heralds, the royal archers, took
their place in the line along with princes of the blood, religious
orders, city and government and university officials.

Twenty years before Francis had made his entry, compelling the
monks to go by the side streets while he caracoled for the ladies
on a white horse. Now, with violins and trumpets and hautboys

and cornets, with the choir-boys and their masters, he walked bare-headed, soberly clad, to express his sorrow for the placards.

After high mass at Notre Dame he himself addressed the assemblage, not as the King but as a subject and servant of their common King, the King of Kings. To Him they did honour, reverence and obedience. France was the only power that had never bred monsters, and its fair name must not be stained. People of lowly origin were spreading damnable and execrable opinions. It was not his fault that these cursed opinions had been spread. Ever since learning had been transferred from Athens to Paris, the city had been renowned for good and holy letters but its light would be dimmed if order were not maintained. The vast majority held to good and sound doctrine, but those who had fallen away should be denounced. If his own arm were infected with this rottenness he would cut it off, and if his own children were so unhappy as to fall into error he would sacrifice them to God. But no one must be falsely accused.

His audience's countenance was swept by succeeding emotions as he carried them from one point to another. He swayed everyone by his own profound emotion. Then the royal company went to dine with the bishop, opposite Notre Dame, and the relics of Christ's passion and crucifixion were returned to safety. While dinner was in progress six heretics were led in front of the cathedral to their passion, and then taken away and burned alive.

This news was not slow to travel over Europe. Though it dismayed the German Lutherans, it had its value for Henry VIII. A few months later he and Cromwell would send Thomas More and Fisher to their doom.

16

It was in the midst of these Christian manifestations that Charles V set out to chastise Francis's ally Barbarossa. "Not only," said Clement two years before, "will the King of France not prevent the coming of the Sultan against Christendom: he will advance it." Hence Charles was doubly anxious to get rid of the Sultan's naval base, dominated by Barbarossa. He had thought, first of all, that the services of a secret agent might be best, and he had arranged to reward an adventurer if this wicked Turk could be poisoned or have his throat cut while drunk. But the hardy old pirate seized Charles's agent in cold sobriety and put him to death instead. It was precisely what Sforza had done with one of Francis's secret agents, two years before, to Francis's enormous indignation. But Charles's private plot having failed, he himself raised the banner of Christ on his laden fleet and proceeded in July to La Goletta. It was his first participation in a battle, and turned out a signally brave and successful one. He then had the resolution to go on to Tunis, which his Germans and Spanish and Italians captured in terrible heat, releasing thousands of Christian slaves, while Barbarossa himself escaped, to prove that the Mediterranean was still his lake by raiding the Balearic Isles.

The world was still near enough to the Crusades to be deeply stirred by this valiant expedition of Charles V. Francis might claim a few achievements overseas. Jacques Cartier had just discovered Canada for him, and the French were contesting Brazil with the Portuguese. But the Emperor had really vindicated his world fame as Emperor. It was true, of course, that such things were going on in the non-Christian world as the building of the Taj Mahal, in 1535. Everything did not depend, for human salvation, on this chastizer of Barbarossa. But he firmly believed in his mission. He was protecting Hungary and Germany from the Sultan. Flushed with triumph though still undemonstrative, he landed in Sicily and then in Naples. He had thoughts of bullying Pope Paul III, who was firmly and scrupulously neutral. But he came up to Rome in all Christian humility, in April, 1536.

17

Francis did not like the victory of Tunis. At the time that the author of Utopia was being executed, he was touring France to inspect his new legionaries, whose uniforms in Normandy he had decided on himself. Montmorency was with him, but Francis fell ill and sent the Grand Master to complete the inspections. Incidentally, his faith in the Grand Master's policy was shaken. He wanted to strike, even when Charles was fighting the Turk. And when Sforza died, late in 1535, at a moment that could not have been more suitable, leaving Milan without an heir, all the old preoccupation was fiercely stirred in Francis's blood.

But to strike at the Emperor directly would be impossible. The procedure in such a case would be to pick a quarrel with a minor power. The Duke of Savoy, Louise's brother, had become a satellite of the Emperor's since the peace at Cambrai. Francis asked parlement to prepare any claims on Savoy that he might derive from his mother. He wanted Bresse and Nice and Villefranche, if not Geneva. With slender grounds for attacking his uncle, he still prepared invasion. It was the signal for Montmorency's dismissal. And Francis talked of bestowing his youngest son on Henry VIII's new daughter, Elizabeth of England.

The turn that affairs were taking broke on Charles V at Rome, when he heard that Savoy was invaded and Turin already occupied. Up till then he could gaze in wonder on the Colosseum in a Rome recovering from the Sack and urgently cleared of its ruins to receive him worthily. Rabelais had just left the city. On his first visit Rabelais had studied the antiques. On his second visit he was hugely diverted by the living circus, especially by the parasites collecting for the Emperor. But he had hurried away with his patron, Jean Du Bellay, because war was threatening. And war was clinched by an indignant speech in Spanish from the Emperor himself. At a papal reception he spoke for an hour and a half, an indictment of Francis. To the horror of all well-bred diplomats he used this hospitable occasion to trounce his rival, to threaten war unless Francis made terms within twenty days or unless he would meet him man to man. This outburst, while hot and vehement, re-opened the European war, since Francis had no intention of yielding Turin and since his weapons were "not long enough" to fight a duel with.

While Charles V gave his ultimatum with the Pope at his side, Benvenuto Cellini was hurrying frantically to finish his cover for a Book of Hours, a present from the Pope. And when the artist presented it to Charles, "Let five hundred golden crowns be given at once to Benvenuto," were the delicious words, at which a papal official stepped up and took the five hundred crowns.

Benvenuto, though recovering slowly from a serious illness, had made a ring to fit the Emperor's present to the Pope, a twelve-thousand-ducat diamond. "These two pieces of work," said the

THE EMPEROR CHARLES V

A portion of the Painting by Titian in the Alte Pinakothek, Munich

furious artist, "on which I had spent upwards of two months, brought me in five hundred crowns." The frugal Pope made the Emperor's gift the sole payment for everything. "I took what I could get, and made up my mind to leave Rome without permission." So Benvenuto Cellini would go to France.

18

The indispensable man for Francis's war was not the volatile Chabot de Brion. The admiral was an old and intimate friend of the King's. He talked to him with an informality, a familiarity, that no one else could venture on, and he criticized Montmorency with great verve. He had become wealthy serving Francis, and he was not above taking bribes from the Portuguese to relax French interests in Brazil. But his insouciance was too costly in the crisis of 1536. Francis removed him and sent for the hard-headed Montmorency. By the time that Charles, commanding veterans who like himself had been bronzed in Africa, resolved to invade Provence in July, the Grand Master had matured his plans for receiving him. These plans were not heroic, but Francis gave them full assent. His own part in the war was to play full back. He gave domination to Montmorency.

Provence was to be sacrificed. Its vines could remain and its fruit trees, because that meant dysentery for the invaders. But the beasts had to be killed, the mills burned, the wells poisoned, so that no invading army could live. Montmorency built a camp at the junction of the Rhône and the Durance, skilfully fortified, policed and drained. He fed his orderly multitudes and paid them. He was up early and held serious and attentive council, himself a Roman captain, a grander version of Gié. He allowed Charles V to do his worst in a country as bare as a board, with the King at Valence, a garrison in Marseille, the Turk on the sea. This forced the Emperor to defeat himself. He withdrew, hopelessly frustrated, half his army wasted away: and his veteran Antonio de Leyva died.

Francis had gone to the second camp after an affectionate parting with Anne de Heilly, and his weary spirits rose at the evident ruthless efficiency of Montmorency. But a terrible blow fell on him in August. His eldest son François, fresh from an ardent game of jeu de paume at Lyon, drank a cool drink handed to him by his squire Montecuculli, and was dead in three days.

Francis was beside himself for a few days. That a cool drink should cause this mortal illness—as with Charles V's father in Spain—at once created a dreadful doubt. Was the dauphin poisoned? His new page, Ronsard the poet, was present at an autopsy. "I saw his body opened, daring to feast my eyes on his lungs, his heart, his blood." He had only been six days with this youth whose sepulchre was "a thousand standards, bucklers, horses, the tears of soldiers," and the suspicion of poisoning was universal. François was an outdoor youth, though he had never recovered from his long imprisonment in Spain, and hated the Spaniards for the bad treatment he had received. But was he poisoned? Montecuculli was at once arrested. The wretch avowed under torture, then disavowed. He was said to have had a book on poisons, and a safe conduct from Antonio de Leyva. He was formally tried by the Council and found guilty of giving the dauphin arsenic, condemned to be "desmembré tout vif à quatre chevaulx." This was done at Lyon. The populace execrated this man from Ferrara. It cut his remains into little morsels, hacked off his nose, tore out his eyes, broke his jaws, trained the head in the mud "and made him die a thousand times after his death."

No one could have great benefit from this death but his younger brother Henri and his younger brother's wife Catherine de' Medici. The younger brother already found intense favour with Montmorency and Diane de Poitiers, and the one person whom Montecuculli tried to implicate was Guillaume de Dinteville, a cousin of Montmorency's. That this great soldier's cousin should have worked with the man from Ferrara seemed unthinkable. Yet the Dintevilles, used by Montmorency for unsavoury work, were an unsavoury crew. Gaucher was taunted with being a sodomite in the next year by Pierre de Plessis and demanded a chance to avenge his honour. A duel was arranged presided over by the King, but Dinteville failed to appear. He and Guillaume were banished for high treason, as soon as Montmorency came into disfavour. As for Montmorency and the dead youth, they were definitely unfriendly. The dauphin did not propose to be managed by a pro-Spaniard. "Attend to your own business," he said to the Grand Master, who reproved him for a flirtation, "and see that it is honest, without interfering with me."

And, said Henri immediately after his brother's death, "the Grand Master has received me in his camp with the greatest honour possible."

It has perhaps never been suggested that Anne de Montmorency had the Dauphin François murdered, but he was the man who had a real motive for the crime, the necessary coolness, firmness and cruelty, and an impeccable situation. He was absolutely indispensable to France. No one could afford to incriminate the man who was saving France. He, young Henri, Diane de Poitiers, might be in the opposite camp to Marguerite, for example, yet even Marguerite, in a defensive war of gravest importance, was compelled to sink her enmity and to fawn on Montmorency. Her days on the Rhône were spent in admiring his camp, in reviewing troops, in listening to spies. She became patriotic, militaristic, gurglingly bellicose. She showed a sweet friendliness to the Grand Master that paid full tribute to his indispensable service as a general, seeing her brother was ill—but a tribute so profuse, so falsetto, that nothing but a strong sense of self-preservation, for herself, for her brother, and for France, could have induced her to resort to it. And her husband, his titular kingdom straddling the Pyrenees, was himself straddling the two powers now at war—a position of great danger to Marguerite. So she talked in high, fluent tones about Montmorency's magnificence as a general, and wanted to don armour and fight in the wars.

"At Rome," said the observant Doctor Rabelais, "a world of folk get an honest living by poisoning, drubbing, lambasting, stabbing and murdering." But this lively fellow said too much. In the month that Montecuculli was executed Rabelais' letters were opened, according to the Montmorency-Tournon system, and the Cardinal nearly threw him into prison for loose talk in wartime. Marguerite and Francis saved him. But what people really felt they seldom dared to express. As for "stabbing and murdering," before the end of the year Etienne Dolet, according to his own story, was attacked by a gang and killed one of them in self-defence. He received a royal pardon but it could not keep him out of prison. It was a time for heresy hunters, for savage reprisals.

19

But it was a trying time for those in authority. Francis was reaching the age at which, as at the end of August, the crisp leaves begin to fall. Duprat had died in 1535, heavy with flesh, heavy with gold, drowsy with the spoils he had gained by gutting the Pragmatic Sanction and the Parlement. He had seen many of the bourgeois dynasties end on the gibbet. He was lucky to decline peacefully out of existence. But younger persons were going—Mary Tudor, Anne Boleyn, Fleurange. It was all very well for John Calvin, now safe in Basel, where Erasmus was dying, to begin his own strenuous chapter with a thundering Epistle to the Roy tresmagnifique, Roy tresmagnanime. But Francis had mortality in his bones. He was harassed and tired. Madeleine, married to James of Scotland, on the first day of 1537, was pale as a lily and would be dead in a few months. Francis could act the soldier at Hesdin, and Marguerite could unite Catherine de' Medici and Anne de Heilly and young Marguerite to send him a round-robin saying "bravo," but he was troubled and unwell.

War in Flanders might seem more logical for him than war in Italy, but he was content to garrison Saint Quentin, Péronne, Corbie, Doullens. The reason for this was simple. Flanders was England's best customer, and he could not hold England as an ally if he proved too aggressive in Flanders. Milan, incidentally, he now needed for his younger son Charles, so that the elder son could have Brittany to incorporate with the crown. The younger son must be placated, and at Italy's expense. Hence Francis, having mended his line in the north, turned to Savoy. But he was miserable at Melun. "Care, worry," diagnosed Montmorency. Anne de Heilly hung on him and kept him from going to the front.

In August, 1537, amusing himself by hunting, he was confronted by serious news from Savoy. An offensive must be undertaken. He was sitting on his horse when he heard this. He remained motionless, his eyes fixed. Then he stroked his beard, passed his hand over his forehead and sighed deeply. To begin all over again! But within half an hour he was hard at it with his staff, working out a plan.

Since his mother died this man was something of a widow. He

FRANCIS I ON HORSEBACK, ABOUT 1540

From the Painting in the Pitti Palace, Florence, attributed to Clouet

had lost aggression. He was carrying on his war, but he welcomed a truce in the north and he would accept a truce in the south once Montmorency forced the pass of Susa, with himself manfully aiding him by sending forward one hundred thousand rolls of bread every day. He could take Barcelonette while Montmorency did the heavy work. It was not the old war-horse. This Francis was gentler, quieter, weaker. He was changing.

He was, in fact, happily at home at Meudon. It was there that "la petite bande" of maids of honour amused him. At carnival one Buzambourg, according to Brantôme, was ordered to take the dishes the King had finished with to refresh "la petite bande." The "gentilhomme servant" made some remark about flesh, flesh for the ladies. They complained to Francis. In fury he ordered the archers to seize Buzambourg and string him up. But that mocking gentleman had "sniffed the wind" and vanished. "Anyone who reflects on the honour of these ladies," proclaimed Francis, "will be hanged without further orders."

And when "la petite bande" and he were separated, the same indulgence he put into a song, remembering perhaps that Anne de Heilly had been "une belle amourette" not so long before:

> My pretty darlings,
> Where have you gone away?
> Will you be changing
> Your place every day?
> To whom shall I my torment tell,
> My torment and my gloom?
> No voice gives answer in the dell.
> The trees are secret, deaf and dumb.
> My pretty darlings,
> Where have you gone away?
> Will you be changing
> Your place every day?

> Ah since the heavens do decree
> That so unhappy I must be,
> I shall betake me to the dale
> And there recount a lovelorn tale.

My pretty darlings,
Where have you gone away?
Will you be changing
Your place every day?

So could he flirt with the whole company that hunted with him
and danced with him and admired him in his new châteaux and
his new costumes. And he showered presents on them, and gathered
kisses.

One of the group who strove most to please him was Catherine
de' Medici who, with her famous new idea of the side-saddle, could
gallop with him through the forest. She succeeded in winning
him, though her failure to give the dauphin an heir would eventually make them discuss her divorce.

But Catherine, smiling and submissive, would know how to
survive. A friend who succumbed was Françoise de Foix. Her
death was reported from Brittany in this year 1537. "Ce beau
corps," Francis remembered. It was later rumoured that her husband had revenged himself on her by killing her. Two surgeons
came to her room in a tower, with six masked men, and her veins
were opened. If this were secretly hinted, Francis took a light tone.
He heard that Châteaubriant was planning to re-marry. "Poor
fellow," he laughed, "he has more need of a good doctor and a
good confessor than he has of a wife." But Marguerite, all alone,
went on a mission to Châteaubriant, at the request of an unhappy
daughter. What was the truth? The Brézé who murdered an un-
faithful wife was compelled by Louis XI to give up his estates.
Châteaubriant would bequeath, for no known reason, immensely
valuable estates to the all-powerful Montmorency. Was there a
crime? It remains mere surmise. And Francis, who soon forgot his
own eldest son, could not agitate himself for his forsaken mistress.
Marguerite's mission he dismissed as a match-making caprice.
"When one wants to hold back the women," he generalized, "they
pine to disobey us, and when we want them to go somewhere,
that is the time they never want to budge."

Here was Francis without guile. Neither he nor Marguerite ever
admitted his guile. The Venetian Francesco Giustiniano talked of

him with Marguerite and persuasively described him in this guile-less humour.

"The Queen of Navarre, sister to the King," he told the Signory, "a woman of a rare talent and wisdom, who takes part in all the councils of the Crown, said to me one day that to bring about an accord between these two men [Francis and Charles] the Lord would have to remake one of them by a tracing on the other, for the Very Christian King had no liking for the transactions and cares of state but prefers hunting and pleasure while the Emperor dreams of nothing but business and how to augment his power. The Very Christian King is simple, open, liberal, yielding to the opinion of his councillors, while the other is very reserved, very stingy, fixed in his aims and guided more by his own opinion than by that of those about him. In short, they are of such different character that the King himself said one day to the ambassador Cappello and myself, in regard to the truces that were being con-cluded, 'The Emperor strives to do the exact opposite to what I do. If I propose peace, he says peace is impossible, but an agree-ment is better. If I talk of agreement, he proposes a truce. We are never of the same sentiment in anything.' "

Here Francis said what he thought, and in this way Giustiniano could rightly call him open and frank. He was ready to commit himself in conversation, even about the Turk. He could declare himself in the wrong. He could regret. He could pardon. But while the details of state were beneath his interest, and no one loved more to escape into those realms where new ideas are flushed as in a forest of the mind, ideas of sport, of painting, of literature, of languages, of exercise, of the art of war, yet with this abundance of discourse, which another Venetian would describe as marked by a very sound judgment and a very wide erudition, there did go a capacity for misleading the auditor which is not usually reckoned liberal. Francis's candour did not preclude insincerity. Treaties apart and allies apart and debts apart and Semblançays apart and Bourbons apart and Berquins apart and wives apart and foreign ex-peditions apart, he could be relied on to be engagingly frank, at any moment, and to lend wings to discourse and warmth to his flow of words. There is something in a tone of voice that carries conviction, some vibration that captures a listener so that he lends himself to a generosity that thrills him. This rather beautiful quality Francis possessed. He was a King and he looked the King. He could not, of course, be blamed for the financiers he was stringing up, nor could the fruit of the gibbet, the rich confiscations, be supposed to have made him sign death-warrants. He learned that heretics were not burned alive in Flanders, so he announced he would change the French method, yet, as a Venetian put it, the rôtisserie went on. But the faculty for conveying as truth that which, at the moment, he felt to be truth was in itself so sincere a gift that its possessor, given the brevity of memory and the superficiality of life, could be reckoned a far more liberal character than Charles with his tape-measure and pencil. Yet it was extraordinary, as the Venetian plaintively noted, that Francis had lost so many of the campaigns he elucidated so convincingly. There was a gap between himself and the actual hardness of human act. He liked life to be "galonné et chamarré, riche en pierreries et en ornements précieux," like his own costumes. And he did not go into the obduracy of fact. He became increasingly less intimate with the bird of actuality, feathered and beaked with mysterious entrails into which an augur peers. Francis's bird of life was by this time nearly all paté. And with his mother no longer on earth to prepare the paté in full sight of him, his complicity in turning the bony into the boneless was less apparent. That hard job he was delegating to Chabot de Brion or to Montmorency. But his conversation flowed out of him frank and liberal and open.

In Republican Venice the bird was not all paté de foie gras. Francis's "choice and dainty" life the Ambassador contrasted with his royal exercise of that "singular gift God has given him of curing the scrofulous by touching them." He mentions the formula, "The King touches thee, may God heal thee," and adds reverently, "Since the crowd swells all the time, one must conclude that it is God who uses this means of freeing the infirm and at the same time adding to the dignity of the Crown of France."

20

With a truce accepted in 1537, and Montmorency named Constable at the beginning of 1538, all was prepared for a peace with

Spain as the culmination of Montmorency's policy. It was a prospect greatly desired by Pope Paul III. That small, clear, experienced
man of the world, whose sister had been Alexander VI's mistress,
was bridging the renaissance and the reformation, the Farnese
abutting on papal princedom but Caraffa and Sadoleto carrying
him over to the Council of Trent. And he came to Nice, to meet
Francis and Charles, and to unite on a Catholic basis the two
powers that could then deal with Merry England.

No peace was possible. What had Francis to counterbalance
Charles with except the Turk and the Lutherans and Henry VIII?
The Pope strove hard. Francis asked for Milan and Milan was
presented to him in profile, in half-length, in three-quarter-length,
close up, but he wanted it tout ensemble and at once. The negotiations boiled down to a ten years' truce. And then, Navarre being
excluded from the arrangements, the Constable managed to bring
Charles and Francis together, at Aigues-Mortes.

Each of them, it was remarked at Nice, had mastered Italian.
They had become no less supple in the language of life. Francis
could still flush with memory and grow furious at the thought that
his son was poisoned, but his common sense forced him to acknowledge the necessity of dealing with Charles. And Charles, who had
not seen his rival since they stood by the roadside crucifix on the
day they parted in Spain, could now forget those challenges and
those recriminations, and embrace his brother and welcome his
sister Eleanor again.

It was a gain in amenity, with Francis benign and Charles hospitable, but no interview can cure a surgical case with physic. Both
Francis and Charles were members of a class that had been born
and reared in the military tradition, and they had organized their
state on that basis, married, shaped their religion, governed their
offspring, created their courts and promoted their Kingdoms' fame
on it, so that the rest could only be pantomime. Montmorency had
the underlying hope that Francis could agree with Charles, so to
divide Catholic Europe between them. Cromwell dreaded this
agreement so much that for counterpoise he persuaded his master
Henry VIII to take Anne of Cleves for his bride, princess of the one
little power that could be a nuisance to the Emperor. Henry had
previously asked for a selection of French brides to choose from,

but Montmorency had deliberately rebuffed him. He had pointed out that the French court did not send out "damoiselles à choisir."

21

The interview at Aigues-Mortes seemed to promise appeasement, and the French in general rejoiced. Much as Picardy and Provence had suffered, a great deal of sympathy was felt for Francis. He had lost his son. He was suppressing heretics. He was becoming a calmer, larger, more benevolent figure, and just as he himself was filling out so Paris was growing, in spite of wartime, with a prosperity that could not be denied.

But under these appearances French policy was anything but settled. Francis had been ill in 1535, in 1537. He was very ill in 1538, and desperately ill in 1539. He was not finished, but he was becoming intermittent in his exercise of power. This chronic abscess "à bas de ventre" showed no signs of being cured, and already he was ceasing to be the dominant personage in the government.

Montmorency he did not completely trust. He had no ultimate faith in this patched-up truce with Charles. But he was willing to give Montmorency his head, much too unwell and much too indolent to combat him unless circumstances became intolerable.

The King had, at any rate, the loyalty of the women. Clément Marot, in 1538, gave the laurel to Anne de Heilly:

> To you I give—without
> On anyone to frown—
> Beauty's golden apple,
> True devotion's crown.

This "ferme loyauté" was now of supreme importance, and Francis's sister was heartily seconding Francis's mistress. With them were Chabot de Brion, a confident and mocking ally, and the young boy Charles, good-looking, "gai et fort aimable." It was the party friendly to England, sympathetic with the Reformation, suspicious of the Emperor. And Montmorency looked on it with something like contempt.

He knew Chabot de Brion was careless as an administrator and he pursued him into disgrace. Anne de Heilly he could not dislodge, and she had as much right to be Charles's partisan as Diane de Poitiers to be Henri's partisan. But Marguerite he intended to defeat, and Henri de Navarre made it possible. That valiant gentleman was no more faithful to France than he was faithful to Marguerite. He had exactly the same dynastic object as the two greater powers that sundered his kingdom, and he made continuous and urgent approaches to Charles V, offering him his daughter Jeanne d'Albret for an imperial alliance. It was easy for Montmorency to hint at these intrigues. Francis sharply rebuked Navarre for his rudeness to Marguerite. The child, Jeanne d'Albret, was taken from her parents, virtually imprisoned on the Loire, and Montmorency meant to plunge her into marriage with a son of Lautrec.

This was intolerable to Marguerite. Loyal to her husband, ambitious for Navarre, she could not free herself from all suspicion. To turn Francis against her was not impossible. But all her forces, her ingenuity, her tact, her endurance and her courage, were matched against Montmorency to save not only her daughter but her brother. She could not rescue Jeanne d'Albret without running the risk of her young husband's doing something to antagonize Francis. But to defeat Montmorency became imperative. The duel was concealed from the public, but under the court surface it surged with passion, while in the centre of it, himself the theatre of a disease no less remorseless and exhausting, Francis kept on, not detached but relatively passive.

22

Almost nothing confers more prestige than to organize a royal visit, and Montmorency was at his zenith when it was arranged that Charles V, faced by a burghers' insurrection in Ghent, should go overland through France to chastise his subjects. The mere fact that Ghent had appealed in vain to France was an evidence of goodwill. But the visit was a greater evidence. And Francis welcomed it from his sick bed, magnanimously sociable, promising not to ask for Milan.

Charles caught a cold, unfortunately, and snuffled from Hendaye to Loches. But he was thoroughly appreciative. He tried a little

pigeon shooting. He was astonished at the size of Poitiers. The
wealth and epicurean delights of the French château were a revelation to him. And the arrogance of the young nobles, who simply
appropriated horses from the country people, must have explained
why the arming of the peasants in Francis's legions had shown the
innate truculence and disobedience of the lower orders. But Charles
wanted no fuss. By the time he reached Loches, where Francis
received him, he was already nearly overwhelmed by hospitality.
He was attracted by his namesake, the younger son, a vivacious
Charles. Marot seemed to think that this boy had not clearly decided whether he was mâle ou femelle, but everyone fancied him
and everyone thought Henri "melancolique."

The effort to capture Charles V made Montmorency go so far
as to betray to him the secret negotiations of the German Protes-
tant princes with Francis. Marguerite, on the other hand, was
amazingly frank with the English on the Imperial policy of the
Constable. The tension increased every day. By the time that Anne
de Heilly sweetly remarked that she happened to be born on the
day that Diane de Poitiers was married, a good many tail feathers
were floating in the air. Unless Montmorency could present Francis
with full and tangible proof of his power to sway the Emperor, his
downfall could not be averted. Francis's methods were not Henry
VIII's. Cromwell's life was staked on the issue. But Montmorency
must either perform or go under.

"C'est un grand coquin," cried Anne de Heilly in triumph. "He
has deceived the King by saying that the Emperor would give him
Milan at once, when he knew the contrary."

Francis did not blame the "grand coquin." But with tears in his
eyes he reproached him. "I find only one fault with you. You do
not love those that I love." In other words, he could not go in
opposite directions at the same time.

23

It was this facile prince, highly benevolent and deeply evasive, who
welcomed Benvenuto Cellini with open arms. Anne de Heilly could
look at Benvenuto with cold practical gaze. "I believe that devil
will sack Paris one of these days." How Benvenuto hated that

ANNE DE HEILLY DE PISSELEU, DUCHESSE D'ÉTAMPES
From the Painting by Corneille de Lyon about 1544 in the Château de Saint-Roch

firm young woman. But how naturally his nose detected for him, all the way from Rome, the perfect emulsion of wealth and taste that Francis would provide for him. Here was an artist who lived in surfaces, who whipped them into exquisite ornamental shapes, who delighted in the effective, the inventive, the external. His was a Florence no longer burdened with the mystery of good and evil, the mystery that Michael Angelo carried from Savonarola into his brooding marble and that Vittoria Colonna could still impart to Marguerite in the long letters she was writing at the moment. Benvenuto Cellini, sincere and combative in his intensely personal life, no less so than Étienne Dolet, was simply incapable of breaking through the crust that the modern state was creating. The moral abdication of Rome, the advent of the Prince, had brought a great epoch to its end. The new epoch had been trampled down by armies. Homicide had become a commonplace. God to Cellini was merely a talisman in case he had trouble with the police. For the rest, he was brilliantly alive to the effects he wished to produce, a creator of masterpieces in which hand and eyes captured balance and rhythm, a daring and inexhaustible craftsman asking no question of his art beyond its own enticement and never false except when he strove to enlarge his miniatures to dimensions never required except by matters of life and death. Capable of almost any sensation, intensely faithful to his task, Cellini walked straight into Francis's heart. It was Cognac, the classicism of the Saint-Gelais, but this classicism without the mièvre provincialism of Mellin chanting to his lute, and without the bastard piety which could sculp Francis as a well-shampooed Christ about to be entombed. Benvenuto was worthy of Pan. His imagination had that natural festivity which flies in birds and sings in running water and spangles the sky. No one could better conceive the swing of a fountain's curve or the grace of a vase. Quick, vehement, beautifully responsive, a natural mastery resided in this true artist. And he had in him just a glint of that early morning before the apple was eaten.

The great King, "my great King," let down the drawbridge and took Cellini in.

So far Rosso and Primaticcio were the best whom Francis could secure to succeed Andrea del Sarto and Leonardo da Vinci. But from the day that Benvenuto first kissed his knee there was a real comprehension between them. Exhausted by his disease, distracted by the new breach with the Emperor—his ambassadors to the Turk being murdered—he still had sympathy for a creative man whom the wizened Pope Paul III had kept locked up in prison. Had Cellini been subversive, threatening the authority of the state, Francis could not have used him. As it was, his radium would burn through any metal, even gold, but from 1540 to 1544 the King held on to Cellini, a true and fecund association.

"Mon ami," said Francis, laying his hand on Cellini's shoulder, "I know not whether the pleasure be greater for the prince who finds a man after his own heart, or for the artist who finds a prince willing to furnish him with the means for carrying out his great ideas."

Cellini answered: "If I am really the man your Majesty describes, my good fortune is by far the greater."

The King laughed. "Let us agree, then, our luck is equal!"

And then Cellini ruefully adds: "My ill-luck willed that I was not wide awake enough to play the like comedy with Madame d'Étampes," Anne de Heilly.

An artist who, presenting a basin and jug, could suddenly exhibit the model of his salt-cellar was more than Francis could have hoped for.

"This is a hundred times more divine thing," he cried out, "than I had ever dreamed of. What a miracle of a man! He ought never to stop working."

Only twelve statues, Francis's own height, were ordered from Cellini. But the golden salt-cellar, a great silver vase, two bronze heads, a lunette to show the genius of Fontainebleau—all of these excited his creativeness and delighted Francis. He gave the artist le petit Nesle, where the Institut now stands. He made him a Frenchman. He called him "mon ami." And had Benvenuto placated Anne de Heilly (who wanted le petit Nesle for her perfume-maker) he could have gone on for ever. But Francis's enraptured reception of the Jupiter made his mistress say: "One would think you had no eyes," indicating the antiques. Benvenuto flamed with wrath and conveyed a beastly insult to Francis's mistress. No wonder the King was driven to command him to hold his tongue, and later, in "a great and terrible voice," to rebuke the knave. He too did not love those whom Francis loved. And the King called him: "You fool!"

24

Amid so many strong, passionate, explosive human beings, demanding extravagant consideration and lusting for power, the weary Francis barely asserted himself, in order to survive.

Montmorency had failed to work out a treaty with the Emperor. Francis thereupon decided to sacrifice Marguerite's daughter Jeanne to a marriage with the Duke of Cleves. It was a companion marriage to that of Henry VIII with Anne of Cleves, and the young girl was just as vehement in her dislike of the match as Henry had been of his own. Her rebellion brought Francis into direct collision with the child and he showed himself just as unreasonably violent in breaking her will as Marguerite's daughter was violent in asserting herself. Marguerite was torn between the two persons she most loved. Her daughter was making herself sick by refusal, and her sacrifice was utterly repugnant to the mother. But at last Francis prevailed. And Marguerite had her daughter flogged to make her submit, knowing full well that in canon law this would be grounds for a divorce. Jeanne d'Albret, on her own side, followed the example set by Francis himself by making a formal protestation before the wedding, on the model of his protestations of Madrid.

Clad in a bridal costume encrusted with jewellery and heavy brocade, this small girl made a final scene in the chapel at Châtellerault. She declared she could not walk to the altar in this fashionable armour. Francis thereupon turned to his proud Constable Montmorency and ordered him to carry Marguerite's daughter up the aisle.

The next day Montmorency resigned.

25

The assassination of Francis's ambassadors to the Sultan was not directly ascribed to the Emperor, but in lieu of satisfaction war was once more renewed. Cleves renounced France, releasing Jeanne d'Albret from the purgatory of her unconsummated marriage. The new war on every front, with Henry VIII as Charles V's ally, did not lead to Montmorency's recall. Francis had warned him in his "great and terrible voice" to stand aside from politics. And Marguerite was enabled to reconcile herself with the brother she still adored.

But he was quite broken in health. Young Boisy, the nephew of Bonnivet, wrote to the exiled Montmorency that "our master is the same as you have always said. Plus y va avant, plus se prant avecque les fames et en a perdu toute honte." To be found shameless by Bonnivet's nephew had its own irony. But if Francis flirted shamelessly with his "petite bande," he had reached a stage where Marguerite could congratulate him on his sublimation of sensual love, at the age of forty-nine.

Yet in 1542 he had gone to Montpellier, to support the attack on Perpignan. And he still asserted himself in council. Chabot de Brion had never recovered from his dismissal. He died soon after he was restored. The stupid Annebault became admiral, the man whom they called âne-bo, ass-ox, a characteristic flight of party witticism.

26

In the March of 1544 Francis was scarcely less circled by war than Louis XII had been thirty years before, and in those thirty years his beautiful strong body had crumbled, his flesh at once gross and feeble, his voice husky, his hair scant, the eyes congested and dim. But he still was the managing director of his Kingdom. He was not afraid to undertake long journeys. The year before, when the Emperor failed to take Landrecies, he was at Saint Quentin. He returned to Fontainebleau, where he could have the baths the doctors had ordered him and where Primaticcio had been working in his atelier for at least a decade. There the Queen Eleanor, sister to his enemy, was deliberately cut off from the main life of the court, grouped with furtive and pious Spaniards, and Anne de Heilly, on the contrary, had her place of honour, though by this time she had discovered that, if the King were sublimated, there were "hommes à choisir." Her brother-in-law Jarnac, Chabot de Brion's brother, was typical of the courtiers who swarmed to the honey-pot. A swaggering bully, la Châtaigneraie, accused him of being gigolo to his mother-in-law, and only Anne de Heilly's intervention saved him from a duel. But the duel, under Francis's own credulous encouragement, was becoming the recognized resource of courtly animosity and emulation, and, of course, of honour. Diane de Poitiers and the Dauphin espoused la Châtaigneraie and great hostilities poured into the menacing clatter of expert swordsmen, the glances of fair ladies, the crackle of gossip, the sweep of contemptuous favourites. While Rosso was still alive, he and the other artists were hardly less combative than the courtiers. Yet, out of this frenzied self-assertion there was flowering this château, on which the King had lavished his preference, especially since the truce of Aigues-Mortes. Its woodwork was Italian. So were its frescoes and its stucco. Where at Charles's Amboise there was an imported Italy, still detached and even stored, here there was an Italy acclimated, assimilated, steeped in the canvas and melted into the walls. It was Francis who had fused these arts into the visible legend of his own fantasy, the "beau corps," the faun, the god, the goddess, the beautiful wild animal, the rich and thronged sensuousness of an ageing Pan. Here, portly, fluent, magnificent, eating well, drinking well, sleeping well, he kindled at the sway and lilt of beauty. He worshipped it, in the kind intermissions of his rotting frame. A flattering would remind him he was a "roi soldat," but the enemy was inside him and gaining. He was yielding his provinces in order to survive.

Fontainebleau was the background to Francis's last war. Something of its indolence had crept into the French strategy. Charles would soon be on the Somme and refugees from Paris would cut across religious processions that once more told God he was a Frenchman.

27

Into this indolence, in March, 1544, broke a wiry Gascon, Blaise de Monluc. He had come from Piedmont, to seek the King's permission for a pitched battle. The French will had been paralyzed since Bicocca and Pavia. They quailed at the thought of another disaster. And Henry VIII and Charles V were linked in the campaign of 1544.

Monluc was from a remote district in France. If the Loire was parterre, and the Angoumois was the balcony, the Agennais was the upper gallery. There, under a benignant sky, in valleys too easily flooded, in a broad tufted region of fruit and root, Monluc developed into one of those hardy adventurers whose clang sounded so strange at Fontainebleau. He was allowed into the royal council chamber to take his orders, to be carried back to Enghien in Lombardy.

Annebault sat with his back to Monluc. Straight across from him was Saint Pol, Bourbon's cousin, veteran of Pavia, prisoner at Landriano. And next to Saint Pol, fresh from his dinner where Monluc had been allowed to wait on him, sat the repleted King. At the back of his chair, a black, introspective Frenchman, stood the future Henri II. And at a distance stood young Boisy, Galliot, several others of this general staff.

"Monluc," said the master, "I wish you to carry back my decision and the council's to Monsieur d'Enghien."

He then gave the floor to Saint Pol, who explained the junction of the two invading armies and the danger of losing a battle.

When he had spoken Galliot took it up, and then the Gascon began to boil and his lid to dance.

"Tout beau, tout beau," admonished Saint Pol, while Francis gave a laugh and the Dauphin, looking intently at Monluc, smiled in encouragement.

"Have you clearly understood, Monluc," asked the King, "the reasons which decide me not to give Monsieur d'Enghien permission to fight and risk anything?"

Monluc understood all right but he eagerly asked permission to speak. This was granted, and with the Dauphin smiling encouragement to him from behind Francis's back the Gascon threw himself heart and soul into his plea for a battle. Here, in the perfumed hall, with a good fire, relaxed after dinner, the spectacle of this vigorous soldier, this hound of war, barking to be allowed to fight.— "Nous sommes en cœur et eux en peur"—aroused the whole council to smiles, but it fired their blood. This man from the Midi, crisp, bright, hard, all fire and dash, woke something long asleep in Francis's poisoned frame.

"But you say the companies are not complete!" he frowned.

They could be made complete. "If we lose, if we lose," said

Monluc boldly. "But I have not heard any of them say, if we *win*, if we *win*, what great good will come to you!"

Francis listened, all attention, and then turned his eyes to Saint Pol.

"Monsieur, would you really change your opinion for this madman?"

"Sire," protested Monluc, "I am no bravache," and fired out another long speech.

The Dauphin laughed hard and spurred him on. Annebault smiled uncertainly but kept mum.

"What," cried Saint Pol to the King, "Monsieur, it seems you wish to change! You are going to pay attention to this mad fool?"

"Foi de gentilhomme, mon cousin, he makes such an argument I don't know what to do."

"I see very well you are already converted."

Francis turned to Annebault. "Sire," answered Annebault, "you wish to hear the truth? You are dying to give them permission to fight. Do one thing. Ask God and pray that He aid and direct you."

Francis lifted his eyes, put his hands together, and said: "My God, I beg You that it please You to-day to guide me what I ought to do for the preservation of my Kingdom." And he was silent.

Then Annebault broke the silence timidly. "Sire, what is your opinion now?"

"That they fight! That they fight!"

And then they all got up.

"Fol enragé," laughed Saint Pol to his old friend Monluc, as the council conferred. Francis then, putting his hand on Monluc's arm, gave him his personal message to d'Enghien, and the Gascon, trembling with proud delight, kissed both the King's hands.

The battle of Cerisole, brilliant, victorious and fruitless, was the outcome of this council meeting.

28

Francis was unafraid when Charles V drove into France as far as Saint-Dizier. His negotiations were in hand. And Henry VIII's capture of Boulogne did not frighten him. But in the next year a desperate blow smote him. His boy Charles, his favourite boy, the one who had least of Claude and most of himself in his vivacious nature, was cut down and died. He had, they said, been in a cottage behind the front where people had died of the pest, and he plunged his sword into a mattress and flourished it and drove at the floating feathers. His illness came so soon after this prank that it was believed he had contracted the pest.

"I was page to the great Duke of Orléans, the third son of Francis," said Ronsard, "who, in the flower of his age, handsome, brave and strong, highly enterprising, set his desires on almost the entire world. He vaunted himself to be the son-in-law of the Emperor Charles. Already peace visited the earth, and this Duke thought himself master of Burgundy and Milan. He boasted himself author of the proud peace. He had the favour of his father and the people, child of Fortune." And then this prince "died of the pest at Fremontier." Gracious, debonair, eloquent, subtle, he was a "fertile storehouse of the inventions of war." Ronsard, five years with him, compared him to Mars and to Paris.

Had Charles survived, he would undoubtedly have led his brother Henri a very stirring existence.

But he was the fifth of Francis's children to die. Louise and Charlotte died as babies, then François and Madeleine, and now Charles. The father prayed against it, then himself "closed his eyes and bent over him and wept on him, and, half-dead, attended the dead."

29

While this personal misfortune rolled over Francis, submerging him for a time, a tragedy of public dimensions had taken place in the hills to the east of the Rhône. There lived the Vaudois, simple heretics whose austerity had not made them persuasive elsewhere, but whose unconformity had aroused the zeal of local military lords. To these men the Cardinal Tournon, schooled in illiberality, had given free hand, and the villagers refusing to abjure, eight hundred of them had been massacred. It had not been debated in advance by Francis's council. It was something that happened be-

FRANCIS I, ABOUT 1544

From the Drawing attributed to Clouet in the Musée Condé, Chantilly

cause he had kept no control on his own loose and easy acquiescence. It was a slip of the absolutist's machine.

Quite often he had intervened in the name of clemency, of recent years. Marguerite was overjoyed when he forgave the insurrectionary town of La Rochelle. That was a symptom of good personal government. The massacred villages of the Vaudois, Mérindol and Cabrières, were a symptom of its other aspect, in a period when the psyche had become undermined by the pale spirochete of war. Even Calvin was infected by the same germ, declaring his adversaries worthy of "a thousand fires and a thousand gibbets." And the Council of Trent, called a few months before Luther's death, would be the prelude to its vast dissemination.

Meanwhile Francis upheld the massacres of the Vaudois, and Étienne Dolet, condemned for blasphemy, sedition and the sale of prohibited books, was, on August 3, 1546, hanged at the Place Maubert. His invocation of the Blessed Virgin saved him from having his tongue rooted out and being burnt alive.

At this time Francis wrote a letter to Michael Angelo, asking him for a copy of that great commiseration, the *Pietà*.

30

The execution of Étienne Dolet, the massacre of the Vaudois—these aggressive acts could not touch Francis where he lived. They were ominous events. Neither his alert mistress nor his contemplative and compassionate sister could fail to weigh their gravity. But within the court itself there was too much to favour such aggression for Francis to put forth his failing strength to resist it.

His faithful women knew that for years an inimical group had been accreting about the dauphin. On the edge of this group, immobile by prudence, was planted the formidable Anne de Montmorency. For ten years this solid, circumspect man had been the avowed ally of Francis's successor. He was the contemptuous enemy of Anne de Heilly and Marguerite, and for that reason banished from court. But if he was absent, his group was present, and the principal of it, the calm goddess of it, was Diane de Poitiers, now forty-seven years old. This clear, bold, possessive female had no reason to love Henri's father. She had early seen in Henri the means of attaching herself to the source of power. She had come between Henri and his young wife, Catherine de' Medici, from the start; had attached the inhibited boy to herself on his return from Spain and given him that warm milk of comprehension which is so dear to the parched ego, and rewarded by such fidelity to its fountain. Both Diane de Poitiers and Anne de Montmorency were too level-headed and too conservative to break with an existing order, but by working through the closed-in Henri they could surround Francis with an ever-present danger, and they could circle insolently around his weary, relaxing form. The Lorraine family, the Guises, were allied with Anne de Montmorency and Diane de Poitiers. It was a compact, ambitious company with curled lip, but still standing in the wings.

In this situation, under this presence, Francis bore himself as King. Like his own predecessor, Louis XII, he now knew what it was to see eagerness gleam in the eyes of his heir. They were waiting for him to go. But gnawed by disease as he was, wearied by government, he was still too old a hand to be dispossessed before his time. He asked for peace, and such flagrant acts as execution or massacre could not unsettle him so long as he could keep undisturbed in his walled garden, or move in his kingly orbit like a great bearded Neptune whose satellites swing obedient in their round.

Anything for peace! This was Francis's mood at the end of 1546 and the beginning of 1547. And if his own body could not give him peace, then at least he could go seeking his distraction, taking with him his thousands of courtiers and living from one château to another.

It was the existence he had chosen to create since he lost a tangible empire outside. He poured out wealth to give him this ambulant court, so that wherever he travelled he would still be at the centre of his beloved habits, surrounded by pretty darlings, with lovely objects to console him, and beautiful forms to give him the illusion of peace. Thus he lived in the garden he had created from a kingly workshop, the dearest achievement of his life.

And in this elegance, this sumptuousness, this mingling of the sexes, Francis proved himself an Orléans to his finger-tips. He could not deny the æsthetic man in him, the worshipper of beauty. It might be a hollow, pompous beauty, with something in it of the ostentation of Chambord; or it might be florid and ebullient like Fontainebleau. But it poured out a temperament, a faculty for rising above the commonplace of existence and declaiming a conception of royalty, a conception of lordly magnificence and pride.

So he persisted, in the intervals of court intrigue, and hot baths and poultices, and the stink of disease.

31

The surgeons had tried to help Francis repeatedly but his disease did not relax. He could not bear to stay quiet and be the invalid. And then a bad shock came. He shook his head over the news from England that his old friend Henry VIII was dead in January, 1547. He took it as a bad omen for himself. He sighed in grim earnest, and fell pensive. But he could not remain pensive. He struck camp. He shifted from Compiègne on January 1, to Pierrefonds, Villers-Cotterets, Saint-Germain-en-Laye, Villepreaux, Limours, Rochefort, Meudon. At the end of February, worn out, he settled at Rambouillet.

Marguerite he had summoned in December. He wished to talk over the German Protestants with her. But she was an invalid herself, in Navarre. From there she sent Francis a doublet that she had embroidered for him, a Christmas present. He was much in her mind.

The news she received was so inquieting that from afar she apprehended her great sorrow. She yearned, she prayed, for a messenger to come with good news. No matter how travel-stained he might be, she would embrace him with joy. Torn between confidence in God and the anguish of a love that had never slackened, she spent feverish weeks. Then, in the convent where she was staying, she had a dream. A pale, worn face bent over her and a gentle voice said, "My sister! my sister!" She woke, bathed in tears, terrified. No news arrived. For days she waited. One day in the cloisters she came on an old half-witted nun who was praying and weeping. She stopped to console her. "Alas, Madame, it is for you I weep." Then Marguerite understood. They had been hiding the news.

32

In his last days Francis sent for Henri, the only boy of his who remained. Both François and gay Charles still remained coffined until there would be a great state funeral: they had gone before their father. They would now accompany their father to Saint Denis in a triple funeral, and the sceptre must pass to a son wholly unlike him, a "triste personnage."

When Francis turned his dying eyes on his melancholy son, he could feel none of the joyous excitement in life that he himself had so passionately experienced. Here was a man who would never fight a Marignano. The dying King foresaw the future. He warned his son, significantly, not to be dominated by a woman. By inculpating women, he would have lived by and for women, he was guilty of a characteristic infidelity. But it was not Anne de Heilly he was thinking of. It was Diane de Poitiers. He could see her seated refulgent behind the throne of Henri II.

He turned from his earthly throne to the Heavenly one.

His sins, his multitude of sins, he confessed to his Creator, imploring an indulgence that he himself had denied to many a rebel. And then he breathed wearily that he was ready to go, he had had his full life, he was glad to die. "Jesus! Jesus!"

In an adjoining room Anne de Heilly sobbed and wailed in loud abandonment. He had been the oak and she the vine. Without him, where would she be?

In the same room smouldered the dark dauphin, and Diane de Poitiers shone. The genial François de Guise stood by the door.

"The old sport is passing out!" he cried to them. "Le vieux gallant s'en va!"

Francis was dead. Everyone knelt and said prayers.

It was March 31, 1547. He had reached fifty-three years and a half.

33

He was so human. Even in that late portrait from which he blinks, a wicked old satyr gone to seed, there is something redolent and rich. He might be a timeworn ostler or a rascal, stewed in wine, who lived by selling onions. He had lived fully, this royal rascal, as he himself huskily confessed on his deathbed, and he had savoured his existence. He was never a prig. He abounded in his sense of those with whom he spent his varied life, men as well as women. He had romped with them when young and rhymed with them in maturity, played rough pranks, run his race, chased his boar, lifted his lance to ride forward against a foe. This juice that is in life he had pressed it with delight. When Gargantua was read aloud to him, he must have twinkled with pleasure. He knew himself to be an animal, a great healthy animal in his vigour, proud of it and abundant and quivering.

He had thousands of special tokens in gold coined for him when he first went to Italy. He enjoyed such childish magnificence. But he was not merely a parvenu. He could be ravished by the art of Leonardo. He could be thrilled by a binding by Grolier. The pencil of Clouet, that suave pencil which caresses a likeness into being, it was wielded for Francis, every likeness held in his jewelled hand. He could visit Brou, Margaret of Austria's cathedral, and his exercised eye would see the soft stone crumbling. On France he had written his signature in châteaux. He understood the technique of the architect, as patron and as connoisseur.

And for all his gusto, for all his discriminating senses, he could at times surpass an æsthetic absorption in his own being to stand humbly convicted of his weaknesses. "The older," he admitted as he took precedence of the polite Emperor, "and the more foolish!" He could deplore himself, not a failing in princes.

But this tolerant and practised human being, this man without iron prejudices, was yet a member of an iron caste. His school was soldiering, and even if he had once knelt to Chevalier Bayard soldiering was rape, theft, murder, as well as fight. The Gascons from his galleys were often from the gallows: they spared no one. And his nobles, Lautrec, Bonnivet, Fleurange, Montmorency, had steeped themselves in homicide. To invade was to outrage, and outrage was high humour. The Italians who could enact the Perfect Courtier could also gouge out the eyes of their prisoners. The sacredness of life could not be imagined except by a Thomas More or an Erasmus. So that in Francis's leer, in that amusing wickedness of the satyr, there is something hard, self-regarding, dangerous and repellent. In the last resort he would prove a friend to no one, not even to his mignonne.

It might have been a grander career, given his charming aptitudes. What the Renaissance offered to human understanding was a release of energy out of all proportion to the institutions that are supposed to contain and harmonize the liberated man. Once the Church had ceased to direct the fertile imagination which Heaven drew into cathedral and crusade, once faith in Heaven was questioned by science and disconcerted by classic art, the overpowering exigence of mankind could no longer be directed into channels leading from the passionate to the divine. Mankind burned with a desire to know itself, to feel itself, to govern itself, outside its Father's dominion. In Italy alone the fervour of human faculty was so intense that in a few generations men transcended every restraint imposed by the artifice of theologians, the skill of lawmakers, the force of arms. Philosophy ran molten, but no more molten than bronze or paint. The disinherited instincts surged forward into a tame and deferential society that had been ruled by pious tradition, and sins that Thomas Aquinas had clamped into place ran scarlet and naked through the Vatican.

It was impossible for society to arbitrate the problems of imagination in the mere interests of the family and the state. The imagination by itself undertook to span the universe and to domesticate an ego that quivered with insurrection and blazed with inner fire. What world could at one and the same time complete Michael Angelo, Leonardo da Vinci, Cesare Borgia, Alexander VI, Julius II, Erasmus, Machiavelli, Loyola, Rabelais, Ferdinand, Maximilian, Charles V, Henry VIII, Francis I?

The human experiment had suddenly become so charged with significance, so boldly conceived, so extravagantly enterprised, that neither captaincy nor scholarship, neither poetry nor sculpture, could bring life into that spiritual oneness which now flashed on genius like lightning through the seams of clouds. The attempt of the Renaissance to capture power on the terms of charity, to include within the fullest expressiveness the docility of the subject, to stand outside custom and inside law, to give to worldly splendour the last glory of the arts while soaring above the glory of the world—this attempt, sincere beyond sainthood because loyal to every experiment, carried Italian life to heights brilliantly intrepid and tragically insecure. The human spirit broke under this double responsibility to beauty and truth. The Church, the triumph of averages, resumed the task that the adventurers had ravished from it, restoring mediocrity, re-establishing fear.

The Church was the inner problem presented to Francis. Through the extreme suppleness and vivacity of that beautiful intellectual instrument, the Italian mind, a body of thinking had been organized from century to century which concerned itself with human conduct and man's higher fantasy. A life without this high fantasy may be enjoyable but it cannot in the long run escape being vulgar, and the Church had done much to domesticate the divine. But the Renaissance broke open the gates to a possibly greater fantasy, and within these gates Francis stood for a moment, shimmering in glory.

He did not hold the gates open. While the whole North of Europe shook under the Reformation, most of it breaking away from Mother Church, France held to it, and held to it by reason of Francis's concordat. It was the choice the soldier had made.

It was a costly choice. Francis's tomb at Saint Denis might be wholly Pagan, and the Catholicity he preserved might be wholly formal. But it was a choice, to be maintained by fire and sword.

Three coffins were borne to Saint Denis, his own, that of his boy François, that of Charles. The Valois would march on with the dark Henri. They would march down and down until at last, in abysmal night, the benign spirit of Marguerite would rescue the tribe through her grandson Henri Quatre. She would redeem the race, as so often she had redeemed her brother.

INDEX

INDEX

Acciajuoli—Italian crisis, 328–329.
Adrian of Utrecht—adviser to Charles V, 320.
Ailly (*see* d'Ailly).
Alarcon—Francis a prisoner, 297, 300; good treatment, 325–326; Pope a prisoner, 337.
Albret (*see* d'Albret).
Aleandro—Papal Nuncio, 227–228, 283–284.
Alençon, Duke of—Marguerite, 90–91; marriage, 101–103; broken arm, 105; the new king, 133–134; governor of Normandy, 134; Valenciennes, 246; Pavia, 281; the attack, 289; fails to advance, 291; flight, 301; returns home, 302–303; Louise, 302–303; broken, 303; death, 303.
Alexander VI (*see* Papacy).
Alviano—Venetian ally, 156; Swiss attack, 160.
Amboise—the castle, 45; rebuilding, 55; Louis d'Orléans, 59; death, 162; Francis returns to Amboise, 174; (*see* also d'Amboise).
America—and Spain, 32–33.
Angelo, Michael—36–39; 383; Florence, 382–383; Medici tombs, 382–383; the *Pietà*, 425.
Anne of Brittany (*see* Brittany).
Anne of France—death of Louis XI, 16; Regent, 16, 25–26; Maximilian, 25–26, 27; Brittany, 25–26; la Trémoïlle, 26; breach of faith, 28–29; retirement, 30; character, 45–46; death of Charles, 65; demands on new king, 67; death of Anne of Brittany, 105; funeral, 106–107; the succession, 115–116; Charles de Bourbon, 131–132; building a great family, 132; relations with Bourbon, 237; dying, 255–256; death, 257.
Annebault—becomes Admiral, 420.
Anselm—Jean d'Angoulême, 10.
Antwerp—and Venice, 70.
Aragon, Carlotta of—Borgia, 77 (*see* also Catherine).
Artillery—modern, 70.
Asti—69.
Augustine—Jean d'Angoulême, 10.
Azincourt—battle (1415), 7, 8.

Babou—succeeds Semblançay, 258.
Barbarossa—Charles V, 402.

435

Bayard, Chevalier—Charles VIII, 37; Francis's army, 151–152, 153–154; knights Francis, 162; fighting on the East, 243; defence of Mézières, 245; killed, 278.

Beaurain, Lord of (*see* de Croy).

Bellay, Guillaume du—sent to Pope, 331.

Bellay, Jean du—Francis's new policy, 207–208; Wolsey's downfall, 357.

Berquin, Louis—Luther's pamphlet, 240; terrible plight, 330; arrest, 347; conviction, 352; appeal, 353; burnt alive, 353.

Bibbiena, Cardinal—Holy League, 147; Bologna, 169; Paris, 198; Field of the Cloth of Gold, 215–217.

Boëtius—Jean d' Angoulême, 10.

Bohier, Antoine—Louise of Savoy, 189.

Boisy (*see* Gouffier, A.).

Boleyn, Anne—Henry VIII, 5; Mary Tudor, 125.

Boleyn, Sir Thomas—British Ambassador, 205.

Bonnivet—French Court, 90; Marguerite, 90, 100; Francis, 94, 110–111; return to France, 101; sensuous, 102; the new king, 120; the army, 151–152; King's visit, 191–192; Marguerite, 191–192; Françoise de Foix, 197; London, 198; German election, 205; Francis's general, 232; Spain, 234; advance on Fuenterrabia, 246; driven back, 275–277; siege of Pavia, 283–284; the attack, 289; his efforts at Pavia, 291–292; death, 292.

Borgia, Cesare—the Pope's son, 41; Rome, 71; Louis XII, 71; Cardinal, 71; Duke of Gandia murdered, 71; resigns as cardinal, 72; Court of France, 72–74; effect on Italy, 74; effect on France, 74; character, 74–75; his plans, 77; display, 77; marriage, 77; Milan, 86; death of the Pope, 86; a prisoner, 86; death, 86; married sister of Henri of Navarre, 332.

Borgia, Lucrezia—81.

Bourbon, Cardinal of—assists Francis, 346.

Bourbon, Charles de—King Francis, 104, 106–107, 131; keen soldier, 131–132; alliance with Anne of France, 132; governor of Languedoc, 133; Francis's army, 151–152; attack on Swiss, 159; Sforza, 167; withdrawal from Milan, 187; heir born, 187; Field of the Cloth of Gold, 215; a fine soldier, 232; death of Suzanne, 236; childless widower, 236; Emperor's sister, 236; jealous of Bonnivet, 237; Anne of France, 237; the younger branch, 238; offer of Louise of Savoy, 238–239; Valenciennes, 246; claims by Francis, 254–255; and by Louise of Savoy, 255–256; negotiations with Emperor, 256; sounding Henry VIII, 256; comes to Court, 256; English help, 261; Montbrison, 261; double treachery, 265; illness, 266; more trickery, 266–267; off to Spain, 268; safe at Besançon, 269; succeeds Colonna, 275; needing help from England, 278; ready to invade France, 278; crosses Var, 278; claims to be Count of Provence, 278; followed by Montmorency, 280; Marseille left, 280; retreat to Lodi, 281; relief of Pavia, 282; approach from Lodi, 286; Pavia, 288; dismembering France, 310; Eleanor, 321; given Milan, 321; no money, 326; gives up Milan, 331; joins Frundsberg, 331; death of Frundsberg, 336; on to Rome, 336; attack on Rome, 336; his death, 337.

Botticelli, Sandro—war picture, 85.

Brandenburg, Albrecht—bribing the Papacy, 202.

Brandenburg, Joachim of—betrothed to Renée, 176; German elections, 206;

Bresse, Philip de—Charles VIII, 36.

Brézé, Louis de—Bourbon treachery, 266; appeals to Francis, 274.

Briçonnet, Cardinal—40; Bishop of Meaux, 240; Marguerite, 240; support from Francis, 241–242; influence on Francis, 270–271; influence on Marguerite, 277.

Brion, Chabot de—Francis, 83, 85, 94;
Italy, 139; supports Francis, 272–273;
hunting, 273; Pavia, 289; prison, 292;
promotion, 325; French nobles, 394;
old age, 405; criticizes Montmorency,
405; his death, 420.

Brittany—Louis XI, 13; Anne of Brittany, 26; Anne of France, 26–27;
peasants, 26; virile people, 26; Anne
and Maximilian, 26; Anne's marriage,
52; Anne's demands on Louis XII,
69; French policy, 69; Anne's marriage to Louis XII, 78; Gié disgraced,
87; accident to Anne, 94; Anne's illness, 105; death, 105–106; funeral,
106–107.

Brognina—Isabella's maid of honour,
168.

Brosse, Jean de—Anne re Heilly, 385.

Brosse, René de—Bourbon, 262.

Buckingham—indiscreet, 238; execution,
238.

Budé, Guillaume—97; used by Francis,
271.

Burgundy—Francis's aims, 235; Charles
V's demands, 309; a protest, 326.

Burgundy—Charles the Bold, 13; the
Swiss, 14; Nancy, 14; death, 15.

Burgundy, Mary of—15; death, 15; her
marriage, 24.

Calvin, John—Francis, 4; in France,
19; birth, 98; at Noyon, 253–254;
voice of Europe, 368; visit to Orléans,
372; Bourges, 372; Paris, 372; his
work translated into French, 384;
flight, 399.

Canossa—Papal errors, 108; return to
Rome, 164; Italian crisis, 328.

Cardona, Ramon de—Viceroy of Naples,
156.

Catalonia—Louis XI, 12–13.

Catherine of Aragon—England, 31.

Cauvin, Jean (see Calvin).

Cellini, Benvenuto—the Pope's flight,
345; present for the Pope, 404; hatred
of Anne de Heilly, 416.

Chambord—Francis's efforts, 180.

Charles—Francis's third son, 416; death,
424; Duke of Orléans, 424.

Charles d'Angoulême—father of Francis,
7; Royal Court, 11; Louise of Savoy,
13, 15; the Court, 15; fear of Louis
XI, 15; betrothed, 47; Guyenne, 48;
his mistress, 48; curious establishment, 50; birth of heir, 54; death of
the Dauphin, 58; death, 61; widow's
court, 63.

Charles VIII of France—14; weak
minded, 16; as king, 16; betrothed,
28; Spain, 30; Naples, 31; Maximilian, 33; Ferdinand, 33; Naples,
36; Sforza, 37; Italy, 39; Turkey, 40;
the Pope, 40; marriage, 53; a son, 54;
death of Dauphin, 57–59; Neapolitan
campaign, 65; diversions, 65; further
children, 65; death, 65–66.

Charles V, of France—Family tree, 6.

Charles, Duke of Orléans (see Orléans).

Charles, Archduke, afterwards Emperor
—Francis, 28; Archduke, 88; betrothed to Claude, 89; Milan, 127;
the new king, 141; betrothed to
Renée, Claude's sister, 142; German
elections, 205; Emperor, 207; Wolsey,
215; character, 218; German education, 226; crowned, 226; Luther, 226–
227; siding with Rome, 228; English
support, 231; war with Francis, 244;
Valenciennes, 246; retreat, 246; visits
England, 249; plans with Bourbon,
263; Henry VIII's help, 264; crosses
Pyrenees, 269; letter from Francis,
298; angered by the Pope, 300;
Spain, 304; troubles, 305; Papal
treachery, 300; money needed, 305;
many marriage engagements broken,
305; news of Pavia, 306; refuses to see
Francis, 313; Francis ill, 313–315;
Madrid, 314; see Francis, 324; meets
Marguerite, 315; interview, 317; Burgundy, 317; his sister Eleanor, 317;
Francis's treachery, 328; sack of
Rome, 337; Lautrec sent to liberate
the Pope, 338; death of Moncada,
348; Francis's pledges broken, 348;
envoys imprisoned, 348; challenges
Francis, 348–349; Doria's assistance,
349; placating Italians, 382; treaty
with the Pope, 382; return to Spain,

393; Turkish danger, 393; Barbarossa, 402; fleet goes to La Goletta, 403; successful battle, 403; Tunis, 403; Naples and the Pope, 403; indictment of Francis, 404; peace with France?, 412–413; meeting the Pope and Francis, 413; ten year truce, 413; meets Francis at Loches, 416.

Châteaubriant, Jean de—husband of Francis's mistress, 183, 185–186; Brittany, 385; death of his wife, 410; murder?, 410.

Châteaubriant, Madame, (see Foix).

Châtillon, Madame—Marguerite's matron, 193; Montmorency, 395.

Chaumont, 100.

Cheyney, Sir Thomas—and Francis, 252–253.

Chièvres—Austrian Chancellor, 142.

Claude of France—birth, 79; bestowed on Archduke Charles, 89; married to Francis, 89; anger of Maximilian, 89; her marriage, 109, 110; children, 182–183; death, 182; dying, 279; death, 279; funeral, 330.

Cleves, Duke of—to marry Navarre's daughter, 419; renounces France, 419.

Cognac—town, 7; Charles d'Angoulême, 49; festivities, 325.

Colonna, Prosper—Papal forces, 154; Charles's general, 233; in Milan, 249; death, 275.

Colonna, Vittoria—Pescara's wife, 320.

Columbus, Christopher—Spain, 29; activity, 31; birth, 31; Portugal, 32; voyages, 32; death, 32; effect in Europe, 32; death, 91.

Contarini—Italian crisis, 329.

Coq, Jeanne le—and Francis, 111; intimacy, 123; new king, 136.

Corfieto, Cardinal—in prison, 190.

Cortès—Charles V, 305.

Croy (see de Croy).

D'AILLY—Jean d'Angoulême, 10.

d'Albret, Jeanne—daughter of Navarre, 415; to marry Duke of Cleves, 419; flogged, 419.

d'Amboise, Georges—Louis XII, 68; Cardinal, 72; Borgia, 76; Louis XII,

78; his power over Louis, 80; Papacy, 86.

d'Angoulême (see Charles, also Jean).

Dauphiny—battle ground, 152–153.

da Vinci, Leonardo (see Vinci).

de Bresse (see Bresse).

de Brézé (see Brézé).

de Brion (see Brion).

de Brosse (see Brosse).

de Cardona (see Cardona).

de Châteaubriant (see Châteaubriant).

de Croy, Adrian—Bourbon, 263.

de Dinteville (see Dinteville).

de Foix (see Foix).

de Genouillac (see Genouillac).

de Gié (see Gié).

de Heilly (see Heilly).

de la Pole (see Pole).

de Leyva (see Leyva).

dé Medici (see Medici).

de Moncada (see Moncada).

de Monluc, Blaise—Fontainebleau, 421.

de Montmorency (see Montmorency).

de Montpensier (see Montpensier).

de Paule, Francis—Charles VIII, 53; Louise of Savoy, 62.

de Poitiers (see Poitiers).

de Polignac (see Polignac).

de Prie, Aimar—Francis's army, 155.

de Saint-Gelais (see Saint-Gelais).

de Selve (see Selve).

d'Este, Beatrice—38–39.

d'Este, Isabella—in Milan, 168.

d'Étaples, Lefèvre—Marguerite, 241.

de Warthy (see Warthy).

Diamond—Great Mogul, 13–14.

Dinteville, Guillaume de—death of the Dauphin, 406–407.

Divorce—the Vatican, 5.

Dolet, Etienne—executed, 425.

Doria, Andrea—famous seaman, 338; naval victory, 348; not paid, 349; goes over to Charles, 350.

Duchâtel—and Francis, 359.

Duprat, Antoine—Francis, 104, 110; Louise of Savoy, 104; new chancellor, 134; president of parlement, 134; Semblançay, 135; Francis's army, 152; Bologna, 169; new policy, 208; Bourbon inheritance, 238–239; succeeds

Boisy, 244; Semblançay, 252; news of Pavia, 301; Conference of Calais, 310; made cardinal, 337.

ELEANOR—sister of Charles V, 317; Marguerite, 317; sent away, 317; engaged to Francis, 321; 378; marriage, 381; welcomed by the French, 382; coronation, 383.

Embrun, Archbishop of—mass for Francis, 316.

England—Louis XI, 12, 22–23; tired of war, 274; Henry VIII and Anne Boleyn, 335; Francis and little Mary Tudor, 335.

Erasmus—and Francis, 4; Luther, 226–227; voice of Europe, 368; character, 368–372.

Este (see d'Este).

Étaples (see d'Étaples).

European war—231.

FAMILY Trees—Francis, 6; Habsburgs, 23.

Ferdinand—Louis XI, 12; Spain, 31; Charles VIII, 31, 33; Granada, 33; danger to France, 41; Naples, 71; Louis XII, 85; Naples, 91; hunting, 96; death, 175.

Ferrara, Duke of—Paris, 198.

Field of the Cloth of Gold—212; English possession, 213; English preparations, 214.

Filiberte—Marguerite's aunt, 277.

Fitzwilliam, William—Francis and war, 234; Francis and money, 235; English ambassador, 243.

Fleurange—and Francis, 83–84, 94; wounded, 103; Francis, 108–109; Mary Tudor, 115; Italy, 139; army, 151–152; the Swiss, 158; knighted, 163; Cremona, 167; Pavia, 289; the attack, 290–291; a prisoner, 292; promotion, 325.

Florence—34; Charles VIII, 39; plague, 345.

Foix, Françoise de—intrigue with Francis, 183; Bonnivet, 196; Paris celebrations, 200; jealousy, 258; sent from Court, 259; visited by Francis, 386–387; death, 410.

Foix, Gaston de—91–94; Marguerite, 100–101; death, 101.

France—Modern France, 14; war, 19; type of people, 20; parlement, 21; religious epoch, 22; defeat, 24; Netherlands, 24; the East, 29; invasion of Italy, 30; danger from Spain, 41; marriage and politics, 51; change of ideal, 55; illness of Dauphin, 57; his death, 58; death of Charles VIII, 65; Louis XII, 66; no son, 68; Cesare Borgia, 72, 77; war in Italy, 85; national character, 122; returned soldiers, 310; economy, 310 (see also Francis).

Francis—as King, 3; family tree, 5, 6; birth, 10; parentage, 16; warfare, 17–18; the Church, 18; Habsburgs, 25; Charles V, 28; Columbus, 32; his mother, 41; Jeanne de Pol, 50; birth (1494), 54; death of father (1496), 61; death Charles VIII (1498), 65; Dauphin, 65; Duke of Valois, 74; intrigues, 79; mishap with pony, 81; boyhood, 83–84; Borgia discussed, 84; Gié (1504), 87; d'Amboise in control, 88; marriage to Claude, 89; Artus Gouffier, 90; his sister Marguerite, 90; at Court, 92; character, 93; women, 94; Chinon, 94; hunting, 95–96; Françoise, 97–98; fever (1511), 102; war, 104; extravagance, 107; marriage, of (1514), 108–109; no sentiment, 108; appearance, 110; women, 111–112; Mary Tudor, 114; his mother-in-law, 115; death of Louis XII, 116; only twenty, 120; mother's training, 121; visits ex-queen, 124; marriage proposals, 125; Milan, 127; importance of Henry VIII, 128; funeral Louis XII, 128–129; Vive le roi, 131; helping his family, 133; extravagance, 134; Semblançay as treasurer, 135; le Coq's brother, 136; Paris restive, 136; his power as King, 137; the Church his rival, 137; consecration, 139; Suffolk, 140; royal festivities, 141; entry into Paris, 142; quarrel over Mary

Tudor, 145; petticoat government, 146; audience for Venetians, 146; Milan, 147; Wingfield's opinion, 147; tires of Paris, 149; royal journey, 149; hunting, 149; first child (1515), 150; off to Italy, 150; arrival at Lyon, 150; modern artillery, 151; rise in prices, 151; the Swiss, 152; army of mercenaries, 152; Alps, 153; Papal troops, 154; Embrun, 154; Swiss retreat, 155; Milan and Naples, 155; twenty-first birthday, 156; unreliable Medici, 156; new armour, 157; Swiss advance, 159; utter exhaustion, 160; Venetians arrive, 160; retreat to Milan, 161; piles of dead, 161; victory, 162; knighthood, 162; Milanese women, 166; entry into Milan, 167; plague, 167; Italian ladies, 168; his first child, 168; to meet the Pope at Bologna, 168; arrival, 169; meets Leo, 169; Papal absolution for nobles, 170; good terms, 170; meets Marguerite and Louise, 171; reception in Marseille, 173; Rhône, 173; stops at Lyon, 173; return to Amboise (1516), 174; *Mona Lisa*, 175; Treaty of Noyon, 175; betrothal of baby Louise, 175; Hohenzollerns, 176; mercenary Germans, 176; struggle with parlement (1517), 177–178; love of splendour, 180–181; hunting, 180; lack of money, 180; building Chambord, 180; a royal palace, 181; coronation of Claude, 182; more children, 182; death of Claude, 182; Lautrec's sister, 183; fresh mistress, 185; death of Trivulzio (1517), 188; Duprat's tariffs, 189; the Medici marriage, 191; the Dauphin (1518), 192; visits Bonnivet, 192; tiring of Françoise, 197–198; negotiations with Wolsey, 198; Paris, 198; ambassador from England, 198; celebrations at the Bastille, 199; German elections (1519), 203; threat to Turks, 205; bribery, 205–206; Papal backing, 207; loss of elections, 208; fresh policy, 208; death of Boisy, Vinci and de' Medici, 209; Wolsey's power, 210; hunting mishap, 211; visits the An-

goumois, 211; Field of the Cloth of Gold (1519), 212; his mother, wife and sister, 213; also his mistress, 213; the meeting, 215; Marguerite and Wolsey, 216; visit to Henry VIII, 216; Françoise in trouble, 219; three accidents (1520), 225; Romorantin, 225; preparing for war with Charles, 226; European war, 231; still after Milan, 232; heavy cost, 232–233; Reformation in Germany, 233; ill-health, 234; need of England, 235; French nervous, 253; death of Bourbon's wife, 236; Francis's claim to Bourbon inheritance, 237–238; Reformation activity in France, 240–241; support from Francis, 242; Wolsey at Calais, 242; war with Charles, 244; Bapaume destroyed, 245–246; Valenciennes, 246; foothold in Spain, 246; Milan abandoned (1521), 247; death of Leo, 247; need of money, 248; Pope Adrian, 248; Lautrec reaches Lyon, 250; insulted, 250; missing money, 251–252; Francis accused by England, 252; deadly need of money, 254; selling offices, 254; despoiling Reims Cathedral, 255; claims upon Bourbon, 255; pressure on parlement, 255; Bourbon comes to Court, 256; disastrous year (1522), 257; Françoise dropped, 259; Anne de Heilly, 259; grievances of nobles, 262; Bourbon treachery, 265; warning from de Brézé, 266; Bourbon's illness, 266; importance of Italy, 266; Bourbon treachery, 266–267; escape of Bourbon, 268–269; fixed at Lyon, 269; Henry VIII lands an army, 269; Emperor's army crosses Pyrenees, 269; no money, 270; the new Pope, 270; all Europe involved (1523), 270; opposition of parlement, 271; pillage, rape and murder, 272; illness, 273; Francis goes to Blois, 273; Claude ill, 273; hunting, 273; Anne de Heilly, 273; Saint Vallier condemned to death, 274; England tired of war, 274; degradation of Saint Vallier, 274; reprieve, 275; parlement again,

276; illness at Blois, 276; Four Years' War, 276; death of Bayard, 278; ready for invasion, 278; recalcitrant parlement, 278–279; Claude dying, 279; her death, 279; retreat of Pescara, 280; forcing troops forward, 280; approaching Italy, 280–281; Milan, 281; plague in Italy, 281; importance of Pavia, 281; struggle for the town, 281–282; bitter cold (1525), 282; Papal Nuncio, 283; Clarice Visconti, 284; aid from the Medici, 285; crisis approaching, 285; secret treaty with the Pope, 285; difficult position, 286–287; determined attack, 288–289; artillery fire, 290; Francis unhorsed, 291; a prisoner, 292; heavy slaughter, 293; Francis paraded publicly, 297; important papers lost, 297; It was Friday, 297; Pizzighittone, 298; letter to Charles, 298; the King is imprisoned, 300; Pescara as attendant, 300; a golden bullet, 300; Montpezat, 300; Four Years' War over, 302; death of Alençon, 304; plans for escape, 308; writing verse, 308; the Pope's messenger, 308; Charles V's terms, 308; restitution of Burgundy, 309; Impossible!, 309; danger from returned soldiers, 310; parlement acts, 310; it is economical with Francis in prison, 310; to go to Naples, 311; plot for escape, 311; in Barcelona, 311; friendly journey to Madrid, 311; appeal to Louise to come, 312; in Madrid, 312–313; in the Alcazar, 313; Charles refuses to see Francis, 313; lack of exercise, 313; fever and torpor, 313–314; arrival of Charles, 314; Francis sinking, 315; Marguerite arrives, 315; the King is unconscious, 316; Mass said, 316; an abscess breaks, 316; complete recovery (1525), 316; importance of Burgundy, 317; Marguerite returns, 318; plans for escape, 318; plans betrayed, 318; suggested abdication, 319; Francis gives way, 321; engaged to Eleanor, 321; his children as hostages, 323–324; return to France, 324; Bayonne Cathedral, 325; with his mother, 325; Anne de Heilly again, 326; Burgundy to protest, 326; the Pope exonerates Francis, 327; proposal for Holy League, 327; Bourbon helpless, 327; alliance with England, 328; worn out, 328; festivities on the Loire, 329; funeral of Claude (1526), 330; indignation at Papal outrage, 330; Marguerite's marriage, 333; betrayal of Semblançay, 334; the question of another marriage, 335; French envoys to England, 336; serious news from Italy, 336; death of Bourbon at Rome (1527), 327; Rome looted, 337; attack on parlement, 338; the King's supremacy, 338; Wolsey at Amiens, 339; meets Francis, 339; Mary Tudor to be given to his son, 339; death of Machiavelli, 340; war in Lombardy, 344; Pavia sacked, 344; the Pope's flight, 345; appeal to nobles, 346; the Louvre, 346; Francis's extravagance, 346; to dwell near Paris, 347; the broken Virgin, 347; Naples to be attacked, 347–348; naval victory, 348; envoys imprisoned by Charles (1528), 348; challenge to Charles, 348; Doria annoyed, 349; death of Lautrec, 350; death of Louis Berquin, 353; Marguerite of France, 353; the changing public opinion, 354; religious evolution, 354; the Ladies' Peace, 355; death of Margaret of Austria, 356; Wolsey's power weakening, 357; selling titles, 359; plague in Paris (1531), 359; Francis goes to Chantilly, 359; death of his mother, 360; his mother's loyalty, 363; his loss of aggression, 364; no variety in his methods of war, 364; Marignano responsible?, 365; improved firearms, 365; money needed, 365; his craving for Milan, 366; the French temperament, 367; the clerical struggle, 368; Francis and Rabelais, 375; Treaty of Cambrai, 377; Montmorency's influence, 377; alliance with Eleanor, 378; his children's ransom, 379; sent to Bayonne, 379; bad coins found, 379;

delay, 379; Spanish tension, 380; four
years' absence of the boys, 381; children restored (1530), 381; married
to Eleanor, 381; hunting, 382; Anne
holds aloof, 382; new queen welcomed by France, 382; coronation of
Queen Eleanor, 383; Eleanor and
Francis's mistress, Anne, 383; Chairs
of Literature founded, 383; Calvin's
books translated into French, 384;
Henry VIII's divorce, 384; antagonism
to the Church, 384; death of his
mother, 384; royal entry into Rouen,
385; three mistresses (1532), 385;
Brittany problem, 385; Châteaubriant,
385; the King is the guest of Françoise, 385; Francis gives Anne to de
Brosse, 385; Anne drops Francis, 387;
circumventing the Emperor, 387;
Francis's love of novelty, 388; rebuilding Chantilly, 388; the English
and women, 388; interview with
Henry VIII (1532), 390; meeting
Pope Clement, 391; Milan again,
392–393; internal difficulties, 393;
French nobles and new army, 393–
394; cheap fighting men, 394; Marguerite and the French clergy, 395;
indictment of Mass, 396; departure of
Marguerite, 396; public executions,
397; the Pope cries a halt, 397;
Henry VIII and religion, 398; Concordat with Leo, 399; religious persecutions, 399; flight of Calvin, 399;
Montaigne, 401; religious procession
in Paris (1535), 401; heretics burnt
alive, 402; effect in England, 402;
effect of victory at Tunis, 403; Duke
of Savoy, 404; Montmorency dismissed, 404; Savoy invaded, 404;
Turin occupied, 404; Montmorency
returns (1536), 405; Provence to be
sacrificed, 405; death of his son
François, 406; arrest of Montecuculli,
406; quartered alive, 406; was he to
blame?, 407; Calvin in Basel, 408;
Francis's powers failing, 408; Catherine's side-saddle, 410; no heir for
Henri of Navarre, 410; death of
Françoise de Foix, 410; murder?,
410; fascination of Francis, 411;
peace with Spain?, 412–413; meeting
the Pope and Charles (1538), 413;
ten year truce, 413; loyalty of women
to Francis, 414; the struggle between
Montmorency and Marguerite, 415;
Francis meets Charles at Loches, 415;
he welcomes Cellini, 417; Anne's
jealousy, 418; Montmorency resigns,
419; Francis broken in health, 420;
war on every front, 420; Fontainebleau (1544), 420; Anne de Heilly
again, 420; importance of the duel,
420; de Monluc, 421; plea for war,
422; battle of Cerisole, 423; capture
of Boulogne, 424; death of his son
Charles, 424; massacre of villagers,
424; Michael Angelo, 425; execution
of Dolet (1546), 425; Montmorency
and the Dauphin, 426; Diane de
Poitiers, 425–426; death of Henry VIII
(1547), 427; removal to Rambouillet,
427; Marguerite an invalid, 427;
Francis sends for his son Henri, 428;
warning against women, 428; Anne
de Heilly, 428; death, aged fifty-three
(1547), 428; triple funeral, 431.

Françoise—Francis and the girl, 97;
intrigues, 98.

Frederick of Saxony—German elections,
205; Luther, 206; Papacy, 227.

Frundsberg, George von—supports Bourbon, 282; Pavia, 288; the attack, 291;
Lutheran army, 331; his death, 336.

Fugger, Jacob—banker, 202; German
elections, 202; money wanted, 305.

GAILLARD family—Robertet, 135.
Gandia, Duke of—murdered, 71.
Gattinara, Mercurio—envoy of Austria,
142; snubbed, 143; Wolsey, 244; con-
ference at Calais, 310; peace terms,
320.
Genoa—revolt, 91.
Genouillac, Galliot de—artillery, 151;
Swiss attack, 160; Pavia, 289.
Geraldini—Columbus, 32.
Germany—modern Germany, 14, 24;
unsettled, 188; Luther, 188; complex

State, 202; new Emperor, 202 (*see also* Charles V).

Gerson—Jean d'Angoulême, 10.

Ghiberti—Italian crisis, 330.

Gié, Marshal de—Charles VIII, 37, 61; Louise of Savoy, 63; Louis XII, 68; Francis, 78; his prejudices, 80; his power, 80; Duke of Nemours, 87; too hasty, 87; banished, 87.

Giustinian, Sebastian—visits Francis, 210.

Gonzaga, Federico—Francis in Milan, 167.

Gouffier, Artus—guardian of Francis, 90, 101, 110; known as Boisy, 134; death, 209.

Gouffier, Guillaume (*see* Bonnivet).

Granada—conquest, 30, 31, 33.

Guicciardini—crisis in Italy, 326, 328.

Guyenne—Charles d'Angoulême, 48.

HABSBURGS—14; war, 22; Family Tree, 23; start, 24; Austria, 25; Valois, 28; German elections, 205; victory, 208; Luther, 227; harsh peace, 322.

Hackett, John—English ambassador in Flanders, 352.

Heilly, Anne de—Francis's mistress, 259; again, 273; joins Francis, 326; Francis and Eleanor, 378; Francis's wedding, 382; coronation of the queen, 383; Anne and Eleanor, 383; given to de Brosse, 385; drops Francis, 387; jealous of Cellini, 418; Fontainebleau, 420; death of Francis, 428.

Henri—Francis's son, 406; Dauphin's death, 406; favours Montmorency, 406; no heir, 410; Montmorency, 425; death of the King, 428.

Henry VII—Marguerite, 92.

Henry VIII—and Francis, 4; France, 24; hunting, 96; San Sebastian, 103; France invaded, 104; Francis, 127; bribery, 144; Marignano, 164; *Virgin Mary* galley, 164; Field of the Cloth of Gold, 212–215; bringing his queen, 213; arrival at Calais, 214; supports Charles, 243; attacks Francis, 252; help for Bourbon, 264; army in France, 269; suggested marriage with Marguerite, 332; heir needed, 335; Anne Boleyn, 335; divorce delayed, 345; resolved to marry Anne, 389; interview with Francis, 390; religion in England, 398; Anne of Cleves, 413; death, 427.

Howard, Kathryn—Henry VIII, 5.

Hugo, Victor—Francis, 4.

Humbercourt—Francis's army, 151, 153; death, 162.

Hundred Years' War—12–23.

Hungary—Maximilian, 27.

Huss, John—Nationalist, 17.

IL MORO—(*see* Sforza).

Italy—Louis XI, 12, 17; French invasion, 30; Milan, 69; her art value, 70; Borgia's policy, 74; war, 85; importance, 266, 270; Francis approaches, 280; plague, 281; Morone's plans, 310; crisis, 328; Papacy a difficulty, 328; importance of Milan, 328.

JEAN d'Angoulême—grandfather of Francis, 7; brother of Orléans, 8; prisoner in England, 8.

Jean d'Angoulême—uncle of Francis, 10; return to Angoulême, 10.

Jeanne of France—16; divorce, 73; nunnery, 73; abbess, 94.

Joan of Arc—17, 23.

KISSING—a French custom, 39.

LA MARCK—(*see* Marck).

Lannoy—at Pavia, 288; the attack, 290, 292; Francis a prisoner, 292; in charge of Francis, 311; Bourbon fury, 311; in Madrid, 314; peace terms, 320.

Languedoc—Charles de Bourbon, 133.

la Palice—103; Francis's army, 152, 154; at Pavia, 281; the attack, 289; death, 292.

la Trémoïlle—Anne of France, 26; Charles VIII, 36; Louis XII, 105; Francis's army, 152; crossing Po, 167; Pavia, 289; death, 292.

Lautrec—104; Francis, 110; the King, 120; governor of Guyenne, 134; Francis's army, 152; Treaty with the Swiss, 156, 157; misses the battle, 162; his sister and Francis, 183; quarrel with Trivulzio, 187; marriage, 211; Francis's general, 232; Lombardy, 234; need of money, 247; abandons Milan, 247; attacking Milan, 249; Swiss troops, 249; final defeat, 250; character, 250; insulted, 250; war in Lombardy, 344; Pavia sacked, 344; Adriatic, 345; siege of Naples, 349; illness, 350; plague, 350; death, 350.

Leyva, Antonio de—in charge of Pavia, 281; hardships, 282; heroic defence, 288; holding Milan, 344; death, 406.

Loire—the Valley, 55; the river, 56–57.

Lombardy—campaign, 91; plague, 281; war again, 344.

Longueville—104; Mary Tudor, 108; Jane Popincourt, 125.

Lorenzo de' Medici—Papacy, 34; death, 34.

Lorenzo il Magnifico—64.

Lorraine, François de—with Francis, 279; death, 292.

Louis d'Orléans—Asti, 39; Milan, 39; grandfather of Charles d'Angoulême, 50; death of the Dauphin, 58; heir to throne, 59; quarrel with Charles VIII, 59; control of Francis, 61; death of Charles VIII, 65 (see also Louis XII).

Louis XI—and Orléans, 10; a Political Workshop, 11; France as a unit, 12; feudal lords, 12; bribery, 12; Charlotte of Savoy, 13; Burgundy, 14, 15; Nancy, 15; Habsburgs, 15; a son, 14; death, 15; crippled children, 16; the Church, 16, the Catholics, 17; warfare, 17.

Louis XII—(see also Louis d'Orléans) divorce, 5; parentage, 10; appearance, 10; gout, 21; parlement, 21; the crown, 65; no heir, 65; ill health, 66; Duchy of Milan, 69; need for divorce, 71; Borgia, 72; divorce, 72; Milan, 73; Louise of Savoy, 73; capture of Milan and Naples, 78; marriage, 78; birth of daughter, 79; character, 80;

Ferdinand, 85; offensive against Spain, 86; facing defeat, 86; Gié's treachery, 87; illness, 89; betrothal of Claude, 89; Maximilian's anger, 89; Milan, 91; hunting, 96; death of Anne, 105; the Papacy, 107; remarriage, 109; Mary Tudor, 113–115; Francis, 115; his children, 115; the succession, 116; death, 116; burial, 128–129; Notre Dame, 120; The King is dead!, 131.

Louise of Savoy—mother of Francis, 41; ward of Anne of France, 46; character, 46, 47; betrothed, 47; Jeanne de Polignac, 48, 49; need of heir, 52; Anne of Brittany, 53; throne of France, 53; birth of Francis, 54; death of Charles d'Angoulême, 61; Marshal de Gié, 61; care of Francis, 62; her father's death, 64; her household, 64; death of Charles VIII, 65; no heir for Louis XII, 66; Paris, 68; the Papacy, 69; Louis XII's divorce, 73; protecting Francis, 79; marriage proposals, 81; Gié, 81; Artus Gouffier, 90; Duke of Alençon, 90; loses Francis, 92, 93; left alone, 93; superstitious, 94; Bonnivet, 102; Duprat, 104; death of Anne, 105; Mary Tudor, 115; anxiety about heir, 116; Francis's accession, 123; Duchy of Angoulême, 133; Duprat, 134; Venice, 147; a pilgrimage, 163; Cardinal Bohier, 189; said to be hoarding, 211; Field of the Cloth of Gold, 213, 217; helping Francis, 235; claim to Bourbon, 237–238; offer of marriage, 238; Semblançay, 251; suit against Bourbon, 255; death of Claude, 279; collapse, 279; news of defeat at Pavia, 301; her appeals for Francis, 302; attacks Alençon, 302; death of Alençon, 304; in control of France, 310; plots for Francis's escape, 311; Dauphin to be hostage, 322; joins Francis at Bayonne, 325; friendly to Wolsey, 338–339; tired of losing struggle, 351; anxious for peace, 352; anger against the Pope, 355; seeks Margaret of Austria, 355; death of Margaret, 356; illness, 356; her death, 356; feminine loyalty to Francis, 363.

Louise—Francis's child, 168; betrothed, 175.

Loyola, Ignatius—226; religious war, 234; Charles V, 307; the Voice of Europe, 368.

Luneberg—in Paris, 198.

Luther, Martin—France, 171; Germany, 188; sale of indulgences, 202; attacked by the Pope, 203; power in Germany, 204; Frederick of Saxony, 206; Charles V, 227; the Papacy, 227; a Papal Bull, 228; the people behind him, 288; excommunicated, 240; Henry VIII's anger, 240; Marguerite, 240–241; attack on immorality, 260; Berquin's death, 352–353; the Voice of Europe, 368.

Machiavelli—and Francis, 4, 16, 23; France, 122; Bourbon conspiracy, 262; Charles V, 305–306; crisis in Italy, 327–328; death from plague, 340; character, 340; his philosophy, 340, 341; admiration for French politics, 342; not for the French people, 343.

Madeleine de Boulogne—the Medici, 190–191; death, 191.

Mainz, Archbishop of—negotiations with Francis, 176.

Mantua, Duke of—death of Medici, 331.

Marck, Robert de la—and Francis, 83; Francis, 188; his son Erard, 189; attacks Charles, 226; Pavia, 302.

Marcourt—indictment of the Mass, 397.

Marignano—Swiss routed, 164.

Margaret of Austria—28; betrothed, 28; Anne of France, 29; Netherlands, 95; German elections, 205; the Ladies' Peace, 355; her marriage to Louise's brother, 355; frequent visits to Louise, 356; revised treaty of Madrid, 356; death, 356.

Marguerite of France—Francis's sister, 90; marriage intrigues, 90, 91; Francis, 93; Françoise, 97; Gaston de Foix, 100; Bonnivet, 100; marriage, 101; death of Gaston, 101; Bonnivet, 101–102; Francis's women, 112; the new king, 133–134; favours, 134; consecration, 140; partisan of Francis, 148; character, 147–149; anxiety about Marignano, 172; opposes King's new mistress, 184; at Court, 186; visited by Bonnivet, 192; did she love him?, 194; celebrations in Paris, 199; Field of the Cloth of Gold, 213; Wolsey, 215–216; her influence on Francis, 220; her difficulties, 220–221; no children, 220; what Francis was to her, 223; was his appeal sexual?, 224; turns to religion, 240; Bishop of Meaux, 240; Luther, 240–241; Fitzwilliam, 243; anxious about Francis, 245; illness of Louise of Savoy, 276; influence of Briconnet, 277; death of Claude, 279; Pavia disaster, 302; death of Alençon, 304; joins Francis, 312; suggested marriage, 312; in Madrid, 314; meets Charles, 314; nine days' journey, 315; Francis recovers, 316; Toledo, 316; interview with Charles, 317; sees Eleanor, 317; returns to Francis, 318; plans for escape, 318; failure, 318; disgrace, 319; her black dog, 319; plight of Louis Berquin, 330; plans for marriage, 332; Henry VIII, suggested, 332; Navarre, 332; her marriage, 333; child born, 347; Louis Berquin, 352; his death, 353; her mother's illness, 359; death, 360; mysticism, 376; Marguerite and Anne de Heilly, 383; idealising her mother, 384; friendship with Montmorency, 395; conflict with French clergy, 395; leaves Court, 396; Calvin, 396; favours Montmorency, 406; opposed by him, 414; Jeanne d'Albret, 415; an invalid, 428.

Marot, Clément — Marguerite, 148; Francis, 174; death of Semblançay, 334; devoted to Marguerite, 395.

Marriage and Politics in France—51.

Maximilian—Louis XI, 11–13; Mary of Burgundy, 14; Family Tree, 23; marriage, 24; Netherlands, 24; defeat of French, 24; failure as general, 25; Bruges, 25; Anne of Brittany, 25, 26; Anne of France, 25; Hungary, 27; animosity to France, 28; Spain, 30; Charles VIII, 33; Sforza, 71; marriage,

71; anger at Claude's betrothal, 89; hunting, 96; France, 103–104; reaches Milan, 173; retreat, 173; death, 201.

Medici family—lending money, 70; alliances, 107.

Medici, Alessandro de'—and Charles's daughter, 382–383.

Medici, Caterina de'—birth, 191.

Medici, Giovanni de'—Emperor Charles, 233; needed by Francis, 285; at Pavia, 285; wounded, 285; death, 331.

Medici, Giulio de'—and Pope Adrian, 270.

Medici, Lorenzo de'—the Pope's captain, 156; marriage, 191; death, 209 (see also Lorenzo).

Milan—the Duchy, 69; Venice, 70; Louis XII, 73; capture, 78; military unrest, 157; entry of Francis, 166–167; plague, 281; held by de Leyva, 345.

"Mistresses"—in France, 5.

Mona Lisa—175.

Moncada, Ugo de—terms for Francis, 308; the Pope's weakness, 330; treachery, 330; killed, 348.

Montaigne—401.

Montchenu—and Francis, 83, 94; Italy, 139.

Montecuculli—arrest, 406; quartered alive, 406.

Montferrat—Francis in Milan, 167.

Montmorency, Anne de—and Francis, 83, 84, 94, 97; new policy, 208; takes Novara, 249; following Bourbon, 280; Pavia, 281; the attack, 289; in prison, 292; Charles in Madrid, 314; promotion, 325; acting for Francis, 349; taking Boisy's place, 377; wish for peace, 377; undervalues Navarre, 377; brutal with Doria, 377; ransom for King's children, 379; arrival at Hendaye, 381; Bordeaux, 381; understanding with Charles, 382; Jacqueline, 385; great wealth, 388; Turks, 393; Marguerite's friendship, 395; dismissed, 404; recalled, 405; death of the Dauphin, 406; a power in France, 406–407; favoured by young Henri, 407; attacks Marguerite, 415; resigns, 419; influence on the Dauphin, 425.

Montpensier, Gilbert de—Charles VIII, 36.

Montpezat—Francis a prisoner, 300.

Morette, Sieur—Francis's army, 154.

Morone—independence of Italy, 310.

Monlac—(see de Monlac).

Nancy—great battle, 14.

Naples—in danger, 31; Spain, 70; capture, 78; abandoned, 86; death of Nemours, 87; to hold Francis, 311; to be attacked, 347–348; besieged, 349.

Navarre—war, 103–104; lost, 105; lost to France, 226; its importance, 332.

Navarre, Henri de—with Francis, 279; in prison, 292.

Navarro, Pedro—Francis's army, 151; Sforza, 167; Florence, 330; dying, 350.

Nemours, Duke of—death, 87.

Netherlands—Maximilian, 24–25.

Norfolk—Field of the Cloth of Gold, 215.

Novara—defeat of Louis's army, 155.

Orléans—the town, 7.

Orléans, Charles, Duke of—a prisoner, 8.

Papacy—dissatisfaction, 17; Alexander VI elected, 33; the Medici, 33–34; election of Adrian VI, 36; family, 35; Popes from 1455 to 1534, 35–36; uneasiness, 39; Turkey, 40; Charles VIII, 40; Louis XII, 69; murder of Duke of Gandia, 71; Borgia, 72; death, 86; Pius III, 86; Julius II, 86; death, 105; Leo X, 105; illness, 110; Francis as king, 147; papal forces, 154; Leo's anxiety, 157; dismay, 164; Leo to meet Francis, 168; Bologna, 168; absolution for nobles, 170; Leo's plans, 190; Vatican crime, 190; thirty-one new cardinals, 190; selling indulgences, 202; attack on Luther, 203; German elections, 206; Luther, 226–227; Leo committed to France, 228; Pope Adrian and Francis, 233; excommunication of Luther, 240; Leo as prince and priest, 246; death of Leo, 247; Adrian VI, 248; siding with the Emperor, 270; Medici tradition, 270; new Pope, 270; indecision, 280; Papal Nuncio, 283; secret treaty with Francis, 285; dealings with Charles, 304; messenger sent to Francis, 308; secret plans, 310; exonerates Francis, 326; proposes Holy League, 326; Italian crisis, 328; betrayed by Moncada, 330; Bourbon troops march on Rome, 336; Rome attacked, 337; death of Bourbon, 337; Rome looted, 337; plague, 337; the Pope a prisoner, 337; Vatican and divorce, 339; flight to Orvilto, 345; Clement meets Francis, 391; French executions, 397; Concordat with Francis, 399; Paul III, 403; peace between Spain and Francis?, 412; meeting between Francis and Charles, 413.

Paris—Villon's emancipation, 8 (see also under Francis).

Paule—(see de Paule).

Pavanes—burnt to death, 346.

Pavia—importance to Francis, 281; bitter cold, 282; attack opens, 290; disaster for Francis, 290.

Pescara—the Emperor's general, 233; Spanish troops, 280; at Pavia, 288; with Francis in prison, 300; Naples, 310; influence on Charles, 320; his wife, 320.

Petrucci, Cardinal—and Leo, 190; poison, 190.

Philip of Bresse—Louis XI, 13.

Philip of Spain—91.

Philip II—Charles's son, 306.

Pizarro—Charles V, 304.

Pizzighittone—Francis a prisoner, 298.

Poitiers, Diane de—influence on the Dauphin, 425.

Pole, Richard de la—with Francis, 279

Polignac, Jeanne de—mistress of Charles d'Angoulême, 48; a curious household, 50; death of Charles, 61; Louise of Savoy, 63, 78.

Pompérant—with Bourbon, 268; Pavia, 292.

Pont-Remy—negotiations with England, 277.

Popincourt, Jane—and Mary Tudor, 125.

Prie—(see de Prie).

RABELAIS, Francis—and Francis, 4, 74, 75, 234, 254; the Voice of Europe, 368; Paris, 372; character, 372; Rights of Man, 373; comparison with Francis, 375; Rome, 404; the Dauphin, 407.

Rabodange—and Duke of Orléans, 10; Louis XII, 72.

Ravenna—death of Gaston de Foix, 101.

Reformation, The—233.

Renée of Savoy—Swiss Treaty, 156; Pavia, 289; mortal wound, 292.

Renée of France—Claude's sister, 142; given to Brandenburg, 176.

Rennes—28.

Riario, Cardinal—poison, 190.

Robertet, Florimond—and Francis, 104, 110; the new King, 135; new policy, 208.

Roman Empire, Holy—23; the end, 24.

Roses—from Persia, 56.

Rovere, Giuliano della—37; as Pope, 86.

Russell, Sir John—with Bourbon, 261, 267.

SAINT-Gelais, Jean de—and Francis, 63, 78; used by Francis, 271.

Saint-Vallier—Bourbon, 262; with Charles, 264; dines with the King, 267.

Sarto, Andrea del—and Francis, 179.

Savonarola—Florence, 17; the Medici, 33; the Bible, 35; Florence, 39.

Savoy—its importance, 13; Charlotte of Savoy, 13, 39 (see also Louise).

Savoy, Duke of—death of Louise, 404.

Schinner, Cardinal—Swiss army, 156; Milan, 157; plague, 281.

Selve, Jean de—judicial inquiry, 271.

Semblançay—and Duprat, 135; Francis and money, 180; new policy, 208; Francis's Treasurer, 233; money troubles, 235; in disgrace, 251; replaced, 258; on trial, 272; fresh arrest, 333; destruction of papers, 333; sentence of death, 334; hanged, 334.

Severino, Galeazzo San—Francis's army, 151–152; Pavia, 289; death, 292.

Sforza, Bianca—Maximilian, 71.

Sforza, Caterina—284.

Sforza, Francesco—Louis XI, 69.

Sforza, Ludovico—Charles VIII, 37; Naples, 38; Milan, 71.

Sforza, Maximilian—163; fear of Charles, 310; loses Milan, 321; remains in Milan, 382.

Shore, Jane, 15.

Sickingen, Franz von—and Francis, 176, 188; German elections, 203, 206; Luther, 226–227.

Soderini—adviser to Pope Adrian, 270.

Solyman—advance on Mohács, 327.

Sorel, Agnes—and Francis, 5.

Spain—Louis XI, 12, 17, 22; Columbus, 29; Granada, 30, 33; French rivalry, 65; Italy, 71; an offensive, 86; anarchy, 175; Charles V, 304; news from Pavia, 306; ransom for Francis's children, 379; dangerous tension, 379.

Stein, Albert von—in French pay, 158.

Stubbs, Bishop—and Francis, 4.

Suffolk—Mary Tudor, 113–115; hunting, 115; France, 140; marriage, 143–144; Field of the Cloth of Gold, 215; army in France, 269; Pavia, 289; the attack, 291; death, 292.

Swiss, The—and Burgundy, 13; Milan, 85; advance of Francis, 159.

TÉMÉRAIRE—14.

Torquemada—307.

Tours, Archbishop of—death, 333.

Trivulzio, Marshal—and Francis, 145; the army, 151–152; Dauphiny, 153; stern fight, 162; lent to Venetians, 167; quarrel with Lautrec, 187; death, 188.

Tudor, Mary—marriage, 109; arrival, 113; Francis, 114; Suffolk, 115; death of the King, 123; whether enceinte, 124; visit from Francis, 124; fresh marriage, 125; Suffolk, 126; her marriage, 143–144; the diamond, 144; French heirloom, 144; bribing Henry VIII, 144.

Tudor, Mary (the younger)—to be bride of Francis's son, 339.

Tudor Parliament—the popular aspect, 20.

Turkey—the Papacy, 40.

URBINO, Duke of—Venice, 329; his army, 330; following Bourbon, 336.

Utrecht—(see Adrian).

VATICAN—(see Papacy).

Vaudois—massacre of villagers, 424.

Verger—Gié's château, 81.

Vendôme—sent to Paris, 274.

Venice—uneasy, 39; France, 70; Antwerp, 70; intrigues, 91; audience with Francis, 146; hiring an army, 329–330; the army under Urbino, 336.

Villon, François—at Court, 8; Paris, 9.

Vinci, Leonardo da—38; and Francis, 166, 174; his influence, 179–180; death, 209; his life's work, 209.

Visconti, Clarice—at Pavia, 283.

Visconti, Valentina—39; Asti, 69.

WAR—as a trade, 20.

Warthy, Perault de—in charge of Bourbon, 267.

Warty, de—(see Warthy).

Wingfield, Sir Robert—and Francis, 147.

Wolsey—Mary Tudor, 108; death of Louis XII, 124; Mary Tudor's marriage, 126; missing jewels, 144; cardinal, 158; Marignano, 164; tires of Maximilian, 175; negotiations with Francis, 198; Bonnivet, 198; in control, 210; Henry and Francis, 212; arrival at Calais, 214; diplomatic meeting with Emperor, 215; Calais, 242–243; bid for Papacy, 243; claims on France, 256; Italy, 270; difficulties with Charles, 277–278; distrusts Bourbon, 278, 310; peace terms, 310; divorce for Henry VIII, 335; arrival at Amiens, 338; friendly with Louise, 339; opposition to Anne, 357; his fall from power, 358.

Würtemberg, Duke of—women, 196; German elections, 205; Pavia, 302, 317.